DATE DUE		
JAN 2 9 1992			
MAR 2 6 1994			

Class and space

Other titles in the series include:

An Introduction to Urban Geography, J. R. Short
The Geographer at Work, P. Gould
Cities and Services: The Geography of Collective Consumption, S. Pinch

Class and space

The making of urban society

· *Edited by NIGEL THRIFT*
and PETER WILLIAMS ·

ROUTLEDGE & KEGAN PAUL
LONDON AND NEW YORK

First published in 1987 by
Routledge & Kegan Paul Ltd
11 New Fetter Lane, London EC4P 4EE

Published in the USA by
Routledge & Kegan Paul Inc.
in association with Methuen Inc.
29 West 35th Street, New York, NY 10001

Set in 10/12 point Ehrhardt
by Hope Services Ltd
and printed in Great Britain
by T. J. Press Ltd
Padstow, Cornwall

Library of Congress Cataloging in Publication Data
Class and space.
Bibliography: p.
Includes index.
1. Social classes—Great Britain—History.
2. Social classes—United States—History.
3. Anthropo-geography—Great Britain—History.
4. Anthropo-geography—United States—History.
5. City and town life—Great Britain—History.
6. City and town life—United States—History.
I. Thrift, N. J. II. Williams, Peter, 1947– .
HN400.S6C54 1987 305.5'0941 87–9868

British Library CIP Data also available
ISBN 0–7102–1150–3

Contents

1 The geography of class formation 1
NIGEL THRIFT and PETER WILLIAMS

PART ONE THE NINETEENTH CENTURY

2 Introduction: The geography of nineteenth-century class formation 25
NIGEL THRIFT

3 Class, place and industrial revolution 51
CRAIG CALHOUN

4 Class, behaviour and residence in nineteenth-century society: the lower middle class in Huddersfield in 1871 73
RICHARD DENNIS

5 Home ownership, subsistence and historical change: the mining district of West Cornwall in the late nineteenth century 108
DAMARIS ROSE

6 Constituting class and gender: a social history of the home, 1700–1901 154
PETER WILLIAMS

PART TWO THE TWENTIETH CENTURY

7 Introduction: The geography of late twentieth-century class formation 207
NIGEL THRIFT

8 The growth of scientific management: transformations in class structure and class struggle — 254
JOHN URRY

9 Knowing your place: Class, politics and ethnicity in Chicago and Birmingham, 1890–1983 — 276
DENNIS SMITH

10 Spatial development processes: organized or disorganized? — 306
PHILIP COOKE

11 The affluent homeowner: labour-market position and the shaping of housing histories — 330
RAY FORREST and ALAN MURIE

Bibliography — 360
Index of Names — 398
Subject Index — 406

Tables

2.1 The structure of industrial employment in Sheffield, 1851 33
2.2 Decennial rate of population increase in Leeds and Sheffield 34
2.3 Some examples of employment patterns in four Leeds woollen factories, 1858 43
2.4 The structure of industrial employment in Leeds, 1851, 1861 and 1871 44
4.1 A comparison of census, directory and pollbook sources from Clara Street, Hillhouse 87
4.2 Social stratification by household, Hillhouse, 1871 91
4.3 Occupations of fathers and co-resident sons, Hillhouse, 1871 93
4.4 Rates of neighbouring between occupational groups 95
4.5 Marriage choices in Hillhouse, 1871, 1878–80 98
4.6 Proportion of heads resident in Hillhouse in 1871 who were on the electoral role in 1867–68 100
4.7 Voting behaviour in Hillhouse, 1868 102
4.8 Church membership, occupational status and voting behaviour in Hillhouse, 1871 103
5.1 Mining parishes in the Camborne–Redruth District: employment in mines, 1883, smallholdings, 1889 and inhabited houses, 1891 118
6.1 Average age at death in 1842 188
7.1 Leisure time in minutes per average day in Britain for people aged 25–45 (1937, 1961 and 1975) 212
7.2 The dual politics thesis 213
7.3 Employed population by sector, 1971 and 1981 218
7.4 Socio-economic structure of service class in manufacturing and services only, 1971 and 1981 218
7.5 Employees in employment, service-industry activities, Great Britain, 1974 to 1984 219

7.6 Persons in employment by social class in Great Britain, all sectors, 1981 220
7.7 Inter-class recruitment of men, aged 20 to 64, into service-class positions in England only, 1972 221
7.8 Social class by gender in Great Britain, 1971 and 1981 221
7.9 Ethnic groups in different socio-economic groups in Great Britain, 1981 222
7.10 The distribution of income between classes 223
7.11 Indicators of service class consumption culture in Great Britain, 1982 224
7.12 Participation in selected social and cultural activities in previous four weeks by socio-economic group, 1983 225
7.13 Class composition of the electorate, 1964 and 1973 227
7.14 Voting according to class, 1983 General Election 227
7.15 Voting in the 1983 General Election by social class and consumption sector 229
7.16 Social composition of three environmental groups 230
7.17 Change in total service employment, 1971–81 234
7.18 Areas of increase in service-sector employment in Great Britain, 1978–81 236
7.19 The CURDS classification of local labour market areas 238
7.20 Change in resident service employees by socio-economic group, 1971–81 239
7.21 Location quotients showing over- and under-representation of socio-economic groups employed in manufacturing and services, 1971–81 240
7.22 Winchester in 1981 247
7.23 Changes in social class in two districts bordering Plymouth, 1951 and 1981 250
7.24 Service-sector employment in Devon, 1971–81 250
7.25 Some centres in the Plymouth commuter-shed, 1981 251
8.1 Administrative/production employees in American manufacturing industry, 1899–1929 268
8.2 Sectoral distribution of the American labour force, 1900–30 269
8.3 New middle-class positions in the US labour force, 1900–30 269
11.1 Profiles of affluent home-owners 342

Figures

1.1	The chief approaches to class	2
2.1	Location of Sheffield and Leeds	30
4.1	The location of the study area	82
4.2	District and landownership boundaries in Hillhouse	88
7.1	The location of service employment: services employment as a percentage of total employment, 1981	233
7.2	The location of public schools belonging to the Headmasters Conference and the Society of Headmasters of Independent Schools	243
7.3	The location of key service-class retail outlets	244
7.4	Locations in Hampshire mentioned in the text	246
7.5	Locations in Devon mentioned in the text	249

Acknowledgments

We are grateful to Jo Little for her help in the preparation of parts of the volume and to Maureen Hunwicks who typed the papers. Our thanks to John Urry for commenting on a number of the chapters and to Elizabeth Fidlon from Routledge & Kegan Paul for her patience and support. Finally, we would like to acknowledge the contributions in this area by R. S. Neale whose untimely death was recently announced.

Contributors

C. Calhoun, Department of Sociology, University of North Carolina, Chapel Hill, North Carolina 27514, USA.

P. Cooke, Department of Town Planning, University of Wales Institute of Science and Technology, Cardiff, CF1 3EU, Wales.

R. Dennis, Department of Geography, University College London, London WC1E 6BT, England.

R. Forrest, School for Advanced Urban Studies, University of Bristol, Bristol BS8 4EA, England

A. Murie, School for Advanced Urban Studies, University of Bristol, Bristol BS8 4EA, England.

D. Rose, Institut National de la Recherche Scientifique-Urbanisation, Montreal, Quebec H2X 2C6, Canada.

D. Smith, Sociology and Technology Policy Division, Management Centre, University of Aston, Birmingham B4 7ET, England.

N. J. Thrift, Centre for the Study of Britain and the World Economy, Department of Geography, University of Bristol, Bristol BS8 1SS, England.

J. Urry, Department of Sociology, University of Lancaster, Lancaster LA1 4YW, England.

P. R. Williams, Institute of Housing, London N1 9XJ, England.

Preface

This book is about the place of space in the study of class formation. It consists of a set of papers that fix on different aspects of the human geography of class formation at different points in the history of Britain and the United States over the course of the last 200 years. During this period, of course, a capitalist economic system has been in operation which dictates the basic forms that class relations have been able to take.

Why a book on the geography of class formation? Three reasons stand out. First of all, human geographers have been curiously inactive in the study of class even though it is difficult to deny that class (howsoever formulated) is a crucial determinant of the geography of modern capitalist societies. Although recently this situation has begun to change there is still a long way to go before class takes its rightful place as a part of the pantheon of social forces that human geographers routinely acknowledge. A second reason is that the study of the geography of class is necessarily a cross-disciplinary affair, as the book attempts to show. It must integrate the work of human geographers with that of social historians, sociologists, social anthropologists and other social scientists in an enterprise which emphasises the essential unity of social science. This making of a common social scientific cause is crucial for the future of human geography (and indeed social science). Finally, and most important of all, the geography of class is fundamental to the understanding of the processes of class formation. Classes do not wax and wane in a geometrical abstraction but on the ground as concrete situations of conflict and compromise – in a geographical reality. Classes are organised (or disorganised) over space at a variety of scales and the degree and form of this spatial organisation will affect their integrity in myriad ways, ways which the chapters of this book begin to document.

• 1 •

The geography of class formation • *NIGEL THRIFT AND PETER WILLIAMS*

Introduction

This chapter provides an introduction to the subject of *Class and Space*. Its purpose is to briefly survey the literature on class and the geography of class in capitalist societies. The chapter is based on the presumption that the analysis of classes should start with the social relations of production but, as will become clear, the analysis cannot end there. Other perspectives on class are valuable too. Quite clearly, the insights provided by, for example, the Weberian approach are important for the analysis of classes in modern capitalist societies. As Abercrombie and Urry (1983, p. 91) put it concerning the middle classes:

> As 'Weberians' have become worried about the Boundary Problem, and 'Marxists' have recognised the importance of middle classes, the theoretical waters were bound to become muddy. In these circumstances it is more profitable to worry less about the way in which one discourse is privileged over another and more about the manner in which an adequate theory of the middle class can be constructed.

This chapter is split into three main parts. The first part provides a general introduction to the theory of class, concentrating on the chief determinants of class formation. The second part is intended to establish the role of geography in the study of classes. In the third and final part of the chapter we briefly review the contributions to the volume placing them in the context of our discussions here.

1 A space for class

The first problem in any discussion of class is how class is to be defined and it is therefore with this problem that the discussion must begin.

Defining class

Figure 1.1 shows some of the chief approaches to the definition of class within capitalism. Wright (1979b) has analysed these approaches in terms of three sets of oppositions. First, a distinction can be drawn between *gradational* and *relational* theories of class (Ossowski, 1963). Gradational approaches are usually based on the notion that classes differ by quantitative degrees on attributes like status or income. It is this gradational approach (usually based on official gradational classifications) which underlies much of the little work done in human geography which includes class as a variable. But such an approach is without any real explanatory power. Explanation requires a conception of class in relational rather than *relative* terms, that is as a set of social relations between classes which define their nature. Of course, relationally defined classes can have gradational properties – capitalists are rich and workers are poor. But it is not these properties as such which define classes. Rather, it is the other way round. The social

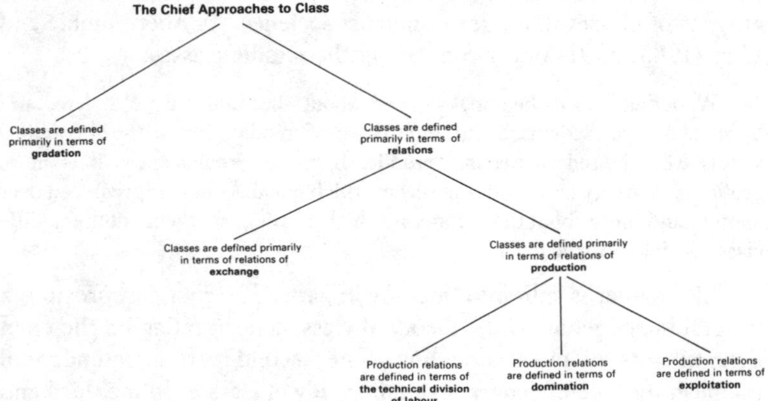

Figure 1.1 The chief approaches to class
Source: Wright, 1979b.

relations between classes explain at least the most essential features of their gradations (Wright, 1985).

Given a relational conception of class, a second distinction can be drawn according to whether class is seen as primarily determined by social relations of exchange ('the market') or social relations of production. The conception of class based on market relations is usually attributed to Max Weber, although this attribution is all too often allowed to degenerate into a crude caricature of Weber's ideas (c.g. Wright, 1979b). In fact, in Weber's scheme of things class consists of two dimensions: market interests, which always exist independently of men and women and influence their life chances, and status affiliations. The two dimensions represent the two different strategies that are open to a class and their emphasis changes through history (Giddens, 1973). This Weberian conception of class has been widely used in political theory (e.g. Parkin, 1972) and urban studies (e.g. Rex and Moore, 1967; Saunders, 1979, 1981). The conception of class based on relations of production is usually associated with the name of Marx. However, there are at least three ways in which class can be so defined and still remain consistent with a definition based on social relations of production and only one of these is, in fact, Marxist.

These three definitions provide the final set of distinctions that can be drawn. First of all, class can be defined according to *occupation*. In this case the theoretical backdrop is usually provided by a variant on the theme of the increasing technical division of labôur (e.g. Bell, 1973; Berger and Piore, 1980). Second, class can be defined according to possession of, or exclusion from, the *authority* to be able to issue commands to others (e.g. Dahrendorf, 1959), that is as a set of relations of *domination*. Lastly, class can be defined as the contradictory relation between capital and labour which allows surplus value to be appropriated, that is as a set of relations of *exploitation*. This is the Marxist view that there is a causal relationship between the affluence of one class and the poverty of another.

Of course, all classifications of approaches to class have their problems and Wright's is no exception. First, a number of the relational views of class incorporate to a greater or lesser degree Marx's view on class. Some of them were first put forward as reactions to, explicit critiques of, or simple additions to Marx. Thus Marx is often criticised for either not realising that there were other dimensions to class than production, or, because of his position in history, not having access to later developments which show that his theory of class needed adjustments or additions. Second, many authors fit uncomfortably into any classification. Giddens's (1973) theory of class structuration, for example, incorporates elements of both Marx and Weber's concepts of class and, in consequence, is far less easy to assign to a market or a production relation approach than Wright assumes (see Giddens, 1979b).

This chapter takes as its starting point (and only the starting point) the Marxist definition of class; that is class is based in social relations of production that are exploitative. Quite clearly, this definition means that certain social groups like women or religious or ethnic groups are *not* classes. This is emphatically *not* to downgrade these social groups. Indeed, one of the major points of modern Marxist analysis has been to take proper account of their importance. It is certainly *not* to suggest that these such social groupings are excluded from membership of classes. That would be absurd. Similarly it is *not* to suggest that these social groupings have no effects on the formation of classes. They clearly do have important effects. Wright (1985, pp. 129–30) sums up the Marxist position particularly well with regard to women:

> Class is not equivalent to 'oppression', and so long as different categories of women own different types and amounts of productive assets, and by virtue of that ownership enter into different positions within the social relations of production, then women *qua* women cannot be considered a 'class'. A capitalist woman is a capitalist and exploits workers (and others), both men and women, by virtue of being a capitalist. She may also be oppressed as a woman in various ways and this may generate certain woman non-class interests with the women she exploits, but it does not place her and her female employees in a common gender 'class'.

Doing class analysis: some basic concepts

It has become something of a truism that Marx never developed any systematic account of class: the text of the final chapter of *Capital*, Volume 3 entitled 'Classes' breaks off after just one page. This has been the opportunity for a whole host of (often dogmatic) recoveries of what Marx really meant about class to be developed by subsequent writers in the Marxist tradition (Giddens, 1979b). In this chapter, however, our concern is not with any kind of historical salvage operation but rather with the extension of some of the basic Marxist concepts of class.

Marx's account of class under capitalism is constructed at two levels of abstraction. At the highest level of abstraction Marx provides an analysis of the contradictory, exploitative and antagonistic relation between capital and wage labour that sustains capital and labour as classes and guarantees the presence of some degree of class conflict. At the lowest level of abstraction Marx provides a series of concrete historical analyses characterised by a large cast of classes, class functions and other social groupings. For example, 'in the *Eighteenth Brumaire of Louis Bonaparte* he refers to at least the following actors in social conflicts: bourgeoisie, proletariat, large land owners, aristocracy of finance, peasants, petty bourgeoisie, the middle class, the lumpen proletariat, industrial bourgeoisie, high dignitaries' (Wright, 1985, p. 7).

The overriding problem still is how to get from the most abstract two class account of the relations of production that Marx provides in the model world of *Capital* to the multiplicity of classes in constant formation and deformation that characterise Marx's accounts of real societies. There is no easy solution, of course. Currently five major concepts are fairly consistently utilised in a class analysis, namely class structure, the formation of classes, class conflict, class capacity and class consciousness. These concepts are likely to become more or less important in class analysis depending upon the spatial and temporal scales that are chosen. Class analysis at the grandest of these scales tends to put the emphasis upon long-term changes in the relations of production over large areas of territory. Such an approach can reveal fundamental shifts in *class structure* arising out of the changing trajectory of capitalist development. Alternatively, comparative studies of the class structures of different countries can be revealing. Class analysis can also be carried out at more restricted temporal and spatial scales, for example in a region over the course of forty or fifty years. In this case, much more attention must be paid to the exact mix of institutions that both generates and is generated by shifts in class structure. At this level of resolution, the formation of class*es*, the detailed to and fro of *class conflict* and the strength of *class capacity* all become more apparent. Finally, class analysis can be conducted at smaller spatial and temporal scales, often within a specific community. Here close attention tends to be paid to the exact class practices that institutions generate and the way that these practices mesh to create subjectivity and the particular actions needed to produce, sustain and question daily life. Hence the definition of *class consciousness* becomes particularly important. Of course, each of these five concepts can be deployed at any spatial and temporal scale, and they often are. The argument here is only that the nature of the scale chosen at which to practice class analysis is more likely to throw particular concepts into relief than others.

The way in which these five concepts are thought of is important and this chapter therefore continues by giving a modern interpretation of these concepts. Clearly, class structure is the most abstract of the five. Class structure is best conceptualised as a system of places generated by the prevailing social relations of production through the medium of institutions which set limits on people's capacity for action. For example, it will place limits on the resources (and especially the forces of production) that institutions have available and that people can call upon. The basic feature of class structure is still, and will be as long as a society remains capitalist, the exploitative relations of production that are based upon the amassing of the surplus labour of one class by another via the 'free' exchange of labour power. This relation ensures the existence of a class of wage labourers and a class of capitalists.

The problem then becomes what other relations of production are to be treated as distinctive determinants of class structure. Marx would certainly have included the form of possession of the means of production (property rights) and the degree of domination over production (the control of the labour process). Other commentators add in other relations. The criteria differ. For example, some commentators include the point at which they envisage the capitalist mode of production appearing in full flight. Thus Wright stresses the importance of the control of investment (money capital). Other commentators also include relations forged within the development of capitalism which hail the arrival of new 'submodes of production'. For example, control of business organisations becomes an important determinant of class structure under corporate capitalism. The list can be extended much further (see Walker, 1985a) to encompass the division of labour, the form of the labour market, and so on. While this may seem a rather frustrating exercise it is not a trivial one. On decisions as to what relations of production are chosen as distinctive determinants of class structure rests the system of class places which is generated with which to pursue class analysis. The exercise becomes particularly important in defining a middle class or middle classes (see below).

There are certain clarifications of the concept of class structure which need to be addressed. First, it is important to realise that stating that a particular class structure limits institutions or people's capacity to act in certain ways is by no means the equivalent of saying that class structure alone determines action. There is no unproblematic mapping of class structure onto social and political life. Other autonomous or relatively autonomous social forces quite clearly act within the limits described by class structure such as race, religion, ethnicity, gender, family and various state apparatuses, not only blurring the basic class divides but also generating their own social divisions (Wright, 1985). This is a conclusion to which the Marxist literature has come slowly and painfully over the last twenty years – class is not the be all and end all of social and political life. Its ability to set limits to action can be quite limited (although, given the nature of capitalist societies it is never non-existent). Not only that. These other social forces can act through distinctive institutions to alter the relations of production in ways which can be quite important. Think only of the differences in the cultures of Japanese capitalism and United States capitalism (Morgan and Sayer, 1985). Second, class structure cannot and must not be seen as some kind of *deus ex machina* hanging over the stage of social life, and periodically descending to point actors in the direction of particular class places. Class structure is always and everywhere tentative. It has to be reproduced at each and every instant. Clearly institutional momentum will often ensure this but it can by no means be guaranteed. Third, the existence of class structure can only be the beginning of any class analysis which is not on the grandest of scales. Class structure is only one element of class and it is unfortunate that in the literature it has too often become an end in itself.

In many ways, the concept of *the formation of classes* is of more importance. We take it that class formation refers to how people are recruited to class places through institutions which are numerous, diverse and overlap. The concept is more problematic as well because it involves such a high degree of contingency; there are many possible ways in which a system of class places can be formed according to the number of institutions that can be found in a particular society, at a particular time, the mix of those institutions and the degree to which each institution embodies class practices. 'Thus in each concrete conjuncture struggles to organise, disorganise, or reorganise classes are not limited to struggles between or among classes' (Przeworski, 1977, p. 80). What is clear, then, is that any analysis of class formation as a historically contingent process arising out of reciprocal actions must step outside the social relations of production and venture into social relations of reproduction. Further, these social relations of reproduction cannot be seen in the narrow sense as just concerned with the reproduction of labour power. Many of them are bent towards reproducing practices which may only tangentially interact with class practices or, indeed, may be divorced from them; 'culture' rears its problematic head. Quite clearly, the implication is that the analysis of class must be broadened out to the analysis of social class*es*.

The study of the formation of social classes requires the development of at least three associated concepts; class conflict, class capacity and class consciousness. It may well be true that the basic exploitative and antagonistic divide of class structure between capital and labour guarantees some degree of class conflict for that divide generates a gradation of wealth. But class conflict involves much more than this. It involves struggles among classes (and alliances between them) which are not constituted just out of the relations of production around issues which are not just concerned with the relations of production. More than this even, it involves struggles about whether classes will take shape at all. Thus the distinction between 'class struggle' and 'classes in struggle'. Until quite recently, with a few exceptions, the importance of class conflict tended to be underemphasised in Marxist writings – class conflict too often tended to be thought of as something ant-like going on at the interstices between the two warring blocs of capital and labour. In the last few years, however, under the stimulus of Thompson's (1965) *The Making of the English Working Class* and then Przeworski's (1977) raising of Kautsky (see also Przeworski, 1985) the importance of class conflict has been reaffirmed, most especially in work on the evolution of the labour process as encapsulating a history of struggle at the point of production (e.g. Friedman, 1977; Burawoy, 1977, 1985; Stark, 1980) but also in the more general context of the history of working-class politics (e.g. Foster, 1979; Cleaver, 1979; Groh, 1979; Joyce, 1980).

Once classes are thought of as being formed by the battles they have to fight, then the mode and degree of class organisation becomes a crucial determinant of classes' ability to reproduce themselves. Certain types of organisations will be more or less effective, enabling a class to exert more or less of its powers in the service of particular causes. Conventionally, the effectiveness of a class organisation in linking individuals together into a social force is referred to as class capacity (Wright, 1979) or class connectedness (Stark, 1980). Recently work on class capacity has become more common. Stark (1980, p. 98) sums up the general thrust of this work as well as any other:

organisations may be informal (based, for example, on interactions within the work situation or on the networks of kinship or residence) or formal (craft organisations, trade unions, professional associations, firms, state agencies, political parties, etc.). But in both cases their interests, capacities and resources are not posited *a priori* by the analyst but emerge historically, subject to changes in direction and magnitude based on the shifting patterns of relations (of conflict and alliance) within and between organisations. A relational analysis which focusses on the interaction of organisations (rather than on the attributes of individuals or the global properties of modes of production) is not incompatible with class analysis, but, in fact, is inseparable from it . . . it becomes apparent that a class never exists as a single collectivity-in-struggle but as a multiplicity of collectivities-in-struggle. The study of the forms and dynamics of these groups is the task of class analysis.

This is not, of course, to say that certain classes in capitalism do not start with some organisational advantages. Offe and Wiesenthal (1980) have shown how the organisation of the capitalist class is beneficially affected by the fact that its *raison d'être* – the search for greater and greater profits – fuels a process of concentration and centralisation which in turn means that it inevitably becomes collectively organised. Collective organisation follows from the economic 'monologic' of capitalism. On the other hand, the working class always and everywhere faces an initial problem of becoming collectively organised and then the continuing problem of staying collectively organised:

Offe and Wiesenthal . . . demonstrate that the associations of labour are defensive; they are responses to the collective organisation of capital. The latter also organise further in response to the associations of labour, in either informal cooperation or employers' associations, sometimes mediated by the state. Thus capital possesses three forms of organisation; the firm itself, informal cooperation between firms and the employers association; labour, by contrast has only one. It would appear never to be worthwhile for labour to engage in collective action – capital would always seem certain to win since there are far fewer individuals involved, they are more united and they possess clearer goals and greater resources. Thus Offe and Wiesenthal maintain that for the associations of labour to be viable an alternative form of organisation has to develop, which they term 'dialogical'. This involves, not merely aggregating the individual resources of the association members to meet the common interests of the membership but also, and more distinctly, defining a collective identity (Abercrombie and Urry, 1983, p. 134).

So far then, classes can be seen as formed out of conflict. The prevailing social relations of production structure that conflict but they are also changed by it. In the struggle between classes, organisation is a crucial determinant of success. But, as Offe and Wiesenthal point out, there is one more term that must still be added into this formula and that is class identity or consciousness. Class consciousness provides, or should provide, the essential element of subjectivity that is so far largely missing from the discussion (although implicit in it) by posing the question 'to what extent are members of a class likely to be conscious of the fact?' (Thompson, 1965, p. 10). That will depend, of course, to a large extent upon the level of class conflict and class connectedness.

Writers, at least from Lenin onwards, have envisaged a road to a final working-class calvary which passes through one or a number of stages of class consciousness (Gregory, 1984). We can distil the essence of a simple model here. In the most primitive stage there is class perception or 'consensus' (Morris, 1976), a simple awareness of the existence of classes, and of the differences between them, brought about by shared experiences of economic misfortune. In the next stage this class perception metamorphoses into class awareness or a Leninist 'labour consciousness' (Foster, 1974) or 'conflict consciousness' (Giddens, 1973), the awareness of conflict, of the need to protect living standards against exploitation and to maintain organisations like trade unions that do this. The result is to create a sense of identity within occupational groups and sometimes, briefly, within a class as a whole. But it is a sectionalised interest that comes together only over particular issues like working hours and then falls apart again. Then there is 'revolutionary consciousness' (Giddens, 1973; Foster, 1974) in which a sense of solidarity with all other members of the class is created. Sectional identities break down. There is not only opposition to the capitalist system. New and socially incompatible ideas are also developed. There is a 'profound process of mass cultural change' (Foster, 1974, p. 124). Finally, true class consciousness develops. A revolutionary consciousness permeates the whole of a class, a consciousness of the class as a whole as the dissolution of all classes. Truly, this is a class-for-itself. As the class-in-itself and the class-for-itself merge so the now brittle carapace of class shatters and is flushed away by the tide of revolution.

But there are difficulties with this sort of millennarian model. First, Marxist writers differ in what they identify as the cusp beyond which stretches the terrain of *class* consciousness. For Thompson (1965), class consciousness is triggered somewhere between class perception and class awareness. For Foster (1974) revolutionary consciousness constitutes class consciousness. For Neale (1981) only the fourth type of consciousness is class consciousness (and, indeed, this probably comes closest to Marx's own conception). Second, it is difficult to establish when each of these types of consciousness is present. As Foster (1977a, p. 73) puts it 'few things are more difficult to establish than class consciousness'. In particular, there is the problem of what constitutes evidence of any type of class consciousness. This is especially problematic in historical studies, of course. The evidence of Thompson and Foster, for example, can be read in other ways (cf. Dinwiddy, 1979; Donnelly and Baxter, 1975; Stedman Jones, 1975; Musson, 1976). But there are a multitude of other problems of interpretation as well. For instance, can a group be declared class conscious in the presence of an informed Leninist 'revolutionary vanguard' that is disseminating ideas and leading protests or must the whole of the group be inculcated with revolutionary ideas? Or, can the people in one particular place be declared 'class conscious' when all around laps a sea of ignorance and apathy?

However, the real problem goes deeper than these difficulties. A finished, materialist theory of the social determinants of consciousness, indeed of what consciousness *is*, has proved very elusive (Thrift, 1983). There are numerous sources of inspiration, of course. The French tradition gives us Sartre, Castoriadis, Deleuze, Sève, Bourdieu, Faye, Pêcheux, even that anti-Marxist, Foucault (see Thompson, 1984). The Italian tradition gives us Gramsci and the concept of hegemony as well as that unclassifiable intellectual, Ginzburg. The German tradition gives us the Frankfurt School, and latterly Habermas (see McCarthy, 1970; Held, 1980; Thompson and Held, 1982). The Russian tradition gives us Vygotsky and Luria (see Wertsch, 1985). The British tradition gives us Thompson, Williams, Bernstein, Hall, Willis and Giddens (see Inglis, 1982). And lately the meeting of the feminist tradition with social psychology has given some particularly powerful signposts (see, for example, Steedman, Urwin and Walkerdine, 1985).

To some writers, like Althusser, any attribution of agency to individuals is irredeemably bourgeois. But to all the above writers such a conclusion would seem alien. For them, the individual is socially constructed in line with Marx's dictum that social being determines consciousness. Again, for some writers ideology is a distorted representation of reality, passively received. But to the above writers the process of signification gives shape to the reality it implicates; reality is actively and knowledgeably negotiated through languages suffused with class (see Stedman Jones, 1983).

In a sense, it is possible to suggest that theory has lagged behind empirical practice. For there are many excellent detailed empirical accounts of how social being determines consciousness, of how class can enter into the formation of language, self, thought and feeling. For example, there is some of the literature in oral history (e.g. Thompson, 1975, 1982). There is the closely related literature on biography (e.g. Bertaux, 1982). There is the literature on the social psychology of schooling and gender (e.g. Henriques *et al.*, 1984). The list goes on almost endlessly. Abrams (1982) has most ably summarised what is currently perhaps the most exciting frontier of class analysis.

2 Class analysis with space

So far in this chapter, the emphasis has been laid upon outlining the present condition of class analysis. But one of the most noticeable criticisms of this condition is that it still tends to ignore geography. This is not to claim that geography does not figure in current class analysis. It quite clearly does and at a variety of scales. Thus, at the most extensive scale Wallerstein and his co-workers have attempted class analysis on the world scale (e.g. Taylor, 1986). Then again, comparative analyses of class structures within different nation states are common enough (e.g. Wright, 1985) and there are a few national geographies of classes (e.g. Rubinstein, 1980). Regional class analyses have been carried through quite frequently, especially in France (e.g. Judt, 1979, 1985; Agulhon, 1982; Jenkins, 1983). And at the smallest scales, histories of the make-up of particular working class (and most especially mining) communities are far too numerous to list (e.g. Hareven, 1982; White, 1980), and often placed under the label of 'community studies'. Rather, it is to claim that no systematic account of the place of space in class analysis has been given. This omission is more important than it might at first seem because the evidence suggests that now the foundations of such an account are being laid the nature and content of class analysis will have to change, perhaps quite substantially.

In particular, the current interleaving of geography with class analysis has changed the nature of how classes can be thought about. Most significantly of all, classes can no longer be thought of as unified and uniquely determined objects set in an abstract space-less realm. Given the fact that classes are geographical objects, they can never be anything but fragmented and overdetermined. This observation does not downgrade the importance of class as an important focus of investigation. Rather it denies the efficacy of pursuing a line of enquiry in which 'class is a singular' theory 'which is less real if it is less unified' (Walker, 1985a, p. 187). Nor does such an observation lead to the conclusion that classes are necessarily disorganised or opaque to theoretical analysis. What it does mean is that the degree and type of class organisation – its capacity or connectedness – becomes a much more crucial variable in the formation of classes. And this is a variable which must be consciously fought over in a host of very different circumstances. In other words, the relations of production (and reproduction) do not float above places. They are constituted within them.

There are three main areas of work which utilise this geographical viewpoint and which show its consequences. The first and perhaps the most obvious consists of the linking of the general trajectory of capitalist development to the specific historical geography of cities and regions. In the course of making the links human geographers and others are being forced into reconceptualising or certainly extending the Marxist analysis of capitalism. In the following three magisterial paragraphs, Harvey (1982, pp. 373–4) outlines the problems of analysing the complexly determined spatial organisation of capitalism within a Marxist framework:

The historical geography of capitalism has been nothing short of remarkable. Peoples possessed of the utmost diversity of experience, living in an incredible variety of physical circumstances, have been welded, sometimes greatly [sic] and cajolingly, but more often through the exercise of ruthless brute force, into a complex unity under the international division of labour. Monetary relations have penetrated into every nook and cranny of the world and into almost every aspect of social, even private life. This *formal* subordination of human activity to capital, exercised through the market, has been increasingly complemented by that *real* subordination which requires the conversion of labour into the commodity labour power through private accumulation. This radical transformation of social relations has not progressed evenly. It has moved faster in some places than others. It has been strongly resisted here and made more welcome there. It has penetrated relatively peacably in one place and with genocidal violence in another.

It has also been accompanied by physical transformations that are breathtaking in scope and radical in their implications. New productive forces have been produced and distributed across the face of the earth. Vast concentrations of capital and labour have come together in metropolitan areas of incredible complexity, while transport and communications systems, stretched in far-flung nets around the globe, permit information and ideas as well as material goods and even labour power to move around with relative ease. Factories and fields, schools, churches, shopping centres and parks, roads and railways litter a landscape that has been indelibly and irreversibly carved out according to the dictates of capitalism. Again, this physical transformation has not progressed evenly. Vast concentrations of productive power here contrast with relatively empty regions there. Tight concentrations of activity in one place contrast with sprawling far-flung development in another. All this adds up to what we call 'the uneven geographical development' of capitalism.

This surface appearance of extraordinary historical–geographical change cries out for theoretical examination. There is much to do here and unfortunately not much theoretical guidance as to how to do it. The difficulty is to find a way to approach the issue that is both theoretically grounded in basic Marxian concepts and robust enough to handle the evident confusions, antagonisms and conflicts that characterise the spatial articulation of human activities under capitalism. The phenomena to be looked at are, besides, of seemingly infinite variety. They include events and processes as diverse as individual fights over jurisdictional rights to a plot of land; colonial and neocolonial policies carried out by different nation states; residential differentiation within urban areas; fights between street gangs over 'turf'; the spatial articulation of diverse market systems (financial, commodity, etc.); regional patterns of growth within a division of labour; spatial concentrations in the distribution of the industrial reserve army; class alliances built around territorial concepts like community, region, nation; and so on.

Harvey's own answer to these problems consists of a 'third-cut' theory which will integrate uneven geographical development into his theory of capitalist crisis. Harvey's approach, especially with regard to the formation of classes, remains at a quite abstract level. But other researchers have had to become more specific, in the struggle to relate the general trajectory of capitalist development, uneven geographical development and processes of class formation together. In particular they have had to take more account of the relations of reproduction.

Four practitioners of the geographical imagination – Walker, Massey, Cooke and Urry – can be taken as representative of movement along a spectrum with a concern for relations of production at one end and a concern for relations of reproduction at the other. Walker (1985a; see also Storper and Walker, 1983), builds an argument based upon the junction of class with the division of labour, focusing particular attention on class formation as a result of the interaction of classes in the workplace through 'the employment relation' (see also Clark, 1981) and how this employment relation is worked out unevenly in space and time in different industries resulting in specific spatial divisions of labour. Massey's (1984) argument summarised in the classic *Spatial Divisions of Labour* is quite similar in outline but more attention is paid to the role of relations of reproduction in structuring classes, and especially gender relations. Cooke (1982a,b), in a series of papers, bends even more towards acknowledging the importance of relations of reproduction. His regional geography of class relations (Cooke, 1985) entails five main components: the uneven development of the productive base, the labour process and the ownership of capital in a region fuse with the specificities of local social relations and institutions to form a class. Finally, Urry's (1981, 1984) work is even more preoccupied with reproduction. The state and civil society are stressed as crucial determinants of class formation. Warde (1985, p. 199) summarises this concern well:

> No contemporary account of the division of labour can afford to ignore the broad range of social relationships which derive from the process of the (re-)production of labour power. There is significant disagreement among Marxist accounts on the importance of state intervention in the process of reproduction of labour power and how effects of that intervention should be conceptualised – hence the debate over collective consumption. But even those who consider reproduction important take almost no notice of variations among social institutions of civil society which reproduce labour power – households, families, neighbourhoods, etc. Yet there are considerable temporal and spatial variations in the conditions under which labour power is produced, and different sets of social arrangements appear to have pertinent political effects. These effects are germane to the formation of a local surface.

The current level of concern with relations of reproduction leads to the second area of work which has interleaved geography with class, namely the investigations into the constitution of consciousness and subjectivity. This area of research is a useful antidote to some of the research outlined above which can sometimes fall prey to reductionist tendencies and which often only pays lip service to the importance of human agency.

The constitution of consciousness and subjectivity in space has become a recognised focus of endeavour in geography through a mixture of sources including time-geography, humanistic geography and even, to an extent, behavioural geography. It is fairly easy to sketch an outline of the way that consciousness is constituted by social being over space (see Thrift, 1983, 1985, 1986). Particular practices, encapsulating social relations, are generated by institutions which provide people with other people to intermix with through the course of their lives; home, work, school, shop and so on. These practices impart accounts of the world, drawing upon particular institutional stocks of knowledge in doing so. Since institutions both produce and are produced by social divides like class it follows that different persons will be differently constituted by them. There is a 'political economy of development opportunities'.

The process of investing people with particular abilities – to sell their labour power, to be a 'good girl', to be a 'good worker', to identify with a class and all the other dimensions upon which people define themselves – is not a passive one. It is negotiated or even fought over day after day, year after year in all kinds of small guerilla actions and linguistic skirmishes as well as in the larger collective set battles. As Gregory (1984, p. 117) puts it: 'these are not the spectacular confrontations which set the pulse racing; but the transformations which have so long eluded traditional historical geographers lie as much in the ebb and flow of such seemingly mundane conflicts as in the episodic "revolutions" which excite our contemporary imaginations and sensitivities'. It is vitally important to remember that people have a capacity (however small it may sometimes be) to change institutions just as institutions have a capacity to change them.

Clearly space has a lot to do with how different people can be constituted differently. Institutions are not equally distributed in space and in particular locations the prevalent *mix* of institutions will be more or less effective in bending particular people's consciousness in certain directions rather than others. The political economy of development opportunities is a geography.

This, then, is a bare bones outline. The problem lies in fleshing it out. Three concepts can be used to elaborate upon some of the effects of geography on the production of people as members of classes; 'locale', 'locality' and 'distanciation'. *Locale* is probably best defined as the physical setting of institutions (involving the arrangement of space and time and also the meanings that go with this arrangement) within which certain practices are contained. This setting is drawn upon by people to constitute practices but it can also structure the development of these practices in certain ways rather than others (Giddens, 1981, 1984). Each locale is distinctively differentiated (Giddens uses the term 'regionalised') and class will often be one of the determinants of this differentiation. The homes of the different classes, for example, are divided up into rooms which can differ quite substantially in the typical practices associated with them and the meanings ascribed to them (Bourdieu, 1984, Saunders and Williams, forthcoming; Williams, 1986). Of course, the rooms of homes also have gender and age connotations. In the workplace, those in middle-class occupations function in quite different physical settings from those in working-class occupations and these settings say a good deal about what it is to be a member of that class through the limits they impose upon certain activities. Or take even a classical culturally specific institution like the British pub (Clark, 1983). This will usually be divided into a lounge bar and a public bar within which quite different practices are acted out, often with class connotations.

Clearly villages, towns, cities, even regions, are characterised by a mix of institutions which produce strings of practices (including class practices) that are distinctive. The more distinctive the mix, the greater the likelihood that the people producing and being produced by this local mix of institutions will generate strong bonds or acute divisions (and novel strategies to cope with them). In certain places the institutional mix will be so distinctive that it will produce a local economy and culture sufficiently potent that it can be dignified with the label of '*locality*' (Duncan, 1987). Much of the work by geographers and others on these localities has singled out their class characteristics. There is, in particular, the work on small working-class localities distinguished by their isolation and the class homogeneity borne of a community grouped around a single employer (e.g. McIntyre, 1980). But there is also work on 'radical regions' (e.g. Judt, 1979; Joyce, 1980; Cooke, 1983b).

But the power of the local mix of institutions to produce distinctive localities is not as great as it once was. The nature of institutions has changed substantially over time. In particular they have become organised at ever greater spatial scales – the regional scale, the national scale, even the international scale, with the arrival of the modern nation states and the multiple establishment firm. They have become, to use another Giddensian term, '*distanciated*'. That is, practices are no longer necessarily locally generated even though they may still be carried out locally. For example, a trade union is now commonly run at a regional or more likely national level and its different local branches must now co-ordinate their local affairs with those of the union as a whole (although the example of the 1984/85 British Miners Strike shows that the relationship runs both ways).

Technological change in the medium of communications has clearly been an important determinant of distanciation, allowing face-to-face interaction within a specific local institution to be replaced by interaction at a distance. In Giddens's terms again, social integration has been replaced by 'system integration'. The classic case of this tendency is, of course, television. Television has taken particular social practices that used to be locally generated (in the home, for example) and universalised them. The class implications of the following quotation are surely both intriguing and important:

> Many of the traditionally perceived differences among people of different 'social groups', different stages of socialization, and different levels of authority were supported by the division of people into different experiential worlds. The separation of people into different situations (or different sets of situations) fostered different world views, allowed for sharp distinction between people's 'onstage' and 'backstage' behaviours, and permitted people to play complementary – rather than reciprocal – roles. Such distinctions in situations were supported by the diffusion of literacy and printed materials which tended to divide people into very different informational worlds based on different levels of reading skill and on training and interest in different 'literatures'. These distinctions were also supported by the isolation of people in different places, which led to different social identities based on the specific and limited experiences available in given locations. By bringing many different types of people to the same 'place', electronic media have fostered a blurring of many distinct social roles. Electronic media affect us, then, not primarily through their content, but by changing the 'situational geography' of social life (Meyrowitz, 1985, pp. 6–7).

These considerations lead us to the third and final area of work on class in which the geographical imagination is important. That is in the consideration of class capacity. With the historical developments in organisation and communication that took place in the nineteenth century it is no longer appropriate to consider class connectedness as a network of local 'island' communities, joined together only by the arrival of the *Northern Star* or the diffusion of the news of a riot from a contiguous community. Classes now exist at a number of *levels of integration* or *co-ordination* (Smith, 1982; Calhoun, 1982) and within each of these levels the capacity of a class to take part in conflict may be high or low; similarly, between each level the capacity of a class can be high or low. The ability of classes to operate at particular levels of integration depends on either the presence of, or the generation of, the appropriate institutional orders to support such operations. Before a whole class, or even a large proportion of a class, can be mobilised one precondition is the existence of institutional orders able to co-ordinate and span several levels of integration. Typically, however, certain classes are better able to monopolise the orders of certain levels of integration rather than others. For example, in the nineteenth century, the middle class was often successful in capturing the municipal level of administration in Britain but in many ways this was a substitution for its lack of power at the national level (Crossick, 1977).

While the importance of these levels will obviously vary over time with particular issues, there is still a general tendency that since the nineteenth century the importance of the larger-scale levels of integration of classes has become greater while the more local levels of integration have become less relevant (at least, in *class* terms). There are a number of reasons for this tendency. The first is simply the growth in population size and consequently in the overall size of classes. The second is the growth of institutions able to deal with these facts. These have become progressively less likely to be based on local social bonds and personal inter-relationships and progressively more likely to be based on bureaucratic procedures (see Smith, 1982; Calhoun, 1982). Third, time–space convergence and the increasing orbit of modern telecommunications have expanded the spatial reach of all classes (although this has been a differential process with the upper and middle classes able, through their occupations and income, to expand the reach of their classes more easily than the working class).

There are numerous studies of the geography of classes at a range of scales (see above) but the nature and strength of the interconnections that make classes into living, developing systems are still too little treated. Our purpose in this volume is to explore these interconnections through a set of specially commissioned papers analysing different aspects of class formation in space in Britain and the United States.

3 The papers

The first part of the book is concerned with that golden age of class, the nineteenth century. In his introductory chapter, Nigel Thrift outlines some of the key determinants of class formation in space through the period, using the examples of Sheffield and Leeds as paradigms of uneven development. In, 'Class, place and industrial revolution', Craig Calhoun is mainly concerned with the issue of class connectedness. He emphasises the vital role of spatial scale in the forging of class struggle. In particular, he stresses the importance of improvements in transport and communications in enabling the build up of indirect relationships through which collective action at larger scales must be organised. (Note here the parallels with Giddens's (1981, 1984) work on social and system integration.) Some will quarrel with Calhoun's argument that class struggle must be understood as a large-scale phenomenon but clearly this chapter raises a number of important issues for the analysis of class formation in space.

The next two chapters are more specific in their focus, both in time (the later nineteenth century) and in space. Richard Dennis considers the connectedness of lower middle-class life in the Hillhouse district of Huddersfield, West Yorkshire, in 1871. Dennis describes a complex social hierarchy, differentiated to an extent by location and with limited evidence of a 'neighbourhood effect' (Johnston, 1986) appearing in political allegiances. For Dennis, this small segment of the lower middle class had at least a latent class consciousness borne out of the fact that its members perceived the world in a common fashion borne out of the familiar routines of everyday life. In a wide-ranging chapter Damaris Rose concentrates upon a rather different class segment. Her study is of the Cornish tin-miners in a period when they were suffering considerable industrial dislocation leading to their proletarianisation. She is particularly concerned with the effect that the ownership of smallholdings by some miners may have had in boosting their economic circumstances and conditioning their political allegiances. Due attention is paid to the complexities of the issues involved – the nature of the labour process, the effects of gender divisions and the nature of civil society are all taken into account. Thus this paper draws together all three of the traditions of work outlined earlier.

In the last chapter of the first part of the book, Peter Williams considers the role of one institution of reproduction, the home, and the interaction between the home and class formation in the eighteenth and nineteenth centuries. The chapter focuses on consciousness and connectedness and raises a whole set of issues including the importance of gender divisions, the form of domestic production and the general nature of the household. These issues are crucial to the discussions of class and civil society and have definite connections to similar debates on the constitution of twentieth-century civil society (see, for example, Pahl, 1984; Mingione and Redclift, 1985).

The last five chapters which make up the second part of the book are concerned with the twentieth century. In his introduction, Nigel Thrift is concerned with the changing processes of class formation in space, paying special attention to the new service class habitats being carved out of quasi-rural areas. John Urry's chapter is concerned with linking the trajectory of capitalist development and social change. He traces out the interplay between the rise of scientific management and the formation of the service class in the United States in the years bracketing the First World War. Urry stresses the importance of scientific management in providing the nascent service class with a tool of struggle against other classes which it was unable to use as successfully in countries like Britain where other classes had better prepared defences.

In a comparative chapter, Dennis Smith addresses the intersecting roles of class, politics and ethnicity in the making of the history of Chicago and Birmingham in the period from 1890 to 1983. Smith is particularly interested in how feelings of attachment to place and ethnicity (defined in its broadest sense) can either reconcile or disrupt political allegiances moulded on class lines. Like Rose, Smith links each of the three areas of work – trajectory, consciousness and connectedness.

The chapter by Phil Cooke sets the scene for class analysis in the later twentieth century. Cooke focuses on the restructurings of capital that have taken place between the 1960s and the 1980s, and on the social consequences of these restructurings. His main argument is that the thesis that capitalism has now become 'disorganised' is overstated and more attention needs to be paid to the ascendancy of new technological, social and spatial 'paradigms'.

The final chapter concentrates upon the current role of the middle class in structuring urban places. Ray Forrest and Alan Murie are concerned with the upper end of the service class. In particular, they argue that these élite members of the service class have housing histories tailored to their job careers in bureaucracies (whether in the state or private sectors). These careers give them less choice than is conventionally assumed in picking when and where to move but at the same time they provide fiscal privileges in buying a house which are rarely considered in the housing literature.

These are a diverse range of chapters illustrating some of the ways in which the formation of class and the formation of space are inextricably intertwined. What is certain, is that there are many theoretical issues still to be addressed and many empirical case studies left to be documented. There is much to do.

Part One
The Nineteenth Century

• 2 •

Introduction: *The geography of nineteenth-century class formation* • *NIGEL THRIFT*

The purpose of this introductory chapter is to show how the determinants of class formation changed over the course of the nineteenth century in Britain in unexpected and often quite drastic ways. Such determinants were sometimes crucially affected by geography (see Bedarida, 1979). The problem is to assess exactly how space intervened in class formation. Clearly a framework of analysis is needed. The framework used here and in Chapter 7 is the simple model of capitalist society first put forward by Urry (1981). Urry distinguishes between three spheres of social relations which go to make up a capitalist society, namely relations in the sphere of production, relations in the sphere of state apparatuses and relations in the sphere of 'civil society' (that is, relations within and between households). Urry's main innovation is that, unlike many previous Marxist writers, he makes civil society an equal partner, with the economy and the state, in the determination of class formation.

Within civil society another three overlapping spheres can be discerned. These are the sphere of circulation (that is of distribution, exchange and consumption), the sphere of reproduction (biologically, economically and culturally) and the sphere of struggle (of individual subjects, of groups, classes and so on). The sphere of civil society is always and everywhere differentiated spatially, by gender, by religion, by ethnic groups, by voluntary association and by generation and these distributions form the available bases on which individuals, groups and classes can mobilise. Each civil society is vertically or horizontally organised:

> A civil society is vertically organised when (the) diverse social groupings and associations are class-specific and there is relatively little independent organisation; a civil society is horizontally organised when there are a large number of social groupings and other social practices which are non-class specific and which generate relatively autonomous forms of organisation and representation (Urry, 1982, p. 8).

Within civil society class formation is a process of continual organisation, disorganisation and reorganisation of classes in which the class struggle between capitalists and workers is only one of a number of conflicts. Other classes, less directly based on capitalist relations of production, also fight for pre-eminence. For, while under capitalism, capitalist relations are necessarily important it does not follow that they are always the focus of struggle. There is no essence of class waiting to be expressed. Rather the salience of the class relation and class conflict has to be continually established and maintained. And so does the existence of particular classes.

Following Urry, the form a class takes in society at any one time and its capacity for struggle is therefore related to three major axes of class formation. First, there is the current pattern of capital accumulation and the relations between the functions of capital and labour (sphere of production). This will subsume other sources of determination like the division of labour and authority relations within the enterprise. Second, there is the prevailing form of political organisation and state apparatus (the State). Third, there is the precise form of civil society, including especially its spatial layout (civil society).

It seems obvious that class consciousness, given the validity of this account, will be always and everywhere a diffuse and, above all, a historically contingent phenomenon which has to be continually fought for by members of particular classes, given a certain class capacity, within a particular place. That fight must take place within and as part of overall patterns of socialisation, of class and other group allegiances, of the continual learning *and* relearning of the social relations that constitute the subject (and reproduce wage-labour) as each subject follows their particular life-path:

> friendship, visiting, receptions, the more organised unity of clubs and associations, and the diffuse unity engendered by a particular type of schooling. All these practices bring about a commonality of background and

attitude which crystallises a social class into a collectivity whose members possess not merely equivalent life chances but also a similarity of life style (Scott, 1979, p. 110).

All this, of course, is geographically variable and particular localities produce particular subjects and particular distributions of subjects each with particular potentials for class action and inaction.

This framework makes it possible to order a discussion of how the geography of class formation has changed over the course of the capitalist history of Britain. Britain in the mid-nineteenth-century is often considered to represent a prototypical form of capitalism. Certainly it is, courtesy of Marx, Dickens and innumerable economic and social historians, one of the best documented forms.

The capitalist *economy* at this time was still focused on manufacturing industry where the real subsumption of labour was just beginning to be felt (but see Samuel, 1977a). However, no account of mid-Victorian Britain can ignore the enormous growth of what is now called service industry (see Lee, 1984) and more especially the commercial activities, centred on the City of London and the major provincial cities, and domestic service (which accounted for 13 per cent of the labour force in 1851). In this situation, there was an easily definable working class, although not without its gradients (for example, see the debate on the labour aristocracy) or internal tensions. There was an easily identifiable capitalist class as well, again with its distinctions and tensions (for example, on the schisms between the merchant capitalists of the City and the manufacturing capitalists of the North of England, see Rubinstein, 1980).

The mid-nineteenth century *state* was important as the ultimate source of order, embodied in the Army. But it was by no means the complex, all encompassing phenomenon of today. For example, primary education (which was all the education most were likely to receive) was predominantly in private hands and indirect control over a few others through the Inspectorate (Best, 1971). The police force, only a few years from its beginnings in the 1830s, was still small in number. Welfare for the poor was still heavily dependent upon private charities.

In the sphere of *civil society*, there were strict gender divisions. Women were mainly, and quite literally, given the constant pattern of childbearing, reproducers. Of course, this is not to say that no women worked. In 1851, 25–26 per cent of women were in employment of one kind or another. Mainly these were working-class women in domestic service or enlisted in an army of casual workers and outworkers (see Rose, 1986). Middle- and upper-class women were meant to be virtually idle. But even middle- and upper-class households were still sites of production in every way – the mass market with its panoply of consumer goods substituting for domestic production was embryonic (see Fraser, 1981). Households were diverse as well with the numbers in each household varying considerably (see Anderson, 1985). The life experience was correspondingly heterogeneous. It was also hazardous. There was constant bereavement to remind people of their own likelihood of dying soon. For many of the working class there were the added uncertainties born of facts like the constant movement from one set of lodgings to another in what was a fluid rental market.

The *space* of mid-nineteenth-century Britain was being shaped in three ways. First, there was a dramatic increase in the density of population as a result of rapid population growth. Between 1801 and 1851 the population of England and Wales nearly doubled (Lawton, 1978). Second, there was a massive increase in the concentration of population in cities. In 1801 only 34 per cent of the population of England and Wales lived in urban areas. By 1851 the figure was 54 per cent (Lawton, 1978). The vast movements of population signified by these figures continued unabated until the latter years of the nineteenth century and led to a challenge to the traditional dominance of London and other southern regional centres by the new manufacturing centres of the North. These population movements were also responsible for a general decline in traditional modes of association within the civil society of many (but by no means all) of the new manufacturing areas. Third, there were dramatic changes in the time distances of different areas of Britain from one another with important social and economic consequences. Of most importance was the coming of mass transit. By 1851, the basic railway network of Britain had been built. Although rail fares were still too expensive to permit much working class suburbanisation, the building of the railways allowed the first waves of middle-class suburbanisation to spread outwards, aided by the advent of horse omnibus services in cities like Leeds and Manchester (Bagwell, 1971). The railways had other effects too. In particular, they integrated the operations of the economy and the state. For example, the system of marketing goods was transformed, local differences in prices began to be eliminated and greater promptitude in business and government affairs was encouraged.

Within civil society, knowledge of the world was generally enlarged. The railways acted as a precondition for the establishment of mass circulation daily newspapers. They allowed the development of excursions, such as to the 1851 Great Exhibition in London. They made it possible for postage to become cheaper, encouraging letter writing. And so on.

Thus, the mid-nineteenth century is a time of flux through which the distinctive class and non-class-based institutions of modern societies can usually only be glimpsed. Rather, the class character of mid-nineteenth century Britain is probably best described as a patchwork quilt of different but connected production cultures. It is a patchwork quilt because the degree of the annihilation of space by time is still limited. Thus classes and class formation still tended to be local. 'In the mid-nineteenth century the city was an independent political unit with its own internal consistency and primary political drives; by the early twentieth century it was clearly no longer a discrete focus of politics' (Fraser, 1976, p. 284). And these locally-based cultures were still generated first and foremost by the exigencies of production because there was little opportunity for any other kind of culture to form. Long working hours meant that there was not much time outside of work and what there was was often devoted to subsistence while there was a general dearth of consumer goods (although as recent work on seventeenth and eighteenth century consumer goods industries shows this is not to say that no such goods were available).

In these circumstances an uneven development model of class and class formation works quite well. Knowing the parameters of production (and especially the degree of formal or real control of the workplace) makes it possible to read off the nature and extent of class formation in particular places with some degree of certainty (given that there will always be variations in the history and culture of any place to be taken into account). Places are discrete and the diffusion of class impulses and the building up of class organisation between them are usually able to be traced fairly easily. The examples of Sheffield and Leeds in the 1850s and 1860s, two towns with at this time roughly similar population sizes, show how the uneven development model can work with authority, even with places some thirty miles apart (figure 2.1).

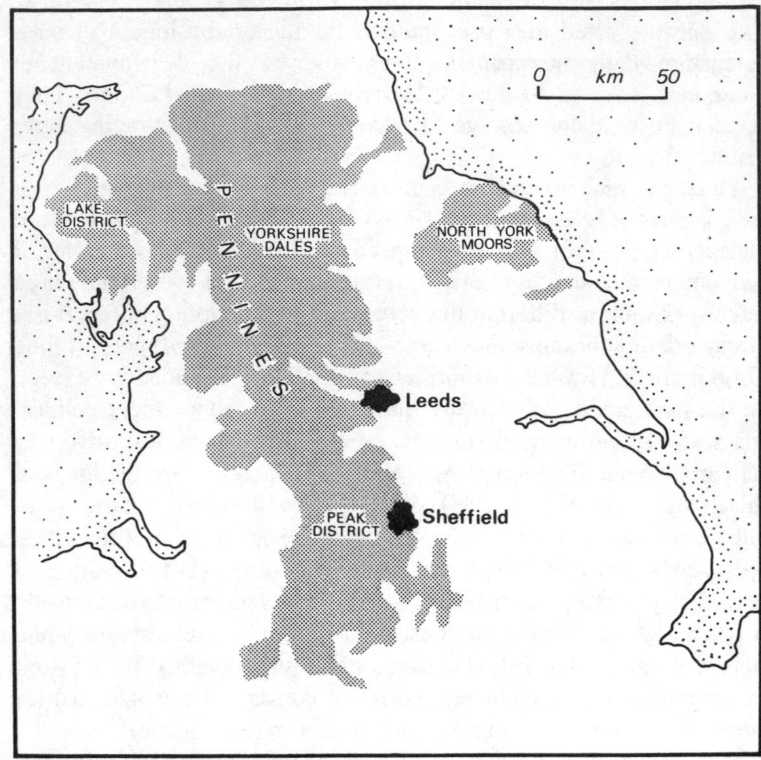

Figure 2.1 Location of Sheffield and Leeds

Sheffield and Leeds 1850–70: A study in uneven class development

At first sight there are many similarities between Sheffield and Leeds in the third quarter of the nineteenth century; contemporary commentators like Engels usually attested to the growing respectability of the working class in both towns, for example. But such similarities are only partial and often trivial. They gloss over the far more substantial differences. In particular, Sheffield in the 1850s and 1860s is the sheltered site of a brief 'golden age' (Pollard, 1959), the Roman summer of a particular form of industrial organisation that is wedged between the 'proto-industrial' form of rural domestic production (Mendels, 1972) and the machine-based factory with its wage-labouring proletariat. This form of organisation, which Marx called 'manufacture', was based on skilled handicrafts (in Sheffield the 'light trades' like cutlery and file-making) and a substantial artisanate. In contrast, Leeds in the 1850s and 1860s is dominated by textiles and although a good part of its industry is still domestically-based as the new engineering trades appear the die is, so to speak, cast. Leeds runs to the rhythm of the factory. It is the site of 'machinofacture'. The two towns are the two sides of a more general Janus-like articulation between manufacture and 'machinofacture'. Sheffield peers back into the past; for all intents and purposes it is a workshop. Leeds faces the future; for all intents and purposes it is a factory.

In what follows, we will consider the fate of two quite different social classes in these two different towns during the 1850s and 1860s; the Sheffield artisanate and the Leeds working-class. The one class had a strong capacity at the local level of integration, based upon a distinctive mode of production and a tightly defined civil society, but an increasingly marginal position in both the local and national systems of production (Reid, 1983; Hobsbawm, 1984). The other class had a weak capacity at the local level of integration but an increasingly central position in both the local and national systems of production. The kind of politics each class could pursue was affected accordingly.

The Sheffield artisanate

In the 1850s and 1860s, contemporary commentators always first remarked on the pall of smoke that hung continuously over Sheffield:

> A thick pulverous haze is spread over the city (wrote an observer in 1861) which the sun even in the long day is unable to penetrate, save by a lurid glare, which has the effect of imparting to the green hills and golden cornfields in the high distance, the ghostly appearance of being whitened with snow (Pollard, 1959, p. 13).

Next, they would notice the splintered spatial layout of the town. It was still possible to see a necklace of small, almost village-like, communities surrounding the central township of Sheffield, although by 1850 these were beginning to be swallowed up in the rising tide of 'back-to-backs'. These small and closed communities housed the skilled handicraft trades making cutlery, tools and handles, for which Sheffield had been famous for so long (even in 1672, there was a smithy to every three households in Sheffield). Steam-power had brought these trades into Sheffield where they clustered in 'wheels' and 'forgings', buildings divided into 'hulls' (rooms) in which there were a number of 'troughs' (workplaces) which gave access to power for forges, grinding wheels and other machines. But the trades needed no complex machinery. They were grouped for the convenience of, not subordination to, such machines. In these small communities was to be found a whole way of life, 'the trade', one that had grown out of proto-industrial origins and was still versed in rural practices and traditions; many artisans still cultivated plots of land. The cutlers even kept going a pack of hounds. Even as late as 1889 an observer could still assert:

> The population of Sheffield is, for so large a town, unique in its character, in fact it more closely resembles that of a village than a town, for over wide areas each person appears to be acquainted with every other, and to be interested in each other's concerns (quoted in Smith, 1982, p. 31).

A set of class-specific institutions form the nodes around which this way of life could be built; the workshop, obviously; the sick clubs (the proportion of artisans contributing to sick clubs was higher in Sheffield than in any other manufacturing town in England); the Sunday schools (often firmly in artisanal hands, see Smith, 1982); the many small inns and beer houses; the numerous Methodist chapels (Methodism was the major denomination in Sheffield and 'democratic' Methodism was very popular); and the distinctively domestic character of the home (it was a male culture; fewer women worked than in Leeds). Workshop–pub–chapel–house, these were the foci of what was almost an enclave mentality and what was certainly a very resistant culture, *a culture that controlled itself* (see Smith, 1982, ch. 3). As Storch (1977, p. 147) puts it:

> What characterised (Sheffield) was not so much different activities but different temporal rhythms. Working-class recreational life was not primarily packed into the Saturday night and the Sunday. In Sheffield there could be a number of Sunday-like days. The streets and street life itself presented rather different aspects to Leeds or Manchester and as we approach 1850 these approaches tend to magnify. Whatever order and regularity could be found where the worker was tied to the discipline imposed by the factory was absent in Sheffield.

Lying in and around these small self-contained, even clannish communities were the 'heavy trades', an embryo steel industry and an emergent engineering industry. In 1850, the 'firms' making steel, the rolling mills (still often water-powered) and the engineering works were not yet marked off from their counterparts in the light trades.

Table 2.1: The structure of industrial employment in Sheffield, 1851

(a) Light Trades (includes women and boys)

Trade	*Forgers & Strikers*	*Grinders*	*Halters*	*All Others* (including warehouse work & handle making)	*Total*
File	900	250	–	2850	4000
Spring knife	550	850	2800	200	4400
Table knife	800	1000	1700	500	4000
Razor	150	450	200	200	1000
Scissors	200	400	–	600	1200
Saw	450	250	–	300	1000
Steel fork	400	250	–	–	650
Edge tool	200	450	–	50	700
Other tools	200	–	–	200	400
Scythe, sickle	200	400	–	200	800
Stovegrate, fender	100	100	–	200	400
Nail	300	–	–	–	300
Needle	–	20	–	30	50
Horn	–	–	–	300	300
Gold & Silver	–	–	–	700	700
Plated, etc.	–	–	–	900	900
Britannia metal	–	–	–	500	500
Totals	4450	4420	4700	7730	21300

(b) Heavy Trades (including boys)

Trade	*Total*
Engineering	800
Wire Trades	330
Crucible steel	1700
Converting	300
Tilting & rolling	1250
Steel puddling	250
Axle and spring	300
Founding	200
Totals	5130

Source: Pollard, 1959, pp. 331–2

Often they were simply adjuncts of the steel-consuming cutlery and tool industries and, as yet, they employed many fewer workers (Table 2.1). But developments in the 1850s and 1860s were very rapid. As the market for steel expanded as a result of demand from the railway and armaments industries (the Crimean War) large factories were built in Sheffield, mainly in the north-east of the town on the lines of communication. In 1858/59 Bessemer built his own works in the town. In 1860 John Brown & Co. laid down four large convertors. The way of things is shown by the employment figures for John Brown; 200 in 1856, 2500 in 1863, 5000 by 1872. An industrial proletariat was in the process of being formed in Sheffield; the steel and armaments industries demanded continual attendance and round-the-clock working; in the depressions unemployment was the norm, not short-time working; skill was only at a premium in certain of the occupations; labour-power was supplied by a flood of immigrants from the countryside and other iron working districts. These immigrants produced a massive population increase in the 1850s and 1860s (Table 2.2) which had a number of detrimental effects on the artisanate. First, the artisanate was rapidly outnumbered and, second, a strong pattern of working-class residential segregation was produced relatively early on (certainly earlier than Leeds) in the shape of working-class housing estates for the steel workers and suburbs for the functionary middle class.

Table 2.2: Decennial rate of population increase in Leeds and Sheffield

	1801–11	'11–21	'21–31	'31–41	'41–51	'51–61	'61–71	'71–81	'81–91	'91–1901
Leeds	33.9	33.3	46.4	23.6	13.1	20.3	25.1	19.3	19.0	16.6
Sheffield	15.2	22.6	41.5	20.6	21.6	37.0	29.7	18.7	13.6	26.2

Source: calculated from Mitchell and Deane, 1962

Gradually, then, a dual economy came into being in Sheffield. In one segment the light trades, in the other the heavy trades. In the 1840s and 1850s there had still been some movement between the two segments. Artisans had moved between grinding files and grinding in the engineering trades for example. And some artisans (for example, John Brown, a factor and cutlery maker) had set up as steel manufacturers (cf. Schorsch, 1980). But as the industrial proletariat (and industrial capitalists) came into being, this interaction diminished and then all but ceased.

The class structure of Sheffield in the 1850s and 1860s had a similarly dualistic character. But it still took its cue from the distinctive organisation of production of the light trades which was able to survive as it was only because there was no real competition. The cutlery industry, for example, was almost a Sheffield monopoly even in the context of the world economy. The result was that 'the concept of a self-contained factory, where each operation was subject to the control of a single guiding hand, was alien to local light industry' (Pollard, 1959, p. 55). Even those few buildings blessed with the name of 'factories', in reality comprised men willing to devote most (but not all) of their time to the employer's work and tenants who merely rented room and power. Scattered round in other locations there would be a network of outworkers all taking on orders from the 'factory' but by no means bound to it. The typical Sheffield artisan owned his own tools, controlled his hours of work, observed Saint Monday (Thompson, 1967; Thrift, 1981), and paid a weekly rent for space at his 'trough' and the use of power.

The distinction between artisan and employer was a blurred one in the light trades in Sheffield. Many 'employers' were still only merchant capitalists who often doubled as landlords as well. They owned one or a combination of capital, raw materials and buildings and, by 1850, increasingly controlled the distribution of finished products. Then there were a few large manufacturers with their decentralized 'factories'. Lying between these worthies and the artisans were 'little masters', artisans who had begun to purchase their own raw materials and employed a few apprentices, and 'factors', middlemen who took on work and then contracted it out again. There was a fairly well marked out channel of mobility:

> the ascent from wage labour to manufacturer was gradual and fairly easy. A man could easily double his income by employing two or three apprentices or other journeymen; he could then invest his additional income in buying materials on his own account and thus become a 'little master' and duly plough back sufficient sums into his business to rise to the position of a manufacturer, with his own trade mark and his established market. The initial required capital was small and importers of iron, local makers of steel and even wholesalers and exporters were in the habit of granting six-month credits (Pollard, 1959, p. 56).

Some masters, reflecting their origins, sat on the committees of the local unions. The employers, then, were nearer to a petty bourgeoisie than industrial capitalists.

This was still a pre-capitalist or, more accurately, transitional capitalist class structure. It made a strong contrast with the classical wage-labouring proletariat/industrial capitalist structure which was becoming increasingly entrenched in the north-eastern part of the town.

Class conflict in Sheffield during the 1850s and 1860s took place in two related arenas, at work and on the stump. At work the single most important fact had been, at least since the disputes of 1810–14 with the masters of the Company of Cutlers, the presence of strong unions in the light trades. The unions, some of which dated from the first half of the eighteenth century, considered themselves to be the direct descendants of the Cutlers' Company, the guild repealed by the masters in 1814. In one case, a union itself owned tools, hired rooms and power and took on contracts at which unemployed workers were set (Pollard, 1971). Indeed the unions used many of the same guild traditions. First, they set limits to entry, to the number of apprentices any union member could have, to the prices charged and to hours worked. Union meetings were compulsory and fines were levied for non-attendance. Second, regular and often very high payments were demanded to support those 'on the box' (unemployed) in times of depression. Third, sanctions were imposed on those who offended against the union, for example by non-payment of dues. 'Rattening' was the most usual sanction, the removal of the bands from grindstones and of an artisan's tools, but more severe measures were sometimes taken ranging in severity from a threatening letter (traditionally signed by 'man in the moon', 'Mary Ann' or 'Nathan') through the hamstringing of the wrongdoer's horse to the use of more incendiary reminders like gunpowder. These measures were needed because the unions suffered from a number of weaknesses; typically, each union was small and unstable. Some members of the union had to be kept on the box in order to keep the price of labour up, and factors and small masters constantly abused the system. However, if the capacity of the unions to engage in conflict was diminished by these problems, the employers were usually no better off. They had, at best, only formal control of the workplace. And, because of Sheffield's complex industrial structure, there were a large number of different types of employer, each with different and often conflicting interests. Employers' Associations were, with a few exceptions like the File Manufacturers' Association (which won the major dispute of 1866), weak, ineffective and transient. The light trade unions reached the peak of their power in the 1860s when membership stood at 6000. After 1866 union power was severely curtailed, first by the defeat in 1866 after a sixteen-week dispute, of the filesmiths and file grinders over the introduction of machinery; and then, in 1867, by the 'Sheffield Outrages' (see below). But the decline in union power was, more generally, a symptom of the decline in the Sheffield light trades as a whole, which was the result of the introduction of machinery into the United States and the rest of Britain that was able to make cheap saws, cutlery and files in bulk and the invention of new materials which affected the handle making trade in particular.

The nature of the light trades' unions is nowhere better encapsulated than in the so-called 'Sheffield Outrages' of the 1850s and 1860s (Pollard, 1957, 1959, 1971) a series of assaults, gunpowder attacks, even shootings, which resulted in the Royal Commission of Inquiry of 1867. The minutes of this inquiry are a poignant exhibition of mutual incomprehension on the parts of union members and commissioners. On one side the union members remained generally unrepentant (indeed some of them demanded the legal right to distrain goods if dues were not paid). The perpetrators of the 'outrages' were never expelled from their unions. On the other side, the commissioners, in a national atmosphere of anti-union hostility, considered that they were investigating a criminal conspiracy and yet they were forced to realise that they were dealing not with criminal figures but with sober, respectable and eloquent artisans. In these minutes are enshrined the clash between an essentially pre-capitalist moral economy (Thompson, 1971) and a capitalist economy. For 'the trade' was a life hewn out of community, not work and non-work. The artisans:

> had a very clear consciousness of 'the trade' as almost a physical entity within which they worked. It was within their trade that they were apprenticed, that they spent their working lives, that their wages and their work load was settled, and that their welfare provisions, in case of sickness or unemployment, death or legal costs, were met – or if the trade was 'out of union' – failed to be met. One could not escape one's trade, even by leaving the union and it was this that the Commissioners failed to grasp, and that caused some of the most persistent misunderstandings in their examination. Repeatedly they questioned the unionists about men who had left the unions by failing to keep up with their weekly subscriptions, and repeatedly they were at cross-purposes with witnesses who appeared to give them unclear or shuffling answers. What the unionists were trying to explain, and what the commissioners genuinely failed to see, was that one did not cease to be a member of one's trade simply by not

> paying up; one would fall out of benefit, but the workmen in Sheffield, both those who continued to pay, and those who had stopped paying, knew better than to imagine that one could thereby sever one's connection with the economic reality of the 'trade'. In at least one case, the union lent its members who had fallen out of benefit by not paying, sufficient money to make them 'financial' again, i.e. entitled to benefit just before calling a strike, and such action was clearly unintelligible to men who thought of unions as clubs which one could join or leave at will.
>
> Similarly it was hard for the Commissioners to believe that rattening . . . until such time as the man was straight again with the union, was undertaken also without official orders by the union. Yet normally such action could be taken entirely at the initiative of individuals, who only afterwards might or might not use the good offices of the union secretary to secure a payment, nominally called expenses, but in reality constituting a fine, for their trouble (Pollard, 1971, pp. xi–xii).

As at work, so in the realm of politics, there was a blurring of the lines of battle. The polarized class structure of the capitalist economy had not come into being and indeed would not until the heavy trades, with their wage-labouring proletariat, gained ascendency in the Sheffield urban economy. So no truly independent working-class politics existed until the last quarter of the nineteenth century. A Sheffield Labour Association was not formed until 1885, a 'Socialist Club' only in 1887. But this should not be taken to imply that the level of political activity amongst the artisanate was low or that politics were never radical. Sheffield already possessed a long history of radical politics before 1829 (Donnelly and Baxter, 1975). From 1791 to 1820 there is a continual record of demonstrations, petitions, riots, arrests, even deaths. Tom Paine walks the streets. Troops had to be garrisoned in the town in 1791. In 1795 soldiers fired into a crowd, killing two. There were large demonstrations in 1812 and again in 1819 (against the Peterloo Massacre). There is some evidence of revolutionary movements. Indeed Williams (1968) has compared Sheffield during this time to the French Revolutionary Fauborg Saint-Antoine. While this is an exaggeration there is no doubt that the town's reputation was not just the work of a few radicals. The Sheffield Society for Constitutional Information, before it was suppressed in 1795, surpassed in size the London Corresponding Society. A petition for reform in 1817 bore 21 000 Sheffield signatures.

However, after 1820 and, more particularly, after 1848 this radical voice was slowly muted. This muting was partly the result of a coalition between the more radical members of the petty bourgeoisie and the more conservative members of the artisanate that had started before 1837 and now carried through the 1850s and 1860s. Such a coalition could hold only if the interests of the two classes appeared to be the same and because of Sheffield's economic structure this was more often the case than in most other places. First there was the fact that employers and artisans were not so very far apart in either income or outlook; many artisans were hopeful of rising into the ranks of the small masters and manufacturers and many small masters and manufacturers had come from the ranks of thc artisans. Second, the climate of opinion in the town was not generally hostile to artisans. Artisans could take their employers to court and win. Unions had not, since 1814, had to fight so very hard for recognition. Third, because of the absence of factories there was no need for a parting of the ways between the working class and petty bourgeoisie over the Factory Acts, as occurred in other towns like Manchester. Fourth, because of their relative prosperity again, both classes had certain common goals; for example suffrage. Even before the Reform Act of 1867 many artisans possessed the franchise. In 1866 one-quarter of the electorate were artisans or merchants. After the Act artisan electors formed a majority. Finally, artisanate and petty bourgeoisie had, to some extent, a common culture, bolstered by many of the religious and educational institutions in the town as well as the classically middle-class institutions like the Mcchanics' Library, and summed up in one world, 'respectability'. In 1843 Holland could already note:

> the fortunes here are already small, and the command of the necessaries and comforts of life is largely enjoyed by the population. Morality, intelligence, order and social feeling exist perhaps in greater proportion than in any other large town (p. 63).

In 1847 Porter made some similar observations:

> It is worthy of remark that this comfortless condition of the poor is not seen in all localities. In some places where no other appearances in the state of society would seem to indicate it, there is to be found an extraordinary degree of respectability in this particular. The town of Sheffield, for instance, contains a large manufacturing population, by no means remarkable for orderly conduct. The town itself is ill built and dirty, beyond the usual condition of English towns, but it is the custom for each family among the labouring population to occupy a separate dwelling, the rooms in which are furnished in a very comfortable manner, the floors are carpeted, and the tables are usually of mahogany; chests of drawers of the same material are commonly seen, and so

in most cases is a clock also, the possession of which article of furniture has often been pointed out as the certain indication of prosperity and personal respectability on the part of the working man (p. 533).

Certainly, during the 1850s and 1860s, the artisanate had a potentially considerable voice in the political affairs of the town. Yet this was continually undermined by the coalition. The coalition held through the anti-Corn Law agitation, for example, and even through the trauma of Chartism, for which there was considerable support in the town, not least from the small masters, shopkeepers and well-to-do artisans. In November 1846 two Chartists were elected to the newly incorporated (1843) town council as part of the Chartist or Democratic Party now led by the extraordinary Isaac Ironside (see Smith, 1982). In November 1847 six more Chartists were successful. In March 1848, 10 000–12 000 people assembled to welcome the Paris Revolution. In November 1848 seven Chartists were elected to the council even after the failure of the Charter. By November 1849, twenty-two out of fifty-six seats on the Town Council were filled by Chartists. In 1851 Ironside set up the Central Democratic Ward Association, a formidable apparatus based upon 'ward-moots', regular local neighbourhood meetings. But the caucus broke up in 1852, and they fought their last municipal election in 1854. In the remainder of the 1850s and through the 1860s Town Council representation was predominantly conservative, although Ironside kept control of the Highways Board for a time. But even given this record between 1843 and 1893, the Town Council was almost exclusively petty bourgeois (and later upper- and middle-class) in origin. Of the 385 men who held office in those years, 151 were manufacturers, 59 were professional men and 26 were publicans, brewers and builders. After 1854 only 7 were artisans (Smith, 1982).

Parliamentary representation in Sheffield was continually Liberal until 1914 and the men in the light trades were among the last to identify their unions with the Labour Party. The artisans were, it sometimes seemed, instinctively Liberal voters.

To summarise, for the artisanate the main nexus of class conflict in the 1850s and 1860s continued to be the trade unions. It was the unions that the artisans spontaneously identified with. It sometimes seems that this identification may have been at the cost of more general forms of politics. But, as we have seen, the Charter gained considerable support amongst the artisanate and it may well be that the lack of this more general issue during the 1850s and 1860s combined with the attacks on unions during these years and general economic prosperity to keep the artisanate quiescent in the more general political sphere. In the growing 'heavy trades', in contrast, the men 'had not yet found their bearings; apart from certain skilled engineering trades, they had not even succeeded in forming stable trade unions' (Pollard, 1959, p. 121). And, of course, most men in these trades did not meet the property qualifications needed to get the vote.

As for class consciousness, considerable problems exist in identifying its existence in Sheffield in the 1850s and 1860s. The artisanate's immediate loyalties lay with concrete, local collectivities and, in particular, the unions. Given this fact and Sheffield's radical tradition it seems certain that there was a more generalised 'labour' consciousness. But, just as certainly, Sheffield's sectionalised economy prevented any transformation of this type of consciousness into 'revolutionary' consciousness, except briefly on particular occasions amongst small and generally isolated groups. Class consciousness was turned inwards rather than outwards, into struggles within Sheffield's peculiar local economy and not outwards to the existence of the economy as a whole.

The Leeds working class

In the 1850s and 1860s over Leeds too, the contemporary commentator would have noticed a smoke haze. In 1844 Kohl noted that 'Leeds like all the great manufacturing cities in England is a dirty, smoky disagreeable town . . . Leeds is perhaps the ugliest and least attractive town in all England.' But whereas in Sheffield the smoke came spiralling up from the town's numerous small workshops, in Leeds it belched from the chimneys of large factories. It was on the factory that Leeds' prosperity was built – it was from the wealth directly or indirectly generated by the factories that the upper and middle classes were now laying a veneer of grandiose public buildings (Briggs, 1963) over the less-than-inspiring town centre and building homes for themselves in the new suburbs on the high ground to the north and west of the city. And it was in and out of the factory gates that a wage-labouring proletariat walked each day so causing the new and much remarked upon phenomenon of a 'rush hour'.

The early wealth of Leeds was based on the textiles industry (Rimmer, 1967). And in this industry the factory had come quite early into existence. In the woollen industry by 1794 the cloth workers were already petitioning thus:

Some merchants have commenced in the Erection of immense Buildings in which all the Machinery and Contrivances they (i.e. the clothiers) have invented for facilitating Labour, are consolidated and connected in such a manner, and in such Quantities, as to be worked by a much less number of Hands, for the sole advantage of the Merchants, some individuals of whom are likely to sequester at once the Profits of Two or Three Hundred Master Clothiers and their Families.

The first steps in this direction in Leeds had been taken by Benjamin Gott, the youngest partner in a mercantile house. To meet the growing demand for blankets and army cloths for the war in France, in 1792 he constructed a large factory complex based on the famous Bean Ing mill which, by 1797, already employed 1200 workers (Crump, 1931; Heaton, 1920; Rimmer, 1967; Connell and Ward, 1980). By 1805 there were five woollen factories in the borough, responsible for 6 per cent of all cloth production. But although the woollen manufacturers were amongst the first to install steam engines in these mills until about 1820 most products still continued to be made by hand. There was only formal control at these workplaces. Moreover around these early woollen factories there still existed, as in Sheffield in the 1850s, a much greater network of outworkers and domestic handicraft workshops. Even in 1822, domestic output was still of greater significance than factory production in the woollen industry. For example, in that very year Baines could note that:

The first stages of manufacture are carried on in the villages and hamlets of the surrounding country, where the wool goes through the respective operations of spinning, weaving and finishing . . . of late years, however, manufacturers of cloth have been established on a larger scale and the use of machinery has much increased.

It was only after 1825 that the woollen industry rapidly converted to factory production and as late as the 1850s much of this production was still not integrated on the one site. In particular, cloth finishing was still partly the preserve of special finishing mills and domestic outworkers (Table 2.3).

In the newer flax industry, in contrast, factory production was the norm from the beginning. In 1792, for example, over 1000 workers worked in Marshall's mill at Holbeck. By 1842, a handful of factories each employing more than 500 hands and having more than 10 000

Table 2.3: Some examples of employment patterns in four Leeds woollen factories, 1858

	Men (over 13)	*Women and children (under 13)*	*Total*
Woollen factory	38	142	180
Finishing mill	88	105	193
Woollen factory with putting out			
on premises	83	53	136
off premises	127	40	167
			303
Woollen factory and finishing	200	370	570

Source: Baines, 1859

spindles dominated the flax industry. Here there was real control of the workplace.

By the 1850s and 1860s both of these textile industries relied on factory production. In 1851 the 32 firms of the flax industry employed 9500 workers, many of them still children, the majority female and Irish, and accounted for a tenth of the gross output of British flax mills. The woollen industry employed twice this number (cf. Baines, 1859).

But the textiles industry was now at its peak, notwithstanding the rise of the shoddy industry centred on Batley. Through the 1850s and 1860s the textiles industry would be gradually replaced by other industries, at least in terms of employment (Table 2.4), partly as a result of the greater and greater capital intensity of the mills, partly as a result of relocation to other areas and partly as a result of competition from other areas and most notably, in the case of flax, Belfast where much lower wages were paid. Thus Gott & Sons closed down in 1870 while Marshall & Co. tranferred to New England. In particular, the predominantly male and more skilled engineering industry became important. By 1851, one in twelve males found employment in metal working and engineering. The industry, originally started to produce machinery for the textile industry, had by the 1850s and 1860s graduated to machine tools, locomotives, cranes and boilers. Whilst initially it was a skilled handicraft industry, run on Sheffield lines, by 1850 it had become factory-based. This was true too of most of the other industries which by 1850 were giving Leeds a more diverse

Table 2.4: The structure of industrial employment in Leeds, 1851, 1861 and 1871

Trade	1851	1861	1871
Chemicals and oils	748	927	944
Engineering	7415	12208	13082
Precision metals	190	299	367
Textiles	28889	28311	17506
Skins and leather	1023	1767	2339
Dress	9184	9822	9315
Food, drinks, tobacco, lodging	9727	5752	6439
Woodworking	1546	2078	1957
Paper, books and printing	783	1222	1196
Building	4179	5665	6768
Totals	63684	68051	59913

Source: Connell and Ward, 1980, pp. 156–7

industrial base, industries like chemicals, footwear and printing (cf. Rimmer, 1967; Connell and Ward, 1979). It is not surprising, therefore, that the average number of workers employed per firm crept increasingly upward. In 1800, it had been eight, in 1840 it was ten. By 1880 it was fifteen.

By the 1850s and 1860s the class structure of Leeds had started to stabilise, taking on a classically capitalist form. There was a large wage-labouring proletariat, many employed in factories. There was a remarkably large petty bourgeoisie, mainly comprising shopkeepers, master manufacturers and moderately wealthy professional men, which by 1832 perhaps one-fifth of the population of Leeds could already lay claim to belonging to. And there was a capitalist class made up of an élite of merchants and the major manufacturing families.

However the existence of this classical structure did not guarantee class-based struggle by the working class. Far from it. The new proletariat was disorganised, its class consciousness attenuated and its protests often undermined by middle-class involvement. The evidence for these statements can be found in the history of trade unions, reform movements and local government in the town.

Throughout the 1850s and 1860s trade union organisation in Leeds was weak or non-existent. In the 1860s a Trades Council was set up but it survived only with the support of skilled and craft unions and did not flourish until the 1890s. This is not to say that there were no strikes or lockouts in the factories. There were and there had been right from Gott's attempt to introduce presses and gig-mills to Bean Ing in the 1770s. But the strikes were nearly always isolated outbursts. One exception was the so-called Plug Riots of August 1848. All mills in the town were stopped.

> There was a clash with the police at one of the mills, and Prince George and the Lancers were brought up to disperse the strikers. During an attack on the mill of Titley, Tatham, and Walker, in Water Lane, the Riot Act was read, two pieces of artillery were paraded, and thirty-eight people were arrested. On Thursday morning the town was quiet, except for a run-out at the coal pits at Hunslet and Middleton. The pits were again visited on Friday when fourteen prisoners were taken. A meeting on Hunslet Moor was dispersed by police and soldiers. About 1200 infantry arrived in the town, and White Cloth Hall was used as a temporary barracks, and General Brotherton was sent from London to take command of the district (Harrison, 1959, p. 89).

But these riots were 'basically a violent reaction of unemployed operatives, spurred to desperation by hunger and destitution' (Harrison, 1959, p. 90), not organised protests.

The course of reform movements in the town shows the problems of middle-class involvement. Leeds had a strong radical tradition. But it was based on a continual tension between the middle class and working class. Nowhere is this better shown than in the course of Chartism in the town. In the early nineteenth century a whole series of reform organisations had sprung up in Leeds; the Association of the Friends of Radical Reform (founded in 1819), the Leeds Radical Reform Association (1829), the Radical Political Union (1831) and, of course, the Chartist movement founded as the Leeds Working Men's Association in 1837. In the Chartist movement working-class and middle-class representatives vied for supremacy, each with rather different goals (Harrison, 1962). The working class wanted universal suffrage, the middle class wanted economic and social hegemony and so clung to household suffrage. But the two goals were to some extent contradictory since the working-class vote could swamp the middle-class vote (see Fraser, 1976). In the 1830s Leeds became, briefly, one of the most important northern centres of militant working class Chartism with the publication of the *Northern Star* and the existence of the famous (or infamous) physical force wing led by O'Connor. But it was a short-lived ascendancy culminating in the grim winter of 1839–40 and O'Connor's arrest and subsequent imprisonment. When the Chartist movement revived in Leeds, as it soon did, it was in more respectable middle-class garb as signified by the setting up of institutions like the Leeds Total Abstinence Charter Association and the Leeds Charter Debating Society. It is significant that when the Plug Riots occurred, Leeds Chartists were not much in evidence. What organisation there was came from other urban centres like Bradford and from the Irish population of the city. Chartism in Leeds staggered on after the riots as a general union of reformers until 1853 when it was drawn under the wings of the Liberal Party, as the Leeds Advanced Liberal Party, and the various manhood suffrage movements and, in particular, the Leeds Working Man's Parliamentary Reform Association established in 1860.

What is most noticeable about Leeds local government in the 1850s and 1860s was how little it had to do with the working-class. The history of local government in Leeds until well into the nineteenth century is one of fierce struggle between the gentry and the middle class (country versus town, Tories versus Liberals) and, within the middle class, between the 'old' upper middle class and the newer lower middle or middling (Neale, 1968) class of shopkeepers, small proprietors and substantial artisans. It is a history that is interspersed with various attempts by elements of the working class, allied with this lower middle class, to gain control of various local government institutions under the banner of Chartism. The first conflict, between the gentry and the urban middle class was settled early and is indicated by the fact that Leeds was predominantly Liberal from 1835 to 1986 and by the gradual turning-over of the old parochial institutions (the vestries, the church wardens, the poor law commissioners, and improvement commissions and the highway surveyors) to Liberal control. But there was some working-class involvement in the latter battle, especially through the involvement of the Chartists. Fraser (1976, p. 107) has described the board of highway surveyors, from the time of the Chartist takeover in 1843 to its demise in 1866, as 'the political resort of the humble', an accurate enough description as long as the humble are equated with the lower middle class. For example, the final board of 1866 consisted of nine craftsmen or tradesmen, eight retailers and two professional men. Property qualifications debarred the proletariat. They could be represented. They could not take a direct part. The second battle, between the different segments of the middle class, took place at both the parochial and municipal scales and became particularly important in the 1850s and 1860s after the demise of Chartist councillors in 1853. Thereafter the Chartists fought as Radicals or Liberals. Before 1850, the lower middle class groups had already gained ascendancy in parish politics, as the constitution of the board of highway surveyors shows. But, after 1850, the lower middle class also began to increase their presence upon the city council and it is true that 'although only an extremely small proportion of the working class were able to vote in municipal elections, they were represented after 1850 by their lower-middle or middling-class neighbours, some of whom had been their allies, in the protest movements of earlier decades' (Ward, 1980, p. 161).

It would be a mistake to describe the working class as quiescent in Leeds in the 1850s and 1860s. Strikes and internecine conflict continued at work but outside the narrow confines of their own workplace working-class people did not, in general, become active in Leeds in forming unions or in other class-based political activity except in periods of great economic depression. There are a number of reasons why the working class in Leeds lacked social organisation. First, much political effort was drained off in, alternately, alliance with the middle class and fighting off the effects of alliance with the middle class. Too often fundamentally middle-class political organisations like the Liberal Party were allowed to become substitutes for a home-grown political base. Second, the working class was itself split in various ways thus making organisation more difficult. There was the existence of more and more skilled workers in engineering and allied trades who could afford to have some middle-class aspirations; there was the high proportion of women and juvenile workers in some industries and there was a small but significant Irish-born population. Finally, the conditions for working-class communities had not yet grown up in Leeds. The high rate of population increase (Table 2.2), much of it from immigration, coupled with a high rate of population turnover and intra-urban residential mobility to act against the formation of these communities. Ward (1980) has shown that there is little evidence that (unlike Sheffield?) residential differentiation increased in the 1850s and 1860s; it may even have decreased.

These three facts combined with the lack of independent institutions upon which to base working-class social and political solidarity. Trade unions were weak or non-existent. Co-operatives, friendly societies and various forms of chapel or educational self-help had certainly grown up but they were, to some extent, neutralised by first state intervention, particularly in schooling (see Frith, 1977) and second, strong middle-class involvement, either directly in institutions like schools or through counter-institutions like the Mechanics' Institutes.

Pubs were few and far between, large and consumer-oriented (the number of inns and beer houses was 80 per cent higher in Sheffield). The working-class way of life was not its own.

In other words the capacity of the working class in Leeds in the 1850s and 1860s was not great. As a class it remained socially unconnected. The situation was still too fluid, perhaps. High rates of geographical mobility combined with a class structure in which the boundaries between classes were still very diffuse. The ability of the working class to engage in class forms of conflict was therefore severely limited.

It was not until the 1880s and the remaking of the working class (Stedman Jones, 1974) that the Leeds working class became an organised political entity able to conduct a coherent class politics on the basis of more fixed class-boundaries and a classical pattern of residential segregation; Ward (1980) has shown that a small group of working-class residential 'stayers' was already emerging in the 1850s and 1860s. Perhaps these formed the nucleus of the new working-class communities that were able to gain experience of politics over a longer period and capitalise upon it. It is surely no concidence that the Socialist League and the ILP were essentially formed in the West Riding in the 1880s or that Leeds working-class people took such a great part in this formation.

Discussion

With the maturation of capitalism . . . three sets of changes affecting the city occur: (a) the city is supplanted by the nation-state as the dominant power container; (b) the contrast between the city and the countryside . . . is *progressively dissolved* . . . (c) the factors influencing the social patterning of urban life are for the most part different from those involved in cities in non-capitalist civilisation. Taken together, these represent a profound discontinuity between the city in class-divided societies and capitalist urbanism. The mass migrations from the land into urban areas associated with the rise of capitalism mark not just a population movement from one type of social milieu to another, but an *over-all transformation of those milieux themselves*. The development of capitalism has not led to the consolidation of the institutions of the city, but rather to its eradication as a distinct social form (Giddens, 1981, pp. 147–8; author emphasis).

In the 1850s and 1860s Leeds and Sheffield were still in the midst of Giddens's 'great transformation'. It would be possible to see the Sheffield artisanate as resembling a sandcastle gradually being washed away by the tide, while the Leeds working class is a part of the new pattern on the shore that is only just being uncovered as the tide of change begins to recede. But changes in the relations of production must not be painted as this remorseless. They are always fought over. How and how well they are fought over depends on the capacity of a class for conflict. For different reasons neither the Sheffield artisanate nor the Leeds working class had much capacity to resist these changes in the 1850s and 1860s. The Sheffield artisanate had a class capacity which was integrated at the local level and showed *some* signs of penetration of the conditions of production. But it was a capacity that was disabled, in the changing conditions of the nineteenth century, by precisely what held it together, a way of life based on the immediate locality. This made it difficult for this class to fight at any other level of integration and but for the brief flowering of Chartism, it did not (see also Prothero, 1979). Yet this was at a time when the level of integration of relations of production and political activity were both moving remorselessly upwards, helped by the very rapid time–space convergence of the period (Giddens's 'distanciation'). The artisanate was therefore ultimately rather easily outflanked by classes in struggle at other, and particularly the national, levels of integration.

The Leeds working class, in contrast, had little or no capacity for conflict in the 1850s and 1860s at any level, except briefly around the issues of Chartist politics again. But, then, *pace* Edward Thompson the English working class was not made by 1832. And it was still in the making in the 1850s and 1860s in Leeds (and north-east Sheffield). Only in the 1880s did the English working class become 'remade' as a *social class* (cf. Stedman Jones, 1974) and this was in the context of a *national* politics. It was between 1880 and 1920 that England came nearest to being a vertically structured society in which a coherent working class existed:

It is surely no coincidence that the period which witnessed the growth of a relatively uniform proletariat should have given birth to a parallel political proletarian movement in the creation of the Labour Party. By the 1920's the rise of the Labour Party, the product of a more sharply defined proletarian social and political consciousness, had fundamentally altered the nature of British politics. Just as the political imperative flowing from bourgeois dominance in the mid-nineteenth century decreed that the natural location of politics should be the city itself, so the corollary of proletarian consciousness in the 1880–1920 period determined that politics should be fought on a national scale. City politics, where proletarian numbers eventually delivered power into Labour hands, then became a cog in a national political process, wherein mid-Victorian England national affairs only occasionally deflected the flow of dominant city issues (Fraser, 1976, p. 284).

We can see in the examples of Sheffield and Leeds in the 1850s and 1860s two paradigms of the uneven development of class formation in nineteenth-century Britain; Sheffield still craft-oriented, all irregular hours and Saint Monday; Leeds the coketown domain of the factory, regular hours and the Saturday half-holiday. All over Britain during the nineteenth century these different histories of class formation are repeated in outline in other communities, although sometimes earlier and sometimes later.

• 3 •

Class, place and industrial revolution • *CRAIG CALHOUN*

Looking at the period of the 'classic' industrial revolution – about 1780–1840 in Britain, slightly later in the USA and on the European continent – a number of recent social historians have noted the importance of local community relations to what they call class struggle (see, among many, Thompson, 1968; Foster, 1974; Aminzade, 1981; Smith, 1982). By contrast, I shall try to specify the historical process further by suggesting that two different sorts of social relationships are at stake. Community is built of direct relationships; class, on the contrary, is made possible as a form of social solidarity only by the development of large-scale systems of indirect relationships. In Marxist theory in particular, class refers to social collectivities constructed not haphazardly on the local scene but at the level of the whole social formation under terms dictated by the dominant mode of production. Class is not at issue wherever there is hierarchy, nor class struggle wherever workers challenge the authority of bosses or employers. To be salient in the class struggle engendered by capitalism, classes – bourgeoisie, proletariat – must be organized at the same level as capital accumulation. Because of their smaller numbers and greater resources, élites (including members of the bourgeoisie) are likely to achieve some such organization before classes or 'masses'. It is as weak to describe workers' struggles caught within the bounds of locality – in Oldham alone, say, or even all of Southeast Lancashire – as comprising 'class struggle' as to describe the local industrial organization as comprising (rather than reflecting, or being shaped by) capitalism; each must be understood in terms of a larger scale and more complex sort of integration.

My argument, then, is as follows:
(1) It is necessary to distinguish between class struggle and popular mobilizations on the basis of community or other direct interpersonal relationships.
(2) It is necessary to recognize that even at the level of capitalism, classes are not things, but must be composed of interpersonal relationships. These relationships are indirect rather than direct.[1]
(3) Communications and transportation infrastructures are an essential part of the material basis for class struggle (and other large scale collective action) but were only developed adequately to this purpose as capitalism's continuing industrial revolution progressed past the level it had attained in the first third or even half of the nineteenth century.[2]
(4) Class struggles tend to be caught within certain limits imposed by capitalism and capitalist democracy while movements based on direct social relationships (free social spaces) have more potential to avoid the reification of abstract, indirect relations and therefore to develop alternative, sometimes radical, visions. My presentation is more theoretical than empirical; the historical examples I give are mostly British.

Class and the transcendence of locality

It is the nature of capitalism to create an enormous and normally expanding system of production and distribution of commodities:

> The bourgeoisie has through its exploitation of the world market given a cosmopolitan character to production and consumption in every country . . . in place of the old local and national seclusion and self-sufficiency, we have intercourse in every direction, universal interdependence of nations. . . . The bourgeoisie, by the rapid improvement of all instruments of production, by the immensely facilitated means of communication, draws all, even the most barbarian, nations into civilization (Marx and Engels, 1848, p. 488.)[3]

Marx expected the working class to attain international solidarity on a scale comparable to the international organization of capital and capitalist enterprises. The spreading scope of capitalism is accompanied, however, by the introduction of a split between that large-scale integration and various local systems of direct relationships. Though one's work in a capitalist society will nearly always tie one into such a large-scale system of indirect relationships, one's bonds of affect and mutual support may remain local.

In the new class-segregated communities, individuals and families address the marketplace. Whereas precapitalist communities were shattered by the penetration of new kinds of markets protected by the umbrella of the states, capitalist communities are defined by market relations. 'Household and occupation,' Weber stresses, 'become ecologically separated, and the household is no longer a unit of common consumption' (Katznelson, 1979, p. 230).

Production and consumption, work and community become largely distinguishable phenomena, carried out through distinct sets of relationships. Moreover, the organization of consumption no more necessarily unifies people who live near each other than that of production necessarily unifies those who work at a common trade or for a common employer. Not only do production and consumption engender cross-cutting patterns of association, but each gives only a weak disposition to solidarity. This puts new organizational problems before any attempt to build solidarity on the basis of positions within the relations of production. As the capitalist system grows, the object of any working-class struggle is removed from direct relationships, from immediate locality. Neither workplace nor residential community includes the 'enemy' to be confronted nor is composed of a sufficiently broad network of relationships to reach all those concerned. Large-scale organization of indirect relationships becomes essential.[4]

That class struggle should be understood as taking place on such a large scale is suggested by Marx, who defined the working class as coterminous with capitalist exploitation.[5] To see class everywhere and in every epoch renders the term an abstract tool for categorization, devoid of specific historical content. There is nothing inherently wrong with using the language of class in this broad way; it simply should not be thought that such usages bear much relationship to Marxist theory, with its stress on historically delimited abstractions, and its primary concern for the class relations of capitalism. In developing a theory of social *action*, one learns more by keeping some concept to refer only to collectivities or relations at the level of the 'system' as a whole, large-scale integration.[6] In this sense, the notion of class is distinctively (though not uniquely) relevant to the modern period. Class refers not just to any interest group, but to a particular sort of collectivity which influences our actions more than those of our ancestors; the dominance of which, indeed, is only made possible by modern technology and social organization.[7] But, Marx and most of his followers have failed to consider the organizational difficulties of working-class organization on this scale, its dependence on formal organizations and on the presence of a developed infrastructure of communication and transportation.

In the early nineteenth century, class struggle, at least the struggle of proletariat against bourgeoisie which Marx proposed, was impossible. It was not just unclear, immature or doomed to defeat. In an important sense, it was impossible. The problem lay not with insufficient class analysis, but with an inadequate infrastructure.Capitalist societies had not yet built the transportation and communications systems which would enable co-ordination of activity at the class level.

By the end of the century, this had changed in most of Europe. Precisely as capitalism was being internationalized on a new scale, and just as joint-stock corporations were coming to predominate, so too class struggle became an option. Just as the corporation was an organizational response to larger-scale social and economic integration, drawing on new technologies of control and co-ordination as well as new social arrangements making systems of indirect relations easier to bring off, so class-based organizations were an attempt to give workers the ability to mobilize for struggle on a comparable scale.[8] Neither class struggle nor corporations were the only options open; they were not inevitabilities amenable to scientific discovery, but they were *newly practical* options. This aspect of the discontinuity of industrial revolution is of interest not just for purposes of historical chronology but because of what it can tell us about the nature of modern class struggle and other modes of popular politics.

Capitalism and large-scale social integration

One of Marx's most important points about capitalism was that it creates a social 'totality' in a sense in which one was not present before.[9] This totalization is the integration of indirect relations into a singular system. This does not do away with the direct interpersonal relationships which predominated before capitalism; they continue to co-exist with it, and new sorts of direct relationships are created in capitalist societies. Modern society is not distinguished, Katznelson insightfully has observed, by the contrast between *gemeinschaft* and *gesellschaft*, but rather by that between a society in which *gemeinschaft* and *gesellschaft* were intimately bound to one another, and one which severed them (1979, p. 206). The split between work and community has been as fateful as that between classes:

> Emerging competing class capacities came now [i.e. with capitalism] to depend on the character of the connections made between the motion of capitalist accumulation, the ways they informed the social relations of work, community, and citizenship, and the ideological and organizational links made between these differentiated arenas of social life (Katznelson, 1979, p. 229).

The dynamics of value and commodities, labour and capital, unify an ever larger range of economic activity, eliminating various local specificities and autonomies in favour of the single dominant integrative principle of capital accumulation through appropriation of surplus value. As Engels wrote:

> [Before capitalism] exchange was restricted, the market narrow, the methods of production stable; there was local exclusiveness without, local unity within; the market in the country; in the town, the guild.
>
> But with the extension of the production of commodities, and especially with the introduction of the capitalist mode of production, the laws of commodity production, hitherto latent, came into action more openly and and with greater force. The old bonds were loosened, the old exclusive limits broken through, the producers were more and more turned into independent, isolated producers of commodities. It became apparent that the production of society at large was ruled by absence of plan, by accident, by anarchy; and this anarchy grew to greater and greater heights. But the chief means by aid of which the capitalist mode of production intensified this anarchy of socialized production was the exact opposite of anarchy. It was the increasing organization of production, upon a social basis, in every individual productive, establishment. By this the old, peaceful, stable condition of things was ended. . . . The local struggles begot in their turn national conflicts. . .
>
> Finally, modern industry and the opening of the world market made the struggle universal (1880, pp. 96–7).

In looking at specific workplaces, Marx and Engels stressed the importance of the sort of social organization of production which numerous manufacturers were pioneering and Charles Babbage and Andrew Ure were analysing and propagandizing during their lifetimes.

Outside of the factory, however, they paid relatively little attention to patterns of social organization *per se*. Indeed, they tended to assume that capitalism would not allow coherent national or international economic organization, or the state as we know it.[10] Their economic analyses were focused almost exclusively on the indirect relationships created among people by the system of value and capital.

By contrast the key political groups and movements of Marx's and Engels's lifetimes – those which formed the basis for their ideas of working class radicalism – were based predominently on direct relations. This was true of struggles in France at least through the Paris Commune of 1871 (note the local specificity of that ill-fated red republican venture), true also of all pre-Chartist and most Chartist struggles in Britain, and of German mobilizations through the early days of the social democratic party. Only near the end of his life did Engels have to grapple with the development of a complex party organization designed to mediate relations and co-ordinate activity (including electoral participation) among members of a truly large-scale working-class movement.

Nonetheless, Marx's analysis of the fetishism of commodities is one of the most important bases for coming to grips with the nature of indirect social relationships. The commodity form is a template for analysis of reification, including the reification of social relationships. Fetishism of commodities occurs because:

> the social character of men's labour appears to them as an objective character stamped upon the product of that labour; because the relation of the producers to the sum total of their own labour is presented to them as a social relation, existing not between themselves, but between the products of their labour . . . it is a definite social relation between men, that assumes, in their eyes, the fantastic form of a relation between things (Marx, 1867, p. 17).

The relationships formed in the production and circulation of commodities are a basic model for considering the potential reification of all sorts of indirect relationships. Marx and Engels, however, did not give comparable attention to analysing the fetishism of organizations – e.g. the treatment of a capitalist corporation as a fictive person in courts of law, or the treatment of the proletariat as a singular entity in Marxist–Leninist theory. Nor did Marx and Engels attempt to explore in any depth the place of either direct or indirect social relationships in political action. There is, thus, no strong account of social organization *per se* in any of Marx's or Engels's writings. One result of this is that as classes are deduced from the economic theory, their collective action is presumed to follow simply from rational recognition of common interests. Marx and Engels offer scattered comments on how concentration in cities, organization in large factories, or experience of local struggle might help to build class consciousness. But they bequeath as a problem to generations of later Marxists the question of just what sorts of relationships create classes capable of struggle within or against capitalism.[11]

Classes, as Przeworski suggests, are not settled data prior to the history of concrete struggles:

> Classes are organized and disorganized as outcomes of continuous struggles. Parties defining themselves as representing the interests of various classes and parties purporting to represent the general interest, unions, newspapers, schools, public bureaucracies, civic and cultural associations, factories, armies, and churches – all participate in the process of class formation in the course of struggles that fundamentally concern the very vision of society. . . . The ideological struggle is a struggle *about* class before it is a struggle *among* classes (1977, p. 371).

Classes become important social bases for collective action when society is knit together through large-scale systems of indirect relationships. The working class and the bourgeoisie are the broadest (but not the only) classes demarcated by reference to the relations of production. Not all the conditions of class formation, however, are economic, ideological, or even political. Social organizational conditions encourage some directions of class formation and discourage others. The very centrality of the sorts of parties Przeworski mentions is given in part by these organizational conditions. There must be some framework for achieving class solidarity. The more sustained and contrary to existing institutional arrangements any course of collective action is, the greater the intra-class social solidarity it will require.

Communities offer pre-existing relationships as a potential foundation for collective struggle; in much of Europe, overlap between community and class forms of organization has been a key source of strength for class struggle. Where classes have less prior social solidarity on which to draw, they are weaker. 'Pureness' of class foundations may not be a predictor of social strength at all. Unlike communities and other collectivities formed through direct interpersonal relationships, classes take on subjective existence primarily through the creation of some manner of complex organizations; these organizations mediate the relationships of members of the class to one another. Direct relationships alone cannot give the class collective agency. The organizations of class struggle – from trade unions to labour parties – replace (or supplement) communities and related informal associations in the same way that corporations (especially those which split ownership from management) replace partnerships and owner-operated businesses.

In fact, the archetype for both processes is the development of the modern state.[12] Over a period of hundreds of years, the development of absolutist and eventually parliamentary states reduced the role of personal control and co-ordination in favour of formal organizational structures. The direct, personal relations of domination characteristic of both feudalism and the cities which grew in late medieval Europe were replaced by the indirect relations of bureaucracy. Though medieval cities were socially quite different from their rural surroundings, the relations of artisans, merchants and other urban dwellers shared with feudalism proper a dependence on direct personal relationships. The cities formed self-contained and largely autonomous wholes within the parcelled framework of feudalism. Katznelson points out how 'citizenship began to give way to class as the defining relation of city life' when expanding market relations intersected with the rise of the absolutist state:

> Although market relations at the local level were divorced from the communal meanings of citizenship at the very moment they were joined to the growing political authority of the absolutist state, both the national (indeed, international) and local processes that changed the character of the social structures of late medieval cities shared a common pivot – an enlarged and defining role for market relations (1979, p. 219).

The state was not only a model for corporations and class organizations, but part of the process which produced them. It not only made a broader organization of markets possible, but it sundered the autonomy and unity city life had maintained in both economic and political spheres. Aside from differences in content, this made possible a transformation of the scale of state functioning. States became simultaneously more permanent, more efficient and more powerful. Marx recognized much of this, and made numerous suggestions of the importance of what has since come to be called the relative autonomy of the state apparatus (Marx, 1871 among many; Poulantzas, 1973, sect. IV). That is, while still maintaining that states rule on behalf of a ruling *class*, he qualified the rather broad assertion of the *Communist Manifesto* that the state is simply a committee managing the interests of the ruling class. Marxists since have taken this line of reasoning much further (Poulantzas, 1973 and Anderson, 1975, for example) and in some cases have drawn on Weber's famous analyses of the development of the modern state apparatus.

Similarly, Marx and Engels noticed the importance of the emergence of joint-stock corporations, seeing them as at once purer forms of capitalist enterprise and steps on the way to socialization of production (Marx, 1885; Engels, 1878, pp. 380–1). But Marx had little of substance to say on the subject primarily because corporate enterprise only came to predominate after his death. Generations of thinkers have grappled in detail with the question of how the growth of corporations is to be assimilated into the Marxist theory of capitalism. Perhaps the most famous issue is that of whether the displacement of owners from the direct operation of the companies, and the creation of a class of managerial employees, fundamentally changes the nature of the enterprise or the class structure.[13] As in the case of state apparatuses, corporations built out of indirect relationships proved more permanent, efficient and powerful, by and large, than their more personalistic predecessors. As was the case for states, corporations also greatly increased the scale of social integration in the respective spheres of operations.

One might have expected Marxist thinkers to apply some of the same logic to conceptions of classes and class struggle. In fact, they have failed to do this, largely because of a persisting confusion between the relational conception of classes of exploiters and exploited which is yielded by the Marxist theory of capitalism, the notion of class-in-itself turning into a transcendentally rational class-for-itself which Marx derived from Hegel, and the actual radical movements which have demonstrated the potential for insurgency and even revolutionary transformation (and which have even on occasion spoken the language of class) but which have not been founded on the basis of class (Calhoun, 1982, 1983a). Whatever the reasons, though Marxists have debated the relationship between class and party at length, they have not considered that it might be much like that between state and citizenry, or corporate management and widely dispersed owners.

Classes – at least the Marxian proletariat and other 'mass' or popular classes (the sort with which Przeworski is also concerned) – are too large and widely dispersed to be mobilized on the basis of direct interpersonal relationships. For these collectivities to provide the basis for sustained, effective insurgencies their members must be linked to each other through some mediating agency. Trade unions work in this way for their members, and are thus in direct line of development of class struggle (as Marx thought) and not necessarily to be distinguished from a more revolutionary class consciousness (as Lenin suggested). Trade unions and working-class political parties do vary in the extent to which they *represent* loosely organized constituents, or *organize* those constituents for direct participation in action (the latter comes much closer to Marx's conceptualization of class struggle). In either case, this sort of mobilization differs significantly from that which is based on direct relations such as those of the local community. Moreover, it depends on a level of communications and transportation infrastructure which had not been developed prior to 1840 if, indeed, it was sufficient then.

This reconceptualization of popular political movements turns on a recognition that the industrial revolution was far from over and done with in the middle of the nineteenth century. On the contrary, industrial revolution – as Marx and Engels rather presciently remarked in the *Communist Manifesto* – is an ongoing process essential to capitalism:

> The bourgeoisie cannot exist without constantly revolutionising the instruments of production, and thereby the relations of production, and with them the whole relations of society (1848, p. 487).

This must include not just material technology but the social organization of labour – factories themselves and assembly lines as well as steam engines and spinning jennies. In an 1895 introduction to a new printing of Marx's 'The Class Struggles in France, 1848–50', Engels observed how mistaken he and Marx had been to think that the 1848 revolution marked a climax or even near climax in the political struggle against capitalism. The reason was that, far from witnessing the 'death-throes of capitalism' he and Marx had been witnessing its birth pangs. Capitalism went on developing, revolutionizing the European and world economies in the second half of the nineteenth century (and up to the present day). Only in the course of this development, did capitalism create class societies and the social conditions necessary for collective action on classwide bases. Even then, class definitions were not settled, but subject to continuous struggle during continuing industrial revolution:

the proletariat could not have been formed as a class once and for all by the end of the nineteenth century because capitalist development continually transforms the structure of places in the system of production and realization of capital as well as in the other manners of production that become dominated by capitalism (Przeworski, 1977, p. 358).[14]

Infrastructure and class formation

It was not in the early days of industrialization, but rather in its hey-day from mid-nineteenth century on, that the organizations of class struggle and the infrastructure on which they depended began to mature in the advanced Western societies. The strong bonds of traditional communities provided a basis for most of the radical reaction against capitalism essential to the failed revolts of early nineteenth century Europe and for most successful social revolutions. At varying rates from mid-century on, formal organizations with the administrative and technological ability to transcend place have come to predominate as the bases for such class struggle as characterizes 'mature' capitalism.[15] This struggle developed along with railroads and telegraphs, though the technologies which made it possible also made its repression easier. It developed along with clipper ships and steam power, though the escapes they made feasible offered migration as a viable alternative to continued struggle. But even forced migrations could join with newly efficient postal services, cheap printing presses and all the new infrastructural technologies to spread the theories and practices of class struggle. Trade unions and workers' political parties grew through diffusion, not just parallel invention. Though the European idea of socialism never triumphed in America, Europeans and their ideas played vital roles in generations of American radicalism and labour struggle. Though the ideology might not have been new, the organizational strength of the British general strike of 1926 could hardly have been achieved a hundred years earlier.

Consider just how substantial the advances in infrastructural technology during the nineteenth century were, and what differences they made for the capacity to co-ordinate collective action on a large scale (e.g. that of Great Britain).[16] In the mid–1750s, it took ten to twelve days to travel from London to Edinburgh; by 1836 less than two days were required (Bagwell, 1971, p. 42). As late as 1751, the fast coach between Oxford and London took two days; coaches could make the trip in six hours in 1828; railroads did not cut the trip to under two hours until the late nineteenth century. Modern road building, river channel improvement, canal construction and steamboat transport were all underway by 1830, and going strong by 1870.[17] Clipper ships and other improved sailing vessels enjoyed their brief glory from 1830–60. The original Liverpool–Manchester railroad was opened in 1830. Nationally, operating mileage and especially passenger transportation remained negligible until mid-century. Only then, and only fairly gradually until about 1870, did it take off as an important means of travel (Bagwell, 1971, p. 110). It is also worth noting, as Bagwell's data indicate, the gradual process by which rail transport ceased to be a luxury and became a part of ordinary life for more and more workers and other third-class passengers. In 1871 approximately 200 million third-class tickets were sold; by the 1910s the number exceeded 1200 million. During this period there was negligible change, by comparison, in first- and second-class ridership, which remained under 100 million.

Communications technology did not develop much faster. Though printed periodicals were common by the late eighteenth century, and popular consumption of them was politically important by the early nineteenth century, the heyday of the mass popular press did not arrive until the middle third of the nineteenth century, if then (Hollis, 1970; Perkin, 1957; Webb, 1955). Postal service based on a uniform, relatively low rate was introduced to Britain in 1840 (the International Postal Union followed in 1874). The Dover–Calais telegraph inaugurated direct long distance communication in 1851.

In short, through most of the eighteenth century, England was intensely localized; neither transport nor communication could lead to a ready co-ordination of activity – economic or political – around the Kingdom. Despite fears to the contrary from contemporary élites, the eighteenth-century politics of riot was based on this localism, and declined as a political tactic with national integration and increase in size of population aggregates (Bohstedt, 1982). Riots certainly occurred in nineteenth-century cities, but new means of both coercion and co-optation were available to contain them, and the absence of communal ties minimized the extent to which effective bargaining could take place between rioters and élites. It took the better part of the nineteenth century, however, before infrastructural developments really offered effective transcendence of locality to most English people.[18] Goods transportation and the extension of markets helped to pave the way for greater movement of people, communication, and national social integration. But we must not be misled by the numerous excited accounts of contemporaries who found fast stage coaches or even the first railroads to be indicative of an extraordinary ease of communication. This sort of national integration was limited, and closely focused on a few élites able to afford both the costs and the time for travel until well along in the nineteenth century. Any national 'working class solidarity' before this integration could only have been of the loosest sort; one must assume, therefore, that accounts of working class action before mid- to late nineteenth century refer to local groupings, not the national or international class defined by Marx's *Capital*.

In fact, the chronology of popular activity supports this contention quite well. The early nineteenth-century improvements in road transportation helped to make Chartism possible. It was a transitional movement, drawing its support largely from members of declining and threatened craft communities, but also providing the first occasion for large-scale national political participation by members of the industrial working class. From the 1830s, unions began to achieve stable development, leading eventually to enduring national organizations. Doherty's National Union of Cotton Spinners dates from 1829; the Operative Builders' Union from 1831; the Grand National Consolidated Trades Union offered its prototype for national union among trades in 1833. All of these unions were dependent on close-knit local groups and dominant personalities, though they began the process of elaborating formal organizations. In 1851 they were joined by the 'New Model Unions', led by the Amalgamated Society of Engineers, and through the 1850s and 1860s there was a series of small but significant political victories giving a clear legal basis to trade union organization (e.g. The Friendly Societies Act, the Molestation of Workmen Act and the amendment of the Master and Servant Act). At the end of the 1860s the Trades Union Congress got off the ground, though it did not have any permanent organization until the formation of its Parliamentary Committee in 1871. The 1870s were also a period of final struggles for the old, intensely local, jealously craft-based unions (see Postgate, 1923, ch. 14, on the builders).

From this point on the organizations of labour are familiar because they have endured; they have endured in part because they were able to establish permanent organizational structures based on contributions from workers relatively stably employed in the occupations which capitalist industry fostered (rather than those it persistently or recurrently attacked). British unions never achieved the level of national industrial co-ordination of those in some other countries; the craft and local heritages remained stronger. Nonetheless, they were enduring national actors by the 1880s, based on organizations representing large collectivities of workers only loosely integrated among themselves, related largely, in fact, through the indirect means of common union membership. On these grounds, similarly, were based the Independent Labour Party (founded in 1893) and its fellow tributaries into the stream of the modern Labour Party.

The limits of class struggle

In Britain, class struggle was incipient in Chartism and grew through the remainder of the nineteenth century. It followed a similar trajectory, beginning somewhat later, in most of the other capitalist democracies. Class struggle grew as a part of capitalism, but not because exploitation or suffering became more intense. It grew because of the growing number of workers *within* capitalist industrial organizations (as opposed to those living and working in traditional or transitional craft communities and work structures).[19] It grew because political arrangements allowed it, by creating in capitalist democracy an arena for class compromise.[20] And class struggle grew because new infrastructural technologies made it possible to create viable large-scale organizational structures.

This gives us a crucial insight into the nature of class (and related) struggles. The contraposition often made between political and economic struggles stems from capitalist democracy's sundering of work and community. It is not a matter of stages of maturation in a social movement. In particular, it is not the basis for a division between 'trade union' and 'class' consciousness, nor between reformism and revolutionary radicalism. On the contrary, at least within relatively open and democratic English society, both trade unionism and working-class politics were generally reformist.[21] This was not an accidental limitation, nor an ideological aberration, but was the result (at least in part) of the nature of mobilization and organization of large collectivities through indirect relationships.

It is implausible to abandon popular struggle through complex organizations in a society which remains organized on an extremely large scale through a centralized system of indirect relationships. But it would be a mistake not to recognize (a) that such struggle is characteristically limited, and (b) that there is an enduring role for more directly democratic struggles based on community and other direct relationships.

The limits to class struggle and other action on the basis of indirect relationships come largely from the essential role played by large formal organizations. These organizations are necessary to the co-ordination of action at the same level at which capital and political power are centralized. They are, however, distinct from the classes they represent. Their members may come to act on interests different from and sometimes conflicting with those of their constituents. Those constituents are encouraged to view the 'goods' offered by such organizations as only some among a range of options, a view accentuated by the extent to which such large organizations depend on members' financial contributions rather than their personal participation. Because such organizations are typically separate from local community life, and themselves constitute an alternative community only for a relatively small number of activitists, they appear as non-essential consumer goods rather than an essential part of life. And such organizations must work within the framework of capitalist democracy, competing for a variety of short-term gains as well as potentially more fundamental changes in social organization. These issues apply even where leadership of such organizations works in the best of faith to avoid Michels's 'iron law of oligarchy' (1949).[22]

There is also little in the ordinary experience most supporters have of class-oriented or other similar organizations – trade unions, political parties, etc. – to build an alternative social vision. Members may certainly read theoretical, historical or literary works proposing or inspiring alternative visions, but the activities of membership itself are the activities of organizational life, purchases of goods and services, indirect social relationships, and centralized systems of co-ordination much like those of capitalist organizations and conventional political parties. This is not an avoidable flaw but an essential part of collective action enduringly organized at this scale.

Participation in movements based on direct social relationships, by contrast, offers an often intense experience of a different kind of social organization. It is more likely to involve the whole person, rather than a single role, a segmented bit of time or a simple financial donation.

Whatever the ideology or traditions of such a group, its very social relationships suggest an alternative social vision. Especially where they draw on pre-existing communities, such movements also seem extensions of the relationships essential to ordinary life, not consumption goods chosen by discretion. This gives them a strength and a potential radicalism missing from most organizations based on indirect relationships and thus from most class struggle.

'Populist' movements and others based on direct relationships have, of course, their own intrinsic limits. The most notable, perhaps, is their virtual inability to sustain integration and co-ordination of activity at a level comparable to that of capital or established political élites for any length of time. Closely related is their lack of an organizational framework through which to pick up the reins of government should they succeed in ousting incumbents. If victorious in revolution (rather than more moderate struggles) they are unlikely to become rulers. Such potential insurgencies are limited also by the extent to which capitalism has disrupted local communities and other networks of direct relationships, by the split between community and work, and by the compartmentalization of different segments of most of our lives in modern capitalist societies.

Because capitalism produces social integration of unprecedented scope, centralization and intensity of co-ordination, capitalist democracy must work primarily through organizations of indirect relationships. There is, moreover, little hope that a viable socialism could assume capitalism's material wealth without its pattern of large-scale social integration; there is also little reason to idealize a more fragmented past. But this does not mean that direct democracy is entirely obsolete or limited to the narrowest of local matters. In the first place, a populist political campaign (distinct from class struggle) might well succeed in capturing a greater governmental role for localities, and in making local governmental institutions more participatory. This in turn might help to build the social solidarity for future struggles, in some of which direct, communal relationships might provide crucial support to participation on class lines. Beyond this, social movements based on direct social relationships are – whatever their explicit aims – exercises in direct democracy. Just as a variety of labour laws, guarantees of civil liberties and similar provisions legitimate and provide part of the basis for class struggle in capitalist democracy, so nurturance of community-level institutions may build the 'free social spaces' crucial to direct democracy.[23]

The socialism of class struggle is based on indirect relationships, and generally oriented to reforms which would not challenge the overwhelming predominance of such relationships which capitalism has brought about. Such socialism must be complemented by direct democracy if a stronger and more stable place is to be made for direct social relationships. Class struggle is an essential means of action within the sphere of large-scale social integration, but it is neither a radical challenge to it nor exhaustive of the bases for democratic collective action in pursuit of the genuine interests of workers (and others). Because class struggle is a *part* of capitalism – or at least capitalist democracy – it shares capitalism's tendency to transcend direct relationships, including those of locality. It depends upon advances in the technology and social organization of communication in order to achieve its space-transcending co-ordination of collective action.

Notes

1 The issue is avoiding the reification of relationships into entities (cf. Lukacs, 1924). As Therborn writes:

> Classes are not actors in the same sense as individuals, groups or organizations are, decision-making actors bringing about events or 'monuments', such as programmes, codes, etc. A class can never make a decision as a class. . . . Classes act through the actions of individuals, groups, and organizations (1983, p. 190).

Compare the way in which Abercrombie and Urry reject the reification implicit in the structuralist approach, only to casually accept the notion of classes as entities:

> We shall treat class places as elements of real entities – classes – while the causal powers of those entities are actuated, among other things, by the processes of class formation (1983, p. 109).

In order to understand and transcend the reification of class, we need to distinguish direct from indirect relationships. Direct relationships include both what sociologists have called primary relationships (knitting together whole people in multi-dimensional bonds) and secondary relationships (linking only through specific roles). Indirect relationships, by contrast, are mediated through complex organizations and often through impersonal means of long-distance communication; though ultimately enacted by individuals, they minimize the transparency of the connection.

The individuals may never meet; indeed, as in markets, they may never be aware of each other's specific existence, though of course they will know that someone buys their products.

2 That is, both (a) capitalism achieved a greater scope and internal integration, and (b) the infrastructural developments necessary to working-class action lagged behind those enabling co-ordination among élites and the successful administration of capitalist enterprises and capitalist democracy. Similarly, though I shall not discuss it here, infrastructure is inadequate to class struggle (in this sense of nationally or internationally integrated movements) in many or even most Third World countries today.

3 See Headrick (1981) for a modern account of the importance of technological innovations, including communications and transport, to the capacity of European imperial powers to penetrate, effectively administer and exploit their colonies around the world.

4 Any purely localistic account of class struggle must face the question (which Foster, 1974, for example, slides over) of just how purely local movements can be described as based on the working class created by national or international capitalism. The account tends to become, in Foster's case, paradoxically voluntaristic, and the conception of class to lose all distinctive analytic purchase. One of the virtues of Perkin's (1969) analysis of the 'rise of a viable class society' over Thompson's as well as Foster's account of class struggle is that it makes clear the importance of the emergence of class solidarities on a national scale:

> The essence of class is not merely antagonism towards another class or classes but organized antagonism with a nationwide appeal to all members of one broad social level (p. 209).

While Marxists may, of course, regard the notion of a 'broad social level' as an imprecise account of class foundations, Marxist historians have, unfortunately gone to an opposite extreme and forgotten the importance of the scale on which Marx envisaged class relations and class struggle.

5 This is the fundamental idea of the relations of production – that the bourgeoisie and proletariat are defined by their relationship to each other, the necessary exploitation of the latter by the former (Marx and Engels, 1848, Sect. I; Marx, 1867, pp. 717–18; 1885, p. 33; 1932). See also, however, Przeworski's observation that 'the concept of proletariat seems to have been self-evident for the founders of scientific socialism' (1977, p. 353). One must question, however, Przeworski's belief that this was because class identities were quite clear in the mid-nineteenth century; though the debates were less arcane, arguments over the demarcations of boundaries were common and even the 'proletariat' was not clear-cut. On his chosen example of France in 1848, see Calhoun (1983b) and references cited therein.

6 On some of the genealogy of the term 'class', including development away from usage to designate any classificatory category, see Calvert (1982). Marx himself vacillated between gradational and relational concepts of class, though the weight of his account settles on the latter. The proletariat, thus, is not just 'lower' or 'poorer' than the bourgeoisie, it is defined in the relation of exploitation by and struggles with the bourgeoisie. In the *Class Struggles in France* and the *Eighteenth Brumaire*, nearly every grouping with distinctive 'objective' interests is referred to as a class. In this weak sense, peasants, though 'like a sack of potatoes', are a class. But in the stronger sense of *Capital*, peasants lack both the internal solidarity and the distinctive relation to another class which participation in the 'totalizing' system of capitalism gives to the working class.

7 In Marxist theory the bourgeoisie and proletariat are the key classes, but another theory might hold that other classes connected primarily by indirect relationships are the primary collective actors in systems of large-scale social integration and conflict. In eighteenth-century England, and in general in the cities and small regional economies of pre-industrial capitalism, there were groupings and collective actions of workers which may plausibly be described in the language of class (cf. Neale, 1983a, pp. 292–4). Though these may share some elements of 'orientation' with later working class organizations and mobilizations, they are crucially different in as much as their small scale (both numerical and geographical) allows for their cohesion to be achieved entirely or almost entirely through direct relationships.

8 Harold Perkin's (1969, pp. 107–24) discussion of a revolution in social organization, including a dramatic rise in scale, makes clear this discontinuity (which other historians have sometimes, surprisingly, minimized).

9 We need not make an extreme, categorical assumption about totality, but rather need only to accept the tendency of capitalism towards totalization. A variable is more useful than an *a priori* assumption. That is, capitalism tends to create a singular 'whole' in a way not characteristic of such segmentary social forms as feudal and many tribal societies. The insight is related to Durkheim's (1893) distinction of mechanical from organic solidarity, though Marx's specification of a causal mechanism producing wholeness (capitalist integration – organic solidarity) goes beyond simply a societal division of labour. Durkheim's conception is flawed by failure to recognize that different criteria for solidarity are employed in his analyses of mechanically and organically solid groupings. The latter have more solidarity only through *indirect* relationships; they generally have *less* through direct relationships. For that reason, they lack much of the socio-psychological closeness of constituent groups within mechanically solid societies. Durkheim fails to give any weight to the significance of scale or population size. Marx, interestingly, had a concept of relative population

density based on communications and transport technology which might almost have been linked to a Durkheimian notion of 'dynamic density':

> A relatively thinly populated country, with well-developed means of communication, has a denser population than a more numerously populated country with badly developed means of communication. In this sense, the northern states of the U.S.A., for instance, are more thickly populated than India (1867, p. 473).

Marx applied this, however, primarily to the circulation of commodities and the division of labour in production, not to political relations or social solidarity as such. Nonetheless, Marx and Engels did make centralization of the means of communication and transport in the hands of the state one of the general measures proposed by the *Communist Manifesto*.

10 See Przeworski (1977, p. 395) though one must question the extent to which Marx and Engels developed their views through an accurate appreciation of capitalist intransigence (Przeworski's implication) as opposed to a failure to grasp the directions of capitalist development, even during their lifetimes. Certainly the political economists Marx was happy elsewhere to take as examples of the bourgeois thinking of the day were advocates of many of the state-building innovations against which Marx expected opposition to be longer-lasting and fiercer than it was. That Marx and Engels did not anticipate the dramatic growth of the capitalist state is no doubt connected to their expectation of the withering away of the state in socialism.

11 Wright (1980) points out how Cohen's (1978) powerful reconstruction of Marx's technological determinism reproduces precisely this problem of 'class capacities'.

12 See Kantorowicz (1957) on the origins of the corporation in the legal theory of the late medieval state.

13 Cf. Berle and Means (1932); Berle's later statement (1960); Burnham (1941); and many others since. A summary of debates on how this affects the Marxist theory of class structure can be found in Abercrombie and Urry (1983). Much of this debate is an unhelpful taxonomic quarrel over who has what class interests; Marxists have given much less attention to the organizational capacities which make this sort of capitalist enterprise possible (though for recent exceptions see Mandel, 1975; Scott, 1979; Burawoy, 1983).

14 Przeworski goes on to consider the important question (beyond the scope of this paper) of whether increasing labour productivity diminishes the size of the classical proletariat and creates a new split:

> the process of proletarianization in the sense of separation from the means of production diverges from the process of proletarianization in the sense of creation of places of productive workers. This divergence generates social relations that are indeterminate in the class terms of the capitalist mode of production, since it leads

exactly to the separation of people from a socially organized process of production (1977, p. 359).

15 The extent to which direct relationships supplement indirect class relations is a major predictor of political strength of self-proclaimed class movements – e.g. socialist or labour parties – and the weakness of such juncture between class and community is a major reason for 'American exceptionalism' from the European socialist model. See my brief discussion in Calhoun (1984). The instances of class struggle to which we may point are only approximations to the 'pure' vision of solidary class action embodied in Marx's theory.

16 In considering the circulation of commodities (if not in his political writings), Marx clearly recognized the importance of the new infrastructural technology:

> The chief means of reducing the time of circulation is improved communications. The last fifty years have brought about a revolution in this field, comparable only with the industrial revolutions of the latter half of the 18th century. On land the macadamised road has been displaced by the railway, on sea the slow and irregular sailing vessel has been pushed into the background by the rapid and dependable steamboat line, and the entire globe is being girdled by telephone wires (1894, p. 71).

Of course new technologies of transport and communications also allowed for the creation of larger corporations and an international division of labour. This then could be used to manipulate workers' collective action by creating a conflict of interest between workers of rich and poor countries.

> The global telecommunications revolution, combined with dramatic improvements in transportation systems has made it much easier for the bourgeoisie to organize capitalist production globally, producing parts for consumer goods in 'world market factories' in the third world. This has meant that it is easier for the bourgeoisie to manipulate national and global divisions within the working class and to isolate technical-coordination from direct production (Levine and Wright, 1980, p. 66; see also Mandel, 1975 and Bluestone and Harrison, 1982).

It must be remembered, however, that these developments, though technologically novel, merely continue a trend in which the integration of capitalist organization stays one step ahead of the integration of the working class. On a more localized nineteenth century counterpart, see Gregory (1982).

17 See Heaton (1960), and Bagwell, (1971) for general sources on transportation developments.

18 Much the same story, with slightly later dates and a few other qualifications, based especially on the centrality of Paris, could be written for France; see Price (1975).

19 This is part of the material basis for accounts, like Perkin's (1969), of how a 'viable class society' could develop in nineteenth-century England. Of course, the proportionate decline of employment in capitalist industrial organizations is greatly changing the terms of class struggle, though not necessarily its essential nature – at least as struggle has so far defined the collectivity 'working class'.

20 In 'capitalist democracy' (Przeworski, 1980a,b; Przeworski and Wallerstein, 1980), bargaining and struggle are shaped by capitalist social organization as well as hegemonic culture in such ways that non-revolutionary opportunities to satisfy real, felt interests are open to workers and other groupings (which might overlap with or include that of workers). See also Thompson (1965) on the enormous investment workers have made in the institutions of non-revolutionary reform.

21 Part of the impact of New Model Unionism and the growth of modern working-class institutions was a separation between political and economic organizations which had not obtained earlier. See Stedman Jones (1982) on the essentially political definition of Chartism.

22 Increasing size of collectivities has a built-in tendency towards increasing oligarchy (Mayhew and Levinger, 1976). Size is also generally correlated with an increasing division into sub-groups (Blau, 1977). One should note, though, that Blau's deductions concern rates of interpersonal interaction – i.e. direct relationships. No collectivity can mobilize effectively completely without direct relationships. The question remains open, however, of to what extent intermediate associations of individuals linked by direct relationships will be incorporated (and will serve to incorporate their members) into the larger whole. I have argued elsewhere that this is essential to democratic participation in large organizations (Calhoun, 1980).

23 See Evans and Boyte (1982) for an explication of the idea of 'free social spaces'. The role of black churches in the USA civil rights movement is one of their archetypical examples. The notion goes beyond freedom *from* the incursions of established authorities to freedom *to* develop social strength.

• 4 •

Class, behaviour and residence in nineteenth-century society: *the lower middle class in Huddersfield in 1871* • *RICHARD DENNIS*

Introduction

While geographers have continued to chart the transition 'from Sjoberg to Burgess', plotting the distributions of the extremes of social stratification, or measuring the segregation of different occupational classes by way of dissimilarity indices and location quotients, social historians have paid more attention to the dynamics of class structure among the 'middling' and respectable who accounted for the majority of urban residents in nineteenth-century society. All too often, the two groups of researchers have passed in the night, barely aware of each other's existence.[1]

It is hard to imagine a point of contact between historians, concerned with the ephemeral and diverse situations in which class consciousness is expressed, and geographers, resolutely determined to allocate everybody, permanently, to mutually exclusive and mappable classes. Even if individual acts of class consciousness – strikes, tracts, elections, marriages – are interpreted as surface expressions of more permanent relations of production, it is unlikely that the bourgeoisie and proletariat of Foster's Oldham, or the multiplicity of classes in Neale's Bath, will bear much resemblance to the social-economic strata I–V that inhabit the pages of Pooley's Liverpool (see Foster, 1974; Neale, 1968, 1981; Pooley, 1977, 1979; Shaw, 1977, 1979) or Shaw's Wolverhampton. One problem is that geographers have reduced society to social strata and locale to residential segregation. Another is that they have reduced urban society to Disraeli's two nations, examining *only* the rich and the poor, new and exclusive suburbs and squalid slums.

What follows is an attempt to heed David Cannadine's summons to explore the relationships between 'shapes on the ground' and 'shapes in society' (Cannadine 1982a), examining not only patterns of residence but also various forms of social and spatial behaviour; and to focus on the middle ground of small businessmen, shopkeepers, white-collar workers, little masters and labour aristocrats who have been so conspicuously absent from recent geographical studies. The setting is one small part of one industrial town, Huddersfield in West Yorkshire, at one date, 1871. The smallness of the sample and the lack of a temporal dimension necessarily limit the significance of some of the results, but the methods of analysis may, and I hope will, be used in more comprehensive studies in the future, as research in Huddersfield is extended to cover a longer time-span and a wider range of behaviour, and in comparative studies in other towns and cities.

1 The lower middle class and the labour aristocracy in mid-Victorian society

In recent historical debate on the nature of class in nineteenth-century society, terms such as 'lower middle class', 'petty bourgeoisie', 'labour aristocracy' and 'artisan élite' have featured prominently (see Gray, 1981; Morris, 1979, Neale, 1981). The maturing of the industrial revolution was associated with a substitution of capital for labour, a process of 'deskilling' in which skilled craft workers were superseded by machine operatives who were frequently younger than the workers they replaced, and frequently female; but it also depended on the emergence of an élite of skilled workers who built and maintained the machinery, or who maintained discipline and authority in the workplace (Hobsbawm, 1964). Foster described the process in the emerging engineering and reorganised cotton spinning industries in Oldham in the 1850s, arguing that a labour aristocracy was subverted to bourgeois values of liberalism and patriotism by various forms of 'direct and indirect, overt and covert' bribery, the price that the local bourgeoisie were obliged to pay to regain cultural and political control from a previously unified working class (Foster, 1974). Other authors have disputed this interpretation, noting that ideologies are constructed from within as well as without, that the labour aristocracy, willingly espoused values of respectability, temperance and self-help (Crossick, 1978). Labour aristocrats themselves promulgated new kinds of values and new forms of behaviour. But what values? 'Respectability' could mean temperance and adult education classes, but it could also mean participation in the democratic processes of trade unions, and self-help through joining friendly and building societies, the meetings of which necessarily involved a moderate indulgence in 'social drinking'.

If historians are unsure how to define the membership and values of the labour aristocracy, they are even more confused over the other 'middling' elements of mid-Victorian society, which gave the lie to Marx's vision of two conflicting classes, absorbing and destroying the ranks between them. Crossick (1977) identified two elements in an emerging lower middle class: a petty bourgeoisie of shopkeepers and small businessmen, and a new white-collar group of clerks, managers, travellers and teachers. The first group can be partitioned again between retailers, now separated from the business of production and, in many cases, inhabiting dwellings remote from their town-centre shops, and master craftsmen, perhaps employing a handful of journeymen, apprentices and assistants. The usual impression is that none of these groups constituted a 'class', because there were too few of them in any one place to exert any common influence, because theirs was an ethic of individualism associated with the ambition of upward social mobility, and because they were recruited from the ranks of the working classes with whom they remained on intimate terms as a sort of social security policy, protection against the insecurity of their new status. So, we should not expect these groups to occupy distinctive lower-middle class residential areas, let alone separate areas for retailers, little masters, clerks and managers, partly because in most towns there were too few of them to constitute a distinct housing class and partly because their members were frequently inter related, both to one another and to members of more easily defined working and middle classes.

Commentaries on the spatial distribution of the lower middle classes within cities are vague in the extreme. London and large, provincial cities, along with some smaller administrative and commercial centres had a larger lower middle class that was more likely to occupy extensive and homogeneous suburbs, but elsewhere, lower-middle-class housing was 'located on the fringes of areas changing in social composition' or as buffers around genuinely middle-class suburbs (Crossick, 1977; See also Gaskell, 1977; Cannadine 1980; Thompson, 1977). Crossick argued that many housing schemes 'were pitched ambiguously at a lower middle class and artisan market' although, within such mixed developments, 'there would have been considerable differentiation by housing type, street, or neighbourhood'.

Crossick's own research was initially concerned less with the lower middle class than the artisan élite. In Kentish London the transition from skilled worker to master or white-collar worker probably transformed neither life style nor social milieu (Crossick, 1978). Masters retained their union membership, and skilled craftsmen such as builders and tailors married into retailing and even white-collar families, perhaps reflecting social networks based on business relationships (craftsmen's contacts with their suppliers and wholesale customers) or the pattern of recruitment of non-manual workers from the ranks of manual workers. Overall, 'a degree of social contact is evident between skilled artisans and occupational groups later known as the lower middle class. Artisan involvement with small shopkeepers, and to a lesser extent managerial and clerical workers, is a commonplace of political and social movements from the early nineteenth century' (Crossick, 1978, p. 130).

Over time, however, the lower middle class grew in numbers, began to despise manual labour and moved to exclusively lower-middle-class areas. Recruitment into white-collar work through secondary education threatened the status of the labour aristocracy, whose position at the peak of manual labour counted for nothing when the children of labourers could by-pass them en route to middle-class respectability.

Latterly, Crossick has turned his attention to the petty bourgeoisie. It is hard enough defining the group, let alone uncovering its relations with other social strata, since the term covered shopkeepers and small manufacturers, ranging 'from the parlour shop to the High Street grocer, from the sub-contracting small master to the well established small firm', while some occupational groups that we conventionally classify as professional, such as dentists and general practitioners 'were far more skilled craftsmen building a small business than anything else' (Crossick, 1983, pp. 309–10). Consequently, the limits of the petty bourgeoisie should be defined less in terms of income than in terms of role and attitudes. Most petty bourgeois were cost-conscious, rate-cutting economists, necessarily protecting the viability of their own fragile businesses. When they had capital to invest outside their own businesses, they put it into (local) housing. Their outlook was local, at a time when the prosperous, established middle classes were abandoning local affairs for Westminster, and urban residences for country retreats. So the petty bourgeoisie became increasingly important in local government and local culture. They could never withdraw socially from the working classes, since the latter were both their customers and their tenants. We might expect, therefore, that the petty bourgeoisie would be 'closer', both in terms of residence and social interaction, than either the 'new' lower middle class of office workers or the labour aristocracy, to the mass of the working-class population. While craft manufacturing businesses tended to pass from one generation of a family to the next (or, at least, children followed the same craft as their father, even if they became employees in that craft), shopkeeping was apparently a less stable or persistent occupation. Shopkeepers' sons might find white-collar jobs, but shopkeepers themselves might be recruited from the ranks of downwardly-mobile middle-class children.

If Crossick has demonstrated the potential closeness of the petty bourgeoisie to the working classes, Foster has stressed the increasing separation of the labour aristocracy from the majority of less favoured workers. Foster contrasted the situation in Oldham in the early nineteenth century when all occupational groups from labourers to skilled craftsmen, and including little masters, were broadly united, and class structure comprised '12,000 worker families selling their labour to 70 capitalist families' (Foster, 1968, p. 284), with later decades, when this broad working-class consciousness disintegrated, when there was increasing residential segregation between skilled labour aristocrats and unskilled operatives, and between patriotic, Protestant English and Catholic Irish. Labour aristocrats in Oldham were more likely than the rest of the working classes to attend church, practise temperance or abstinence, and attend evening classes. They also maintained close links with a 'petty petty bourgeoisie' of corner-shopkeepers, many of whom were themselves retired spinners or engineers (Foster, 1974).

How typical was either Kentish London or Oldham of class relations in the rest of England? Morris commented on Foster's argument that 'What matters is the lack of evidence for the same sort of behaviour in other textile towns. This is a caution, not a rejection. Studies of towns like Bradford and Huddersfield may produce results more compatible with Oldham, for they were also single-industry textile towns into which the military commanders in charge of internal security in the 1830s were afraid to send their troops' (Morris, 1979, pp. 42–3). Crossick's Kentish London was both suburban, in its proximity to and railway connections with the metropolis, and provincial, in its uncharacteristic range of local industries, associated with the Thames, the Naval Dockyard and the Royal Arsenal. Not surprisingly, therefore, the authors of overviews, like Gray, have been reluctant to commit themselves:

> Studies of marriage and participation in local organisations reveals a certain amount of contact between skilled workers and white-collar employees and small businessmen. Ideologically there might be an apparently shared commitment to respectability and independence. Many of the lower-middle class groups were also, it seems, recruited from skilled workers or their children. . . . But there is also evidence of a clear separation from lower-middle class groups. The social experience of industrial labour and the collective forms of organisation and activity characteristic of skilled workers distinguished them from clerks and small shopkeepers. . . . Despite their apparent social proximity to the lower-middle class and their separation from other workers, the upper strata of the working class had a clear sense of class identity (Gray, 1981, pp. 41–2).

Because 'labour aristocracy' and 'petty bourgeoisie' are concepts we cannot simply count heads and map the distributions of their members. Classes are not ever-present realities, but are constantly shaped and re-constituted by the reactions of individuals to particular events. As E. P. Thompson has argued, 'classes do not exist as abstract, platonic categories, but only as men come to *act* in roles determined by class objectives, to *feel* themselves to belong to classes, to define their interests as between themselves and as against other classes' (Thompson, 1965, p. 357; quoted in Billinge, 1982). More simply, again in Thompson's words, class can only be defined 'in the medium of *time* – that is, action and reaction, change and conflict . . . class itself is not a thing, it is a happening' (Thompson, 1966, p. 939).

So, most social historians focus on the *acts* of class consciousness, revealed in letters, newspaper reports, political and economic tracts, and rarely consider it necessary or feasible to establish precisely *who* participated in them, beyond listing the principal protagonists. Even those who produce inclusive models of class structure, such as Neale (1968), recognise such a degree of fluidity that individuals cannot be assigned unambiguously to a unique class, and that the criteria for defining classes will change as the sources of conflict and political debate change.

Yet the significance of class as an analytical concept is surely enhanced if we can show that individuals aligned themselves in the same way in a variety of roughly contemporaneous decision-making contexts. So this paper seeks to show whether the impressions of class structure provided by different indicators of social interaction in Huddersfield were sufficiently coincident to justify our dividing the population into a single set of classes relevant to the whole of life.

2 Mid-Victorian Huddersfield

Patrick Joyce has discussed the difference between the textile industries of Lancashire and West Yorkshire, noting that 'in the West Riding working-class political organisation took precedence over trade union organisation, the Chartist political inheritance continuing as a vital presence in a radical tradition which reached more deeply into popular life than was the case in Lancashire'. He attributed these differences to 'later and less complete mechanisation', and smaller-scale, less persistent and less paternalistic employers in the West Riding woollen industry (Joyce, 1980, p. 33). One of Huddersfield's local historians, writing in the 1890s, felt obliged to temper his otherwise laudatory account of economic and social progress with the observation that 'At times the relations between employers and employed have been strained, at times, unfrequent and at long intervals, there have been serious ruptures' (Sykes, 1898, p. 434). Disputes between workers and individual millowners in the early 1880s led to the formation of the Huddersfield Woollen Manufacturers and Spinners' Association, an attempt by employers to introduce uniform wage rates, and a 12-week strike in 1883 (Sykes, 1898). It might be expected that class structure in Huddersfield in the 1870s and 1880s would have resembled that in Oldham forty years earlier. Contrary to Foster's account of a town dominated by large and impersonal spinning mills controlled by a handful of large capitalists, Oldham was actually the smallest-scale in employment terms of all the cotton towns, and its radical character in the early decades of the nineteenth century grew out of its small-scale employment structure, in which little masters occupied an ambiguous position (Gadian, 1978;

Musson, 1976). In his letters to the *Morning Chronicle*, Reach (in Ginswick, 1983) noted that small capitalists in Oldham each rented only one floor of a mill and were unable to survive periods of slack trade without laying off part of their workforce. Consequently industrial unrest in Oldham was attributable to the precarious economic situation of little masters rather than an unfeeling lack of interest on the part of large capitalists. Some of Reach's informers claimed that little masters were popular with their workers because they drank in the same pubs and managed their houses in the same way; but Reach believed that large capitalists were preferred as employers because they offered cleaner and more secure working conditions, and because there was no jealousy between employed and employers where each had such obviously different origins (Reach, 1849; reprinted in Ginswick, 1983). We might expect similar attitudes to and similar ambiguities in the status of master craftsmen and small businessmen in Huddersfield in the 1870s.

Yet we must beware of assuming that social interaction revolved around economic relations, or that explicitly class-based organisations played any significant role in mid- or late-Victorian Huddersfield. In 1875, when there were an estimated 900 members of 16 trade unions in and around Huddersfield, there were about 2000 members of the Huddersfield Industrial Society, the town's principal co-op, about 5000 members of the Band of Hope Union and a thousand students enrolled at the Mechanics' Institute (Co-operative Congress, 1895). In 1894, for which more precise figures are available, there were 3500 union members, of whom 2000 belonged to the Weavers' Association, but there were another 7000 non-unionised weavers, compared to 16 000 members of co-operative societies, 11 000 Band of Hope members, 4500 juvenile and 400 adult members of the Church of England Temperance Society, and at least 6000 members of friendly societies (Co-operative Congress, 1895; see also Balmforth, 1910; Singleton, 1970). Unfortunately, lists of members of such organisations have rarely survived. We know rather more about the membership of élite organisations, such as literary and scientific societies, and non-conformist churches, than of friendly societies, let alone being able to reconstruct patterns of informal leisure activities, such as the patronage of local pubs.

Although Huddersfield had been an important market for woollen textiles in the eighteenth century it was not incorporated as a municipal borough until 1868, when its population was approximately 70 000.

Improvement acts in 1820 and 1848 had established commissions responsible for lighting, watching, cleaning and the upkeep of highways, but their jurisdiction extended only 1200 yards from the town centre, and much of the township of Huddersfield, not to mention four adjacent townships which all became parts of the borough in 1868, was controlled by ten other local government bodies (Sykes, 1898; Singleton, 1970). Hillhouse, a northern suburb that provides the geographical focus for this paper, straddles the 1200-yard boundary, part subject to the Fartown Local Board, and part under the jurisdiction of the Huddersfield Improvement Board (Figure 4.1).

Even more critically, while landownership in Huddersfield was dominated by the Ramsden family, much of Hillhouse lay within the freehold of the Thornhill estate. In 1884, 51.5 per cent of the township and 41.4 per cent of the borough of Huddersfield were owned by the Ramsden family, who pursued an idiosyncratic policy of urban development (Springett, 1979). From 1853 until 1900 the Ramsdens prohibited the building of back-to-back houses on their estate, at a time when this was the characteristic form of working-class housing in the West Riding. Until 1859 most working-class property on the estate was erected on tenancies-at-will: in theory, tenants had no security of tenure and there was little incentive to build dwellings to last, but ground rents were very low. Only mills and middle-class houses were built on leasehold land, for which a higher ground rent was payable, and even in these cases, leases of only sixty years, renewable subject to the payment of fines, were granted. In 1859 the Ramsdens switched to 99-year leases and after 1987 they granted terms of 999 years. Meanwhile, other landowners had been making land available freehold or on long (999-year) leases. Builders of both low quality back-to-back and high quality middle-class villas and terraces were attracted to these other estates, partly because of the absence of control at the bottom end of the market, and partly because they found the combination of long leases and restrictive covenants an acceptable basis for more substantial developments (Springett, 1982).

Between Hillhouse and the centre of Huddersfield land on either side of Bradford Road lay within the Ramsden estate. A series of yards and terraces paralleled the road, mostly erected on tenancies-at-will between 1847 and 1853. They provided an ideal environment for petty bourgeois house ownership, a tradesman or master craftsman occupying a house fronting the main road, perhaps using the yard for the pursuit of

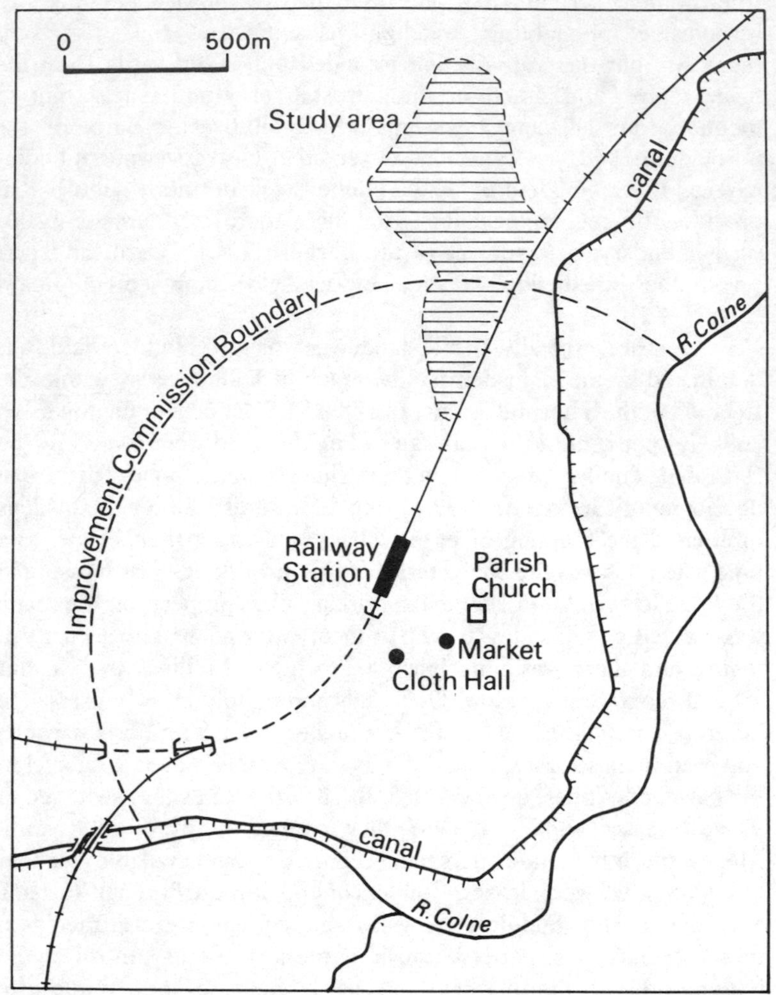

Figure 4.1 The location of the study area

business, but also letting a handful of cottages bordering the yard to individual working-class families.

North of the Ramsden land lay the Thornhill estate. Until 1852, the Thornhill family were limited by entail to granting leases of not more than twenty-one years. Under the terms of the Thornhill Estate Act, 1852, land could be let on 999-year leases. Thereafter, three areas of the estate were developed: middle-class detached villas in Edgerton, working-class cottages in Lindley, and lower-middle-class terraced houses in Hillhouse (Springett, 1978). The Estate Act stipulated extensive covenants concerned with painting, repairing, drainage, roadmaking and property insurance, but in the case of Clara, Eleanor and Honoria Streets, the three residential roads at the heart of the Hillhouse estate, it was also specified that houses 'should have a forecourt . . . kept entirely as a garden or lawn enclosed by a low wall . . . or ashlar edge stone surmounted by iron railings or open work as approved by the Trustees'. Not only the front gardens but also the wide roads distinguished the estate from contemporaneous developments elsewhere in the town. A total of forty-seven building leases were granted between 1853 and 1866, most leases involving fewer than five houses. Houses facing onto Bradford Road were completed by the time of the 1861 census, but most of the estate was developed and occupied during the early 1860s.[2]

Ratebooks, which can be used to establish levels of ownership-occupation, have survived for Huddersfield only for 1847, before much development had taken place in Hillhouse, and 1896, by which time houses which had probably originally been owner-occupied had become privately rented. It was a common occurrence in the late nineteenth century for owner occupiers who moved house to retain ownership and let the property they vacated.[3] Nonetheless, Springett notes that the lower-middle-class area of Fartown exhibited an above-average level of owner-occupancy in 1896, compared to low levels in the 'village nuclei' of pre-1850 cottage and yard property including the old village of Hillhouse (Springett, 1979).

The implication of this admittedly incomplete building and ownership history is that we might expect to find self-employed craftsmen and little masters owning and occupying the houses and yards on Ramsden property nearer the town centre, while the Thornhill estate would have been more likely to attract junior professional and managerial workers.

3 The measurement of social stratification

Most geographical analyses of residential segregation have employed Armstrong's five-class categorisation of the employed population, modified from the Registrar General's 1951 classification of occupations

(Armstrong, 1966, 1972). Unfortunately, Armstrong's classification invariably produces a large and unwieldy class III, whatever the industrial structure of the town under consideration so that inevitably, researchers end up by contrasting the sizes and locations of the extreme groups in the social hierarchy, amalgamating classes I and II to form a unitary middle class of merchants, manufacturers and professional workers, and uniting classes IV and V in a 'lower class' of semi-skilled and unskilled workers (see Dennis, 1984). Apart from a few petty employers and some of the more specific junior non-manual employees such as agents and bookkeepers, all the people who are the subject of this essay are allocated by Armstrong and his followers to class III, along with the majority of factory workers and industrial craftsmen with supposedly 'skilled' jobs.

Two exceptions to this near universal acceptance of Armstrong's classification have been Cowlard's work on Wakefield, and Ward's study of Leeds (Cowlard, 1979; Ward, 1980). Cowlard modified Armstrong's classification, incorporating manuscript census information on the employment of resident domestic servants, or of children returned as 'scholars', as evidence of high status, and on the accommodation of lodgers, or the employment of married women and young children outside the home, as evidence of low status. He divided each of Armstrong's five primary classes into three sub-classes, creating a stratification which, he claimed, mirrored the essential continuity of the Victorian social hierarchy, in which marginal differences in status, skill and income were jealously defended. Whether his classification provides any indication of 'class' would depend on the correlation between social status, housing conditions and tenure, lifestyle and behaviour, including voting behaviour and institutional membership. While a household's relative status may remain the same over time, its 'class' may vary according to circumstances. Cowlard attempted to provide a single measure of status, whereas Armstrong argued that each indicator of status (occupation, education, housing tenure, rateable value, servants, lodgers, women-at-work) should be examined separately (Holmes and Armstrong, 1978).

Ward's study of Leeds identified three classes and eight strata within those classes: a middle class divided into higher and lesser professionals and large and petty proprietors, a working class divided into skilled, semi-skilled and unskilled elements, and between the two, a class of self-employed retailers. Ward was particularly anxious to identify the most substantial businessmen and professionals as a separate category since he suspected that contemporary descriptions stressing the increasing segregation of the classes in Victorian cities simply reflected the personal experience of this tiny upper-middle-class group (Ward, 1978). So his model of society is pyramidal: the two upper-middle-class strata accounted for only 4 per cent of household heads, lesser professionals and petty proprietors for another 10 per cent, and self-employed retailers for around 13 per cent. Ward's distinction between business and the professions is also important, implying the existence of two parallel rather than hierarchical middle classes, with distinctive rules of access (through capital or education) and distinctive values (potentially reflected in the support of different political parties and different religious beliefs).

Unfortunately, neither Cowlard nor Ward used sources other than the census enumerators' books, which are notoriously ambiguous in identifying variations in status within an industrial category. Employers were asked to return the number of their employees, but in practice, this information was supplied only erratically. So it is difficult to distinguish between a 'woollen spinner' who was the proprietor of a spinning mill, a self-employed master spinner, and a factory operative. Despite Ward's claim to have identified 'self-employed retailers', such a group is difficult to locate, except in the case of shopkeepers whose addresses were recorded as 'draper's shop', 'grocer's shop', etc. So many teenage retailers, whose true status was that of assistant or apprentice, are returned in the census that we must suspect that some household heads returned as retailers (or as craftsmen) were not their own masters. Nor is it easy to distinguish between 'retailers' and 'craftsmen' on the basis of the census alone: was a tailor somebody who made trousers or somebody who sold them?

In the present study, the *principal* source of occupational data was the 1871 census, but in an attempt to distinguish between self-employed and employee retailers and skilled workers, William White's Directory of Leeds and surrounding districts, published in 1870, was also consulted.[4] White's Directory included both a listing of principal inhabitants street-by-street, and an alphabetical listing of individuals and businesses. Entries include both private individuals and those who were proprietors of businesses undertaken from a workplace separate from their residence. This information could be matched with the census for the following year. It was assumed that persons with craft or trade occupations who featured in the directory were the proprietors of businesses, while those with the same occupational description in the census, but absent from the directory, were employees. No doubt there were inaccuracies in this procedure, particularly since the directory was published in the year preceding the census, but the linkage proved valuable in very many cases (Table 4.1). It also demonstrated the ambiguity of occupational definitions, especially on the border between business and the professions. For example, Joseph Johnson, enumerated in the census as 'commercial traveller', an occupation normally accorded lower non-manual status, appeared in the directory as 'woollen merchant', a partner in the firm of Johnson, J. and Sons, woollen merchants. Aged only 31 in 1871, he was presumably one of the sons and quite possibly did fulfil the relatively junior role of traveller for the firm. Nonetheless, his status and, no doubt, his income would have exceeded that of an employee-traveller. Even fully professional posts, such as accountants and solicitors, cannot be divorced from the businesses which provided them with work, and we might expect such connections to influence their political attitudes and their institutional affiliation.

4 The social geography of Hillhouse in 1871

Some aggregate statistics illustrate the distinctive characteristics of the Hillhouse district. While the sex ratio in Hillhouse (109.1 females per 100 males) was little different from that for the whole borough (108.5), the presence of resident domestic servants in about 14 per cent of households indicates the above-average social status of the area. Nearly 26 per cent of all male household heads and over 19 per cent of all adult males in Hillhouse in 1871 appeared in the pre-Reform Act pollbook for 1868. By comparison, fewer than 13 per cent of adult males in the whole parliamentary borough had been eligible to vote in 1868.[5]

The origins of Hillhouse residents were more diverse than those of the total borough population. It is generally argued that, with the exception of the Irish, long-distance migrants were of higher occupational status than the local-born (Lawton, 1978; Jackson, 1982). In Hillhouse the Irish were under-represented and the proportion of non-Irish, non-Yorkshire-born was 13.1 per cent, compared to 8.3 per cent in the entire borough.

Table 4.1: A comparison of census, directory and pollbook entries for Clara Street, Hillhouse

Name	*Census occupation*	*Directory occupation*	*Directory workplace*	*Voting behaviour*
Wm. H. Bedford	engineer employing 14 men and 1 boy	ironfounder and insurance agent	Harrison & Bedford, ironfounders & engineers, Phoenix Iron Works, Leeds Road	Con.
James Hirst	flock mart	flock dealer	Marshall's Yard, Westgate	Lib.
George Savile	hairdresser employing 3 men and 3 boys	hairdresser	Savile & Barlow, hairdressers & perfumers, Lion Arcade, John William Street	Con.
Charles Smeeton	draper	draper	Cooper & Smeeton, wholesale & retail drapers, 1 Kirkgate	Con.
Henry Marriott	chemist	manufacturing chemist's manager	—	Lib.
Enoch Heppenstall	dyer	dyer	Heppenstall Bros., cotton & woollen dyers, Turnbridge, Quay Street	Lib.
Thos. G. Woodhead	woollen manufacturer	woollen cord manufacturer	Woodhead, J.D. & Bros., woollen & Bedford cord mfrs., 23 King's Head Bdngs., Sheepridge & Turnbridge	Lib.
Samuel K. Hirst	woollen manufacturer	manager	—	Lib.
Joseph Mellor	livery stable keeper	cab proprietor	S. & J. Mellor, cab proprs. and Livery stable keepers, Chancery Lane	Con.
Edwd. J. Billing	clerk	cashier	—	—
Edward Dawson	draper	—	—	—

Sources: census enumerators' books, 1871, RG-10-4370;
William White's Directory, 1870; *Huddersfield Poll Book, 1868*

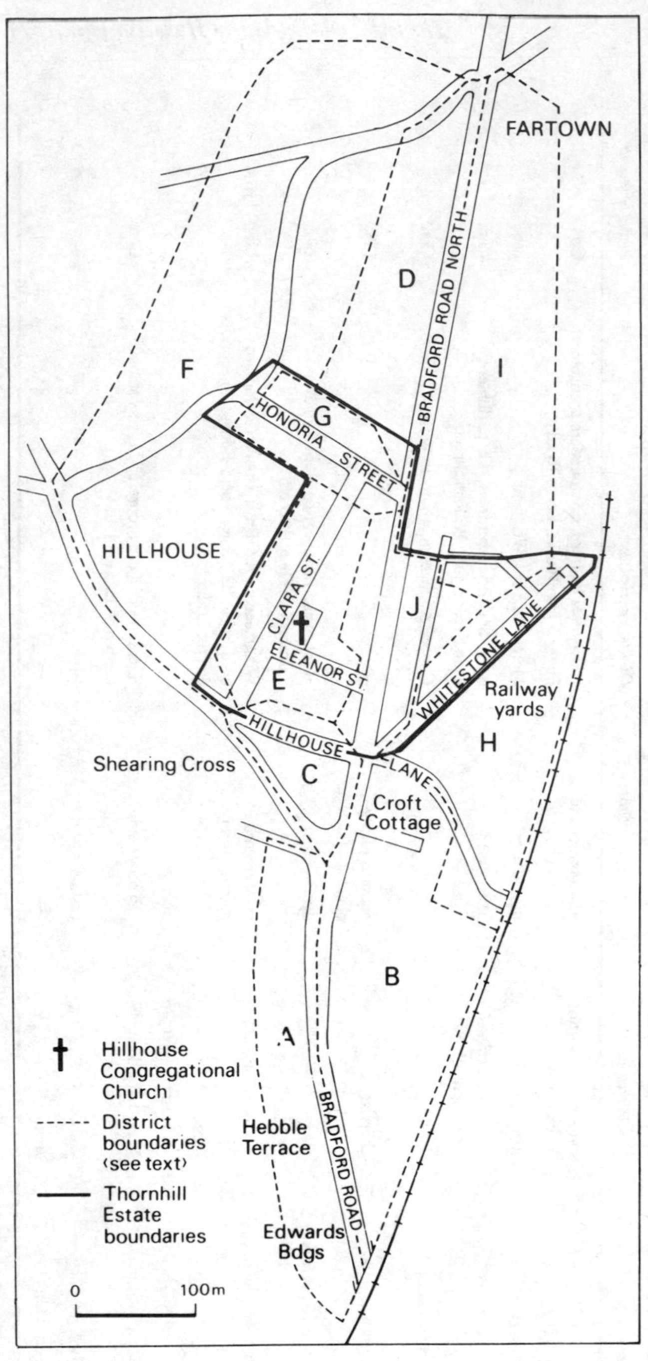
FARTOWN
D
BRADFORD ROAD NORTH
F
I
G
HONORIA
STREET
HILLHOUSE
CLARA ST
J
ELEANOR ST
E
WHITESTONE LANE
Railway
yards
HILLHOUSE
H
Shearing Cross
C
LANE
Croft
Cottage
B
A
Hillhouse
Congregational
Church
District
boundaries
(see text)
Hebble
Terrace
BRADFORD ROAD
Thornhill
Estate
boundaries
Edwards
Bdgs
0
100m

The study area, comprising two entire enumeration districts and parts of two others, was divided into ten districts, each of approximately fifty to sixty households. Districts E (Clara and Eleanor Streets) and G (Honoria Street) comprised the most substantial terraced houses on exclusively residential parts of the Thornhill estate. Districts A and B (Bradford Road and Croft Cottage) included terraces and yards on Ramsden land, mostly erected by the early 1850s on tenancies-at-will. Districts C and F (Shearing Cross and Hillhouse Green) covered the old, pre-industrial core of Hillhouse village. The remaining districts included terraces on or to the east of Bradford Road North, mostly on Thornhill land, but developed more haphazardly, including some shops and, adjacent to railway yards, some industrial premises (Figure 4.2).

The proportion of male heads resident in 1871 who had been entitled to vote in 1868 varied from only 10 per cent in districts C and F to 50 per cent and above in districts E and G, reflecting the higher status of Thornhill estate streets and variations in rates of residential persistence and the age of property. Dwellings in old Hillhouse were low-rented because of their age, even allowing for their modest size. District B (the east side of Bradford Road) also boasted large numbers of electors, a function of both status and the newness of property. Entitlement to vote, which in Huddersfield was entirely dependent on the occupation of property with an annual value of at least £10, was as much a function of the age of dwellings as of their size and the imputed status of their occupiers.

Other status indicators are equally ambiguous. Average household size varied from 5.4 persons in Honoria Street to 4.0 in Hebble Terrace, but large households were associated with both the employment of servants and the accommodation of lodgers, often of the same occupation as the household head. The sex ratio and the proportion of households with resident servants are more direct indicators of status. In each case Honoria Street (G) appeared to rank highest in status, with Clara and Eleanor Streets (E) close behind, and Shearing Cross (C) and the area east of Bradford Road North (I) bringing up the rear.

In studies of working-class areas, the proportion of wives in paid employment is another critical index of status. Among the very poor, particularly those with large families and where there was no further scope to economise on rent, wives were obliged to seek work as

Figure 4.2 District and landownership boundaries in Hillhouse

streetsellers, washerwomen or sweated labour; but it was *apparently* less acceptable for the wives of respectable artisans to seek paid employment than for the family to move to more modest accommodation or adopt a more frugal lifestyle: *apparently*, because one hundred years later it is impossible to determine the true extent of female employment. Male heads who completed census schedules may have omitted women's work which they hoped was only temporary. Enumerators may have deliberately ignored or unconsciously neglected to record wives' occupations. In one Hillhouse enumeration district not one wife was recorded with an occupation. Overall, only 16 of 454 wives were returned as employed, and no pattern can be discerned among them. Husbands whose wives worked included such generally well-paid workers as tailors, a police sergeant, a warehouseman and an engine driver, as well as more obviously needy workers like highway labourers and cart drivers. Nor were their family circumstances at all similar. Two employed wives had no dependents, most had only one or two dependent children, two took in a lodger each, two cared for elderly mothers. However, these fragments do reinforce the image of old Hillhouse (C) as the poorest part of the study area: the only district with more than 10 per cent of wives in paid employment.

4.1 Residential segregation and social stratification

Clara and Eleanor Streets (E) contained twice the proportion of professional workers, merchants, manufacturers, clerks, agents, salesmen and tradesmen present in Hillhouse as a whole (Table 4.2). In Honoria Street (G) there were fewer shopkeepers but more members of the substantial middle class. Self-employed craftsmen and skilled workers in textiles, building and engineering were substantially underrepresented in Clara and Eleanor Streets. Master craftsmen were present in larger numbers in Whitestone and Hillhouse Lanes (H), where an industrial zone was located, while skilled employees were concentrated to the east of Bradford Road North (I), especially engine drivers and firemen in terraces close to the locomotive sheds. Self-employed masters were also well-represented in older housing closer to the town centre (A, B), while textile workers occupied the oldest area of all (F), a legacy of Hillhouse's function as a centre of domestic industry when it was still a free-standing village, but also within easy walking distance of Close and Cloughhouse woollen mills, immediately to the north.

Table 4.2: Social stratification by household, Hillhouse, 1871

Occupation of household head	*District*										
	A	*B*	*C*	*D*	*E*	*F*	*G*	*H*	*I*	*J*	*Total*
	per cent in each occupational group										
1 Middle class	5	7	2	3	16	5	28	7	2	11	8
upper professional	0	2	2	0	0	2	3	3	0	5	2
merchants, manufacturers, managers	5	4	0	3	16	3	25	3	2	6	6
2 Lower middle class	41	43	30	25	54	23	44	38	27	37	36
clerks, salesmen, agents	12	13	4	12	29	8	22	12	16	15	14
shopkeepers, dealers, carriers	8	15	14	6	21	5	13	7	4	14	10
lodging house keepers	3	0	4	0	0	2	0	0	0	0	1
master craftsmen*	17	15	8	6	5	8	9	20	7	8	10
3 Skilled workers†	42	43	48	51	25	67	19	50	62	46	46
textile workers	5	17	12	17	5	33	13	18	27	14	16
engineering, metal workers	3	4	12	6	0	7	0	7	9	5	5
building workers	8	7	4	12	3	12	0	5	4	6	6
railway employees	2	2	2	3	3	2	0	8	9	0	3
other skilled workers	24	13	18	12	14	13	6	12	13	22	15
4 Semi-skilled & unskilled	12	7	18	20	2	5	6	3	9	3	8
5 Not known	0	0	2	2	3	0	3	2	0	3	1
Total	59	46	50	65	63	60	32	60	55	65	555

For the locations of districts A–J, see Figure 4.2.
Female-headed households were classified according to the occupation of adult male members of household, where present.

Notes:
*listed in directory and assumed self-employed, or recorded in census as employing others.
†no evidence from census or directory that they ran their own business.

Tradesmen were scattered through several districts. In retrospect, the distinction between 'local' shopkeepers, who lived above or behind their shops, and town-centre tradesmen, who resided away from work, deserves more attention. We might expect this distinction to carry through into patterns of family employment (wives and children of 'local' shopkeepers would help out in the shop even if they were not recorded as doing so in the census) and social interaction (town-centre tradesmen encountered a wealthier clientele than corner-shopkeepers). Certainly, the separation of residence and workplace constituted an important status symbol for the petty bourgeoisie. Arnold Bennett described how Darius Clayhanger, the proprietor of a small printing works and shop, regarded his move to a suburban house: he 'was achieving the supreme peak of greatness – he was about to live away from business. Soon he would be "going down to business" of a morning. . . . Ages ago he had got as far as a house with a lobby to it. Now, it would be a matter of two establishments' (Bennett, 1910). In Hillhouse, just over one-third of shopkeepers and dealers definitely worked away from home. Two-thirds of them lived in Clara, Eleanor and Honoria Streets. Of the remaining thirty-seven tradesmen who, definitely or presumably (in the absence of any contradictory information) worked at home, only three lived in districts E and G, in two cases occupying corner-shops on the very edge of the residential zone.

There is, therefore, some evidence that little masters did *not* live in lower-middle-class streets; and that businessmen and white-collar workers were heavily concentrated in the newest, purely residential streets, where their neighbours were town-centre retailers and dealers. Skilled labour was more scattered, with local concentrations reflecting proximity to work or the availability of housing in which domestic industry could be undertaken.

In many households more than one person was gainfully employed and it may be erroneous to assume that status depended solely on the head's occupation. It is difficult to compare directly the occupations of fathers and co-resident sons, since most employed children were only in their teens or early twenties and may not have attained their adult occupational status. Yet a comparison of the occupations of 144 father–son pairs reveals a remarkable consistency of status. The classification of sons' occupations was necessarily made on sectoral rather than status lines, since co-resident children were most unlikely to be employers or self-employed. Nonetheless, an approximate ranking may be made, from clerical (and potentially professional) employment, through warehouse and shop work, to industrial and labouring jobs.

Nine out of eleven sons of middle-class fathers were engaged in relatively high-status occupations, fifteen out of twenty-two tradesmen's sons were in trade or non-manual employment, and five out of eight clerks' sons were themselves clerks, but only one out of sixteen sons of self-employed craftsmen had penetrated the world of non-manual labour, a lower proportion than that found among the sons of skilled employees (Table 4.3). While the children of the self-employed were

Table 4.3: Occupations of fathers and co-resident sons, Hillhouse, 1871

	Son's occupation								
Father's occupation	*Clerical/ Teaching*	*Retailing/ Dealing*	*Warehouse-man*	*Textiles*	*Railway/ Engineering*	*Building Trades*	*Other Craft*	*Semi- & Unskilled*	*Total*
Middle class	4	3	2	–	–	–	–	2	11
Lower middle class									
clerks, etc.	5	1	–	1	–	–	1	–	8
trade	3	10	2	2	–	1	1	3	22
craft	1	–	–	6	3	2	4	–	16
Skilled employee									
textiles	1	6	–	20	–	3	6	2	38
other	5	3	1	6	6	5	5	1	32
Semi- and un-skilled	–	2	–	5	2	1	2	5	17
Total	19	25	5	40	11	12	19	13	144

expected to maintain the family business, the sons of labour aristocrats sought advancement through secondary education and commercial training. Theoretically, Table 4.3 confirms the validity of using the head's occupation as an indicator of household status; empirically, it confirms the separateness of the petty bourgeoisie: master craftsmen and their families and, to a lesser extent, shopkeepers, were excluded from a chain of social mobility linking labour aristocrats to the white-collar lower middle class.

The most detailed scale at which residential segregation can be studied is that of neighbouring. Comparing each household with its immediate neighbour (the following household recorded in the enumerator's book, but omitting households where the following household was located in a different street), the impression is of a surprising degree of local homogeneity. Observed values were compared with expected patterns of neighbouring, using a cross-product formula to generate expected values. The highest ratios of observed to expected levels of neighbouring were nearly all located on or close to the diagonal of the matrix, indicating neighbours of similar status (Table 4.4). This was particularly true among the middle classes, where merchants, manufacturers and their managers were very unlikely to have building, engineering or textile workers as neighbours. Contrary to the trend at district level, there was some tendency for clerks and commercial travellers to live next door to self-employed craftsmen, but neither shopkeepers nor little masters showed much inclination to live next to skilled employees. None of these patterns should be exaggerated: few cells of the matrix registered zero values. Somewhere in Hillhouse almost every combination of possible neighbours could be found.

Three reservations must be made about the analysis of segregation, especially at the microscale. Firstly, it is doubtful whether people had much choice over the identity of their neighbours. Even today, with high levels of owner-occupation and low rates of residential mobility, and when the choice of where to live is a critical, long-term investment decision, few of us know much about the status of our neighbours when we first move to a new home. Nor can we normally influence the choice of any new neighbours once we are ourselves established residents. In the late nineteenth century, when residential mobility was frequent and easily and cheaply accomplished, incoming households would have paid little attention to the character of immediate neighbours. On the other hand, during a period of rapid social change,

Table 4.4: Rates of neighbouring between occupational groups

Occupation of household head		*Occupation of neighbour* (1)	(2)	(3)	(4)	(5)	(6)	(7)	(8)	(9)	(10)	*Total* no. of heads*
1 Middle class: professional	(1)	–	**4.8**	1.0	**2.6**	**2.9**	–	–	–	–	–	7
merchants, mfrs.	(2)	–	**3.5**	1.2	1.4	1.2	0.8	–	0.5	0.8	0.4	33
2 Lower-middle class: clerks, etc.	(3)	**2.4**	1.1	1.4	1.0	1.3	0.8	0.8	0.2	1.0	1.0	75
tradesmen	(4)	–	0.8	1.3	**1.8**	1.2	0.9	0.6	0.3	1.0	0.6	59
master craftsmen	(5)	–	0.6	0.9	1.3	**2.0**	0.6	1.3	0.8	0.7	1.4	54
3 Skilled employees: textiles	(6)	0.7	0.6	1.0	0.5	0.7	**1.6**	1.2	0.9	1.3	0.4	85
rlys. & engineering	(7)	**2.5**	0.7	0.4	0.2	0.4	1.0	**1.7**	**1.6**	**1.5**	**1.5**	48
building trades	(8)	**1.7**	0.5	0.8	0.3	0.6	**1.8**	0.7	**1.7**	1.0	1.4	35
other	(9)	1.4	1.0	1.3	1.0	0.4	0.8	1.4	1.7	0.9	0.9	82
4 Semi- and unskilled	(10)	–	–	0.5	1.4	1.1	1.0	0.5	**2.0**	0.9	**1.9**	45
Total no of heads		9	32	79	59	53	86	47	35	80	43	531*

Notes:

*includes heads whose occupation was unknown

The table compares the occupation of each household head with that of the head listed next in the enumerators' books. The 'neighbouring rate' for each pair of occupations is recorded, defined as the observed frequency/expected frequency. Expected frequency is the product of row and column totals, divided by the total number of observations. For example, out of a population of 531 households and their neighbours, there were 33 heads in the business middle class (2) and 79 neighbours who were clerks, etc. (3). So, if neighbouring occurred randomly, the expected number of businessmen with clerks as neighbours would be 33 × 79 / 531 = 4.91. The observed number was 6, so the rate was 6 / 4.91 = 1.22.

the size, value and location of property were all important status symbols, and mobile households, unconstrained by the judgements of council officials and building society managers, may have had *more* freedom of choice than movers in the 1980s. Moreover, because turnover rates were so high, there would never be long to wait for a vacancy in one's desired area (for a review of residential mobility studies see Dennis 1984, pp. 250–69).

Secondly, the frequency of residential mobility meant that neighbours on Census Day might not remain neighbours for very long, so we should not place too much emphasis on a single snapshot of population distribution. Persistence and mobility were not examined directly in this study, but several cases were noted where addresses in the 1870 directory or 1868 pollbook did not coincide with those in the 1871 census, although there was no doubt that the same people were being described. Ward argued that segregation was more significant where it was associated with persistence, as among certain of the skilled working class in Leeds, whose prolonged residence in exclusively working-class areas he interpreted as the beginning of the working-class 'urban villages' described by writers such as Robert Roberts and Richard Hoggart (Ward, 1980; Roberts, 1971; Hoggart, 1957). We might also expect shopkeepers and little masters who lived where they worked to be persistent, while town-centre tradesmen and white-collar workers would move house more frequently. The latter were unlikely to be owner-occupiers and would aim to preserve or enhance their status by moving to the newest, most fashionable houses with the most modern facilities. Several Hillhouse residents recorded addresses in 1868 in older middle-class streets south of the town centre; others had moved by the later 1870s from Clara and Honoria Streets to newer houses (often semi-detached villas or shorter terraces) in Birkby, a few hundred yards to the north and west.

Finally, we must question the social significance of residential segregation, even at the scale of streets. It is meaningless to claim the existence of residential differentiation if contemporaries failed to recognise the segregation groups as distinct social strata. The residential segregation of occupational groups is only significant if it is accompanied by evidence that they held different values, behaved differently, and inhabited separate social milieux (further discussion of the meaning of segregation is included in Dennis, 1980, 1984).

4.2 Marriage as an index of social interaction

In twelve months following Census Day, 1871, sixty-one marriages were solemnised in Huddersfield Registration District in which at least one partner recorded their address on the marriage certificate as 'Hillhouse', 'Fartown' or 'Bradford Road'. Nineteen involved Hillhouse brides marrying Hillhouse grooms, so the total number of marriage partners whose choice of a spouse could be examined was eighty. The normal procedure in marriage studies has been to compare the occupations of partners' parents, but the occupational descriptions recorded on marriage certificates are even less detailed than those in the census (Foster, 1974; Crossick, 1978). They rarely allow us to distinguish between employers and employed, masters and journeymen, factory and workshop employees, except in those few cases where parents were traceable in census and street directory. Consequently, marriage data can be used to examine interaction between workers in different industries (e.g. between building trades and textile workers), or between skilled and unskilled (assuming that 'labourer' denotes lower status than a specific occupational term like 'mason' or 'weaver'), but not between labour aristocrats and little masters.

To supplement this tiny sample, all marriages contracted in 1878, 1879 and 1880 were also examined. The number of partners identified was 219, fewer than expected given the rapid growth of the area during the 1870s, and perhaps indicating that in-migrants were seldom established families with children of marriageable age. Indeed, the two samples proved rather different: in 1871 white-collar and middle-class households were over-represented by comparison with all household heads in the census study area, reflecting the rural origins of some marriage partners, whose fathers, described as 'farmers', were assumed to be middle-class; in 1878–80 the middle and lower middle classes were apparently under-represented, reflecting partly a shift from partners who were the children of farmers to those who were the offspring of the urban working classes, and partly the lack of a census to which marriage certificates could be linked.[6] In 1871 it was possible in at least some cases to establish whether a 'spinner' was proprietor, master or employee; in 1878–80 it had to be assumed that he belonged with the majority who were employees.

Previous studies have presented interaction matrices in which one axis represents brides, the other grooms. In contrast, in Table 5 the vertical axis represents Hillhouse partners, the horizontal axis, their spouses. Where both partners lived in Hillhouse the marriage is entered twice. So the matrices display the choices of individual marriage partners, *not* the pattern of marriages; they should be read only row-by-row.

For all its imperfections, Table 4.5 demonstrates the social separateness of the middle class and the absence of barriers to marriage between the children of skilled and unskilled workers. In 1871, 25 per cent of spouses of all Hillhouse partners were drawn from the middle and white-collar lower middle classes, but 52 per cent of the spouses of middle-class partners came from these groups. Corresponding figures for 1878–80 were 12 per cent and 25 per cent. The pattern is reminiscent of Foster's findings for Oldham in the 1840s. Yet the implication of Foster's liberalisation thesis is that by the 1870s there should have been a much more stratified and fragmented pattern of intermarriage. As Joyce (1980) suggested, industrial and social relations were very different on either side of the Pennines in the second half of the century, and it is quite possible that the social structure in woollen towns was half a century 'behind' that in cotton towns.

Table 4.5: Marriage choices in Hillhouse, 1871, 1878–80

Hillhouse partner's father's occn.		*Spouse's father's occupation % 1871* (1)	(2)	(3)	(4)	(X)	*Propn of all Hillhouse marriage partners %*
middle class*	(2)	**52**	24	14	5	5	26
tradesmen, shopkeepers, craftsmen	(2)	22	17	39	17	6	23
skilled workers	(3)	9	9	**64**	9	9	41
semi- and un-skilled	(4)	29	14	43	0	14	9
unknown	(X)	0	0	100	0	0	1
Total		25	15	44	9	8	100
		1878–80 (1)	(2)	(3)	(4)	(X)	%
middle class*	(1)	**25**	4	63	8	0	11
tradesmen, shopkeepers, craftsmen	(2)	13	**23**	58	3	3	14
skilled workers	(3)	9	12	**61**	16	2	53
semi- and un-skilled	(4)	10	10	60	**18**	3	18
unknown	(X)	**29**	0	57	14	0	3
Total		12	12	60	14	2	100

Note:
*including white-collar workers

4.3 *Voting behaviour*

Several historians have investigated class- and community-related patterns of voting behaviour, employing locally published pollbooks which, prior to the Secret Ballot Act of 1872, recorded the names and addresses of supporters of each candidate (Morris, 1983). For example, Patrick Joyce (1975) showed that in mill communities in Lancashire in the general election of 1868, the first election held after the enfranchisement of adult male householders under the 1867 Reform Act, there was a clear distinction between Liberal streets around mills run by Liberal employers and Conservative streets around Conservative mills. Voting behaviour transcended occupation and status. All grades of textile worker voted Liberal in Liberal neighbourhoods, Conservative in Conservative neighbourhoods; and the voting patterns of millworkers were paralleled among their neighbourhoods engaged in other occupations, especially retailing. Several interpretations of these findings are possible: in a public ballot shopkeepers may have voted with the neighbourhood for fear of 'exclusive dealing'; millworkers may have voted with their superiors for fear of losing their jobs or at least being denied promotion; or there may have been a genuinely deferential spirit, acceding to the creed of the local élite, irrespective of the secrecy of the ballot. Workers apparently subscribed to a community of work and neighbourhood rather than one of economic class; they exhibited a form of class consciousness, where class was a 'false consciousness' based on deference and collaboration, contrary to any polarisation of capital and labour.

Unfortunately, Huddersfield was uncontested in the 1868 General Election, which followed soon after a by-election held on the pre-Reform Act roll, in which the franchise was restricted to £10 householders. I have already shown that, within Hillhouse, voters were concentrated in the newest housing. But possession of the franchise naturally also varied with occupational status. The established middle class comprised 8 per cent of households in Hillhouse, but 22 per cent of the electorate. Skilled workers constituted 46 per cent of household heads, but only 14 per cent of voters. The electoral system especially favoured those with commercial interests: 81 per cent of merchants and manufacturers, but only 44 per cent of professional workers were enfranchised; 80 per cent of substantial tradesmen, 39 per cent of retailers who traded from home, 35 per cent of self-employed craftsmen and 35 per cent of white-collar workers had the vote (Table 4.6). All these percentages should be increased to allow for the three-year gap between election and census, and for households headed by women or those who had been minors in 1868.

A parliamentary inquiry in 1866 estimated that 12.5 per cent of electors in Huddersfield could be described as 'belonging to the working classes', where 'working class' normally excluded shopkeepers and their assistants, and overlookers, superintendents and foremen, 'unless actually employed in daily manual labour in the same manner in every respect as the men who are under them'.[7] By comparison, 14 per cent of electors in Hillhouse were skilled workers. Yet Hillhouse was an area in which the middle and lower middle classes were over-represented and the working classes under-represented in the total population. Evidently, skilled workingmen were more likely to be on the electoral roll if they lived in Hillhouse than if they resided elsewhere in Huddersfield. Overall, about 1.6 per cent of the adult male population of Huddersfield were working-class *and* enfranchised, compared to 2.7 per cent of adult males in Hillhouse.[8] Occupational status cannot be evaluated independently of locality: to be skilled

Table 4.6: Proportion of heads resident in Hillhouse in 1871 who were on the electoral roll in 1867–68

Occupation of household head	*% heads*	*% electors*	*Percentage of heads in each group eligible to vote*
1 Middle class	8	22	63
professional	2	3	44
merchants, mfrs.	6	19	68
2 Lower middle class	36	64	40
clerks, etc.	14	23	35
shopkeepers (1)	4	13	80
shopkeepers (2)	7	12	39
master craftsmen (2)	10	16	35
3 Skilled employees	46	14	7
4 Semi- and un-skilled	8	1	2
5 Not known	1	0	0
Total	100	100	

Notes:
(1) residence separate from business premises
(2) residence and business premises on the same site

working-class in Hillhouse was not the same as being skilled working-class in more solidly working-class areas.

Huddersfield was considered a Liberal stronghold for most of the nineteenth century. Indeed, the Colne Valley has retained that reputation to the present day. Prior to 1868 contests were usually between Liberals and Whigs, both groups reflecting the interests of textile merchants and manufacturers. Most elections were close-run affairs, in which personality mattered more than party. In 1857, Edward Akroyd, the Halifax manufacturer, won the seat for a Whig–Tory alliance, although it was less Akroyd's popularity than the unpopular pacifism of his opponent, Richard Cobden, that cost the Liberals victory. Two years later, when Akroyd stood again as a Whig, he was defeated by a last-minute Liberal nominee, Edward Leatham, by only nineteen votes (779–760). When a local businessman, Colonel T. P. Crosland, a 'Liberal/Conservative', displaced Leatham in 1865, the result was disputed on the grounds that Crosland's party had offered bribes. One witness to the ensuing parliamentary inquiry claimed that while Crosland was popular among respectable people, non-electors were 'dead against' him. Not surprisingly, with the extension of the franchise, Huddersfield became consistently Liberal (Brook, 1968; Sykes, 1898).

Crosland died in March, 1868, and in the subsequent by-election Leatham regained the seat for the Liberals, this time defeating a candidate who was labelled simply 'Conservative'. Roy Brook, Huddersfield's local historian, suggested several reasons why the newly enfranchised workingmen and small shopkeepers maintained the Liberal tradition after 1868 (Brook, 1968). Manufacturers continued to favour free trade and their workpeople followed suit, perhaps in the deferential way that Joyce found in Lancashire. Nonconformists voted Liberal because Liberals favoured non sectarian education; and Huddersfield was strongly nonconformist; and there was strong personal support for Leatham. Yet if this was true we might have expected Leatham to have won more than the 53 per cent of votes he actually polled in the first post-Reform election in 1874.

In fact, the evidence of the 1868 pollbook disproves any simple alignment between business and Liberalism. Hillhouse as a whole was substantially more Conservative than the rest of Huddersfield, perhaps because of the absence of *substantial* millowners and merchants, who mostly lived in north-west suburbs of the town. Yet those there were in Hillhouse were far from all Liberal supporters (Table 4.7). Nor were tradesmen. There was little difference between small shopkeepers and large retailers and wholesalers. Little masters, like skilled artisans, showed some leaning to Leatham, while the junior non-manual group displayed a substantial Conservative bias. Contrary to the pattern of residence, therefore, there was an apparent community of interest between craftsmen and journeymen, and between different grades of businessmen, but a distinction between those with *direct* business interests (merchants, manufacturers, shopkeepers) and those *employed* by business (clerks, cashiers, commercial travellers).

There was, however, one aspect of voting behaviour which justified Brook's conclusion: the association of Liberalism and nonconformity.

4.4 *Nonconformity*

On Census Sunday, 1851, nearly 57 per cent of church attendances in Huddersfield were at nonconformist places of worship. Almost one in six worshippers and Sunday schoolchildren attended two Independent

Table 4.7: Voting behaviour in Hillhouse, 1868

	Number (per cent) in each occupation group voting for:					
	Leatham (Lib.)		*Sleigh (Con.)*		*Neutral*	
Hillhouse census area	55	(44)	54	(44)	15	(12)
Other Hillhouse electors traced in directory	19	(42)	21	(47)	5	(11)
Middle class	17	(46)	15	(41)	5	(14)
professional	2	(40)	3	(60)	0	(0)
merchants, mfrs.	15	(47)	12	(38)	5	(16)
Lower middle class	57	(43)	60	(45)	15	(11)
clerks, etc.	12	(30)	23	(58)	5	(13)
shopkeepers (1)	11	(48)	11	(48)	1	(4)
shopkeepers (2)	11	(46)	10	(42)	3	(13)
master craftsmen	13	(48)	9	(33)	5	(19)
Skilled and unskilled	10	(56)	7	(39)	1	(6)
Other Hillhouse electors untraced in directory	14	(30)	22	(48)	10	(22)
Total Hillhouse electorate	88	(41)	97	(45)	30	(14)
Total Huddersfield	1111	(49)	789	(35)	365*	(16)

Notes:
* includes some electors who had died between the compilation of the roll and the election
(1) residence separate from business premises
(2) residence and business premises on the same site

churches, at Ramsden Street in the town centre and Highfield in the heart of élite Huddersfield.[9] The continuing strength of the Independents was illustrated by the establishment of three suburban churches in the 1860s by members sent out from Highfield. One of these, Hillhouse Congregational Church, was erected in 1865 on the corner of Clara and Eleanor Streets. From its location and parentage we might expect its congregation to have included the highest status Hillhouse families.

By 1871, Hillhouse Congregational boasted 129 members, of whom 74 per cent were female.[10] Nearly four-fifths lived in Hillhouse, most of the remainder travelling from the surrounding villages of Birkby, Cowcliffe and Sheepridge or from the town centre. Because of the female bias, few who lived outside the census study area could be identified in directories. Information from census and/or directory was available for 61 members, 74 per cent female. Members were assigned to the occupational group associated with their household, except for domestic servants who were classified according to their personal

Table 4.8: Church membership, occupational status and voting behaviour in Hillhouse, 1871

Occupational status	*Members, Hillhouse Congregational*	*All nonconformists resident in Hillhouse* (%)*	*All nonconformist electors†*	*Percentage in each occupational group voting Liberal*
Middle-class	18	13	34	100
Lower-middle-class	49	50	50	75
clerks, etc.	21	20	22	57
shopkeepers	18	19	22	86
master craftsmen	10	11	6	100
Skilled workers	20	27	16	80
Servants, labourers, etc.	13	10	0	
Total	61	83	32	84

Notes:
* including members of Hillhouse and Highfield Congregational, Bath Buildings Baptist, Fitzwilliam Street Unitarians and Queen Street Wesleyan Methodist churches.
† including wives and children of electors.

status (Table 4.8). While all the middle- and lower-middle-class groups were over-represented among church members, junior white-collar workers were less dominant than tradesmen. Little masters were even less in evidence.

Given the dearth of adult males, it is not surprising that only seven members were personally entitled to vote. But all seven cast their votes for the Liberal candidate. A further eighteen members came from households in which their father, husband or employer was enfranchised. Fifteen came from Liberal-voting households, three from Conservative households. The numbers are tiny, but it is worth noting that the Liberal bias embraced all social strata: white-collar, skilled workers, shopkeepers and businessmen.

The pattern is reinforced by fragmentary data on the membership of other nonconformist churches.[11] Sixteen Highfield members lived in Hillhouse: four were the wives of enfranchised petty-bourgeois husbands, of whom three voted Liberal, one was neutral. Members of other town-centre churches – Wesleyans, Baptists and Unitarians – were also traced, confirming a substantial degree of long-distance commuting to church among the residents of Hillhouse. In general, these members were of *lower* status than those who attended Hillhouse Congregational: there were no substantial businessmen but several skilled workmen or their families among them.

Evidently, nonconformity in general and Congregationalism in particular was strongly associated with the self-employed bourgeoisie. Almost nobody of less than skilled-worker status, apart from a few servants of middle-class families, was admitted to membership. And its adherents were strongly Liberal in their politics. Although nearly half of all Hillhouse shopkeepers voted Conservative, few of them belonged to old dissenting congregations. The direction of causation between nonconformity, occupation and Liberalism may be left for others to debate, but the statistical correlation is more suggestive of some form of class consciousness than any of the other aggregate evidence reviewed in this essay.

5 Concluding comments

I have offered some slight but suggestive evidence that, in respectable Huddersfield, there were significant divisions between craft and large-scale retailing, and between trade and profession, with respect to their patterns of residence and interaction. Town-centre tradesmen lived close to white-collar workers in new streets of terraced houses with gardens. But tradesmen were more likely to attend the Congregational church and clerks and salesmen were more likely to vote Conservative. Their children were unlikely to marry into the ranks of either skilled manual workers or self-employed craftsmen.

Yet no pattern of behaviour was exclusive to particular occupational groups. One-third of white-collar electors voted Liberal; merchants did live next door to skilled workers; on occasion their children did intermarry. We cannot regard any occupational group or collection of groups as class-conscious. However, it is worth reiterating that Hillhouse as a whole contained more lower-middle-class residents than other parts of Huddersfield, that it was more Conservative than the rest of Huddersfield, and that the most Conservative group in Hillhouse was the white-collar lower middle class. This dominant character influenced the attitudes of residents who belonged to other occupational groups: we may hypothesise that shopkeepers who elsewhere were Liberal, were more inclined to vote Conservative in Hillhouse, either to curry favour with Conservative-voting customers or because there was some genuine neighbourhood effect. In this context, Liberal Congregationalists constituted an important but culturally deviant minority.

Herein lie some shortcomings of the geographical case-study approach adopted in this essay. While it is impracticable to study the whole population of Huddersfield it would be desirable to compare the lower middle classes in Hillhouse, where they were in the ascendancy, with other areas, where they were less significant, or where the balance between white-collar, trade and craft was different. Further research should also examine both area and individuals over time, considering patterns of both ecological and personal mobility. In a population for whom self-help was the dominant ethic, among whom we should not expect any explicit awareness of 'class', the best indication of class structure might be the *permanence* of residential patterns, social interaction and institutional allegiance. If people *continued* to live as neighbours or belong together, we are justified in concluding that they regarded their interests as identical.

The evidence appears to confirm Cowlard's view of 'the essential continuity of status in Victorian society' in which occupational groups can be ranked in order of status, but variously aligned with other groups above or below themselves according to circumstances (Cowlard, 1979). Yet this assumes that occupation mattered more than location. It could also be argued that households of diverse occupational status constituted a single class where they chose to live as neighbours and where their patterns of behaviour were not significantly different. Almost by definition, people who are neighbours must belong to the same class. Class is community.

There have been no heroes or villians in this essay. In contrast to Foster's identification of class leaders in Oldham, I have not discussed specific individuals or their involvement in particular events. No doubt a survey of obituaries, correspondence columns and news reports in local newspaper would permit the identification of critical political, religious and trade union personnel and their activities, and class might be defined by association with such figures and participation in such events. Yet to highlight such people and their activities would be to overdramatise the essential continuity and repetitiveness of lower-middle-class life. A distinction may be drawn between status, defined in terms of occupation *and* interaction, which has continuous significance, and class, which only acquires meaning at moments of conflict or collaboration. Nonetheless, class consciousness lies latent in everyday patterns of work, association and residence.

Moreover, if 'class itself is not a thing, it is a happening' we must ask what contemporaries regarded as historically significant happenings. The contention of this essay is that for the modestly respectable majority, such happenings were their regular and repeated acts of work, worship and leisure, and occasional, but still personal, events such as marriage, or moving house or job. If these happenings failed to add up to class consciousness, they certainly facilitate the reconstruction of class perceptions that underlay a latent class structure.

Acknowledgments

Thanks are due to Alick Newman of the Cartographic Unit, UCL, who drew the maps, and to Jane Springett for her advice and information on the development history of Hillhouse.

Notes

1 See, for example, the collections of papers published by the Institute of British Geographers (Whitehand and Patten, 1977; Dennis, 1979) and the reactions of historians (Beresford, 1979; Daunton, 1980).

2 I am grateful to Jane Springett for providing me with the results of her unpublished research on the Thornhill estate.

3 Rates of owner-occupation declined in Cardiff from 9.6 per cent in 1884 to 7.2 per cent in 1914 and, within two model estates in Halifax, from 60 per cent to 43 per cent and from 31 per cent to 26 per cent between 1876 and 1881. See Daunton, 1976; Daniels, 1980, pp. 188, 224.

4 William White's Directory and Gazetteer of Leeds, Bradford, Halifax, Huddersfield, Wakefield and the whole of the clothing districts of the West Riding of Yorkshire (Sheffield, 1870).

5 A photocopy of the original pollbook was available in the Institute of Historical Research, University of London.

6 The research was undertaken prior to the release of the 1881 census, and permission was sought to consult marriage registers only up to 1880.

7 PP 1866 LVII: Return of the several cities and boroughs in England and Wales, arranged . . . according to the proportion of electors belonging to the working classes. . .

8 These estimates were derived by multiplying the percentage of electors

who were working-class by the percentage of adult males who were electors: 12.5 × 12.8 for Huddersfield, 14 × 19.1 for Hillhouse.

9 Pp. 1852–3 LXXIX: Population (Great Britain): Religious Worship (England and Wales): Religious accommodation and attendance in large towns; manuscript returns are in the public Record Office, HO-129.

10 Information from yearbooks in the possession of the church secretary.

11 Information from membership and baptism registers in the possession of Huddersfield (Kirklees) public library.

• 5 •

Home ownership, subsistence and historical change: *The mining district of West Cornwall in the late nineteenth century*[1] • *DAMARIS ROSE*

We'll have our Rights, our house, our land
The stewards shall not prey;
With 'One and All' and hand in hand
And who shall bid us Nay?
Chorus:
And have they fixed the where and when
That Conybeare shall die?
Here's twenty thousand mining men
Will know the reason why!
Conybeare's guarantee we hold
At leases he'll let fly!
And there's twenty thousand Cornish bold
Resolved to win or die!

(Radical Library Party campaign song,
Camborne Election 1885).[2]

1 Introduction

The area of Cornwall from which this song emanated was at the centre of one of the oldest and most intensely worked mining districts in the world. Its economy was completely dominated by the mining of tin and copper, and was perenially subject to the booms and slumps of the world market. The copper industry peaked in prosperity in the late 1850s and in 1862 about 50 000 men, women and children – one-seventh of the population of the entire county – was working in about 340 mines (Brayshay, 1980; Todd, 1967).

In 1866, however, the copper industry went into a recession from which it never recovered. While the effects of this were partially staved off by a switch back into the traditionally mined tin (Todd, 1967), the tin-mining industry went into a long, slower and more uneven decline in the last quarter of the nineteenth century. Massive depopulation set in: Cornish miners, many with their families, migrated in droves to other parts of Britain and overseas, where work was to be found.

This paper explores one specific and important aspect of everyday life in the mining district – housing and land tenure. It examines the distinctive roles these played in defining, through the domestic economy of mining families, the particular circumstances of the mining working class from the period of capitalist expansion of the industry through the phases of industrial decline – including the political outlook of miners and the strategies they used to respond to de-industrialisation.

In the 1880s the major mining districts, Redruth and Camborne, supplied the strongest local support for a campaign for land reform that was nationally orchestrated by Radical Liberals. The latter saw the solution to rural poverty, unemployment and the social unrest these generated in terms of entrenching an independent peasant and quasi-peasant class in districts of agriculture and rural industry, such as Cornwall. This struck a chord because there had long been a tradition among Cornish workers of moving between mining and small-scale farming or fishing. Many Cornish miners demanded an end to the insecure form of leasehold tenure under which many of them built their own houses and operated subsistence smallholdings, calling instead for access to freehold forms of land tenure that would enable more secure owner-occupancy.

The leasehold reform agitation of the 1880s was the last major manifestation of collective action among Cornish miners, inside or outside of the wage-workplace. Attempts at unionisation were unsuccessful. Cornish miners were reputed to always solve their economic problems through individualistic means, such as dual occupations and migration to places where more money could be earned. Average wages in the industry were lower than in most other mining districts of Britain and, in a cash economy, would have been inadequate to support the average-sized family unless more than one household member was employed full time. Occasionally, however, the most skilled miners, known as 'tributers', who were paid according to the value of the ore raised, were able to net large sums in a single month (we shall return to this point). These strategies were perceived by contemporary observers to function as 'safety valves' against social unrest. Mining families' domestic economy was seen as 'backward' or, at least, 'traditional', yet these traditions, because of their individualistic orientation, were seen as compatible with the ideology of free enterprise.

In recent 'neo-marxist' debates on capitalist development in industrial and agricultural peripheries, increasing attention has been paid to analysing the social relations underlying 'semi-proletarian' forms – a descriptive term which refers to situations in which a household includes both wage workers and people engaged in subsistence production through work on their 'own' land (see, for example, Goodman and Redclift, 1981). In such situations the wage-worker obtains part of the means of subsistence in a non-commodity form (Conway, 1982). This may also include a house built with unpaid labour. A key concern which emerges from these debates is the way in which such 'hybrid' forms affect the 'structural' position and ideological orientation of the wage worker *vis-à-vis* the capital–labour relation.

In relation to these debates, this study addresses the following questions, in the West Cornwall context: how were the processes of proletarianisation and deindustrialisation, as experienced in the daily lives of miners and their families, mediated through access to domestic property and especially through access to smallholdings? What difference, if any, did freehold ownership – accessible only to a minority – make to miners' families' material circumstances over this period? In the second place, we are not concerned here to establish a 'causal' link between the 'necessary tendencies' of proletarianisation processes, cyclical booms and slumps and the 'contingent' conditions of the locality including miners' access to or ownership of domestic property and means of subsistence. Yet such tendencies structured the outer 'limits of the possible' (Williams, 1977) for workers and may have encouraged them to defend and make use of their access to domestic property in particular ways.

At the same time, 'the effect of a process will vary according to the conditions in which it operates' (Massey, 1983, p. 75). Thus this study also explores the possibility that struggles around domestic property might indeed have an influence on the trajectory of capitalist development in West Cornwall in the later nineteenth century, and the resulting configuration of class relations. Our study paints a fairly detailed picture of the spheres of daily life and wage work – a view which at times must extend outside of the 'immediate' question of property relations – in order to explore the ways in which 'ownership' of domestic property giving 'independent' access to subsistence affected the conditions of reproduction of mining families and mineworkers' labour-power in Cornwall.

This study is divided into several parts. *First* (section 2), an outline of the traditional labour process of Cornish miners and the forms of land tenure and housing production in Cornwall, all of which were seemingly pre-capitalist forms, and which suggested an image of the 'independent' and relatively privileged miner. *Second* (section 3), an outline of the Liberals' land reform campaign of the 1880s and the immediate reasons for its appeal in West Cornwall. *Third* (section 4), a critical reappraisal of the 'class position' of Cornish miners in terms of the historical processes of their subordination to capital, through: an appraisal of changes in the labour process and employment in the mines; and the impact of these changes on the size and security of family incomes. *Fourth* (sections 5 and 6), and following from this, an exploration of the responses of miners and their families to these changes: strategies for the acquisition or maintenance of smallholdings, which became increasingly intertwined with strategies of migrant labour by adult males. In conclusion (section 7), it is argued that the *type* of 'independence' that access to small property could bring changed fundamentally over the period under study; and some methodological implications for analysing the political significance of access to houses on smallholding are drawn out.

2 The 'independent miner': the making of a myth

2.1 The contract system and 'individualism'

Cornish miners have been widely regarded by labour and social historians as a group set apart from the general development of the

English working class, because they maintained traditions of independent production and access to the means of subsistence long after these had been stamped out in other branches of industry. As Maurice Dobb (1963, pp. 242–3) explains, Cornwall was among a number of regions where in medieval times miners had been a privileged group with their own parliament and special rights:

> [In] those mining communities which were anciently characterised by the practice that is known as 'free mining'. . . . The custom was that any inhabitant of the area . . . had the right . . . to stake out a claim for himself, and on payment of a fee to the Crown or to the local possessor of seigneurial rights was free to start mining.

Later on, this system gave way to the 'tribute' system:

> under which the owners of a claim, when they were unwilling to work the mine, leased it to a group of workmen or to a small master in return for a share of the product (Dobb, 1963, p. 245).

Direct contract systems of labour were maintained in form right through the nineteenth century in Cornwall. Tributers did not work for a wage as such. They worked directly on the ore-bearing lode, for a negotiated percentage of the value of the material produced. The breaking of ground and opening-up of the mine was done by 'tut-workers', who contracted with the mine captains to work for a negotiated rate per fathom of shaft, earning less than the tributers (Jenkin, 1962; P.P. 1876, XVII, 479).

E. P. Thompson points out that the traditions of the 'free' miner 'coloured' their political responses; 'they saw their wages as regulated by custom or by their own bargaining (Thompson, 1966, p. 63). One mid-nineteenth-century observer explained the absence of labour/capitalist conflict in terms of the tribute system, suggesting that 'the workman is in a sense his own employer (quoted in Rule, 1970, p. 28). Yet the tribute system could not in and of itself explain the miners' individualistic outlook and lack of propensity to strike, since in other mining regions where similar systems of work and payment were used, such as North Wales, miners did take collective and militant action (Rose, 1984). Did the answer lie instead with the nature of miners' ties with the land?

2.2 *The tradition of dual occupations*

Tin-mining was the 'original' industry of Cornwall, and was important in the time of the Phoenicians. Yet it was equally traditional for miners to have other occupations, the foremost among which was small farming. Between the fourteenth and sixteenth centuries, evidence about a large number of tinners reported as producing very small amounts of tin suggests that:

> in all probability some of these tinners were not wholly dependent upon the mines for their living. Many perhaps were artisans or small farmers. . . . In later centuries, when the mines were said to be decaying, a constant subject for complaint was that the tinners were forsaking the stannaries [tin exchanges] and turning to husbandry (Lewis, 1907, pp. 187–8).

Additionally, in the maritime districts of Mevagissey, St. Ives and Mounts Bay, the pilchard fishing industry provided seasonal employment for about three months in the year. A large proportion of the labour-force was comprised of miners, who were in-between contracts. Moreover, miners often had shares in fishing boats (Jenkin, 1962; Lentz, 1982; Rowe, 1953). According to one estimate, in the early eighteenth century there were over 30 000 workers in the mining industry, but only about half of these were full-time mine-workers (Rowe, 1953).

Crucial to this 'tradition' was the fact that, at least until the mid-nineteenth century, it was the norm for the Cornish miner and family to have some access to land for subsistence production (Anon, 1855; Checkland and Checkland, 1974; Jenkin, 1962). Although the mining industry was centred on three towns – Camborne, Redruth and St. Just in the far west – the mining population was largely rural and dispersed around the mines that were dotted all over the Cornish landscape. Miners' cottages in rural areas were typically surrounded by plots of between half an acre and three acres, on which miners and their families grew vegetables and often raised a cow or a pig (Rowe, 1953). In addition, animal grazing rights on the surrounding rough upland were often available (Jenkin, 1962).

Both smallholding land and cottages were produced under seemingly pre-capitalist conditions, which persisted into the second half of the nineteenth century because of the particular structure of land-ownership, the physical nature of much of the land itself and the system of land tenure.

2.3 Land tenure in Cornwall: the 'life-lease' system, smallholdings and the self-building of cottages

Between the sixteenth and early nineteenth centuries, massive enclosures of common land were carried out in Eastern, Central and Southern England. This land was concentrated in the hands of major landowners and was largely converted to arable cultivation. Former peasants now had to work as agricultural labourers, dependent on wage labour since they had lost their rights to the means of subsistence (Marx, 1976). In upland areas of poor quality land, however, the processes and the timing of enclosures were very different. Common rights of rough grazing, rabbit trapping, geese-rearing and so on were frequently retained much longer in such areas than in places where there was the possibility of converting or a greater incentive to convert to arable (Yelling, 1978).

In West Cornwall, the greater part of the best arable land was probably enclosed by the early seventeenth century (Rowe, 1953). The ownership of land was concentrated in the hands of a few large landlords by this process. Yet much of the rougher land within the large estates was enclosed sporadically and temporarily. Lords of manors who had jurisdiction over lands that had been grazed or farmed 'in common' frequently let portions of such land to tenants, who cleared the land of trees and scrub and took one or more crops from it. After this the land reverted to grass or common pasture for a number of years (Slater, 1968). Thus:

> instead of a process which eliminated the small yeoman farmer the Cornish changes [of the eighteenth century] tended to increase the number of smallholders, especially in the mining districts. . . . It is probable that 25 000 to 30 000 acres of wastelands were reclaimed between 1700 and 1860 (Rowe, 1953, p. 225).

Landowners, especially those in the Camborne/Redruth mining district, encouraged miners to enclose plots of from three to six acres and to build one or two cottages on each plot (Jenkin, 1962; Rowe, 1953). This practice continued during the nineteenth century, but the enclosures tended to become more permanent.

From the perspective of mining capitalists, it was not 'necessary' that workers be denied access to landholdings in order to make them dependent on working in the mines. When the mines were expanding, they were not faced with a major labour shortage. The working-class population of the region was growing rapidly, swelled by an influx of landless and impoverished Irish immigrants (Rowe, 1953). There was a strong existing tradition of skilled mining work, and few miners with small farms had the option of making a living from farming alone – for although the climate was good, the land was marginal and the holdings small. Moreover, the mining companies were run on a joint stock basis on land leased from the major landowners, who did very well out of both mine leases and leases to workers under the lives system.

Miners actually obtained such plots of land in one of two ways. Some miners inherited smallholdings that had been in their families for generations – either through previous enclosures or feudal forms of tenure (Rowse, 1942). More commonly, however, the chain of inheritance was much shorter, owing to the peculiar system of land tenure which predominated in West Cornwall, and was in fact unique to Cornwall, Devon and parts of Wales and Dorset (where it was made infamous by Thomas Hardy's novel, *The Woodlanders*). This form of leaseholding was known as the life-lease system or 'leases for lives'. It was extremely complex, but in general in West Cornwall, it operated as follows.[3] A plot of land, sometimes with buildings already on it, was leased for a period of time determined by the total remaining years of life of three named persons, usually including the lessee. The ground rent – referred to as a 'head rent' – was fixed for the three lives' period. Each time a life 'dropped off', a fine or 'heriot' was payable. After the third person named in the lease had died, the surviving lessee, if there was one, had to give up the land and property on it in good condition, unless the landlord permitted her or him to stay, in which case the terms and conditions were stipulated by the landlord, and usually involved a further fine. Under this system, the duration of tenure was uncertain at the time the lease was taken out; the house and the value of all the improvements made reverted to the lessor at the end of the period; and the leaseholder had to pay for repairs to the premises at the end of the lease. The leaseholder was not entitled to any compensation for the value of improvements.

From the landlord's point of view, this controlled system of enclosure – not to be confused with 'squatting' – was of great advantage. Thousands of acres, much of which farmers would not have considered worth clearing for permanent cultivation, were improved by mining families themselves in their own time (Jenkin, 1934). They cleared away rocks and boulders, levelled the ground and made it suitable for grazing, for potatoes and vegetable plots (P.P. 1888, XXII, QQ 6812–9).

From the leaseholding miners' point of view, this system also had certain benefits even though it made inheritance subject to the whim of the landlord. Where there was no house standing on the property and the land was completely unimproved, the ground rents were very low: a 'nominal' amount, according to Jenkin; a few shillings per year, according to a mid-nineteenth century writer (Jenkin, 1934; Anon, 1855). Cottages were very often built on this land by miners themselves:

> large numbers of houses are built by workmen for their own occupation, on land previously of little or no value, and where, in many cases, the whole labour and expense of preparing the site, erecting the house, and all other outlay on the property, is paid for by the lessee (PP 1889, XV, 21).

Yet many of the building materials were available free, either by common right or by arrangement with the landowners: these included stones gathered from the moor by miners (idem) and waste material from the spoil-heaps of the mine (Jenkin, 1962).

Another reason for the persistence of the tradition of self-building was that, in the first half of the nineteenth century, when mines were opened up in the rural districts of West Cornwall, no speculative market existed to build housing for the miners. While in other remote mining areas in Britain employers often built housing in order to attract a workforce, this rarely occurred in Cornwall (P.P. 1884–5, XXX, Q8144). 'Most of the mines were highly speculative enterprises, and the prosperity of the miners fluctuated far too much for the adventurers of investors to tie up capital in housing' (Weaver, 1966, p. 27). These circumstances combined with the landholding structure to inhibit the development of a commoditised form of housebuilding among Cornish miners.

It is impossible to accurately gauge the amount of housing that was self built; although, for instance, in Gwennap, near Redruth, housing self-built by miners amounted to 700 to 800 miners' self-built houses, amounting to about half the total number of houses (P.P. 1888, XXII, QQ 6775; 7135). Data quantifying the number, size, tenure and location of rural smallholdings (by civil parish) are available only for the year 1889, in the *Return of Allotments and Smallholdings* (P.P. 1890, LV 11). In Cornwall as a whole there was a much higher proportion of land in smallholdings than for the whole of England in 1895 (P.P.

1896, LXVII, 509 ff). While this can tell us nothing definite about the extent of smallholdings by miners, the large number of holdings of between one-quarter of an acre and five acres in districts dominated by mining is suggestive. Holdings of from five to twenty acres were more widely diffused through *all* of West Cornwall, including purely agricultural districts, while holdings of from twenty to fifty acres were not at all characteristic of the mining districts.

Rates of freehold owner occupancy of land varied greatly between the mining parishes (calculated from P.P. 1890, LVII; PP 1893–4, C.V. 187) presumably reflecting differences in availability of freehold as well as miners' abilities to afford purchase. However, in England as a whole in 1895 only 17.2 per cent of smallholdings under 5 acres were freehold owner-occupied (P.P. 1896, LXVII, 509 ff). Thus, the 1889 figures for holdings of less than five acres for Redruth (21.8 per cent) and St. Agnes (48.8 per cent) are strikingly high.

Smallholding miners did not necessarily live with their families close to currently operating mines. When a local mine shut down, miners who owned cottages often had to walk up to eight miles to work in other mines (P.P. 1890–1, XLI, QQ 4374–5). If the local shutdown were permanent selling the house might well be very difficult, and the family might remain there until the last 'life' died. Bearing these considerations in mind and since the employment data are recorded by place of work, we have grouped twelve parishes which, based on the settlement structure and topography of the area, approximately embrace the labour shed of the mines located within daily or weekly walking distance. It has been estimated that 5731 adult males were employed in mines located in these same twelve parishes in the year 1889. In the twelve parishes, there were 15 943 inhabited houses according to the 1891 census (see Table 5.1). Assuming that the average household contained one adult male, more than one in three households in this district depended on mining employment in West Cornwall for the income of the primary wage-earner.

In the twelve parishes making up the Camborne, Redruth and St. Agnes mining district (see Table 5.1), there were 1083 smallholdings in this size class. A smallholding of less than five acres could not provide anything close to a subsistence living for a family on the poor land that predominated in this area; holders of these holdings must have had other occupations. There was one smallholding of less than five acres for every five adult male miners.

While these data simply document the extent of smallholding at one

Table 5.1: Mining parishes in the Camborne–Redruth district: employment in mines, 1883, smallholdings, 1889 and inhabited houses, 1891

		Smallholdings, 1889						
		¼–5 ac			5–20 ac			
Parish	*Estimated numbers of miners etc. working in parish, 1883 (a)*	*no.*	*Freehold owner-occupied no.*	*%*	*no.*	*Freehold owner-occupied no.*	*%*	*Inhabited houses 1891*
Camborne (b)	3,395	81	5	6.2	84	9	10.7	3,264
Crowan	39	34	2	5.9	77	7	9.1	585
Gwennap	443	148	22	14.9	117	18	15.4	1,590
Gwinear	356	24	1	4.2	23	1	4.3	374
Illogan	737	156	18	11.5	76	6	7.9	2,107
Kea	227	101	14	13.9	97	13	13.4	553
Kenwyn		150	18	12.0	136	10	7.4	2,027
Perranzabuloe	52	89	12	13.5	80	9	11.3	578
Redruth (b)	3,336	147	32	21.8	89	13	14.6	2,289
St. Agnes (c)	690	82	40	48.8	121	45	37.2	1,141
Stithians	(d)	33	0	0	37	1	2.7	415
Wendron	137	40	0	0	134	4	3.0	1,020
	9,412	1,083			1,098			15,943

(a) These figures include men, women and children. It is estimated that there were 7019 adult males among the total of 9412 for the Camborne–Redruth mining district in 1883, but only 5731 by 1889.
(b) Major urban centres.
(c) Centre of copper mining, in great decline since mid-1860s.
(d) Included with Redruth figure.
Source: Calculated from P.P. 1884, XIX, 249–55; P.P. 1890, LVII: P.P. 1893–4, CV, 187.

point in time, our knowledge about the landholding patterns and the reports of contemporary observers would support the conclusion that most of the holdings of under five acres were held by mining families. Also supporting this interpretation is the fact that in Cornwall as a whole in 1895 a higher proportion of holdings of 1–5 acres were mixed arable/pasture, compared to England as a whole – suggesting a higher intensity of cultivation for personal use (P.P. 1896, LXVII). This is all the more remarkable in view of the poor quality and upland location of most of the land available in this class. Moreover, there were another 1098 smallholdings of between 5 and 20 acres in these 12 mining parishes, averaging 11.2 acres. The poor quality of much of the land would have made it very likely that many holdings in this size class were those of marginal farmers supplementing their income with mine work. Yet, according to contemporary observers, some people whose main occupation was mining did obtain holdings in the ten-acre range.

Moreover, miners had access to subsistence in other ways. In West Penwith and the Camborne/Redruth area substantial areas of upland were still grazed in common by local people in the late nineteenth century, yet such hill land was not recorded by the Board of Agriculture in its Return (P.P. 1896, LXVII, iv). Additionally, they often still had rights to cut furze on the common lands. This was a major source of fuel. Rabbits could also be shot by those with rights to common land (Anon, 1855; Barton, 1972).

For a Cornish miner's family in the nineteenth century, then, leasing land, improving it and building a cottage on it enabled them to obtain, with their own labour, some access to the means of subsistence, through the home, the smallholding and the common. In other words, the home was still the site of the production of some of the necessities of daily life through family labour, even though mining was the primary occupation of the head of household. While it is impossible to accurately quantify the contribution of the 'average' smallholding to family subsistence, a holding of three acres with a cow, a pig and a vegetable garden might have produced potatoes and other vegetables, milk, butter, cheese and bacon in sufficient quantities to feed an 'average' family, if it were intensively worked. Based on 1880s data from the British Association for the Advancement of Science (cited in Burnett, 1969), these items comprised nearly half of the cash value of the 'average' working-class family's food budget in a cash economy in the 1880s – the major outstanding item being flour or bread. The smallholding miner's household appeared at least in part to have been a peasant household – maintaining 'independent' traditions.

All the same, building costs were far from negligible. The houses in which miners lived were, in the main, cottages of between two and four, and occasionally six rooms (Jenkin, 1962). They were usually made of a mixture called 'cob', which consisted of rough stone to a height of seven to eight feet, with the rest being a clay/straw mixture (P.P. 1884–5, XXX, QQ 8187–8).

At least when new, they provided efficient insulation against the weather and were not inferior to the porous brick typically used for labourers' housing in Cornish towns and elsewhere (Gauldie, 1974). The cost of building a four-roomed cottage made out of cob was estimated in 1885 to be about £50, which was less than the selling price in a town (Weaver, 1966). Stone cottages of four to six rooms cost £60 to £120 – rather less if mine stone from the spoil heaps could be used. Sometimes miners were even able to have larger houses built for them (Barton, 1972), but these were much more expensive, being provided in a commodity form by builders.

For reasons which will be explained later, miners did not take out mortgages to pay for building their houses. Therefore, what enabled a mining family to self-build a cottage of reasonable quality in a rural area was the ability to raise the capital of at least £50. To raise such a sum was not as much out of the question for the skilled miner of mid-nineteenth century Cornwall as might at first be thought. Average wages for the ordinary miners, paid by time rates, were only around 40s. to 50s. for a five week month (Anon, 1855). Boys, women and girls working at the mines earned amounts varying from 10s. to 20s. in the same period. However, as mentioned above, the most skilled miners worked 'on tribute' for a percentage of the value of the metal raised. Tributers' earnings could fluctuate widely, but for a skilled worker in a good lode, earnings of £6 to £8 in a month were not unusual in mid-century (Anon, 1855), allowing the opportunity for savings to be put by toward a house. Once or twice in a lifetime, £40 to £50 might be made on tribute in a month's work (Jenkin, 1962). The 1864 Commission on Mines was told that:

> a good substantial cottage, with a room and a scullery downstairs, and two or three bedrooms upstairs, can be built for about £80. A tributer, if he has had a good venture, will often invest his gains in a house (P.P. 1864, XXIV, 395).

while building a cottage and clearing land for a garden was said in the 1860s to be the miner's chief 'out-of-core' occupation (Jenkin, 1962).

The commonly-held *image* of the mid-nineteenth century Cornish miner, then is one of a worker-peasant, making part of his living through mining, part through the work of his family in subsistence farming, and perhaps in seasonal work fishing – and only partially integrated into the processes of industrial capitalist development. Given the land tenure system and this subsistence production, was it then true that the Radicals succeeded in winning over Cornish miners to their land reform schemes in the 1880s because the miners were trying to preserve an archaic way of life? We shall now discuss the Programme and the immediate reasons for miners' support of it, before making an assessment of this question.

3 The political–economic context of leasehold reform agitation in Cornwall

3.1 The Radical Liberals and land reform: the national campaign

The leasehold reform movement of the 1880s was promoted across Britian by Radical Liberals who sought to abolish the controls that large ground landlords exerted over commercial and residential leaseholders. Nationwide, the leading advocate of leasehold reform was the Radical M.P. Henry Broadhurst, who in 1886 introduced into the House of Commons a bill that would empower all leaseholders to purchase the freehold title to their land, subject to certain charges and conditions (Hamer, 1971). In London and many other parts of the country it was impossible to obtain land for building purposes with freehold tenure. When leases expired the properties reverted to the owner of the land; this led to evictions of householders, or the loss of valuable commercial property (Reeder, 1961). It was argued that if leaseholders were allowed to purchase the freehold of their properties, an obstacle to the development of a capitalist housebuilding industry responsive to demand would be removed. The reformers believed that landlords would then have an incentive to maintain their properties in good repair, which would benefit their working-class tenants, and that the hardships of eviction of householders would disappear. 'Leasehold enfranchisement', as the acquisition of freehold rights was called, was also considered to be of political importance in enhancing social stability, especially through the encouragement of working-class freehold owner-occupation (Reeder, 1961).

The leaders of the Radical movement appealed not only to urban dwellers but also to rural workers – using the theme of a return to a 'Golden Age' of small landowners, yeoman farmers and peasants (Collings, 1906; Hamer, 1971). The redistribution of land into allotments and smallholdings became a major election issue for the Radicals in 1885. It was 'crystallised in the slogan, "three acres and a cow"' (Hamer, 1971), a slogan which seemed to have a strong appeal to Cornish miners but was the object of much ridicule by elements both left and right of the Radicals. The Radicals saw the existing land tenure system in Britain as being 'very near to the root of many of our social evils'. With such land reform, the land system would 'become a guarantee of class concord and harmony' (Hamer, 1971, p. 3). Jesse Collings, one of the movement's ideologues, made an explicit link between individual peasant proprietorship and political stability, arguing that the system he advocated would be a 'bulwark against communistic attacks' (Collings 1906, pp. 272–3).

3.2 Leasehold reform in Cornwall: the local context

The *Select Committee on Town Holdings*, which sat from 1886 until 1892, was set up in large measure because of pressures from the Radical wing of the Liberal Party, and because of the attractive prospect of attracting the votes of city workers and middle-class men (Reeder, 1961). None the less working-class protests did have some influence (Offer, 1981). Yet, leasehold reform found its strongest locally-based and working-class support in certain *rural* areas: not on as geographically wide a basis as its leaders had hoped for, but particularly strongly concentrated in the small towns, villages and rural smallholding districts of the slate quarrying region of North Wales and the tin and copper mining district of West Cornwall (Reeder, 1961).

Cornwall's life-lease system became nationally infamous in 1883 with the widespread distribution, by the Camborne Branch of the Leasehold Enfranchisement Association, situated in the heart of the mining district, of a pamphlet entitled *The Bitter Cry of the Cornish Leaseholder*.[4] It documented many hardships of life-leaseholders and tenants, and was apparently strongly supported by building industry capitalists and their professional associates in Camborne and Redruth, in spite of attempts by large landowners to dispute the claims (P.P. 1888, XXII, Q. 9025 ff).

During the 1885 election campaign, which led to the defeat of the sitting Whig member by a Radical-Liberal, Mr C. A. V. Conybeare, thousands of people attended meetings on leasehold reform – an issue which the Radical section of the Party took up as one of the cornerstones of its platform (Cambourne Election Papers, 1885). At one such meeting, Conybeare's agent drew loud cheers for stating:

> [The] leasehold [reform] bill is of paramount importance, for at present the labouring classes, instead of living in cottages of their own, are obliged to exist in tumbledown old shanties belonging to other people (Camborne Election Papers, 1885).

When the *Select Committee on Town Holdings* was conducting its investigation of 'the Terms of Occupation and the Compensation for Improvements possessed by the Occupiers of Town Houses and Holdings, (P.P. 1889, XV, 1), it visited the county of Cornwall several times during a three-month period in 1888. Members of the Committee were impressed by the 'strong and bona fide desire on the part of the working population to acquire the freehold' particularly among miners (P.P. 1888, XXII, QQ 9095–9105; Q 12,596).

The extent of bourgeois support for leasehold reform in the mining districts of West Cornwall raises some important questions relating to the political orientation of miners whose cause was seemingly taken up by members of the local capitalist class. It is legitimate to ask whether there was a community of interest between miners (self-builders and less-fortunate tenants) and 'progressive' capitalists in the building industry, against the old landed class in West Cornwall. As will be seen, the 'progressive' capitalists took up the causes of slum dwellers, evicted tenants and small occupying-leaseholders who were suffering because of the life-lease system, as indicated by their evidence to the Commissions. One might perceive here a 'natural' basis for a 'class alliance' based on some common interests in opposing the landed class. The 'independent' and 'individualist' tradition of the Cornish miner could also be seen as being sympathetic to a capitalist transformation of the land and housing industry. We shall now examine housing conditions in the mining district, and the relative position of smallholding miners, in more detail, in order to further evaluate this view of the class position of the miner who had a smallholding or who aspired to home-ownership.

3.3 Housing conditions in rural and urban west Cornwall: the 'relative privilege' of the smallholding miner, 1860s–80s

The population of the mining centres of Redruth and Camborne, together with the surrounding villages, grew rapidly from the 1820s to the 1860s, as local mines prospered and many new workers were taken on. In the late 1850s to early 1860s, many new houses were built in response to this influx (Barton, 1972). Growth in Camborne continued until the 1870s, due to an influx of people from neighbouring districts which had suffered from the decline in copper mining.

In *urban* areas, where a capitalist land market was well developed, even small allotments were out of reach for miners:

In many districts, and especially in the West of Cornwall, miners have gardens, but in the neighbourhood of the towns and villages the rent of land is so high as to preclude the possibility of this addition to their comfort (P.P. 1864, XXIV, 396).

In the town of Camborne, in 1864, it was estimated that 800 'labouring men', mainly miners, owned their own cottages, which almost always had small gardens attached; however, the ground rents on these houses were high (P.P. 1864, XXIV, QQ, 10,334–9).

At the same time, there was by now less inexpensive uncleared *rural* waste land available more cheaply than early in the century, and the improved smallholdings that came onto the market were increasingly expensive. From mid-century until the 1870s, several thousand acres of waste lands were enclosed in or close to the mining districts. However, unlike the earlier enclosures, these were carried out on a grand scale, using steam ploughs and other machinery. Moreover, the work was done by unemployed miners and other poor or destitute people, hired by the landowners at either piece-rates or day wages. This land was then cultivated by the landowner for arable crops, or sold off to full-time farmers. New smallholdings were *not* made available on such lands. Instead, 'a certain amount was set aside for [allotment] gardens for the labouring poor'.[5] In other cases the enclosed land was destined for a different use again, foreshadowing the fundamental change in the economy of Cornwall that the twentieth century was to bring:

The Commissioners have . . . ordered the inclosure [sic] of Lizard Common or Downs, in the parish of Landewednack. . . . [T]he principal object of the inclosure is the allotment of the land in severalty in order that it may be applied to building, sites for houses being greatly required in this part, which at certain seasons is much frequented by persons who are attracted by the coast scenery (Barton, 1972).

Meanwhile, the exchange value of smallholdings already improved had greatly increased. By 1875 there were only fifty to sixty acres of land uncultivated at Connor Downs and land 'first let to the miners at 2s-6d per acre' had increased in value to 'upwards of £1.10s' (Barton, 1972). Land on St. Agnes Beacon was being sold in lots of up to thirty acres, rather than the previously typical one to ten acres, and advertisers stressed as a selling point that 'a quick return may be had for cultivation' (Barton, 1972, p. 255). In 1888 agricultural land undamaged by mining activities was rented at £1.4s per acre per year in the Redruth area, where such land was very scarce (P.P. 1888, XXII, Q6784). In the mining parish of Illogan, near Camborne, the ground rent for a cottage on an acre of improved ground was as much as £8 per year by the 1880s (P.P. 1888, XXII, Q6870). In the 1880s, rural cottages without any land cost 50s. to 60s. a year (P.P. 1888, XXII, Q6784). In the towns, rents were higher. In Camborne the average rent for a four-roomed cottage was about 3s. a week (P.P. 1884–5, XXX, Q8181). Such a cottage would have little or no garden thus preventing its occupier from getting access to the means of subsistence in the way of a food supply.

These drastic increases in the costs of housing and land, especially affected *new* entrants to the housing market, as life leases were at a fixed ground rental. Housing and land were increasingly produced in the commodity form after the middle of the century in rural as well as urban areas. These developments must be seen in a context where mining wages did *not*, in general, increase and where cash food prices were increasing until the late 1870s (Burnett, 1969). Combined with the lack of new land for smallholdings, these changes would appear to have increased the gap in living standards and prospects between the miner who already had a smallholding and the miner setting up house for the first time. By the 1880s, a little under a quarter of the average mining family's income of around 16s. to 18s. per week (P.P. 1884–5, XXX, Q8181; Jenkin, 1962) could, therefore, *either* pay the rental of a cottage in town without any land, *or* pay the ground rent for an acre of land in the nearby countryside – where access to land enabled access both to housing and to the means of subsistence.

The average length of a three-lives lease in the mining districts of Cornwall in the 1880s was only thirty-five years (P.P. 1888, XXII, Q6820; 7152). This was partly due to the short life expectancy of Cornish miners resulting from their hazardous work (P.P. 1888, XXII, Q7686) which in turn made it very difficult for them to take out insurance that would protect their families (P.P. 1888, XXII, Q7182). Moreover, without life insurance the owner of a house self-built on the lives system could not borrow much money using the house as collateral (P.P. 1888, XXII, Q7258.) This inability to take out a mortgage removed a common advantage of home ownership in this period (see Mills, 1980, for a discussion of this point) and at the same time made miners particularly inclined to seek opportunities for fairly large lump-sum earnings over a short period.

The uncertainty of length of tenure under the life-lease system was thus one of the major grievances of leaseholding miners (P.P. 1888, XXII, Q7315). If the lease did last for a long time, the holder would benefit to some extent from the fact that the rent had been fixed for many years, while the buildings would be of little value to the landlord. If the lease turned out to be short, however, the benefits to the landlord would be substantial (P.P. 1888, XXII, Q9173–9184). This, together with the fact that all improvements reverted to the landlord, gave miners little incentive to use durable building materials. As a result, rural cottages were often unhealthy and damp and fell into increasingly bad repair as the 'lives' grew old (P.P. 1888, XXII, Q6909–11; 7141–3; *Cornish Post and Mining News*, 16 February 1899; Land Enquiry Committee, 1914).

Further, as the lives 'dropped off', the value of the property to lessees on the market fell drastically, so that they would lose greatly if they sold. The following report of an auction at Camborne in 1884 is indicative in this respect:

> Small farm, Mount Pleasure, 12 acres, house and outbuildings, held on one life, £131; 8 acres land, three lives, £390; 27 Centenary Street, Camborne, small house, two lives, £55 (*Royal Cornwall Gazette*, 29 February 1884).

By contrast:

> [on] the only estate in Cornwall where leases are [continually] renewable . . . people are very anxious to build houses . . . and they put up a good lasting kind of house (P.P. 1888, XXII, Q7204).

Although self-built housing in the rural areas was often not of high quality, living in one's own cottage in a rural area had definite advantages over renting a house in a town. Rented houses were leased from another ground leaseholder on a monthly or quarterly tenancy. Several witnesses to the *Royal Commission on the Housing of the Working Classes* testified as to the poor quality of that available at a rent ordinary miners could afford, and documented the overcrowded conditions of dozens of families living in two-roomed cottages and tenements in Camborne and Redruth (P.P. 1884–5, XXX, QQ 7925–8044; 8130; 8218–8250; P.P. 1893–4, CV500). Rental properties were commonly allowed to fall into disrepair because the leaseholders would not reap the capital value of any improvements under the life-lease system of tenure. As in London, short leases encouraged the growth of 'an entire class of middlemen' who often became slum landlords (Jones, 1976; P.P. 1888, XXII, QQ 12,560–4).

Housing conditions in Camborne and Redruth were exacerbated in the 1880s by a shortage of building land (P.P. 1884–5, XXX, QQ 7914–7924). The precise cause-and-effect relationship in this shortage was disputed. Building industry representatives blamed the life-lease system, arguing that upon the expiration of leases more miners' houses had been demolished than there were new ones built (P.P. 1884–5, XXX, QQ 8125–36; 8189–90). The Medical Officer of Health for Camborne, on the other hand, argued that the population fluctuation caused by the nature of the industry was in and of itself severe enough to create the housing shortage (P.P. 1884–5, XXX, Q8231–9). Investors were reluctant to invest in rental properties for fear of losing not only their income but also the value of their capital assets should the mining industry collapse and the demand for housing collapse with it (P.P. 1884–5, XXX, QQ8098–8100, 8321–2; P.P. 1888, XXII, Q6845). In the opinion of the investigating commissioners, and the Medical Officer of Health, this fear of falling property values was a more important disincentive to building in the towns than the life-lease system itself, although building capitalists stressed that they would build properties for rent to miners if freehold land tenure were available (P.P. 1884–5, XXX, QQ 8075–6; 8127; 8247–9). They also argued that large landowners had actually withheld serviced land during the copper boom in the Redruth area in 1850–62, thus slowing the building of new housing for miners (P.P. 1884–5, XXX, QQ8051–8; P.P. 1888, XXII, QQ6680–4).

Building industry witnesses and professionals in the real estate field told the Select Committee's Cornish hearings that leasehold reform would give themselves the incentive and the opportunity to develop a more extensive building industry and alleviate overcrowding in the towns (P.P. 1888, XXII, QQ6749–51). They specifically complained that the maintenance of a leasehold system controlled by large landowners was impeding both commercial and residential development in the towns of Redruth and Camborne (P.P. 1888, XXII, Q6701).

At the same time, notions of 'improving' the working-classes through small property ownership were prominent in the evidence of several middle-class and capitalist witnesses. The leasehold tenure system prevailing in Cornwall was accordingly singled out as a major obstacle to the development of a more stable society containing a high proportion of working-class home owners (P.P. 1888, XXII, QQ7093–7104). Instability and conflict in the mining districts was held to be due to the near-feudal shackles of the large landowners. It was believed – and hoped – that leasehold enfranchisement in West Cornwall would contribute to the development of a progressive and enlightened capitalism, into which the upper echelons of working miners could be co-opted.

Thus, in view of the nature of the national leasehold reform campaign, its political philosophy, and the 'progressive' position of bourgeois leasehold reformers as opposed to the old landed class in Cornwall, it is tempting to see Cornish miners who supported the campaign and struggled for access to their own smallholdings as having a 'natural' basis for a 'class alliance' with the former and against the latter. The class identification of Cornish miner-smallholders gives the distinct impression of being 'petty bourgeois', and it is tempting to view their support for freehold ownership of a cottage, three acres and a cow in those terms.

However, we cannot reach reliable conclusions about miners' 'class location', goals or political consciousness from the above considerations alone. Although we have described the seemingly precapitalist *forms* of access to subsistence and the apparently 'traditional' labour process, we now need to investigate how the processes underlying these forms were changing in the third quarter of the century, so as to gain a better understanding of the role of access to owner-occupied cottages and subsistence plots in the lives of Cornish mining families. We thus move on to a theoretically informed account of the changes that occurred in the purpose and direction of labour processes in the mining industry, in the context of the beginnings of industrial decline, from the 1860s to the 1880s. We then consider the impact of these changes on family earnings from mining.

4 'Old forms remain, but they are changed at the core':[6] the restructuring of labour processes in Cornish mining, 1860s–80s

4.1 The labour processes of Cornish mining: from independent production to formal subordination to capital

In an overview of the various historical processes through which industrial proletariats may be formed, Maurice Dobb makes the point that analyses of the development of capitalism in Britain and Europe have tended to assume that the dispossession of working people from the land was in all cases the crucial – if not the exclusive – factor in creating a dependent wage-earning class (Dobb 1963). A related and equally common assumption is that those who maintained or achieved the status of petty producers or who had access to independent subsistence, in contexts where capitalist relations of production had overtly penetrated other sectors of the economy, were somehow 'external' to capitalist relations, or existed as anomalous relics of earlier modes of production.

However, complete separation from the land need not be the main factor in creating a class subordinated to capital:

> Even where free land exists, other factors such as debt or monopoly may rob the small producer of his independence and eventually occasion his dispossession. . . . [T]he essentials of the process by which a small producer became a servant of capital and a proletarian . . . [are] nowhere more clearly depicted than in the case of those mining communities which are anciently characterised by the practice that is known as 'free mining' (Dobb, 1963, p. 253).

To explore this argument, we shall now look in more detail at mining labour processes in Cornwall and the ways in which they changed up until the later nineteenth century.

In the production process of tin mining in Cornwall, the tributers' labour processes were increasingly dominated by capitalistic exchange relations from the fourteenth century onwards. This occurred through a complex set of processes of internal differentiation between the parties involved in the industry and the growth of middlemen and distinct classes of ore-purchasers and smelters (Dobb, 1963; Lewis, 1907). However, the erosion of tributers' independence within the workplace itself took place unevenly (P.P. 1864, XXIV, 546).

Mine captains and agents had a wide range of responsibilities in running the day-to-day affairs of the mine, but did little in the way of formal supervision of the labour process itself, which remained minimal (Rule, 1970; Samuel, 1977). The lack of supervision in the labour process, combined with their specialised knowledge, gave both tributers and tutworkers a certain amount of control over their earnings. Mine agents would decide what work was to be done in different parts of a mine, how much could be done in a given time, and the value of each 'pitch'. Then, on 'setting day' – once a month for tutwork, once every two months for tribute, the different pitches would be 'auctioned' off to the lowest bidder among groups of miners (Lewis, 1907; P.P. 1890–1, XLI, QQ3703–7). Thus, the rates of pay were set. This system could be more advantageous to miners than ordinary piece work because, in the absence of supervision, tributers could conceal the true value of a highly productive pitch by holding back the more valuable ores (Samuel, 1977). Tutworkers, presumably, could likwise pretend that a particular lode was more difficult to excavate than it really was, and thus obtain a higher rate per fathom. Occasionally, in mid-century, there were instances of tributers earning £100 or more in a month (Samuel, 1977.) More commonly, a 'lucky strike' might bring a tributer £40 to £50 in a month once or twice in his lifetime (Jenkin, 1962).

From mid-century onwards, two factors combined to reduce both miners' control over their monthly earnings and their 'luck'. First, their opportunities for personally reaping the benefits of a good lode were increasingly usurped. The geological knowledge and engineering skills of captains and agents increased relative to those of the working miner, which tended 'to increase [the former's] caution in the allotment of work to tributers and lessen the latter's chances of making lucky strikes' (Lewis, 1907, p. 204). Mine agents were thus increasingly able to judge the quality of a lode before striking a 'bargain' with a tributer (P.P. 1864, XXIV, 384). Thus tribute work came to resemble ordinary sub-contract work. Similarly, the earnings of tutworkers came to resemble those of ordinary piece workers (Lewis, 1907; P.P. 1890–1, LXXVIII, 7).

Second, miners' earnings were regulated not only by the amount and quality of the ore raised but also by its market value at the time the ore was sold to smelters (P.P. 1864, XXIV, 383). The way in which the industry was organised made it highly susceptible to booms and slumps in tin prices, increasingly so as the nineteenth century progressed. By the mid-nineteenth century, both copper and tin-mining 'served as a veritable forcing ground for speculative investment' (Samuel, 1977, p. 20). These fluctuations affected tributers more than tutworkers. Moreover, although tributers tended to earn more than other groups of mineworkers, they also had to pay all the expenses entailed in obtaining the ore, such as the cost of materials such as gunpowder and fuses, transportation of the ore within the mine and processing at the surface (Jenkin, 1962). They were dependent on advances from their employer to pay for such items and services, which were deducted from their earnings on pay day (Lewis, 1907). Further, if the lode turned out to be poor, their earnings might be non-existent for months at a time. An advance was available, known as 'subsist', but this amounted to five or ten shillings a week – not nearly enough to feed a family in a cash economy (Jenkins, 1962).

In times of bad luck in tributing, or a slump in the price of tin, the cycle of debt was perpetuated, with the tributer becoming increasingly dependent on currying favour in order to obtain loans from the mine purser (Jenkin, 1962). Furthermore, tributers were taken on under the month-in-hand system; thus, in the first two months of employment, they were often forced into debt to pursers, shopkeepers and travelling salespeople (idem; P.P. 1884–5, XXX, Q8094). If a miner was deep in debt, savings from a previous 'lucky strike' would be soon wiped out (P.P. 1884–5, XXX, Q10,343). Further, such growing indebtedness eroded miners' ability to survive work stoppages, debt repayments wiping out any cash savings they might have had.

Thus, in general:

> mineral works developed in a much more unambiguously capitalist direction, with ownership becoming increasingly associated with control. The scope of sub-contract was progressively narrowed and 'bargain' systems of payment gave way to more modern systems of piecework (Samuel, 1977, p. 73).

We have discussed the specific forms such developments took in Cornwall and their impact on the 'independent miner'. We shall now outline the changing earnings from mining of men, women and children in the context of these labour process changes.

4.2 The earnings of men, women and children in Cornish mines

The earnings of miners in Cornwall had always been low, if the tributer's occasional 'lucky strike' is disregarded. The adult male wage was unable to support a family of five throughout most of the nineteenth century (P.P. 1894, XXIV, 295). Several authors concur that the average earnings in the 1830s to 1840s were around 10s. to 13s. a week (Anon, 1855; Barton, 1967; Lewis, 1907; Todd, 1967). By 1890, average earnings for tributers and tutworkers in Cornwall were around 16s. per week (Jenkin, 1962).

Family earnings could be boosted considerably if other family members were employed in the industry (Rowe, 1953). Child labour was very prevalent in the tin- and copper-mining industries, although children very rarely worked underground. Boys of eight years and up would assist tributing miners in various tasks while girls would work as 'bal-maidens', breaking up the ore in surface workshops, or in tin-stream works. For such tasks they were paid between 4d. and 6d. a day in the 1860s (P.P. 1864, XXIV, 395), and about 11d. per day in the 1880s–1890s (P.P. 1894, XXIV, App. CXXIV; P.P. 1890–1, LXVIII).

Adult women were also frequently employed as surface workers. Rowe (1953) suggests that in the early to mid-nineteenth century, 'female labour was increasingly used as mines became larger and wherever more families became entirely dependent on mining as their source of livelihood. . .'. The 'dressing' of ores from the mines was a heavily 'female' occupation (P.P. 1890–1, LXXVIII, 20). In general, between the mid-1870s and mid-1890s adult women made up between 15 and 20 per cent of the surface workforce in the mines[7] and their earnings averaged 5s-10d per week in the mid-1880s.

Although the collapse of copper in the 1860s was partly compensated for by a boom in tin in the late 1860s and early 1870s (Brayshay, 1980), during the 1870s tin prices fell precipitously, the number of operating mines fell from 251 to 138 and the workforce was halved (P.P. 1910, XLIII, Table 27). This decade marked the beginning of a thirty year decline in employment and increasing volatility in tin prices. The mining industry responded to this by cutting wages. According to the *Annual District Report of Her Majesty's Inspector of Mines (Devon and Cornwall)* (P.P. 1876, XVII, 447), '[i]n 1876 the [tributing] miner received about £7 or £8 less for every ton of black tin than [in 1875]'. The wages of tutworkers also fell.

Wages were cut again in the early 1880s (P.P. 1884, XIX, 317), and as fluctuations from year to year and between highs and lows in tin prices in any one year became greater in the 1880s and 1890s (P.P. 1910, XLIII, Table 27), it seems reasonable to assume that miners' piecework earnings became less reliable. In 1886, a fairly good year for tin prices, returns received by Cornish mine inspectors indicate that mean wages for tributers were 16s-2d but that only one-half of them received wages within 10 per cent of this mean – the range being from 13s–2d to 19s. Additionally, the proportion of children employed in the mines fell sharply from the 1880s onwards. This might have further reduced the mining family's chances for reliable and adequate sources of earned income from Cornish mines.

Situating these wage levels in relation to the cost of living, the average minimum subsistence level for a family of father, mother and four children in a cash economy in England and Wales at this time was about 23s a week. Of this, about 70 per cent or 16s would have to be spent on food, about 3s in rent and the rest on fuel and sundries (Burnett, 1969). If paying 'urban' rents and without a smallholding, a Cornish mining family would just have got by, in a 'good' year for tin prices, on the full-time earnings of a tributer or tutworker combined with those of his wife. To cope with slump years, or to move beyond a bare physiological subsistence level, either some other source of income, or a smallholding would be necessary strategies, in the absence of ability to influence rates of wages. We shall discuss such strategies, and assess their effects, in the next section, after some brief methodological observations.

4.3 Tradition and proletarianisation: some methodological comments

This review of changes in the mining labour process and of miners' reduced abilities to control their earnings and family living standards by means of their cash incomes from Cornish mining suggests the need for a shift in analytical perspective in order to understand miners' struggles over access to a freehold cottage, 'three acres and a cow'.

By the 1870s, the labour process of Cornish mining was by no means a relic of a bygone age. The form of the old labour process remained, but it was changed at the core. The independence of the miner was retained only in appearance. It found its echo in the needs and desires of miners and their families to resist total subordination to hard rock mining capitalism in whatever ways remained open to them. As Stuart Hall has astutely commented,

> Tradition . . . has little to do with the mere persistence of old forms. . . . [T]he elements of tradition [can] be rearranged, so that they articulate with different practices and positions, and take on a new meaning and relevance (Hall, 1981, p. 236).

Certainly by the 1880s, and probably even earlier, Cornish miners' struggles for access to a freehold cottage, 'three acres and a cow', were not at all aimed at returning themselves to a mythical 'golden age', whatever the nationally leading proponents of the Radical Programme might have believed or advocated. As Cornish mines provided a decreasingly reliable way of making a living, miners sought other sources of economic security, and, as we shall see, the traditional landscape of cottages and smallholdings became crucial to this process.

5. Industrial change in the mining district: how miners and their families responded

5.1 Collective responses, and their limits

Although some mining historians have tended to represent Cornish miners as being acquiescent to the course of industrial change, and as having responded solely in individualistic terms (see, for example, Jenkin, 1962), the fragmentary evidence that does exist reveals both some history of organised response and resistance, and some clues about why this was, all the same, limited in extent.

For instance, in 1872 miners at St. Ives struck for wages to be paid them every four weeks rather than every calendar month (Barton, 1972).

Later that year the 'five-week month' was abolished throughout Cornwall, but this was a time of temporary boom, and it was reintroduced in 1874 as the depression in tin-prices deepened and the operators sought to cut costs. As a result, the Camborne area saw its first-ever miners' strike and a resolution from its leaders to form a county-wide miners' union with the aim of defending the worker against even more severe measures than the cuts already introduced (Barton, 1972). This was one of several actions against attempts by adventurers to reduce miners' wages (Jenkin, 1962; Rowe, 1953).

At least twice, severe police, military and judicial coercion and repression was used against strike leaders – tactics commonplace in Cornwall (Barton, 1972). Faced with such harsh measures, miners might well have been inclined to seek out more individualistic solutions to the problems of fluctuating wages and economic insecurity.

Miners did take part in other types of collective action, outside the wage workplace and related to the conditions of subsistence of their families. Food riots were one form of collective protest that remained prevalent in Cornwall long after they had become a rarity elsewhere in Britain (Barton, 1972; Jenkin, 1962; Rowe, 1953). This was partly because the organisation of the industry made it difficult to confront employers directly over the issue of wages and because the 'mineral lords' had a pervasive and often paternalistic influence over the working class (Rule, 1971). But food riots must also be viewed in the context of the extreme vulnerability of miners and their families to fluctuations in the price of flour and bread (Burnett, 1969; Lewis, 1907).

Other actions took place in the area of common property rights. In the 1860s and 1870s many of the traditional 'rights of common' of Cornish working people were lost, as enclosures for large-scale agriculture were accelerated, railway lines cut through tracts of common land, and customary rights to keeping geese or shooting rabbits were replaced by a system under which these rights were sold to individuals at high prices. Newspapers reported major protests by miners and other working people against such curtailments of their access to occasional free meat and poultry (Reports quoted in Barton, 1972). Working people also made organised demands at the parish level that particular large-scale enclosure schemes only be approved if some of the land were made available for the poor in the form of small allotments (Barton, 1972).

5.2 Family responses: the domestic economy, family security and smallholdings

Whilst they are still young they take a farm, perhaps at a time when they are unable to get work, and they build a cottage and take in a few fields. . . . They get a cow or two, and a horse . . . and then they have that to fall back on (Witness from St. Agnes, in evidence to *Commission Appointed to Enquire into the Condition of All Mines in Great Britain (not Coal)*, 1864 (Quoted in Jenkin, 1962, p. 269)).

The most important level of response to industrial change was the mining family – which was usually a nuclear family (Brayshay, 1980) and the strategies used by the partners within it to maintain it as an economic unit. Samuel has astutely noted that:

[i]n the absence of satisfactory statistics historians have often neglected the question of *family* earnings [emphasis added] (difficult or even impossible to quantify) and have instead argued from wage rates . . . [which] cannot tell us much about net earnings . . . nor about the kinds of vicissitudes which a labouring family experienced from one week to the next (Samuel, 1975, p. 6).

We have already discussed such 'vicissitudes' in the Cornish context, and we shall now consider 'net earnings' in terms of non-monetary as well as monetary inputs. Family-level strategies will now be examined in terms of the division of labour within the household and the importance of unwaged – domestic – labour to the domestic economy, and in terms of men's attempts to provide security for their families through savings and small property.

It has already been mentioned that adult women, as well as children, had high rates of participation in the mining labour force. In addition, miners' wives also worked on farms (Jenkin, 1962) and, when they lived close to fishing ports, in pilchard curing in order to supplement the family income (Kitteringham, 1975; P.P. 1909, XLIII, 117). Female and child labour, despite low rates of pay, made important contributions to household income. Miners' wives were also responsible for the greater part of day to day household management and domestic labour inside the home. It was said that women's abilities to keep such households orderly and well managed were the only things keeping many mining families out of debt, and conversely that if a miner's wife could not cope the family would be ruined (Jenkin, 1962). The irregular nature of miners' earnings under the bargain letting system made the task of managing household finances difficult (Barton, 1972; Rogers, 1980). The domestic workload of miners' wives was abnormally heavy, and many tasks had to be repeated several times a day, since within one household there might be several adult men – each working a different shift (P.P. 1890–1, XLI, Q3681–7; 4011–5).

Additionally, since men, boys and employed women at the mines worked full eight-hour days, work on the family's subsistence plot, which was done by both men and women, was a further burden – more indicative of a necessity than a luxury. Indeed, miners who took on several acres of land often found themselves overburdened. A Truro magistrate put out a pamphlet in 1827 with the following advice:

> from one eighth to one quarter of an acre will generally be better than more; for without the aid of a lucky start in mining, or some other piece of good fortune productive of means beyond the proceeds of daily labour, no poor man should attempt to cope with several acres, especially of a coarse description. After years of hard struggling, a severe winter, sooner or later, will arrive, and find him ill-provided for the maintenance of his little stock. . . . Besides, when there is too much to be done at home the labourer will seldom be worthy of his hire elsewhere. (Checkland and Checkland, 1974, pp. 287–8).

While this recommendation refers explicitly only to men, it highlights an interesting question as regards the carrying out of the unwaged labour of subsistence production on the smallholding or allotment. How much could a family cope with, along with waged work and other domestic labour, and what were the implications for women, and for the maintenance of the family, when this work of subsistence production became the sole responsibility of the miner's wife due to the husband's absence from the home for an extended period of time? This is a point to which we shall return later.

The Truro magistrate referred to above suggested that miners would be better off banking their small savings rather than tying them up in a cottage and smallholding, advocating that miners limit themselves to 'a well-cultivated garden'. Indeed, by the second half of the century, miners had become assiduous savers. A witness to the 1864 Commission, from St. Agnes, commented, 'I suppose that three quarters of the working men in this parish have money accumulated in the Savings Bank. There is very little drunkenness here (quoted in Jenkin, 1962, p. 269), while Post Office Savings Banks were heavily used by miners. The average of £14–£16 for each account was 'higher than those for many other counties' (*West Briton*, 27 September, 1888).

However, miners tended not to keep such savings as liquid assets. Nor did they speculate in mining shares to any large extent, preferring domestic property: 'a little house is a favourite investment with the Cornish miner who has saved a few pounds' (P.P. 1888, XXII, Q.7062). They rarely took out mortgages but tended to buy outright in cash, using their savings (P.P. 1888, XXII, QQ6902–4; 7095–7100). The reasons for this were threefold. Miners found it difficult to borrow large sums of money since this was contingent on obtaining life insurance, for which they were considered a bad risk (P.P. 1888, XXII, QQ7180–2). Also, those who owned a house outright would not have to worry about meeting mortgage or house rental payments during times of low earnings or unemployment, although, unless they could get *freehold* land, they would still have to meet ground rent payments. A further reason was the occasional opportunity for tributing miners to earn substantial cash sums, as discussed above. While the prospects of such windfalls declined in the latter part of the century, this was in part compensated for, as we shall see, by miners' earnings overseas.

The use of savings for cottage property and smallholdings was a more satisfactory means of providing income security for a family than the available alternatives. This must be understood in relation to the particular working life-cycle of the underground miner. A smallholding would help to keep a miner and his wife when he retired. Retirement came early. Accident rates were high and damp and dusty conditions in the mines put many miners in failing health by their forties or even younger (P.P. 1864, XXIV, 379; Jenkin, 1962).

The high death and disability rates made crucial some form of insurance for miners and their families. To this end, the mine club was one means by which they might avoid dependency on the Poor Law Union. Clubs were administered by mine managers or pursers, who made a compulsory deduction from wages of sixpence a month for the club subscription. Yet, the clubs were often corrupt and the doctors inferior (Jenkin, 1962), while as a Mine inspector explained, this:

> is simply an insurance for non-fatal accidents, from which miners who have been injured at the mine receive one shilling per day as long as they are unable to work. The present clubs have two great defects: first, they make no provision for the dependent relatives of the victim of fatal accidents . . .; secondly, in cases of non-fatal accidents the benefit is not always permanent, for it ceases if the mine is stopped (P.P. 1876, XVII, 485).

Evidence to the *Royal Commission on the Housing of the Working Classes* highlighted the inadequacy of compensation for families. In one case:

> in a court near Plain-an-gwarry [Redruth], there are a mother and six children and a sister sleeping with the mother, the husband having been killed at the mine; that is eight people in one room? – That is correct, the woman has been having £2 a month from the mine; that has been her sole support except what she has had from her friends; she is quite a young woman, left with six children (P.P. 1884–5, XXX, Q8020).

In another case, a miner's widow lived as a lodger with one of her own children and another woman with three children, all in one room:

> her husband went abroad. He was killed and she had £20 from the mine. That was very quickly spent, and she came to this life of a prostitute (P.P. 1884–5, XXX, Q7958).

This woman's other two children were in care of the Poor Law Union.

A house, and a little plot of land, owned by the miner's family, were clearly the best 'all risks' insurance available. The need for security provided a major motivation for the acquisition of a house and land (P.P. 1888, XXII, Q6494). In better times a source of supplementary family security for those fully employed in mining, subsistence plots became essential support in times of recession in the industry, when a tributer had a run of bad luck in tributing, or when a miner changed jobs and thus received no pay for two months (Barton, 1967). As previously mentioned, an intensively worked holding with three acres, a cow and a pig could provide half the cash value of a family's subsistence diet (about 7s.–6d. worth of food), so if a landholding miner's earnings fell by one-half but his wife or two children still had full-time work the family could have held on at a basic subsistence level. If they owned the freehold of the property or had an old lease at a nominal rent they could still have stayed above the minimum physiological subsistence level with an even smaller cash income.

Moreover, as *common* rights to the grazing of animals, keeping of geese and so on were eroded, the use value of *private* ownership or exclusive access to land on which one could grow some food or keep some animals would have been enhanced.

In the later nineteenth century the ownership of a home and a subsistence plot became increasingly important as a means of keeping the mining family unit economically intact, as the mining economy of West Cornwall declined further. This, as we shall now see, was related to another element of the social landscape: the complex patterns of *labour migration* which characterised the lives of thousands of miners from Cornwall and which became integral to the region's economy as industrial decline set in.

5.3 *Labour migration and the family economy, 1830s–70s*

Migration from one job to another, within Cornwall, and from one part of the country to another, had long been features of the mining labour force (Barton, 1972). Yet for miners with families of their own, long-distance migrations were not taken lightly and the decisions involved were complex. The male family head might accept a temporary work contract elsewhere in the country during a slump, intending to return to Cornwall when times were better, and sending remittances home. Alternatively, he might migrate overseas on a tentative basis and send for his family when established, in a 'two-step migration' migration process. A third strategy was the simultaneous permanent migration of a whole family to another part of Britain or overseas.

The migration decisions of a Cornish mining family were partly a function of the economic conditions and work options, as they perceived them, in possible destinations relative to those at home, mediated by the costs of travel relative to their financial means. Yet the question of *housing* for miners' families also figured strongly in these decisions, both as an attraction at the destination for a whole family to migrate and as an enabling factor in Cornwall for two-stage or temporary migrations.

From the 1830s, until the end of the nineteenth century, tens of thousands of adult male Cornish miners migrated overseas. Until the 1860s, the main destination was the United States. A major tide of emigration commenced, without state assistance, in the 1840s, the main flows being to the lead region of South-West Wisconsin (Todd, 1967). Copper-mining tributers emigrated in increasing numbers in mid-century, when they had enough savings, since the Cornish labour market was already becoming glutted (Rowe, 1953). Typically, married migrants to North America would set off alone and would send for their families when established, since one much advertised attraction of mining communities in North America, compared with those in Britain, was the prospect of improved living conditions and access to freehold housing and land (Brayshay, 1977; Todd, 1967; Veness-Randle, 1979).

At the same time, home-ownership in Cornwall could sometimes enable whole families to emigrate to North America. In 1846 the fare from Liverpool to New York was £3 per person. While miners could sometimes raise the money from relatives who had already emigrated, they could, if they were already home-owners, use their homes as collateral, borrowing 'from tradesmen on the security of their cob cottages' (Todd, 1967).

The collapse of copper mining in Cornwall greatly accelerated the outflow of Cornish miners to the western United States, British North America, New Zealand, Australia, the East Indies, Cuba and South America (Todd, 1967; Brayshay, pers. comm. Feb. 1980; Duncan, 1963). In an eighteen-month period in the mid-1860s, over 11 000 copper miners lost their jobs; two-thirds of them emigrated, leaving behind 20 000 dependants, St. Just and St. Agnes being the worst hit (Rowe, 1953).

By the late 1860s, overseas migration from Cornwall had become part and parcel of daily life. Tickets could be bought from small town Post Offices to destinations such as Houghton, Michigan and, later, Johannesburg, South Africa (Brayshay, 1977). By 1871, the effects of this migration were beginning to show in household structure: the 1871 Census showed a large increase in the number of households headed by married women whose husbands had emigrated (Brayshay, 1980).

6 Subsistence plots and migration labour in the late nineteenth century: strategies for family and community survival

If you stand on Carn Marth, you see nothing anywhere but the gaunt, dismantled engine houses of abandoned mines that used at one time to support scores of villages. The young men are [overseas] . . . anywhere where there is work to be got and money to be earned. . . . At home, if [the miner] is fortunate enough to get work at all, he has to count himself lucky if he makes throughout the year an average of a pound a week. He saves or borrows the money wherewith to pay his passage to some foreign mining camp, and straightaway begins to earn something like a pound a day. The day's work keeps him for days. He sends home the rest of the money, and gradually acquires a balance at the bank, while allowing his wife more than she used to get for the needs of the whole family when he was at home. . . . As soon as the balance at the bank gets big enough . . . he takes a holiday and goes back to enjoy the old place for a month or two. So he rarely becomes rich, but he does manage to save certain parts of Cornwall from virtual extinction (*Cornish Post and Mining News*, Oct. 26 1899. Reprinted from the London *Daily Mail*).

Between 1873 and 1898 employment in mining in Cornwall fell from 26 814 to 5193. In the early 1880s, very few mines were even covering their costs and hardly any were paying dividends (P.P. 1884, XIX, 615). In response to this, wages of mine workers were cut, especially in the smaller mines. Larger companies survived by introducing machine drills which increased labour productivity (Burke and Richardson, 1978). Output thus remained relatively steady while employment levels were cut. But another depression set in in the early 1890s due to a combination of foreign competition, excessive speculation and the starting of mines with insufficient capital (P.P. 1893–4, XX, 441). A temporary boom in 1899 yielded a ten per cent increase in wages for miners (P.P. 1900, XIV, 368), and the rising price of tin in the early years of the twentieth century led to a slight recovery in employment levels. However, the industry was as unstable as ever. In 1906 only about six mines out of a total of eighty-eight were paying their way in spite of the high price of tin (P.P. 1907, XIII, 646). By 1908 a downturn had started (P.P. 1909, XXXIII), from which there was no recovery after the First World War.

6.1 The making of a 'labour reserve': the role of subsistence in the 1890s

In such a context of deepening structural decline, one might expect an acceleration of outmigration of a permanent character by individuals, followed by the departure of entire families. However, while population in the mining districts fell drastically between the 1871 and 1881 census counts (the period of most precipitous employment decline), thereafter it stayed relatively stable even though employment levels continued to decline markedly. From the 1870s to the end of the century, migrations from Cornwall took on an increasingly *temporary* character. Cornish miners would journey to many parts of the globe, often making several return trips in the space of ten, fifteen or twenty years (P.P. 1904, XIII). As de-industrialisation set in, the practice of labour migration became less a speculative foray in search of a better life overseas and more a necessity for the economic survival of family units and communities (P.P. 1890–1, XLI, Q4373). For instance, in the village of Lanner (in Gwennap parish) in 1888, 120 miners were abroad, out of a total village population of 2000, and were 'sending home regularly to their wives and families money to pay their rent, rates, taxes and living'. When such men returned, they would bring back from £200 to £400 in savings (P.P. 1888, XXII, Q7266).

Gold mining started on the Witwatersrand in the Transvaal in 1886; thereafter the main flows of Cornish miners were to South Africa until the outbreak of the South African war in 1899. Cornish miners overwhelmingly dominated the skilled labour force on the Rand for the first twenty years of gold-mining (Burke and Richardson, 1978). Sometimes 'families would be sent for, or wives would go out and keep their husbands company for a time, [but] . . . usually they stayed behind, keeping the home going, looking after their children, bringing them up alone . . .' (Rowse, 1942, p. 35). In Cornwall, entire communities became dependent on the earnings of miners working overseas, a situation described graphically in an 1899 newspaper report:

In one little town the drafts from the Transvaal usually arrive on Saturday. . . .

On the days when the mail arrives . . . the post office [is] filled with people who are waiting for their letters, all of which contain money. . . . [If] the mail is late . . . the people . . . are in difficulties. They are out of all kinds of household necessaries, and have no money (*Cornish Post and Mining News*, 20 October 1899).

Yet, why did emigré miners leaving Cornwall in the last quarter of the century not send for their families and settle permanently to the same extent as earlier outmigrants, especially those going to the United States, had done? There was certainly a real, sentimental, attachment to Cornwall which expressed itself in a desire to earn enough in the space of a few years to return home and settle down with their families on 'their own little bit of land with their own house on it' (P.P. 1888, XXII, Q7066), and which was not eradicated by the structural decline of the mining economy (Rowse, 1942). A miner from Redruth, one of two hundred to return to Cornwall immediately after the South African War broke out, told the *Cornish Post and Mining News*: '[w]e went to South Africa to make money, not to settle in the country'. His friend commented, '[t]he Cornishmen . . . longs for the time when he shall have made enough to go back again to those little towns beneath the shadow of Carn Brea and Carn Camborne' (*Cornish Post and Mining News*, 12 October 1899).

Considerable sums were invested in housing by returnee miners. Despite the decline in Cornish mining there was a shortfall of working-class housing in Camborne in 1901. Reporting on an influx of funds from the Transvaal into 'one little town' in West Cornwall, a newspaper correspondent noted that 'the smaller businesses benefit', while despite mine closures and the outmigration of young men, 'it has become constantly more difficult to get houses of the middle-class sort in the neighbourhood' (*Cornish Post and Mining News*, 26 October 1899). Miners who had returned from abroad – and especially from South Africa after war broke out in 1899 – were frequently able to purchase their own houses with the money they had saved if inexpensive building land could be made available. A report to the Camborne Urban District Council urged that the Council satisfy this demand for workers' housing by using the *Small Dwellings (Acquisitions) Act*, 1899, to assist miners to acquire their own houses (*Cornish Post and Mining News*, 11 April 1901).

However, the reluctance of Cornish miners to take their families with them to South Africa was not only due to sentiment. Miners could not send for their families unless their earnings abroad were high enough to maintain their families in overseas mining towns and unless there was adequate housing there. In the first twenty years of gold mining on the Witwatersrand in South Africa, '[n]early all the married workmen and miners left families in England', substantially because of the high cost of living and the absence of family accommodation and adequate schooling opportunities (Phillips, 1905, p. 63).

Although in 1897 miners could earn an average of £26 per month on the goldfields of the Rand, 'it costs miners and others with families about £20 per month to merely live, irrespective of clothing and luxuries . . .' (P.P. 1899, LXIV, 38–9; *Cornish Post and Mining News*, 27 July 1899). Thus in 1897, only 12 per cent of white mineworkers on the Rand had their families with them (Krut, 1979).

During the period of most severe industrial decline, there were therefore severe limitations on the possibility of *entire families* emigrating in order to keep the family going as an economic unit. Families fragmented, literally, in order to survive.[8] The subsistence plot thus took on a new significance in the 1880s and 1890s. The combination of migration of the male 'breadwinner' and access to a smallholding by the rest of the nuclear family gave those who stayed behind access to a cash income, from abroad, supplemented by some access to means of subsistence through unpaid labour, in Cornwall, and an inexpensive place to live which was perhaps a reasonable 'family environment'. This casts further light on miners' struggles for small holdings and agitation for *freehold* land tenure, since *security* and *stability* of living conditions in Cornwall would have been particularly crucial for mining families whose heads were working overseas.

Miners who had already been able to purchase a house and land either out of savings from money earned in Cornwall or from earnings from a previous overseas foray, were in the best position when it came to having to leave their families behind in order to earn a living abroad. If they owned the freehold of their land their families would have no ground rent to pay in their absence. If they owned the house outright but not the land it was built on, they would have to pay ground rent but would still not have to worry about house rental or mortgage payments (P.P. 1888, XXII, QQ6882–4; 6994), while their families could consume the produce of their vegetable patch, and that of the proverbial cow, making it easier to cope until regular money orders came in. Although property values fell in the mining districts in times of recession in the Cornish industry, this would not have affected the desire for freehold ownership by the miner whose family needed the house and garden for its use value rather than its exchange value (P.P. 1888, XXII, Q6845).

The migrant labour strategy was always a risky one for the family as a unit, but especially so if the family had no freehold land. Newspaper reports on sessions of the Poor Law Board of Guardians indicate numerous families left destitute when their husbands died, disappeared, became disabled or unemployed abroad (*Cornish Post and Mining News*, 12 January 1899; 9 February 1899; 23 March 1899; 6 April 1899; 19 October 1899). The life-lease tenure system was particularly onerous for the families of miners overseas because if a lease was held on a miner's life it would be ended if he died or disappeared. The families of those who stayed behind in recessions without resources for their subsistence were vulnerable to being broken up, with some members sent to the Workhouse (Barton, 1967).

However, in spite of these risks, going abroad was preferred by working miners to dependency on the Poor Law because of the prospects of bringing a 'nest-egg' home (P.P. 1890–1, XLI, Q4377). The 'payoffs' of this strategy were highlighted in the results of a 1909 investigation into the relationships between industrial conditions and 'pauperism' in the Redruth and Penzance districts. Miners who returned from South Africa seldom needed poor relief themselves even though they were very often chronically sick (P.P. 1909, XLIII, 108; 117). Such miners usually saved at least £100 and:

> it may also be sometime [sic] before his widow and family have to make application, and in some cases which we have come across they have never done so. In the case of those miners, on the other hand, who have worked in West Cornwall, but not in South Africa . . . there are among them many more cases where the men themselves apply for relief, while such application is almost invariable in the case of their widows (P.P. 1909, XLIII, 108).

Judging by the rents paid by the former miners and their dependants who *were* claiming relief, it is notable that none of them had any access to land.

The practice of temporary migration would not have been possible on such an extensive scale had miners not been able to leave their families in cottages and subsistence plots. Miners played an active, if perhaps unwitting, role in creating a 'labour reserve'[9] economy through their strategies of migration and obtaining access to small pieces of land. The continuance of this type of economy, involving heavy work on poor land, was more a result than a cause of low wages in the Cornish mining industry. An official report on wages in mines and quarries in Great Britain in 1891 suggested that their wage rates had, in general, always been low because of 'the localities in which the mines are usually situated, namely in agricultural districts away from the great industrial centres' where there was competition for labour (P.P. 1891, LXXVIII, 585). Indeed, although one can see clear advantages to employers in miners having subsistence plots, these did not 'anchor' the workforce to one spot as in 'classic' company towns and villages in other areas. Unlike many other single industry districts, no evidence was found for Cornwall of concerted promotion of subsistence plots by those with a vested interest in keeping mining wages low.

6.2 The end of the 'labour reserve' in the early twentieth century

Labour migration itself further eroded the viability of Cornish mining (P.P. 1890–1, XLI, Q4867), since '[t]hose who were left to work the mines have been, for the most part, the men who were too old to go abroad, and the lads who were too inexperienced' (*Cornish Post and Mining News* 30 March 1899). 'If you go into the chapels on Sundays, you see a population made up of women, boys and old men', wrote the *Daily Mail*'s correspondent in 1899 (*Cornish Post and Mining News*, 26 October 1899).

At an aggregate level then, and in the medium and longer term, the patterns of migration, temporary and permanent, of Cornish miners, eroded rather than helped stabilise the mining economy on which miners as a group depended. The very conditions which enabled West Cornwall to survive as a labour reserve economy in the 1890s helped to undermine its chances of recovery as a viable mining-based economy in the 1900s and after. By about 1910, renewed incentives on the part of the new South African government and mine-owners there to promote political and social stability among English mineworkers by encouraging them to bring their families to South Africa (Bozzoli, 1981; Krut, 1979; Phillips, 1905; Van Onselen, 1979), led to an increased outmigration from Cornwall by whole families, as a Mine Inspector had forecast some years earlier (P.P. 1903, XV, 677).

By 1919 there were only sixty functioning mines left in Cornwall; by 1923 only two; and by 1920 the workforce had shrunk to only 2105 miners (Burke and Richardson, 1978). By 1921, mining districts had lost up to 12.6 per cent of their 1911 populations due to emigration (HMSO, 1923). Only 'the quickening demand for flowers and vegetables for transport by rail, and the early traces of a holiday and tourist industry, relieved the general gloom' in West Cornwall in the 1920s (Pelling, 1967).

The labour reserve economy which miners, in their struggles to maintain their families in the context of local industrial decline and the lack of opportunities for emigration of whole families, had actively shaped, did not give miners any *collective* power to resist the near-total collapse of Cornish tin mining from the 1890s on. However, at the level of *individual* miners and their families, the results of the labour reserve economy were more ambiguous.

It has been argued here that in the 1880s and 1890s the combination of temporary migration of adult males and subsistence plots was a strategy for family survival. Yet many family units did *not* survive. In the town of Redruth some miners' widows were forced to seek poor relief despite years of struggle to earn a living themselves and sending their children out to work (P.P. 1909, XLIII, App. Vol. XVI). Even access to land was no guarantee that a family could hold together. While the history of migrant miners' wives in Cornwall has yet to be written, it seems likely that for some such families the burden of unpaid domestic labour for subsistence purposes on the smallholding would have proven too great, as foreseen by the Poor Law Commissioners sixty years earlier, especially if women and children had to take on waged jobs as well during the husband's absence, as many did (Brayshay, 1980). Where migrants returned injured, sick or, occasionally, without enough savings, they would have been dependent on their families' labour, and the subsistence part of the domestic economy might have been weakened too much by the loss of their husband's labour to cope with this additional burden (Rogers, 1980). Further, as previously mentioned, many families lost their breadwinners through accident or death overseas. A small minority of migrant miners deserted their families (P.P. 1901, XLIII, 112), and still others sent back only 'meagre, irregular remittances' (Rowe, 1953, p. 321). Even where children worked for wages in the fields all summer, many such family units could not remain intact.

Nevertheless, many individual miners and their families did benefit from the migrant labour/subsistence strategy. The 1909 investigation 'heard numerous testimonials to the generosity of the remittances by miners to their wives, and to other relations at home . . .' (P.P. 1909, XLIII, 112). Some miners were able to earn enough from their mining ventures to return to Cornwall, settle in their cottages and retire or change their occupation to one that might be termed 'petit-bourgeois'. Out of the total of 342 miners who died in the Redruth Registration District in 1900, 1901 and 1902, over half of whom had worked overseas, 43 appeared to have changed their occupations at some point. A change to mine agent (presumably in an overseas mine) was the most often cited, but quite a number became full-time farmers or small shopkeepers or independent tradesmen (P.P. 1904, XIII, App).

While these figures may, if representative of the careers of miners, indicate significant upward social mobility in some cases, in other instances advancement was very modest and in others again, downward mobility such as miner to labourer, occurred. Moreover, these new occupations were often literally short-lived, especially for those who had worked with machine drills in South African mines – about a third of all the miners who died in Redruth from 1900 to 1902 (P.P. 1904, XIII, 706–10). Several survived only a year in their newly 'independent' lives before dying of rapidly-progressing lung disease (P.P. 1904, XIII, 699–702; Burke and Richardson, 1978; P.P. 1909, XLIII, 113).

7 Conclusion

In this study we have explored the changing roles of access to houses with smallholdings attached, for tin and copper miners and their families in West Cornwall, under leasehold and freehold tenure, from the mid-nineteenth century to the turn of the present century. This was a period of major industrial change causing profound dislocation in the regional economy and in the domestic economy of mining families.

The role of smallholdings changed significantly during the course of the nineteenth century and particularly from one phase of the region's economy to the next. These changes can only be understood with reference to the broad tendencies for proletarianisation, boom–bust cycles and deindustrialisation in the region's economy, and the particular local conditions and struggles which affected how these tendencies operated. We may summarise the changing meaning of 'ownership' of this domestic property by considering how its 'ownership' met the changing needs and desires discussed here. In the first phase (capitalist expansion of mining), customary rights of access to common land combined with very cheap leaseholding on the life-lease system to give access to the use-value of means of subsistence in the non-commodity form, which may have reinforced the partial independence that the skilled miner still had in the labour process. In the second phase (onset of industrial decline), access to subsistence property became more of a means of stabilising an increasingly vulnerable domestic economy, and for new lessees such access was becoming fairly expensive. In the third phase (de-industrialisation and the labour reserve economy), security of tenure at minimal, predictable cost became a crucial use-value of domestic property as well as the ability to produce means of subsistence; and this could best be achieved by outright, unmortgaged freehold ownership of house and land.

7.1 Miners' struggles around domestic property: the question of political significance

Having situated miners' struggles around housing and land in the context of the broad processes of industrial change that formed the backcloth to their lives, it now remains to pose the question, how, if at all, did these struggles and miners' access to land mediate the operation of these processes in West Cornwall? For this is the way that the question of their 'political significance' must be addressed. We shall briefly evaluate whether or not these struggles influenced the policies pursued by mining companies and the nature of miners' responses to industrial change. Considering first mining company policies, there is no evidence that wages were kept low *because* miners had access to a substantial part of their food supply in the non-commodity form. It is possible, though, that miners' propensity to strike was indirectly reduced by the leasehold system, since landlords were very much tied into a repressive local power structure. In any case, if the larger mines had become mechanised earlier, in response to pressure from workers for higher, regular wages, it is likely that more male miners would have been laid-off permanently in the 1870s, with results for the community that would have been worse still.

The 'semi-proletarian' form of the miner-cum-smallholder *was* a legacy of the pre-capitalist period in two senses: the 'tradition' of the independent cottager-contractor not fully committed to wage-labour;

and the quasi-feudal land tenure system, combined with the lack of interest by agricultural capital in the marginal land involved, which enabled elements of the tradition to be perpetuated. Nevertheless, the struggles of miners to maintain these forms were *not* the product of a 'backward-looking' consciousness, enhanced by the ideological campaigns of those who wanted to produce a stable and conservative class of worker-peasants. Miners used these old forms to 'get by', improve their living conditions and occasionally to help them escape wage-labour altogether by saving substantial sums. At the very least, they used these forms to resist or reduce their dependency on wage labour in the context of unreliable and typically very low wages that could not support a family. Thus the real income of a family could be 'topped up' to a subsistence level or raised well above that level, depending on the amount that was being earned from mining at a particular time by a male family head. It is important, however, not to romanticise or accord too much 'autonomy' to such struggles: the continuance of the combination, within a family unit, of wage-labour in mining and subsistence production must be recognised as a response that was *produced* by low wages and by the necessity for temporary labour migration.

The lack of a strong tradition of labour organisation of miners is more likely to have been influenced by the relatively small and scattered workplaces of miners, combined with repression, than by the tradition of smallholdings in and of itself. Outside the wage-workplace, the leasehold reform agitation in West Cornwall in the 1880s *was* a collective struggle, and to a considerable extent a 'grass roots' one, in spite of petty-bourgeois leadership. The key issue in this struggle – security of tenure – was certainly highly defensive, though crucial to the strategies families adopted to deal with deindustrialisation.

After the upsurge of the mid-1880s, political radicalism in the Camborne and Redruth mining districts appeared to be on the wane. The possibility of emigration may have had a depoliticising effect in two senses. Miners seemed to have become less inclined to militancy on labour issues within Cornwall as their energies were devoted toward working and generating savings elsewhere (*West Briton*, 25 October 1888). In addition, in 1895 the Radical M.P., Conybeare, was defeated in a parliamentary election fought in Camborne around local issues only. This was widely attributed to a loss of votes due to emigration by miners, combined with the inability of many of those supporters who remained to pay their rates because they were unemployed; they were thus disenfranchised. A wealthy Tory tin merchant was elected after convincing many voters that he would help increase the price of tin. However, since the industry did not recover 'in 1900 Camborne returned to its customary Liberal allegiance' (Pelling, 1967). But there were no Labour candidates before 1910 and 'the single Socialist attempt – naturally in the distressed mining constituency of Camborne – was a disastrous failure' (Pelling, 1967, p.174).

The opportunities to *exit* from Cornwall's economic problems, either through permanent migration or through temporary migration with the hope of earning enough to become economically independent, are likely to have influenced consciousness. Smallholdings are 'implicated' here, since they made it easier for family heads to migrate, but this influence is not independent of the factors we have already mentioned. Although most responses were at the level of the individual family, it is important to note that the goals of 'independence' which Cornish miners clearly clung to did not in and of themselves generate political individualism; this last was a product of a constellation of circumstances rather than an inherent aspect of regional 'culture'.[10]

The long-term effects of the legacy of struggles which have been the subject of this study remain ambiguous and intriguing. We have seen that migration and emigration produced slight upward social mobility and improved living standards for numbers of mining families, while for others this strategy proved disastrous. But what of the influence on the economy of Cornwall in the present century? Until the late 1960s, it was dominated by self-employment, at rates two and a half times those of England as a whole. In one sense this suggests a petty-bourgeois consciousness; but as Massey (1983b) points out one in which the profit motive never really caught on.

In conclusion, we may also draw out some methodological implications from this case study of the changing role of access/ownership of domestic property, particularly as regards regions and sections of the workforce who seem to be only partially drawn into the web of industrial capitalism. If we consider different situations in which industrial workers have 'semi-proletarian' status because of their access to land, then the significance of this status will be determined by *how* it has been achieved, and by the particular path of industrial development in which it is embedded. As we have seen, the 'meanings' of small property among mining families in West Cornwall changed as the economy moved from one phase to another in the nineteenth century. This study has described and theorised about a very localised 'piece' of historical geography, yet, as Massey (1983b) has aptly put it: '[o]n the one hand, general laws are not unearthed empirically; on the other hand, one can do more with the unique than contemplate it'.

Notes

1 This essay is a greatly condensed version of Chapter 2 of the author's doctoral thesis (Rose, 1984). The suggestions and patience of the editors are much appreciated, and the contributions of all those, too numerous to name individually here, who commented on earlier versions of this work, are gratefully acknowledged.

2 Based on the Cornish folk song, 'Trelawny', Camborne Election Papers, 1885.

3 This somewhat simplified account of the life-lease system was pieced together from evidence to the *Select Committee on Town Holdings* hearings in West Cornwall (P.P. 1888, XXII). Rowe (1953) was also consulted.

4 A year previously, a tract entitled *The Bitter Cry of Outcast London: An Enquiry into the Condition of the Abject Poor* had been published by one Andrew Mearns of the London Congregational Union. As Keating (1976, 91) explains, it 'caused an immediate sensation . . . and provoked the writing of similar pamphlets and articles describing the "Bitter Cry" of cities throughout Britain'.

5 A crucial distinction should be noted between allotments and smallholdings, in terms of what could be achieved by access to the type of property involved in each case. During the debate over leasehold reform, and with reference to farm workers, Lord Balfour made the revealing comment that the two forms were 'entirely unrelated':

> A Smallholdings Bill aims at creating a peasant proprietary; an Allotments Bill aims at improving the position of the agricultural labourer while *leaving him in the position of an agricultural labourer* (emphasis in original) (quoted in Douglas 1976, 103).

This was no doubt one reason why allotments were eventually made much more widely available although legislation expanding access to smallholdings was never passed. For discussion of the failure of land reform legislation, see Douglas, 1976, 49–57; Offer, 1981, 352–6.

6 This phrase is borrowed from Dorothea Lange and Peter Taylor's photo-documentary record of the agricultural transformation of the American South in the 1930s, entitled *An American Exodus*.

7 These and subsequent employment figures were obtained from *Reports of*

H.M. Inspector of Mines, published annually from 1876 (PP. 1875, XVI) to 1913 (P.P. 1914, XLIII).

8 The phrase, 'fragment to survive', has been used with respect to this type of situation by Bradbury (1983). I am greatly indebted to Riva Krut for making me aware of the importance of this point. Hareven (1982), in a study of the relationships between industrial development, family structure and migration in a New England town populated largely by migrants from Quebec, has documented the importance of *two-way* social support networks between geographically fragmented kin.

9 The term 'labour reserve' is generally used in the Marxist literature to refer to a geographical area where subsistence activities, carried out through family-based labour, persist to some extent but are not able to fully support a family. At least one family member has to migrate to wage labour employment in capitalist industry or agriculture, but the wages thus obtained are not adequate to support the wage earner's family, which thus still needs the subsistence plot.

10 Indeed, in the western United States, the first labour union of hard rock miners was organised by emigrants from Cornwall in the 1870's, in a struggle against wage cuts in the 'company town' of Central City, Colorado (Wyman 1979). Moreover, Cornish mineworkers in the Transvaal were extremely militant in the early twentieth century over wages and working conditions (Burke and Richardson 1978) – although to point this out is in no way to condone the racially exclusionary tactics they used to prevent wage cuts.

• 6 •

Constituting class and gender: *A social history of the home, 1700–1901* • *PETER WILLIAMS*

Work and the workplace have dominated our conceptions of the ways social relations and institutions are constituted and reproduced. All else, it seems, has been regarded as secondary and as a reflection of the primary relations established through work. Certainly this situation has begun to change, not least through debates on gender and ethnicity, but it is clear we still have a long way to go. An underlying argument of this chapter is that it is essential to think beyond the workplace to other settings (or locales) where social interaction takes place and where social relations are composed and contextualised. There are clearly any number of these including the school, club and pub but there can be little doubt that the home must rank high amongst them and perhaps stands alongside the workplace as a key social setting. Elsewhere, both separately and together, Peter Saunders and I have argued the importance of the home as a crucial structuring medium with respect to the individual, the household and society (Saunders, 1984: Williams, 1986: Saunders and Williams, forthcoming) and the purpose of this chapter is to extend that work through a consideration of the home through history (1700–1901). The chapter is therefore primarily concerned with examining the ways in which both the physical setting and social roles of the home have changed over time and the significance these shifts have had for changing social relations in general and class, status and gender in particular. Given the possible scope of this subject matter it must be recognised that this is a preliminary survey. The chapter begins with a brief discussion on the salient themes and then proceeds via an historical examination of the home to develop an understanding of the constitutive roles of this arena. The chapter ends with a brief concluding summary.[1]

Social relations and the home

The home has both physical and social 'dimensions' In discussing the home one is not simply referring to the physical structure – the dwelling – be it flat or house but also to the social structure, the home, the human institution which may offer rest, peace, quiet, comfort, health and personal expression as Gilman (1903) refers to it in her seminal book on the home. The home, in short, is a 'locale' where the physical form of the dwelling, its external and internal design and contents both reflect social interactions and social forces and also condition and compose them, blending the 'spatial' and the 'social' into an indivisible whole.

As such a setting, the home is particularly crucial with respect to the establishment and development of people as individuals, the relations between individuals as members of households and families and the interaction with neighbours and the local community (Davidoff *et al.*, 1979). We are brought up in a home, spend a great deal of time within the home and develop our lives through the home as an enabling and constraining physical and social location. Moreover, as the primary setting for ourselves as individuals (in contrast to the workplace where such individuality is rarely to the fore), the home constitutes a key point of intersection between the individual and society (thus explaining in part the strong sentimental and emotional bonds between individual and home as epitomised in 'Home Sweet Home' and 'Home Is Where the Heart Is'). There is not room to develop these arguments in detail here but it is important to briefly sketch out the different ways in which the home impacts on social relations and thus why it is so important (see also Saunders and Williams, forthcoming). In giving some sense of the breadth and depth of its meaning it will also be possible to draw out and highlight a select number of themes which will be amplified upon through the chapter.

The home as a social and physical setting has a complex multi-dimensional character. Typically we think of the home as a physical structure which 'contains' the household and which, as a dwelling, provides a simple indicator of the status of its occupants. It is certainly much more than that, and of course, the notions of home as container and status symbol are much more complex, not least because of the constant intertwining of the social and the physical. The home as a physical structure is also a social structure and the two concepts are interrelated. The design of a dwelling conditions the activities which can take place within that dwelling but itself is a representation of conceptions of the social order. Thus the location and style of rooms, the imagery portrayed by the building, internal and external 'forward' and 'backward' regions of the home (Giddens, 1981) which sanction different types of interaction all act to extend the real meaning of the home. As a physical location in the landscape of a city, town or village, the home is also a social location acting to distinguish and demarcate the residents from others in the community. This process is carried further by the possessions contained within the structure and the ways they are displayed within the constraints posed by the physical form of the home.

The location of the home in the social and physical landscape influences access to public services, education, health and job opportunities. Through social networks (which themselves are influenced by propinquity) a whole range of opportunities can be opened up with massive intergenerational consequences. Indeed, pursuing this a little further the home as a possession, a physical commodity, may itself, through sale, have wealth effects which can substantially transform the prospects of its occupants (or through inheritance, the subsequent generation). Equally, the home consumes financial and human resources and is capable of disabling individuals and families as they seek to maintain the home in the face of its physical deterioration and the financial burdens it imposes.

These conceptions of the home are vitally important but in no sense do they add up to the totality. The home, in a variety of ways, penetrates deeply into the core of our social being. Our notions of privacy, freedom and choice are, for example, centred in part upon conceptions of the home as a location (physical and social) where these ideas may be exercised. The home is a private sphere and privacy can be exercised at home. There are few, if any, alternative arenas where this is so. The same is true regarding freedom and choice of action (albeit for some to quite limited degrees). Given these personal opportunities and the important symbolic qualities of the home there is here a significant stimulus to consumption and the acquisition of possessions. We are aided in this process by advertising and promotion which directs our attention to the virtues of a nice home and the acceptable standards of the day.

Just as the home is central to notions such as privacy and possessiveness so we can see that this can spill over into party and personal politics and a whole series of attitudes regarding behaviour and personal morality. Much of this is learnt in childhood, both in the home and crucially through the home. 'Would you do that in your own home' is a common rebuke to a child conveying a clear sense of what is regarded as an acceptable standard within one's personal domain. Party politics can be evaluated at many levels but one is certainly self interest. It is no coincidence that the reason politicians nervously circle around mortgage interest tax relief as an issue is because of its connection to the home and thus deep into the hearts and pockets of its owner-occupants.

Ownership is clearly very important (note how we distinguish 'private' housing from 'public' housing) but it is important not to lose sight of the fact that home 'is where the heart is' and this is not tenure specific (a point Government seemed to recognise in its council house sales adverts on TV which stated 'Turn your home into your house', i.e. the social institution into a physical commodity). While all households own rights to do what they will *within* the dwelling (within specified limits) it is apparent that the rights to do what they will *with* the dwelling have been hard fought for (and carefully promoted). Again this reveals the conjunction between the social and the physical since many have felt that the true exercise of freedom requires individual possession of the dwelling itself. Indeed, it is this distinction between the owners and non-owners that some are arguing marks out a key social change in Britain in the 1980s and one which has contributed substantially to the breakdown of class as a central social force (e.g. Saunders 1984). This remains a complex and contentious argument and one which requires substantial empirical examination.

Housing and class and indeed 'housing class' have become the subject of some interest (e.g. Pratt, 1982: Rex and Moore, 1967: Saunders, 1978 and 1984) but little of the debate so far proceeds substantially beyond the formal association of class position and housing tenure and in particular to the question of the home and social class and status. As already suggested, the home is a very obvious indicator of class positions and social status. Basic building types such as the terrace, semi-detached and detached houses, often allow for simple demarcation which, when further differentiated by location, amenities, contents and presentation, give firm clues as to the social origins and destinations of the occupants. While we may recognise this relationship we have done little to pin it down beyond the crude association with tenure itself. One central theme of the chapter will be an examination of the home and its class and status dimensions, the ways it acts to create, reinforce or indeed even to cross-cut these basic social processes.

Just as part of the task will be to explore how the home, class and status interact over time, so too will the chapter give attention to the questions of gender, women and the family. It is perhaps entirely predictable that these should also be key questions to explore with respect to the home. In popular perception the home is the woman's domain. Terms such as housewife and cleaning lady, the practice of women taking the husband's name, i.e. drawing identity from a male engaged in paid work, and the assumption in most social analysis and virtually all official documents that there is a head of the resident household and that normally the person concerned will be male are all part of the processes of demarcation which surround the home. The identification of women with home becomes particularly complete in the home journals:

> The home which is his the husband's paradise, is your handiwork, your refuge, your pride, your castle, your very very own, your actual self, a part of you inseparable. It is your heart and brain translated into the arrangement of daily life (as cited in Davison, 1978, 137–40).

As Stacey and Price (1981) and many others argue, women have only a place in the private domestic sphere while as Weinbaum and Bridges (1978) suggest, the housewife is central to understanding women's position in capitalist societies. However it can be argued that in no sense does a focus on that role entirely encapsulate the relations women are embedded in. Indeed such a focus denies their functions in paid work and is a particularly historic approach to a historically changing situation. However, although women's roles have changed substantially over time and space, their relationship to men has stood as a key component in this process. Not that patriarchy is unchanging, far from it, but rather patriarchal relations are a critical dimension, which in combination with capitalist social relations provide a basis for understanding the position of women in British society.

Following Hartman (1979), one can define patriarchy 'as a set of social relations between men, which have a material base, and which, though hierarchical, establish or create interdependence and solidarity among men and enable them to dominate women' (p. 11). Hartman argues that although the class structure ensures that some women occupy social positions over men, the basic pattern is one of male dominance. Furthermore, she states 'the material base upon which patriarchy rests lies most fundamentally in men's control over women's labour power' (loc. cit.). It is this argument which gives purchase on women in the home. The economic opportunities open to women are decidedly inferior to those of men and are maintained as such by men. Thus the segregation of the labour market, the promotion of the concept of a family wage (i.e. a man's wage capable of sustaining 'the family'), the sexual division of labour in the labour market and outside, and the pressure on women to marry to join an economic unit are all relations which are part of a patriarchal process. The form of that process and its historic evolution within the changing structure of capitalist society(ies) are essential to an understanding of the ways women are propelled into the home and the structures that reside there. Our argument then is that 'our society can best be understood once it is recognised that it is organised in capitalist and partriarchal ways' (Hartman, 1979, p. 2).

The sexual division of labour both within paid and unpaid work has given women specific 'responsibilities' and most particularly those associated with the home and child-rearing. Men's mastery over women has ensured that marriage, the act of taking wives (and husbands) and the formal assumption of the rights and obligations that pertain to this, has sustained its importance throughout history although its precise form has varied. The comment made by a South Australian Landowner in 1843 'a wife, if a good one, is a cheap stock and maybe a great saving where a man has all to manage' (cited in Richards, 1974 p. 339) is still relevant today. Moreover it is this patriarchal relation set, in our case, within capitalist social relations that explains the way women have been educated for a role in the home; how they have assumed responsibility for children no longer needed in production, and how the whole process operates whereby women as housewives have been placed upon a pedestal (Hunt, 1980; Sokoloff, 1980).

In a number of ways the family has stood at the centre of capitalist society. Much of our discussion of the home and women impinges upon developments around the family. It has shifted from being a directly productive and reproductive unit of society to one largely concerned with reproduction, these changes paralleling a similar shift in the nature of the home. 'The modern family is a transformation of the domestic community; robbed of its productive functions, it remains *the place* where labour power is produced and reproduced' (Meillassoux, 1975 p. 214). The home is, of course, much more than a simple locale for the reproduction of labour power though this is one important role. Current concerns with the family – its apparent fragility, rising levels of divorce, youth violence and abuse – can be seen as expressions of a continuing debate about the role and future of this social unit. In the late 19th century, under the impact of rapid urbanisation and industrialisation, the family was seen as a haven, an escape from disorder and it was here, to an environment created by women for men, that the bread-winner retreated each day to relax and restore himself for the new day's labour. The family, then as now, was seen as vitally important – indeed for some (including W. Reich) the family was seen as the hearth, the central location where global social relations were produced and reproduced. There is a discernible trend in much recent writing to exaggerate the centrality of the family as a necessary unit of capitalism per se (not least because it ignores the household as the basic social unit around which life is organised). This functionalist line of argument which renders the family as simply a container for the reproduction of the relations of production is inadequate as work on the sexual division of labour reveals. Certainly those 'functions' may exist but much more is involved and families are not inevitably reproduced.

This point raises a further important issue, that of the reproduction of social relations. Much social analysis has been dogged by functionalist argument stressing the inevitability of X or Y. As we expand our conception of production and reproduction and acknowledge the salience of relations outside of the workplace so we need to recognise that our society does not reproduce itself as some automatic process but rather as a historically contingent process marked by conflict and contradiction. Lefebvre (1976) in his book *The Survival of Capitalism* (subtitled Reproduction of the Relations of Production) argues as follows:

There can be no reproduction of social relations either by simple inertia or by tacit renewal. Reproduction does not occur without undergoing changes. This excludes both the idea of an automatic reproductive process internal to the constituted mode of production (system) and that of the immediate efficacy of a generative 'nucleus'. The contradictions themselves re-produce, and not without changes. Former relations may degenerate or dissolve – e.g., the town, the natural and nature, the nation, everyday poverty, the family, 'culture', the commodity, 'the world of signs'. Others are constituted in such a way that there is *production* of social relations within the reproduction, e.g., the urban, the possibilities of the everyday, the differential. These new relations emerge from within those which are dissolving: they first appear as the negation of the latter, as the destroyers of the antecedents and conditions which hold them back (1976 pp. 90–1).

In exploring the salience of the home we do have to recognise the weaknesses of modes of theorisation and research which have effectively written such arenas out of the agenda. Fortunately it is increasingly recognised that we must extend analysis beyond production and more than that we must overcome the dualism between production and reproduction. In doing so we are of course leading ourselves into an extremely complex explanatory framework.

This introductory section has been concerned with arguing the importance of the home as a key constitutive element in a range of social relations. Moreover, it has indicated a concern to give particular attention to questions of class and status, gender, women and the family in the historical account which follows. In addition to these particular themes it is important to signpost three other concerns which will re-arise. The first is the intersection between production and reproduction, workplace and home; the second is the ways in which changes in social relations in general are reflected by and reinforced through changes in the home; and finally as a specific illustration of this process the growth of home ownership and its salience with regard to individualism and privatism.

A social history of the home

In developing a historical account of the home one is confronted by the paucity of material in some areas (e.g. gender and class relations and more generally on the pre-industrial home). Three existing accounts of housing (Burnett, 1978; Daunton, 1983 and Muthesius, 1982) provide substantial assistance and these, in conjunction with the important paper by MacKenzie and Rose (1983), provide a key basis for the account presented here. An additional and common problem relates to how to divide the period 1700 to 1901 into sensible historical eras. Historians divide on whether 1780 or 1815 provides a sensible starting point for discussions regarding industrial Britain. In this chapter, 1815 has been taken as a turning point because by then many of the tendencies apparent since 1780 or before are consolidating and, since the whole account is preliminary, it made sense to focus on developed rather than developing categories and situations. In the sections that follow, therefore, there is a discussion of the pre-industrial home roughly coinciding with the period 1700–1815 followed by the section on the Victorian home which takes the reader over the period 1816–1901.

The pre-industrial home, 1700–1815

An assessment of the nature of the pre-industrial home is a complex task. As already noted, there are considerable gaps in our knowledge and because we are crossing against the general direction of analyses (which emphasise the family, production, etc. rather than a composite, the home) we must often attempt to reinterpret fragmentary evidence. In addition, existing research shows the enormous variety of social forms existing across the British or English landscape. In an attempt to restrict our margins of error we will give most attention to the urban household in the period 1700–80. That is our focus is the home in the late pre-industrial period and as research shows many of the changes in society, observable in acute form in the industrial period proper, are already manifest. In some senses therefore we are discussing a transitional period.

The changing context

In 1700, England was dominantly a rural society with most of its population living in the countryside and employed in agriculture. Over three-quarters of the five and a half million people in England lived in rural areas. But, as Clark and Slack (1976) note 'towns were the essential cogs in the machinery of rural society, providing organization, articulation and diversity'. These towns ranged in size from London, with a population of half a million, through the important centres of

Bristol, Exeter, Newcastle, Norwich and York, all of which were in the range of 10 000 to 30 000 inhabitants, to the myriad of medium and small country towns and villages surviving from the disrupted economy of the late Tudor and early Stuart period. In total, there were about 600 towns with populations of more than 400 to 500 inhabitants (Chalkin, 1974). Though England was not an urban nation in 1700, the pattern of an urbanised society was beginning to take shape and over the eighteenth century these developments proceeded apace. A series of centres emerged over this period which were significantly different from the market and trading towns which dominated the urban hierarchy and served England's agricultural economy. These 'new towns' included Halifax and Manchester which developed as industrial centres, Chatham and Portsmouth as dockyards and Bath and Tunbridge Wells as spa towns for the emergent leisured classes. Amongst the 'industrialising' towns a division of labour was increasingly apparent with centres specialising in textiles, hardware, brewing, shipbuilding, paper-making and other activities. As a consequence of these developments the urban system became increasingly diversified with some towns engaged in distribution and others in production while, because of their growing population, a number of towns began to develop specialised services to meet the needs of their own population. By 1820, there were 15 centres with populations greater than 25 000 inhabitants. Liverpool, Manchester and Birmingham which between them had fewer than 20 000 inhabitants in 1700 had populations of 22 000, 19 839 and 23 688 respectively in the 1750s and together totalled over 400 000 people in 1820. As Chalkin comments (ibid., p. 17, p. 19):

> Nearly the whole century appears to have been a period of commercial development. The trade in agricultural and manufactured products and colonial imports was increasing. Town and village retail shops were spreading. Merchants, wholesales and other middlemen 'increased in numbers, efficiency and degree of specialization'. Greater agricultural output increased the need to process it, such as millers, malters, brewers and tanners, the makers and menders of agricultural equipment, dealers and carriers. Many though not all of these people lived in the towns. Finally, the increased wealth of the middle classes helped the development of a small leisured class, which tended to congregate in regional centres. Altogether the possible contributions to growing urban commercial prosperity were numerous.

The development of towns, the expansion of industry and commerce, transport and banking all contributed to an expanded division of labour and increasing specialisation. Consumption patterns too were changing, reflecting in part the rising wealth of the emergent middling classes and an overall increase in real wages. McKendrick (1982, p. 10) has argued that there was 'a consumer revolution in eighteenth-century England'. He suggests that a substantial increase in the number of households with incomes between £50 and £400 per annum made a major contribution to this revolution. With the rich leading the way by rebuilding mansions and commissioning new furniture from Sheraton and Chippendale, 'the middle ranks spent more frenziedly than ever before, and in imitation of them the rest of society joined in as best they might' (ibid., p. 11). Though consumption was clearly restricted for many it is apparent from the evidence assembled (Burnett, 1969; McKendrick, Brewer and Plumb, 1982; Porter, 1982) that consumption expanded across a society as a whole and was increasingly recognised as a 'motor of production' as well as a force which undermined the established social structure. Thus as McKendrick notes (ibid., p. 32):

> it was not for nothing that the first industries to blossom in the Industrial Revolution were more characteristically to be found in the consumer sector than in the heavy industrial sector. . . . The names of those who made them are so famous that it sometimes concealed how modest were the consumer objects they made: Joseph Bramah and locks, Josiah Wedgewood and pots, Mathew Boulton and buckles and buttons, the Pilkingtons and glass, not to mention the great cotton magnates who built their fortunes on the clothes and underclothes of our Georgian predecessors.

Women and the family and the home

It is apparent from earlier comment on the nature of England in the eighteenth century that it is a period in which market exchange increasingly penetrates social life. Wage-labour was widespread and cleavages around market position and the capacity to pay were becoming more important than custom and tradition (Briggs, 1974; Langton, 1975; Porter, 1982). These processes of separation are closely observable in the home and were reinforced through the household.

Malcolmson (1981) estimates that the 'labouring classes' made up at least 80 per cent of the population in eighteenth century England and that 'no more than five per cent (and probably a little less) of the population were gentlemen, professional men and their ladies, the members of the governing class' (ibid., 19). However, given our focus on urban populations it is likely that we are dealing with that part of society which is most differentiated and in subsequent discussion we attempt to distinguish the varied strata of urban life. Though England was undergoing substantial change in this century it is apparent that, 'the household was the central unit of production. . . . The household was not merely a unit of consumption in which its members spent money that was earned elsewhere: an individual's actual work was normally done, not outside the household, but as part of the household's own productive economy' (ibid., p. 23).

This focus on the household and the intimacies it can imply should not distract us from the very real and important changes going on around it. As Stone (1977) indicates, the seventeenth and eighteenth centuries were periods in which family structures changed significantly. The influence of kinship and community declined and that of the nuclear family increased. Such changes reflected the erosion of the power of landowners and the bonds to the land, the growing importance of state regulation and assistance and a concomitant decline of the community and voluntary relief, and to quote Stone 'the missionary success of Protestantism, especially among the gentry and urban bourgeoisie, both in sanctifying holy matrimony and in making the family serve as a partial substitute for the parish' (ibid., p. 94). The impact of enclosure, the rise of towns and a market economy, the changing division of labour, the erosion of rights and obligations by the wage contract and a growth of 'possessive individualism' all contributed to this process of social reconstruction.

For women and the family the eighteenth century saw further development of patriarchal relations, privatisation and individualism. According to Stone 'the enhancement of the importance of the conjugal family and the household relative to the kinship and clientage at the upper levels of society was accompanied by a positive reinforcement of the despotic authority of husband and father – that is to say, of patriarchy,' (ibid., p. 109). During the seventeenth century, men gained control over women's property thus gathering to themselves assets of considerable value in a market economy. Because the death of a spouse was commonplace (25–30 per cent of all marriages were broken by death in the first 15 years) women were often owners of substantial property. Similarly remarriage was very common and by these means men could 'regain' control. Both the Church and the State assisted this process of creating a society in which women's deference to men was expected and 'normal'.

During the eighteenth century women's rights were more formally protected and promoted in an era of 'affective individualism' and Stone argues the period saw trends towards greater freedom for children and more equal partnerships between men and women. While he clearly demonstrates the rise of individualism it is less apparent that women were freed in the process. Indeed, it seems more likely that a process of subordination operated amongst the upper and upper-middle classes though the situation was less clear amongst the petite bourgeoisie and the working classes. As both he and Malcolmson demonstrate, the very difficulties of working-class existence in early modern England were such that all members of the family were workers and in some respects equal for that. Sturt (1912) commented 'A kind of dogged comradeship – I can find no better word for it – is what commonly unites the labouring man and his wife; they are partners and equals running their impecunious affairs by mutual help'. Indeed, women are not only central to the household's productive activities but also carried all the burdens of extended reproduction. Not surprisingly women played a leading role in the food riots which took place through the century. However, though the distribution of the burdens of life was wide, the power of men was legitimated through the State and the Church and it seems clear that patriarchal relations were reinforced at all levels of society. Stone comments (ibid., p. 247):

> Wives of the middle and upper ranks of society increasingly became idle drones. They turned household management over to stewards . . . (and quoting Marietta Grey) ladies *were* dismissed from the dairy, the confectionary, the store room, the still room, the poultry yard, the kitchen garden and the orchard.

Moreover, the decline of kin and the rise of the conjugal family was widespread eroding the supporting networks available to women leaving them more fully under the sway of men. Working-class women had to work to survive but it was survival in a dominantly male world. Women were involved in work of all kinds in the eighteenth century and, because of the structure of craft production this might mean a woman 'controlled' a household which included kin, servants and employees. In those circumstances women played an important role (see Middleton, 1981). Towards the end of the century, and more sharply in the nineteenth century, opportunities for women begin to narrow as the structure of both the economy and society becomes more stratified (Richards, 1974).

The subjugation of women closely relates to changes in the form and structure of the family. Despite popular beliefs to the contrary, the family during this period generally consisted of five or six people, comprising two adults and three or four children. Infant mortality and rudimentary contraception ensured that large families were rare. Moreover, as research by Laslett (1972) has shown, many households consisted of a single family. The reasons for this arc simple. Most adults died in their forties or fifties so only a minority lived to have grandchildren. Many children also lost their parents with the consequence that family life in the eighteenth century was really quite unstable. Stone argues that parent–child relations underwent a remarkable change between 1660–1800. He discusses in detail what he terms 'the maternal, child oriented, affectionate and permissive mode which came to prevail among the upper ranks of the bourgeoisie'. With growing economic prosperity, higher levels of mobility and the assertion of the family, the wife and children assumed considerable importance both as potential heirs but also as actors in the processes of social demarcation and differentiation. Education, manners, leisure all assumed more importance and thus more time had to be spent in ensuring these functions were accomplished.

Housing and the home

The pre-industrial dwelling played a crucial role in both production and reproduction, though the way this was balanced between these two arenas in a particular home was largely contingent upon the social status of the occupants. The homes of the upper classes were increasingly centres of social reproduction, isolated from the realities of daily production whilst for the working classes the two functions merged into an inseparable totality. For the middling classes a very mixed pattern pertained (see Morris, 1983).

As already noted, the eighteenth century was notable for a consumer revolution led by the upper classes. Their houses, life style and all related trappings underwent substantial transformations. As production became more ordered and organised they were able to physically distance themselves from it and, through the profits gained, to socially distinguish themselves as the leisured class (Flandrin, 1979). This can be well illustrated by a consideration of house design, hygiene and personal habits. Unlike homes of the sixteenth and seventeenth centuries (Hoskins, 1963) the houses' interiors were extensively divided with access being provided by corridors. Stone (1977) argues that the three most significant physical symbols of change are the ha-ha, the corridor and the dumb waiter. Ignoring the ha-ha or sunken ditch, a device used on country estates to maintain the illusion of open parkland yet keep stock away from the house, Stone's arguments are apposite to our present concerns. He comments (ibid., pp. 245–246):

> The corridor, which was a feature of all new houses in the eighteenth century and was progressively added to older buildings made a major contribution to the rise of physical privacy by removing the ever-present and inhibiting threat of a stranger walking through one's bedroom to reach his own room. Four walls and a door are a better protection of privacy than the curtains of a four-poster. The dumb waiter, used in the small private dining rooms, made possible the intimate family meal time conversation, not only away from the crowd of servants in the great hall, but also free from the surveillance of waiters serving at the table.

Concepts of privacy, of personal space and an awareness of the body became more acute and for the upper classes at least 'the modern family began to achieve its independence' (Flandrin, 1979, p. 93). The physical structures reflected and reinforced this process.

Just as the internal structure changed so too did notions of hygiene and personal habits. Piped water within dwellings, baths and lavatories only slowly made their entrance through the century and 'the almost total ignorance of both personal and public hygiene meant that contaminated food and water was a constant hazard' (Stone, 1977, p. 62; Gauldie, 1974). Recognition of social distinctions, a diminished dependence upon the locality and community, all contributed to concern with notions of quality, status and class. An essential aspect of this process was, to quote Stone (ibid., p. 412):

> An increasing privatization of one's body, its fluids and odours. The substitution of forks for fingers in eating, the supply by the host of separate plates and utensils for each course, the substitution of handkerchiefs for fingers or cloths for nose-blowing, the wearing of night clothes, the introduction of washbasins, portable baths – tubs and soap, the substitution of wigs for lice-ridden natural hair are all symptoms of the same evolution.

Progress was admittedly slow. There was no bathroom in Buckingham Palace in 1837 and although the washing of hands and faces became relatively commonplace the washing of bodies only really become widespread towards the middle end of the nineteenth century (see Wright, 1966). Despite the growing prosperity of the middling ranks in the eighteenth century it would seem that relatively few were able to enjoy the leisured life of the upper classes and their enormous consumption of consumer durables, though as McKendrick, Brewer and Plumb (1982), Davidoff and Hall (1983) and others make clear their purchasing power was not inconsiderable. Their houses continued to function both as home and workplace and only the more prosperous of this class could afford a suburban home separate from work (though we should note here the generational process by which a father might move out and a son take over the joint dwelling/workplace (see Morris 1979 and 1983). Housing, it seems, was expensive – Burnett estimates it cost £700 for a substantial new house in London (1969, p. 176) while in provincial cities a price of between £300–500 would have been more common (Chalkin, 1974). Despite this, the internal organisation of the home began to become more sharply defined with numerous rooms set aside for specific purposes – the front parlour, back parlour, dining room, kitchen and, increasingly in urban settings, the lavatory or 'needful edifice' as it was sometimes referred to. This would typically be in the garden.

As already noted we can observe the emergence of a much more precisely defined nuclear family during this period. For those engaged in trade, commerce and the professions this meant a growing tendency to remove apprentices, assistants and clerks from the premises, that is from the home as well as the workplace (Vance, 1967; Langton, 1975). As Stone comments (1977, p. 170):

> Apprentices and unpaid wage labourers were increasingly removed from the households of their masters. As a result paternal control of employers over their adolescent labour force declined, and the non-monetary components of rewards – free food and free lodging – were replaced by wages in money. This in turn signified the cultural erosion of paternalism in the relations of employers and employees, and the increasing isolation of the domestic nuclear household.

Mumford's account of *The City in History* develops this point further when he suggests that the separation of home from work leads to the creation of buildings and areas with specific purposes and ultimately to all the problems of connecting these in space. Thus he comments (1961, p. 437):

> the three functions of producing, selling and consuming were now separated in three different institutions, three different sets of buildings, three distinct parts of the city. Transportation to and from the place of work was first of all a privilege of the rich merchants in big cities: it was only in the nineteenth century that it filtered down to the other classes in the city, and instead of being a privilege, became a grievous burden.

Moreover, he goes on to argue (ibid., p. 438) that this led to:

> the household's becoming exclusively a consumers organization, the housewife lost her touch with the affairs of the outside world: she became either a specialist in domesticity, or a specialist in sex, something of a drudge, something of a courtesan, more often perhaps a little of both. Therewith 'the private house' comes into existence: private from business, and spatially separated from any visible means of support.

While Mumford makes the mistake of dismissing the 'private' world as unimportant, he valuably conveys the rising sense of privacy and the impact that it had on personal relations – including sexuality. For the more affluent members of the middling ranks these changes began to gather pace through the mid- to late eighteenth century. For its lowlier members, e.g. for many shopkeepers and tradesmen, it came much later and many would continue to live in small houses with workshops and premises attached. A number of London's squares had been built by the mid-1750s presenting as Mumford acutely notes a 'visual openness and social privacy. Class barriers now formed the invisible ha-ha' (ibid., p. 454). Moreover, the uniformity of such squares concealed from view the tensions and differences between the occupants – the emergent class solidarity found physical expression (Briggs, 1974).

The sense of change and development which derives from this consideration of the homes of the upper and middle 'classes', is also repeated with respect to the urban working classes. The growth of towns, the changing basis of production – both agricultural and industrial, meant that although earnings may have been rising, the demand for accommodation was such that rents consumed a large proportion of wages. Life continued to be very precarious for most workers though some were able to exploit the rising demand for goods and services and thus escape the miseries of the 'lower orders'. Burnett (1974, 1978) reminds us that great care must be exercised in making generalisations about the life of eighteenth-century workers since there was considerable variation between towns (and between town and country) and there is still considerable debate as to the distribution of the profits from industrialisation. Notwithstanding these issues, the evidence does suggest that, in general, working people led lives of extreme harshness. Their homes functioned as places to work, sleep, store equipment and keep animals. Most families were only able to afford the rent of one or two rooms and possession of a whole house was a rarity. Moreover, even when occupying these small spaces, many families took in lodgers so that ten or more persons might be found in one room (Gauldie, 1974). Conditions were to say the least appalling.

The home most clearly functioned as a workplace. Burnett comments (1968, p. 80) 'children from the age of 4 or 5 were commonly employed in noisome sweated trades which used the home as a miniature workshop'. Although new construction during the eighteenth century provided slightly larger dwellings (Chalkin, 1974; Porter, 1982) they still normally 'consisted of "three boxes" placed on top of each other used respectively for living, sleeping and working, with a cellar' (Chapman, 1971, p. 139) though the '2-up-2-down' became more commonplace by the turn of the century (selling for about £150 each). All members of the household above a minimal age engaged in work, some in the home, the others at nearby places of employment. Male domination of women had to be tempered by the very obvious reliance upon the latter's earnings – even though women were paid only a fraction of what men earned. Though raw unskilled labour continued to migrate to the towns it would seem that the general level of health and impoverishment of the working population posed problems not simply through the spread of infection, and the encroachment of hovels onto any open space but also through the costs of relief, the inadequate disposal of refuse, waste and even bodies, social unrest and the growing tensions between the lot of the working person and the leisured classes. Much of this adversity struck at the new urban élites and acted as a considerable inducement to engage in town improvements and break from the ministrations of the landed aristocracy (Morris, 1983).

The commodity status of housing, even of the rudimentary forms constructed during this period, is well demonstrated by work such as that of Chalkin (1974). Housing was a source of considerable profit for ground landlords, builders and rentiers (Jackson, 1980; Morris, 1979) and industrialists increasingly withdrew from direct housing provision (again indicating the growing separation of work and home). As the form and internal design changed, most obviously for the wealthy classes but also in terms of back to backs and other urban 'innovations' so too did the extent to which houses provided usable space. The production of consumer durables that took place found a home in these dwellings as households gathered around themselves more and more possessions. While the wealthy were able to indulge to extremes, it is apparent from wills and other records that even some working households increased their consumption and that the size and structure of the dwelling was an important adjunct to this process (Porter, 1982).

Perhaps above all else, this brief sketch of the eighteenth century conveys a sense of social change, of diversity and conflict. The changing social and economic structure of England found expression in the form, use and location of the dwelling and the home. Status distinctions reflecting increasingly divergent life paths are expressed in buildings, furnishings and diet. They also find form in the relations between men and women and parents and children. Both women and children it seems were, in varying degrees reflecting their social position, or rather that of their husbands and fathers, moving away from the sphere of production as formally constituted. Far from destroying the privatised nuclear family capitalism seemed at this point to be creating it and the home was becoming an increasingly potent force in the process of social demarcation.

The home in Victorian England

Context

In the nineteenth century the pace of change increased substantially. In 1801, England still had many characteristics of a rural society and although towns were of importance only a small proportion of society could be classified as urban. Within a half a century, by 1851, 54 per cent of the population were living in urban areas. There were 10 centres with populations greater than 200 000 and a further 141 with more than 20 000 people. Towns expanded through infill and suburban development with little co-ordination or planning with consequent effects on health, congestion and an array of what have come to be termed 'social problems'. The individual was paramount and employers simply advertised for workers with little or no consideration as to how they would be housed and certainly no thought for the impacts their mass recruitment would have upon the rural areas that supplied the workers (Thomis, 1976). Moreover, as Thomis comments (ibid., p. 23):

> What people failed to realise, through no fault of their own, was the result of these changes – that these individual achievements were adding up to something that would be later identified as a revolution within society of perhaps unparalleled importance.

Certainly when we consider something as specific as the home this would seem to be so. Its form and content were irreversibly changed by the Industrial Revolution, and indeed many of our current perceptions of the home, property and the family were forged in this era.

Women, family and the home

Stone (1977) argues that from about 1770 onwards the development of the family was marked by a strong revival of moral reform, paternal authority and sexual repression. He suggests that this was one response to the tensions arising out of rapid social and economic change. For middle-class women their identity was submerged within the family – which itself because of improved standards of health was not enlarged through the survival of more children beyond infancy and adults beyond the age of fifty. Over the nineteenth century, middle-class women experienced a gradual erosion of their roles and an increasing subjugation to men, the family and the home. Their productive capacities were increasingly denied through the employment of servants, the creation of a genteel life style and the isolation of the dwelling as a private realm. Women were delegated managerial responsibilities for the home and became consumers rather than producers.

Burnett (1978, p. 95) suggests that 'this new class was the most family conscious and home-centred generation to have emerged in English history'. Certainly the evidence supports such a view and a consideration of the context, of a developing mode of production and class structure, provides us with ample explanation for this behaviour. Thus men, whose positions in the formal sphere of production were constantly changing (and being undermined), can be seen to have found solace in the creation of a private sphere in which they exercised control. Male superiority and the obedience of women and children was one aspect of this process. For women, it was a period in which a highly structured set of expectations and mores evolved regarding an appropriate mode of life. Women, or rather 'ladies', did not work.[2] Instead they were to seek a 'prudent marriage' the prime purpose of which was to have children.

Many accounts of change in the eighteenth and nineteenth centuries ennoble the pre-industrial family and mourn its destruction by the industrial revolution. However, we would argue that, rather than being destroyed, the family was reformed and restructured reflecting the shifting relations between genders and age groups.[3] Allowing for all the problems of the selectivity of historical records and the dominantly male middle-class interpretations of what remains, there can be little doubt that middle-class women's lives changed substantially over the period 1780–1901. This is not to suggest that the process of change was even, for clearly it was not, but at a general level, substantial change is apparent. It took a number of forms. First, there are those changes associated with the transformation of the home and the family which we will discuss later. Production was withdrawn from the home and women were *given* more time to prepare themselves for the pleasure of others. Thus we find a dramatic transformation in questions surrounding the education of women. Education not only had to fulfill its functions for a particular class but also for gender (Ball, 1979; Bryant, 1979; Davin, 1979). Girls were sent to small schools where they were instructed in the 'necessary skills' such as art, sewing, music, deportment, manners and social etiquette. The domestic ideal required that women devote themselves to their men creating an untroubled environment full of happiness and joy in which men could relax after a day in the outside world (Calder, 1977; Stacey and Price, 1981). As Ruskin commented (1865):

> This is the true nature of the home – it is the place of Peace; the shelter, not only from all injury, but from all terror, doubt and division. In so far as it is not this, it is not home; so far as the anxieties of the outer life penetrate into it, and the inconsistently minded, unloved, or hostile society of the outer world is allowed by either husband or wife to cross the threshold it ceases to be home; it is then only a part of that outer world which you have roofed over and lighted a fire in.

Women were educated to maintain this refuge. However, while it is clear that early in the century many women became wives with little or no knowledge of managing a haven of peace, by mid-century there had been a massive outpouring of guides and manuals on domestic management. Certainly the tasks were different than those of the nineteenth century housewife but the demands were still considerable. Thus in books such as Mrs Beeton's *Book of Household Management*, Mrs Parke's *Domestic Duties, or Instruction to Young Married Ladies* or Mr Luckcocks *The English Wife, a Manual of Home Duties* instruction was given in the most detailed way as to their responsibilities and the best ways to 'run a home'.[4] As consideration of these books reveals, domestic life was very complex bounded by endless rituals and strict formulations as to correct behaviour. The wife negotiated this social maze for the family as a whole. But despite all this the middle-class woman is projected as a non-working wife. Clearly our definition of work must be reconsidered!

Of course many middle-class women were not destined to be wives and/or mothers. Many women became companions, governesses while others through widowhood became managers in their own right. Such roles were perhaps understandable to the Victorian male but in general women were excluded from most spheres of work and advanced education (Bryant, 1979). Throughout the nineteenth century middle-class women engaged in campaigns to break these practices (Stacey and Price, 1981). Ironically because middle-class women were closeted in the home so early in the century they also had time to read and learn about the inequities of their own existence. As a consequence, it was they who fought for access to the professions and higher education, recognising the contradictions between individualism and familism.

Related to the form and content of education and the image of women as high priestesses of the temple 'home' were several other important concerns. Control over their own lives became increasingly distant from them. Thus women lost control over childbirth – this was passed over to male professionals and hospitals – and the whole process became technologised. This process took its most complete form in the 'image of the perfect lady' through which, to cite Duffin (1978, p. 26), women were rendered:

> progressively more and more useless. It was her complete uselessness which led to the belief that she was incapable and ultimately disabled such that she must be protected and prohibited from serious participation in society.

Increasingly women were viewed as 'weak, delicate and perpetually prone to illness' – with middle-class women 'pure but sick' and working-class women 'contaminated and sickening' (Duffin, ibid.). This view legitimated the way society restricted middle-class women to the private sphere. They needed rest and protection. As Duffin demonstrates a whole range of medical arguments built up around this process, apparently justifying Victorian attitudes to women. Exercise was discouraged and heavy restricting clothing was to be worn. Moreover the repression of sexuality evident in Victorian England then became the grounds upon which most doctors diagnosed ill women. 'Unnatural sexual desires' were seen to lead to insanity, epilepsy and amnesia and at root the woman's reproductive system was seen as the cause of all her illness. As a consequence a whole range of operations developed including clitoridectomy and ovariotomy which would apparently end such problems. In an analysis of similar processes in the USA, Barker-Benfield (1976) in an appropriately titled article 'The Spermatic Economy' relates these concerns to the contradictions and conflicts surrounding men, and in particular their independent existence in the market place reliant upon their own skills and capacities and yet their absolute reliance upon women in the home. The gradual possession of women's bodies by men was seen to be one way in which men could ultimately regain control of this private and utterly repressed sphere.

The disappearance of women from public life included their removal from local politics and the consequent displacement into good works and charity, and the erection of laws which passed all a woman's possessions on marriage to her husband. Sachs and Wilson (1978) argue that the reforms which came about in 1882 were possible because the older forms of wealth, i.e. land and houses, which many women brought with them to marriage were no longer so significant in the late nineteenth century:

> The growth of limited liability companies, creating new forms of economic power divorced from the ownership of the land . . . made these reforms possible. They relegated everything to do with the home to the private domestic sphere. Since wealth was no longer land-based it need no longer be family based, and the merging of a wife's legal being with that of her husband was no longer necessary (Stacey and Price, 1981, pp. 58–9).

As might be expected, for many women marriage was only a convenience, providing shelter and security but little more. The constraints of social practice and law meant divorce was not a practical proposition. Before 1857 divorce was by a private act of Parliament, obviously restricting it to only the wealthiest people in society. Though the 1857 Matrimonial Causes Act opened the way to middle-class divorce it was not until the mid-twentieth century that the process became a realistic possibility for most people. The blatant suppression of women's rights alongside the liberal treatment meted out to men, most notably with respect to pre-marital or extra-marital sexual relations, is a further affirmation of the woman's role in the home and the absolute attachment made between the home and women.

When we turn to the family similar processes of control and repression can be observed. Thus Calder comments (1977, 42–3):

> It was assumed that wife and children would conform to a man's expectation to return to a home after his day's work, or other activities, that was a well-ordered refuge from the world of friction and fear. If children were present, and very often they were neither seen nor heard as far as their parents were concerned but were left entirely to the care of nurses and nannies, they were expected to refrain from intruding their personalities on the parental harmony. In fact one of the striking features of Victorian attitudes to children is a distinct unease at the idea that children have, or should have individual personalities.

For the middle class, children and the family were at the centre of existence. Families were 'expected' to be large and only later in the century did social and economic pressures bring about reductions in family size. Though boys were treated with some liberality, in general strict codes of behaviour and discipline were enforced, at least as far as a system in which the relationship between parent and child was mediated through servants, governesses and tutors could allow. Children were encouraged to become adults, but until they established their own families and homes they remained firmly within parental control. In that way the family, like the home, could act as a prison. Moreover the family was sanctified as a private domain, beyond the state and the sole responsibility of parents and especially the father. The family worked for itself against the world. Children were successors to the achievements and failures of that family. Their place in life was largely derived out of the family and in that sense it was a crucial element in class structuring. Alliances and marriages between families created stability, the training of children created heirs and successors. In a world of uncertainty and change little wonder the family was so important. Unfettered, the family could provide the springboard to success. Consequently suggestions that the state might interfere in its functioning brought shocked reaction. Cooke Taylor (1842) comments:

> The family is the unit upon which a constitutional government has been raised

which is the admiration and envy of mankind. Hitherto, whatever else the laws touched they have not dared invade this sacred precinct; and the husband and wife returning home from whatever occupation or harassing engagements, have their found *their* dominion, *their* repose, *their* compensation. . . . There has been a sanctity about this . . . home life which even the vilest law acknowledged and the rashest law protected.

This account of middle-class life is obviously generalised. It gives little sense of the complexity of this class and its fragmentation into a whole series of sub-classes, only partly captured by the terms upper, middle and lower middle class. Nor does it convey the dynamic transformations occurring within the class structure with households being propelled up and down an intricate social ladder. Burnett (1969, 232) suggests 'there was always more near the bottom of the class than near the top, more who fell back into manual labour than who penetrated into the privileged ranks of gentry'. In this sense the apparent stability of the Victorian family was misleading. Fortunes were made and lost and it was common enough for relatively wealthy families to fall on 'hard times' and find themselves changing residence, social circles and expectations. The dress maker, pianoforte teacher and the private schoolmistress were all occupations which genteel women might find themselves in should their fortunes change and, instead of residing amongst the affluent classes, they must now make their homes amongst the artisans. This brief comment indicates the difficulties of establishing firm boundaries between the classes. Given we have adopted a relational view of class and one which sees class as an actively constituted process it is little wonder such problems arise.

Let us now turn to consider working-class women and their families. At best estimate the working classes constituted 80 per cent of the population in 1851 with approximately an eighth of the households being categorised as being in the skilled labour class, half as less skilled and the remaining group, agricultural and unskilled. Once again we can only offer a short account of their situation.

The contrasts between the 'typical' middle-class home and working-class home are acute. Working-class women often engaged in paid work in addition to all their duties in the home. In 1851 there were more than a million domestic servants (mainly women) and this was twice the number of women and girls employed in all the textile trades. Even in 1914, domestic service still formed the largest occupational group. Women worked in a whole variety of spheres, for example metal trades, agriculture – especially picking and planting – retailing and a wide array of service industries in addition to domestic service (Burnett, 1974). Until 1887 women worked underground in the mines (John, 1979). The tasks women workers performed were poorly paid and often the hours were long. In some trades their spouses and children would work in the same place so that in many senses, in the early industrial revolution, the family was simply transposed from the home (workshop) to the factory. This allowed men to retain close control of their families (and the employer over the entire family). However, as forms of production changed, separation became more likely, not least because over time, occupations became stratified on gender lines with men dominating the manufacturing processes. Despite the low status of women's work, their wages were an essential part of the family economy and the independence and authority of the male breadwinner was in certain respects undermined in this process. According to Stacey and Price (1981) working-class men sought to remove women from the labour market partly as a consequence of their own diminished self-esteem but also because of competition. Stacey and Price comment (ibid., pp. 36–7):

> The workers themselves looked back to a 'golden age' when women and children worked in the home under the authority of husband and father. . . . Many working men not surprisingly resented their loss of authority, fearing a threat to their masculinity. In this context the belief gained ground that a man's wage should be sufficient for the whole family, that women should not go out to work. The factory system was attacked for breaking up home production, for disrupting the rhythm of home and work, and for substituting the overseer's authority for that of husband and father.

Over the century these pressures took shape in a variety of Acts designed to curb the employment of both women and children. The working-class woman was progressively defined as a non-working woman in the formal sense and at the same time she was required to cope with the consequences of that change and the vagaries of the male wage in terms of creating an environment with the capacity to reproduce social existence. Both in and out of paid work the working-class woman had an extremely difficult existence. For most of the century these women had paid jobs and they had to cope both with factory work and home work. The comments of a factory inspector in the Potteries district graphically illustrate the strains this imposed (cited in Hewitt, 1958, p. 22):

> Half an hour to dress and suckle her infant and carry it out to nurse; one hour

for household duties before leaving home; half an hour for actually travelling to the mill; twelve hours actual labour; one and a half hours for meals; half an hour for returning home at night; one and a half hours for household duties and preparing for bed, leaving six and a half hours for recreation, seeing and visiting friends and sleep; and in winter when it is dark, half an hour extra time on the road to the mill and half an hour extra on the road home from the mill.

As noted already the middle classes viewed the working-class woman's engagement in outside paid labour as contaminating and distinctly unfeminine. The heat and discomfort of the factory, the presence of men in close company, all this was believed to heighten sexuality and to lead to depravity. Moreover, because women were outside the home they were considered to be neglecting their proper duties and it was this absence which many middle-class Victorians saw as the root of poverty and squalor. Writing in 1867, Thomas Wright moralised (cited in Pike, 1967):

The man who goes home on a Saturday only to find his house in disorder with every article of furniture out of its place, the floor unwashed or sloppy from uncompleted washing, his wife slovenly, his children untidy, his dinner not yet ready, or spoilt in the cooking, is much more likely to 'go on a spree' than the man who finds his house in order, the furniture glistening from the recent polishing, the burnished steel fire-irons looking doubly resplendent from the bright glow of the cheerful fire, his well cooked dinner laid on a snowy cloth, and his wife and children tidy and cheerful. If the man whose household work is neglected or mismanaged is of a meek character and has been unfortunate enough to get as a wife one who is termagant as well as a sloven, he will have to devote his Saturday afternoon to assisting in the woman's work of his own house. But when the husband is not of the requisite meekness of spirit, he hastens from the disorderly scene, and roams about in a frame of mind that predisposes him to seek the questionable comforts of the public house, or to enter into some other form of dissipation.

Such a statement now remarkable for its chauvinism is probably typical of the Victorian view, and especially the middle-class view.[5] Essentially all blame was laid at the door of women. It is no surprise to find that the journals published by the middle-class for working-class consumption hammered home such points explaining to workers the failings of their ways. In 1864, one such journal *The British Workingman* urged women:

Wife of the Labouring man Take warning in time. Try to make your home happy to your husband and children. Remember your first earthly duty, and, whatever be the temptations to go out to work, STAY AT HOME.

Working-class women were thus trapped between the urgings of the middle-class and the realities of their own existence; work, home, duties, children, appalling housing and in all probability ill-health and early death. These contradictory pressures were particularly acute for those in service who might spend the day in the relative comfort of a middle-class home, albeit hard at work, and then each evening return to their own marginal existence.

The preoccupations of earning a living resulted in children either being farmed out to 'nurses' during the day or themselves being put to work in a variety of occupations. The family as such was distinctly different from the middle-class conception of it. In such circumstances the exercise of parental and paternal authority was more difficult, though it would be unwise to characterise the working-class home as undisciplined. Poverty and insecurity brought their own rules as is revealed in some of the accounts of working-class life in Burnett's, *Useful Toil* (1974). An inadequate diet, long hours of work and home responsibilities such as looking after younger brothers or sisters, tending animals, or fetching water consumed most of the child's waking hours. In work, children were subjected to harsh discipline and there seem to have been relatively few moments of joy and pleasure in their lives. Education was rudimentary or non-existent early in the century, though later as middle-class concern increased and children were excluded from work, schooling became more widespread though its intentions were clearly limited (Ball, 1979; Davin, 1979). George Godwin, an architect and social reformer wrote in 1859 (1972, p. 43):

> If for example we would have the sons of the struggling classes grow into orderly, sensible and striving citizens we must give them a road out of the slough, show them the value of order and furnish them with weapons for the strife. . . . Every effort to provide means of training for those who would otherwise be without it – every endeavour to give the children of the poor some knowledge of common things, and lead out their better parts, has our heartiest support.

Ignoring, if we may, the apparent disregard of girls in his reforming scheme (though he goes on to discuss a laundry (p. 44) 'where girls may be received and instructed in such operations as would enable them to undertake engagements either in families or in washing establishments, or as wives'.) it is clear that Godwin, along with many affluent Victorians, saw virtue in training the working class, if only so that they would make better use of what they already possessed. For them the working-class family could only be saved by concerted action via charities, good works and the State. McGregor (1957, pp. 96–7) comments:

> Working-class people could not perform the familial duties prescribed by the middle class family code. The very bases of this conception – a clean and decent home and the leisure to pursue family life without the health and education of children, the protection of dependents – were only secured by collective action and public provision.

The overwhelming power of middle-class values in this era makes it difficult to extract the realities of working-class family life. It is as if the very insecurity of the Victorian middle class, alongside their obvious power and affluence, forced them to bind others to their cause. As we shall see in the next section however, the realities of physical provision were far short of the sermonising discussed above.

Production, reproduction and the home

As the discussion so far indicates, the home assumes considerable importance in social relations in the Victorian era. For the middle-classes the home was essentially a private arena far removed from the unpleasantness of the outside world. Though work was recognised as necessary for individual advancement it was also seen as vulgar – selling one's labour, associating with the lower orders and working in unclean surroundings were not things to discuss nor contemplate longer than absolutely necessary. Thus work was an anathema to the Victorian home – at least as far as its middle-class occupants were concerned. That is not to say that work did not get undertaken, as the servants bear witness, rather it was removed and isolated as far as possible. Servants worked below stairs and the mistress of the house undertook her management in as genteel a manner as possible – not from an office but from her morning room – utilising her butler, cook or housekeeper as far as possible.

Thus when we talk of the middle-class Victorian home we are in essence talking of a 'unit of reproduction' – but not one in any sense being restricted to simply reproduction, rather having a much fuller role concerned with the relations within and between social groups, their ideas and development. Indeed as indicated already, gender as well as class and status figures strongly on the agenda. The Victorian middle-class home much more strongly than today's home was a meeting ground for different classes. The working-classes and middle-classes, whether in the form of family, relatives, servants and tradespersons, mingled around and within the home. Indeed, for many children and women this was their only experience of 'their inferiors' leading to many peculiar misconceptions about working class life and their relationship to the occupants of that class, for example the need to lead and set an example.[6]

The reproduction of gender relations appears to have been a central feature of the middle-class Victorian home. Though class is clearly important gender (or gender/class) relations demarcate the public world from private world, inside the home from outside the home, the care of children from the care of animals and transport – indeed a whole range of necessary duties and functions can be demarcated in this way (and continue to be so today). It is ironic that the middle class were concerned to create an environment where they could exercise their own choices and live in freedom. As J. A. Froude commented in 1849 (cited in Calder, 1977, p. 49):

> When we come home, we lay aside our mask and drop our tools and are no longer lawyers, sailors, soldiers, statesmen, clergymen, but only men. We fall again into our most human relations, which after all, are the whole of what belongs to us as we are ourselves, and alone have the keynote of our hearts. There our skill, if skill we have, is exercised with real gladness on home subjects. . . . We cease the struggle in the race of the world, and give our hearts leave and leisure to love.

Men may have viewed themselves in this way but there can be no doubt that their concepts of relaxation were distinctly paternal and few would have contemplated close interaction either with their children or wives. Indeed such a view is sustained if one considers the increasing demarcation of the house into male and female spheres and the rise of the clubs – places where men could relax with men. At home the billiard room, the smoking room, the library or study and the dining room were male preserves, and filled with male furniture – the solid, well-upholstered carver chair in the dining room, the large but integrated press in the master's bedroom (Burnett, 1978; Muthesius, 1982). The father remained aloof from the day to day events of the family and the household and in case his son(s) might be tainted by this process, he (they) was (were) sent to boarding school where a similarly remote regime of female servants and male masters operated.

It is of course relatively easy to paint a picture of the home as a totally male-dominated arena. However, this would negate the efforts of women who challenged the authority of men and sought to create alternatives (perhaps the best account of women's attempts to reorganise the home is given in Hayden, 1981). Moreover, although relations between husband and wife were conducted on what appear to have been strictly patriarchal lines, the wife was also head of a household of servants. Her duties were considerable and though conducted within the general confines of male authority, the female head had considerable powers. Calder cites Mrs Beeton's instructions to 'the wife and mother' (Calder, 1977, p. 40).

Having risen early and attended to the toilet, see that the children receive proper care and are clean and comfortable. The first meal of the day, breakfast will then be served, at which all the family should be punctually present. . . . After breakfast is over, the mistress should make a round of the kitchen and other offices, to see that all is in order, and that the early morning's work has been properly performed by the various domestics. The orders for the day should then be given; and any questions which the domestics may ask should be answered, and any articles they require given out. . . . Prompt notice should be taken of the first appearance of slackness, neglect or any faults in domestic work so that the servant may know that the mistress is quick to detect the least disorder.

The wife's management of children and servants was only one component of her role in the home. A particularly significant function with respect to class as well as gender relations was her control of the 'social diary' – the at homes, dinners, teas and musical evenings, the carefully staged conduct of the children's relationships and the marriages that were the right and proper outcomes. In these ways women were essential in structuring social relations, excluding the unacceptable and encouraging the suitable. The rapid rate of development of the Victorian economy ensured that carefully constructed marriages could guarantee rapid social enhancement or sustain status when all around was failing. This important but neglected aspect of class structuring was largely in the control of women. An elaborate ritual grew up around these processes, the complex laws of 'the calling card', the placing of guests at dinner and the careful choice of who to invite, all were conducted with care, frequent reference to the guides to etiquette and consultation with local matrons of influence and social standing. In a world of impermanence these rituals were an essential element of control.

The boundaries between classes are extremely difficult to define.

Many contemporary commentators used the presence of servants to indicate whether a household was middle-class or not but it was not uncommon for many skilled artisans to have domestic help in the form of a young girl (see Muthesius, 1982). Indeed, it must be understood that the working class was in essence the working classes with a whole range of strata from skilled artisan to unskilled labourer. Mayhew noted in 1862 (p. 243):

> The transition from the artisan to the labourer is curious in many respects. In passing from the skilled operative of the west end to the unskilled workmen of the eastern quarter of London, the moral and intellectual change is so great that it seems as if we were in a new land and among another race.

Mayhew not only regarded the artisans as better educated but also to have a distinctly different life style. As a consequence it is difficult to talk about 'the working-class home' rather there are homes of the working classes (the same is of course true of the middle classes though perhaps their aspirations and pretensions were more clear cut and uniform).[7]

Paid labour was carried out in many working class homes allowing women and children to remain in the home but continue to contribute to the household budget. This work would include a variety of formally productive activities, for example weaving, packaging and preparation, and a whole host of service functions including laundering and child minding. Considering the conditions under which all of the labouring classes lived (and many skilled artisans) the home functioned in a minimal way with regard to social reproduction. As we shall show later, dwellings were inadequate in almost all respects with the central requirement simply being that they were within the means of the family's income – although that could mean up to 50 per cent of earnings. For children, home in the towns meant work for at least part of the day and despite the sentimental concerns of the middle classes this persisted until late in the century. It is easy to understand how Marx and Engels conceived of the relationship between capital and labour when they were presented with working-class life in nineteenth century England – its brutality and futility was starkly revealed. Moreover it is significant that middle-class reformers were more concerned with disease and contagion than they were with the nature of poverty and exploitation. Hard work could cure the latter, education the former.

Town life

The form and content of the nineteenth century dwelling assumes considerable importance with regard to the production and reproduction of social relations. The integration of work and home broke down in the eighteenth century reflecting the changing needs of both production and social reproduction (and in the process revealing that one is not a reflection of the other). In the nineteenth century this dichotomy develops further with the home becoming a separate sphere for the upper and middle classes. The rising affluence of the population as a whole, built of course upon heightened levels of exploitation and value creation, led to the opening up of a range of needs and desires incompatible with the existing dwelling stock. This, in conjunction with the growing complexity of society with regard to social stratification, the growth of cities and the development of technology, created conditions which through the nineteenth and twentieth centuries transformed the home for the majority of the population. Not only does its commodity status become more sharply revealed and a variety of tenure forms emerge to cope with the ever present contradictions between housing needs and housing costs but also the space within the home is increasingly exploited as the products of the new industrial age are purchased to sustain daily life (Fraser, 1981). Such products liberated but they also consumed space and income. Indeed, the home as a 'private sphere' proved itself a veritable Aladdin's cave in terms of its capacity to absorb new products and ideas (see Burnett, 1978; Muthesius, 1982).

At the beginning of the nineteenth century the towns and villages of England were undergoing rapid expansion with new building adding substantially to the number of dwellings in each centre. The gradual separation of social groups, increasingly identified as classes, had taken form not only within dwellings, for example the servant quarters, but also in the external environment, the suburbs and the 'poor districts' (Burgess, 1980; Fraser, 1981). These distinctions reflected and reinforced a whole series of social relations including developments in transport technology, notions of privacy and hygiene, questions of control of the urban environment and the nature of the family.[8]

By present day standards, life in the towns was rudimentary as is apparent from the reports of the Select Committee on the Health of Towns (1840), the Royal Commission on the Health of Towns (1844 and 1845), the Select Committee on the Regulation of Buildings and the Improvement of Boroughs (1842) and Chadwick's report on the Sanitary Condition of the Labouring Population of Great Britain (1842). As the evidence to the Royal Commission reveals, most towns had no regulations regarding drainage, refuse was thrown into the streets and sewers (open drains) were found only in a few main streets. With respect to water, this was generally supplied by private companies and was inadequate according to respondents to the Commission. In the poorer districts water was supplied by carts, pumps and the occasional stand-pipe (this being supervised by a resident who would charge for usage (Gauldie, 1974, p. 77). Little wonder then that Engels was so horrified by conditions in Manchester in 1844 (1969, pp. 42 and 86):

> the courts which lead down to the lake contain unqualifiedly the most horrible dwellings which I have yet beheld. In one of these courts there stands directly at the entrance, at the end of the covered passage, a privy without a door, so dirty that the inhabitants can pass into and out of the court only by passing through foul pools of stagnant urine and exrement.

And later to reinforce the point Engels notes:

> On rereading my description, I am forced to admit that instead of being exaggerated, it is far from black enough to convey a true impression of the filth, ruin and uninhabitableness.

The stench and filth of an early nineteenth century town is hard to imagine today. Human excreta was literally everywhere – on floors and walls, in cupboards. Those living in cellars frequently had to tolerate walls oozing with 'filth' as it seeped through from other dwellings and open troughs which might carry human waste from the upper floors of the house in which they lived. Gauldie (ibid., p. 75) cites the case of a woman taking up residence of a flat in Dundee in 1847 finding a cupboard full of 'about two cartloads of dung'. She declined to clear it out and lived with it – not even attempting to sell the dung which at this time was a valuable commodity.

It was generally believed that disease was airborne and that smell was one indication of a diseased environment. While the experts were right in certain senses they ignored completely water-borne disease and particularly the pollution of wells and well-water by sewage. Overcrowding, industrial and human effluent, poor diet and long hard labour were, in conjunction with polluted water, major causes of high levels of mortality.

Table 6.1: Average age at death in 1842

Towns	*Gentry & professional persons*	*Tradesmen*	*Labourers, etc.*	*General average*
Kendal	45	39	34	36
Bath	55	37	25	31
London (4 poor law unions)	44	28	22	25
Leeds	44	27	19	21
Bolton	34	23	18	19
Manchester	38	20	17	18
Liverpool	35	22	15	17

Source: Hopkins (1979, p. 24).

As can be seen from Table 6.1 life expectancy was low, especially for the labouring class. However it was not until 1849 (the year after a major outbreak of cholera) that a discovery that the infection was water-borne meant that progress was made. Until then 'mephitic air' and 'noxious gases' were blamed as illustrated by the following quotes from the fourth Annual Report of the Poor Law Commissioners 1837–8:

> Among the causes which prevent the great part of mankind from attaining the full age of 70 years or more which the nature of the human constitution allows, certain poisons disseminated in the air hold conspicuous place.

Elsewhere the report states:

> In a mews behind Bedford Square a stable had been let for a time to a butcher and a heap of dung had been formed at the door, containing pigs offal, pigeons dung, etc. During the act of removing this heap, a coachman's wife and her three children, of an adjoining stable, sat for a time at an open window nearly over the place, until the insufferable stench drove them away: two of the poor children died of the poison before 36 hours and the mother and other child narrowly escaped.

The accumulation of filth, human and animal waste, overcrowded houses and undrained land were seen as major causes of poisonous air. But middle-class commentators blamed the Irish, a general lack of cleanliness, the neglect of vaccination and intemperance. In other words, the conditions of the working classes were in part, and for some a large part, a product of their own making. Thus the Reverend W. Elkin of the Bath Poor Law Union commented in evidence submitted to Chadwick:

With the poor, far less obstacles are an absolute barrier, because no privation is felt by them so little as that of cleanliness. The propensity to dirt is so strong, the steps so few and easy, that nothing but the utmost facilities for water can act as a counterpoise; and such is the love of uncleanliness, when once contracted, that no habit, not even drunkenness, is so difficult to eradicate.

The official inquiries launched in the 1840s indicate the growing awareness of the state of the towns amongst some members of the middle classes. Local statistical societies, medical practitioners and churchmen were amongst the most active in pushing for reform. Such activity is indicative of the gulf between different social groups, their living conditions and life chances. Dr Kay's report, *The Moral and Physical Condition of the Working Classes Employed in the Cotton Manufacture in Manchester* is an excellent example of the kind of research undertaken. Written in 1832, his report offers a detailed analysis of the problems of rapid urbanisation and industrialisation. Indeed, as well as identifying health and social problems he points towards the potential political effects of this process (ibid., 42):

The districts, Nos 1, 2, 3 and 4 are inhabited by a turbulent population, which, rendered reckless by dissipation and want, – misled by the secret intrigues, and excited by the inflammatory harangues of demagogues, has frequently committed daring assaults on the liberty of the more peaceful portions of the working classes, and the most frightful devastations on the property of their masters. Machines have been broken, and factories gutted and burned at mid-day, and the riotous crowd has dispersed ere the insufficient body of police arrived at the scene of disturbance.

For the majority of the middle classes, however, oblivion ruled. Wohl (1978) suggests that in London the working-class districts remained 'terra incognita' until the 1850s and Engels (1969) cites the Rector of Bethnal Green as stating 'As little was known about Bethnal Green as the wilds of Australia or the islands of the South Seas.' But while the middle classes lacked any detailed understanding of these areas they were increasingly aware of the risks to their own health should they live in proximity to the 'slums', 'congealed districts', 'rookeries' as the working-class areas were known. Indeed, it is worth noting that Chadwick, despite all his reforming vigour, was more concerned with sewage and sewerage than the housing of the working classes.

During the nineteenth century the pattern of developing 'single class' areas continued apace reflecting the very evident demand from those garnering the fruits of the industrial revolutions, careful land release by landowners and astute salesmanship by builders. These factors, alongside improved transport and the changing organisation of production, allowed many families to migrate to the suburbs. Thus numerous contemporary accounts point to growing segregation and its consequences. In the Report of the Select Committee on the Health of Towns (1840, IV) it was noted:

It must be evident that owing to this rapid increase in the population of great towns, the proportion of humbler classes, of those with little leisure for education or improvement, will be augmented, as the more wealthy and educated withdraw themselves from these close and crowded communities; which thus more and more stand in need of some superintending care.

Dr Kay (1832, p. 20) noted 'the opulent merchants chiefly reside in the country. The dense masses of the population and even superior servants of their establishments inhabit the suburban townships . . .' and in the Second Report of the Commissioners Inquiring Into the State of Large Towns and Populous Districts (1845, appendix, 15) it was stated:

It will generally be found that there are few persons of education or considerable property resident in these crowded districts; with the exception of persons belonging to and busily engaged in the learned professions, and master manufacturers, few others remain.

The out-movement and segregation can of course be partly explained by expansion. There were more and more people in the middle classes and the creation of large and discernibly different districts became possible. But, as noted earlier, this was also a reflection of growing self awareness, of tensions and conflicts in a rapidly changing society and the breakdown of older patterns of social interaction. Their 'choices' were inevitably strongly conditioned by what was happening to the working classes. Cholera outbreaks reinforced a concern with disease and the desire to be distanced from it. Even then safety was not guaranteed as the Report of the Registrar General indicates (cited in the Report of the Select Committee on the Health of Towns, 1840, XV):

all classes of the community are directly interested in their adoption (sewerage systems) for the epidemics which arise in the east end of town do not stay there; they travel to the west end, and prove fatal in the wide streets and squares.

However, distance was deemed one solution. In addition, given that almost all households rented and their agreements with landlords were often quite short (six months or less even for the middle classes) it was quite possible for a street or locality to undergo rapid change, especially if the town or city was being 'industrialised'. As the population figures already given show, towns were expanding rapidly, and the working classes were burgeoning. To landlords they represented good money. No wonder then that the middle classes moved both frequently and outwards. As Kay (1832, p. 11) comments:

> The dense masses of the habitations of the poor, which stretch their arms, as though to grasp and enclose the dwellings of the noble and wealthy, in the metropolis and in our large provincial cities.

It is apparent that the nineteenth century city underwent continuous transformations in terms of its physical form. In this context, both the condition and location of the homes of the middle and working classes also changed though in divergent manner. The simple ecological model of invasion and succession is, in part, correct but it only captures a portion of the events unfolding. For the middle classes, their growth in number and status 'enforced' a whole series of redefinitions in their physical living arrangements, and these we observe in the nineteenth century in terms of the suburb, the detached house, the wall and hedge, the curtain and variety of other devices designed to distance and obscure (see Muthesius, 1982; Daunton 1983). For the working classes, overcrowding and poverty, set alongside self-help and a changing division of labour, saw many consigned to slums which were only eradicated in the early twentieth century (only to be replaced) while for others a grim struggle for life beyond this social abyss developed with a never ending series of carefully structured social gradients stretching before them. The working classes moved out to the suburbs in numbers, aided by the workmens' trains. Indeed, it became a matter of some status to make this move. It also reinforced male dominance because typically this meant withdrawing the wife (and children) from work and removing lodgers. As this happened so the distinctions between work and non-work became sharper.

Housing and home

The condition and location of dwellings is suggestive of developments taking place around the production and distribution of housing. As the mode of production developed and towns and cities expanded the question of housing became important not simply as a need but also as a marketable commodity. Landowners within and around urban centres became very conscious of the new opportunities arising out of this process. Land became valuable for its development value, especially for 'house farming'. A whole industry of owners, intermediaries and agents grew up around the building and market allocation of dwellings. In the nineteenth century it was uncommon for a middle-class household to own their own house. Generally landowners were reluctant to relinquish all title to their urban land holdings and they retained the freehold and sold their land leasehold, often having undertaken development themselves. In any case, development was controlled via covenants in order to ensure that standards were maintained and the sites produced their maximum revenue. As might be expected all landowners hoped to attract the wealthiest classes and there was considerable competition to build and establish 'desirable' areas (Lloyd and Simpson, 1977; Cannadine, 1980).

House sales rather than leases were more common in suburbs and country areas – in part a reflection of cash shortages by landlords but also of the degree of uncertainty regarding the future prospects of such areas. Sales allowed cash to be realised and redeployed. Even so there was little pressure amongst the middle classes to buy rather than rent. Renting was normal and the length of leases, quarterly, half yearly or yearly, allowed households to adjust their housing rapidly to new status and the latest fashions. In addition there was always the question of necessary finance and though building societies were active throughout the century with respect to middle-class (and working-class) housing there were certain risks in staking one's capital on a single house which might itself be engulfed by social and physical change. Only with the establishment of land use controls could the market operate within a defined framework. Given such concerns, it is less surprising that purchase was more common in private suburban estates while closer to the centre of towns leasehold estates seem to have dominated. Either way, the home was a commodity which could be bought and sold, and through which profits could be made. In 1832, William Cobden reckoned that the house he had bought for 3000 guineas in Manchester had become worth 6000 within some four years (Checkland, 1964, p. 265). As urban land and property became more valuable, offering speculative gains equal to or greater than other commodities, so the housing market attracted increasing attention.

The Victorian middle classes were very conscious of style and fashion. The plainness of Georgian design whether it be furnishings or dwellings was treated with some scorn as being too plain. Instead they sought to emulate and adapt Classical and Gothic styles. In very general terms, Gothic designs (including Romanesque, Perpendicular and Tudor) dominated domestic construction (though many examples of classical architecture exist, for example Milner Square in Islington built 1841–43). From the early 1830s it became fashionable to fill rooms with furniture, furnishings and ornaments – all symbols of material prosperity, colour schemes became darker and light was obscured by curtains stressing the sanctuary-like nature of the home (see Curl, 1973; Dutton, 1954 and Gloag, 1962).

Through the nineteenth century we can observe a whole series of design and technological developments around the home as entrepreneurs sought to ensure that their products gained universal support and middle-class households insisted on 'the very latest'. The key advances were in the areas of lighting and heating, water supply and sewage disposal – all of them areas around which considerable competition existed both for the design and provision of the service (see Daunton, 1983 for a useful summary). Concerns with hygiene found expression in the direct supply of water to individual dwellings, the installation of baths and the use of the flushing water closet. Water was piped into dwellings, often into a basement cistern and from there it had to be pumped to outlets in the house. These would include the one bath, the maid's pantry and the kitchen. Servants then distributed water to individual rooms. Only later in the nineteenth century did piping within the dwelling become more common – reflecting in part the growing difficulties of finding servants to carry out these onerous tasks.

The pattern of household technological development tended to follow a path from the homes of the nobility to the middle classes and thence to the working classes. The water closet was introduced to the homes of the aristocracy in the eighteenth century. According to Girouard (1978, p. 265) the 'breakthrough came with Joseph Bramah's water closet, patented in 1778' and by 1797 it was claimed that 6000 of these had been installed. However, a wide array of systems existed and although the flushing water closest came to predominate in middle-class houses by the end of the nineteenth century this was not before a whole range of other systems had been discarded, for example the dry earth closet, the hand flushed hopper closet, the waste-water closet as well as the pit privy and the pail closet.

Gaslighting was installed in various mansions late in the eighteenth century but it was not widespread in middle-class homes until the 1840s. In part its introduction was slow because of the smell and fumes generated. Only with the introduction of the bunsen burner did an efficient lighting system emerge. Even then burnt gas worked fast to blacken the interior of the houses. Later in the century gas was used for heating water and for cooking. Electric light only began to supplant gas in the 1880s following the invention of the incandescent burner in 1879. Electricity was much more popular – it had no smell, was more flexible and transportable though according to Burnett (1978, p. 250) the advance of electricity was slow. Each of these innovations sparked off inventive applications to the home and served to create whole new industries concerned with 'domestic appliances'. Moreover, with the development of better heating systems, more efficient fireplaces and radiators and well-lighted dwellings the Victorian middle classes gave birth to a home entertainment industry of considerable proportions (e.g. games and instruments).

Concerns with hygiene were not restricted to the introduction of the water closet or running water. Woodwork was varnished and wallpaper made its appearance in quantity in the middle of the century reflecting not only a concern to decorate but also the belief that wallpaper sealed the wall surface which had been tainted by noxious air. It could also be wiped over and ranges of sanitary wallpapers made by firms such as Heywood, Higginbottom and Smith were developed. Equally the questions of 'ventilation' and 'bathing' became important. The former was resolved by ventilation bricks and other devices for moving air within the dwelling whilst bathing was more frequent although until the 1880s it was rarely taken in a fixed unit. This was a consequence of the absence of drains and a water supply in the upper floors of houses, and for the middle classes a weekly bath and daily washing was more common than a daily bath.

In all these applications of new technology to the home considerable stress was laid upon scientific advance. The whole concept of the home became subjected to concerns of scientific management and the application of advanced technology. Just as work could be revolutionised so it was argued could the home. In 1802, Count von Rumford founded the Royal Institution for the Application of Science in the

Common Purposes of Life and although this can be seen as the founding of domestic science it was not until mid-century that the process began in earnest. The kitchen was an obvious area for the application of new ideas, but because this was the domain of servants, relatively little attention was given to it until late in the century (though Catherine Beecher's treatise on 'Domestic Economy' was written in the USA in 1842 and Alexis Soyer of Crimea and Reform club fame wrote his *The Gastronomic Regenerator* in 1846). Thus Chapman has suggested that as a consequence of this neglect of the kitchen 'the housewife who did her own work had, for a long time, to put up with a standard of comfort, convenience, decoration and equipment fit only for a servant' (ibid., 1955, p. 19).

There can be little doubt that the employment of servants had considerable impact upon both domestic technology and design. The backstairs, the cellar kitchen and other devices were all intended to keep servants out of sight and to retain 'the family' privacy (and to regulate and control servants). Similarly the reluctance to install plumbing, free standing kitchen ranges and to switch from coal to gas or electricity must all be seen within the context of the cheapness of the alternative – the servant. Only as the economy developed and new opportunities arose for working-class men and women did the pressure mount for alternative technologies demonstrating once again the interconnections between the spheres of home and work. In addition, while servants may have hindered technology, their very presence and their ability to clean and polish allowed Victorians to indulge in the consumption of knick-knacks (and encouraged the extravagant displays of possessions).

The social and economic relations operating within the home also find expression in the external design of the dwelling and in the physical organization of middle-class neighbourhoods. As Burnett (1978, p. 109) comments, 'privacy, respectability and distinctive social identification were the leading external characteristics of the middle-class house'. Obviously there were a myriad of designs applied during the Victorian era, but at the most general level the detached and semi-detached house predominated. As would be expected privacy demanded detachment or at least the illusion of it and this would be reinforced by dense shrubbery, walls and in the house itself, lace curtains. For those unable to afford a detached dwelling, 'the semi' was a reasonable compromise particularly when the entire structure was designed to look like one house. The tradesman's entrance, the external coal hole and the bay window were all mechanisms of demarcating the middle-class house from the working-class dwelling (as were 'the avenue' or 'road' distinct from the 'street'). But as Burnett notes (1978, p. 108):

> The bay-window was important in order to distinguish the house from a flat-fronted, working-class terrace, but the bay-window invited prying eyes as well as sunlight which faded the carpet and upholstery, and therefore needed to be screened by inner curtains and floral displays.

The dwelling and the home stood at the centre of middle-class Victorian life. Through the century its form and content changed, e.g. later furnishings became lighter and 'more open' but it preserved its role as a vital component of class formation and expression. Pugin noted 'every person should be lodged as becomes his station and dignity' (cited in MacLeod, 1974, p. 12) and one can find numerous reflections of such views in the form and content of the middle-class house. Ironically, despite Victorian family-centredness, this was also the era of 'the club', with male preserves separate and protected from female intrusion. This served to reinforce the dual nature of the Victorian home – at one level a very class-conscious home, and at another a very explicit expression of gender relations with 'the contented home' as a necessary appendage of the male even though his direct role in its functioning was often only as an authority figure.

Tenure relations and the home

As an inspection of the plans for middle-class housing reveals, servants were consigned to the attic or the cellar, there to dwell in rather mean accommodations giving some indication of the actual extent the middle classes felt they should go in fulfilling their sacred duties to the working classes. It is a matter of some dispute as to whether such accommodations were worse than those the working classes obtained in the housing market. The conditions for the mass of the population were exceedingly poor and it is quite clear from the evidence that, unlike the middle classes, their housing situation deteriorated as more people crowded into the cities and the housing shortage increased. At the same time it would also be correct to say that there were widening divisions within the working classes and the poor as a consequence of a more differentiated work force, the uneven nature of economic change, specific local social patterns and the varied impact of education. This allowed some groups to generate either the income or other resources to markedly improve their housing situation and what becomes apparent during the nineteenth century are these two trajectories of change – one an upgrading of housing and social life, the other diminution and deterioration.

The dominant tenure for all the working classes was renting either a whole house or more commonly part of a house. For those on the most marginal incomes cheap lodgings were available (as other households sought to earn an income from the space they rented), sharing a room or bed with several others. For the poorest, shelter was obtained where possible under bridges in parks, in empty buildings – the vagrant population was large as indicated by Mayhew's *London Labour and the London Poor*. Rented housing was provided by a range of entrepreneurs including members of the wealthy classes and indeed members of the working classes – all concerned, it seems, to extract maximum value for their ownerships. Their right to do so, as part of a more general view of the sanctity of private property was to raise innumerable contradictions in the later attempts to tackle the housing problem (Offer, 1981). Although it appears builders were most interested in constructing homes for the wealthier middle classes, a considerable volume of working class homes were built in the nineteenth century including terraced housing, back to backs, model dwellings, tenements, and workshop houses. The initiative for these came from philanthropists, employers, building clubs, speculators and late in the century, local authorities. There is not room to trace this process in detail here (see Burnett, 1978; Gauldie, 1974; and Wohl, 1977 for useful summaries of developments) but throughout the tension remains between housing as a profitable investment (albeit a modest profit) and housing as a need.

Wages fluctuated considerably during the nineteenth century but 'rents rose continuously throughout the century' (Burnett, 1969, p. 218) and for many households rent consumed an increasing portion of its income (up to half in poorer districts; see Checkland, 1964, p. 243) forcing households to occupy smaller and smaller amounts of space (Wohl, 1977, p. 44). Although house building was not a particularly attractive investment, renting could produce a substantial revenue, particularly if little was spent on maintenance. As the Chadwick Report makes clear most households had little choice but to take what was available (1842, p. 231);

The workman's 'location' as it is termed is generally governed by his work, near which he must reside. The sort of house, and often the particular house, may be said to be, and usually is a monopoly . . . he must avail himself of the first vacancy that presents itself. . . . The individual labourer has little or no power over the internal structure and economy of the dwelling which has fallen to his lot. If the water be not laid on in the other houses in the street, or if it be unprovided with proper receptacles for refuse, it is not in the power of any individual workman who may perceive the advantages of such accommodations to procure them. He has as little control over the external economy of his residence as of the structure of the street before it.

Although many reformers stressed the benefits of moving to the suburbs, only selected groups of workers could realistically make such a choice. The cost of travelling back to work often offset the reduction in rent, but more importantly for casual labour, local contacts were crucial for work and uncertain employment resulted in many families being 'locked into' circuits of credit via pawn shops which made movement difficult. As today, middle class perceptions about the ease with which movement could be undertaken were completely unrealistic. According to middle-class commentators in the nineteenth century most of the working classes were content to live in rented central area slums (Wohl, 1977, p. 42, pp. 318–20). Chadwick commented (1842, p. 232):

Under the slavery of the existing habits of labourers, it is found that the faculty of perceiving the advantage of a change is so obliterated as to render them incapable of using, or indifferent to the use of the means of improvement which may happen to come within their reach. The sense of smell, for instance, which generally gives warning of the presence of malaria or gases noxious to the health, appears often to be obliterated in the labourer by his employment.

Concern to capture maximum revenue from rented housing was reflected in the construction of a careful gradation of dwellings – each type offering discernible improvement both to the occupier and the passerby. It is difficult to ascertain within the hierarchies of Victorian society what status was ascribed to property *ownership* as opposed to renting. Since most households rented, the distinction between classes was the type of size and location of the dwelling rather than its tenure. Having said this it is apparent that in certain localities particular classes of workers sought and were able to become owners rather than renters. Evidence is fragmentary. Discussing the situation over the period 1810–1914 Offer comments (1981, pp. 119–20):

House-ownership was an aspiration of well paid workers in regular employment. Apparently one fifth of the workers in Kenricks, a Birmingham hardware firm, were freeholders in the 1850s; a few of the skilled legal copiers interviewed for Charles Booth's survey in London were house owners. West Yorkshire and Tyneside, where the building society movement was better developed, appear to have had a high proportion of home ownership. 'In Oldham', said the preamble to the Unionist housing bill of 1912, 'out of 33 000 inhabited houses, over 10 000 or about a third, are owned, or in the course of being purchased by artisan proprietors'. The South Wales coalfield apparently had a very high incidence of working-class home ownership coming up to 60 per cent in some localities, and Cardiff had an overall percentage of 9.6 falling to 7.2, between 1884 and 1914. In York, at the turn of the century 608 working-class house owners (occupying almost six per cent of working class housing) were headed by 120 widows, 30 spinsters and 58 retired men, and tailed by eight labourers.

Rose's study (1984) of home ownership and industrial change in what were basically single industry communities in the late nineteenth century revealed relatively high levels of working class home ownership in Dowlais, Penrhyndeudrath, Blaenau Festiniog, and Hawick as well as in parts of Northumberland and Durham. Northampton which was also part of her study, was suggested to have the highest levels of ownership in the country (and low crime rates and high church attendance as a consequence). Daunton (1983) calculated ownership rates for the same period for six cities revealing considerable variety between them (Birmingham 1.3 per cent of property, Blackburn 11.1 per cent, Halifax 13.8 per cent, Middlesbrough 14.0 per cent, Gateshead 17.0 per cent and Sunderland 27.3 per cent). His evidence from the South Wales coalfield pointed up similar variety with ownership rates reaching 60 per cent in some valleys but dropping as low as 5 per cent in Cardiff.

These different studies plus more evidence from single towns (e.g. Bedale, 1980; Bell, 1907) suggest that the working classes had become home owners in some numbers and that this had come about through choice, necessity and careful manipulation. Indeed, given the limited options available to them in certain areas, it may well be that working class ownership rates exceeded those of the middle classes. The building societies, then as now, claim a considerable role in the promotion of ownership. What becomes clear after reviewing the evidence (for example submissions to the various inquiries into Friendly and Building Societies) is that most societies were controlled by the middle classes (if not from the outset, then shortly thereafter) and that, via ownership, the directors were seeking to promote Victorian ideals of thrift, stability and family life as well as ensuring some resolution of a continuing housing crisis. A Mr Taylor in evidence to the 1871 Inquiry commented that his society had funded over 13 000 purchases in Birmingham and 'we have streets more than a mile long in which absolutely every home belongs to the working classes' (Inquiry into Friendly and Benefit Societies 1871). He suggested that, as in Northampton, Birmingham required less police than it used to because of the 'increased frugality and temperance engendered by the societies'. When questioned 'You mean that such habits are increased by the possession by persons in that class of life their own houses' [sic] Mr Taylor replied (ibid., p. 49)

> Yes, they save their money, and instead of spending it in public houses, they spend it upon property. They go home at night and cultivate their gardens or read the newspaper to their wives, instead of being in public houses. We are the greatest social reformers of the day.

This discussion of the home in the nineteenth century reveals the flowering of the home as a concept and as a focus of middle-class Victorian life. In essence, in a rapidly changing world, the home was for the middle classes in general and male adults in particular, a haven, a mark of achievement and a reason for purposeful action in the world beyond. The middle classes were emerging as a numerically large and socially and politically important group. Inevitably, given its varied origins, the group was in reality fragmented into sub-groups but it was united around a concern to project certain values and amibitions (thrift, self help, duty, christianity, the family, sobriety, etc.). The home was essential to this process both as a setting for it and as an illustration of it. In these terms the home was central to the process of class constitution just as in other ways it was crucial to the process of segregation and demarcation within that 'class'.

Equally with respect to gender relations there is almost an indivisible link between class and gender in the middle class Victorian home. The emergence of the lady of the house as a class-gender category, as Davidoff and Hall (1983) refer to it, is of critical significance. This concept has carried through into the twentieth century and has really only begun to be broken in the post-Second World War period with the rise of middle-class female paid employment. Even so the imagery (and reality) of women and the home is very strong. Women are typically described as housewives (even when in paid employment) and the home continues to act as one of the most strongly gender demarcated regions of life. For the Victorian middle classes (if not today) this association and its promulgation as the highest of values was yet another example of attempted male control over females.

For the Victorian working-classes the home was also much sought after, partly because for the whole family it offered some prospect of a life outside of work. MacKenzie and Rose (1983) argue that the century was characterised by a struggle to create the home as a separate sphere and that this was achieved by numbers of the working class through home ownership. Rose (1984) demonstrates the reality and meaning of this even though it is important not to neglect the fact that working class ownership grew within the context of middle-class paternalism and a determination to resolve prudently the housing crisis. Ownership was inevitably one element in the process of status change. Being a 'man of property' was regarded as important (not least because of security in old age) but it did not mean a household immediately departed the working class (indeed because of the propensity by most households to rent, it was neither necessary nor sufficient). Given the poor quality of much rental housing and the limited attempts by government to tackle this situation (beyond clearance) the conditions and uncertainties surrounding the home merely served to reinforce the necessity to achieve advancement in the work-place through individual effort and organised struggle.

The limited space available enforced a mixing of genders and ages in a way which was avoidable in middle-class homes. Women bore the burden of household work themselves with children carrying out some duties (but men much less so). Despite the different conditions in the homes of different classes a similar tendency to 'contain' women in the working class home is apparent. Partly a response to middle-class moralising, partly male protectionism and union pressure to establish family wages this became an increasing reality even though many women still needed to take on paid work in the home (Alexander, 1979).

Conclusion: the home in history

The numerous dimensions and variations to consider make any

attempt at a generalised account of the home a risky business. However, what this account and others (MacKenzie and Rose, 1983) have sought to demonstrate is that the home, as an arena, is far from a tranquil passive haven and that over time, it has been an active constitutive force in the formation of gender, class and status relations and in the structuring of production and consumption. In arguing for the central importance of the home it is vital to recognise that its relationship to society is not simply functional whereby the home is manipulated by capitalists to serve the interest of capital (nor the triumph of labour). It is far too complex to be reduced to that. Certainly we can see that, over time, the home was increasingly commodified with respect to the dwelling structure, its contents and the activities which took place within it. Through the nineteenth century home ownership and private renting replaced job-related accommodation. The home was increasingly separated from the workplace (at least for the male). Households increasingly bought rather than made (or exchanged) the equipment within the home and the range increased beyond all comprehension (the contrast between most eighteenth- and nineteenth century homes would have been considerable in terms of possessions). The functions of homework were also commodified with cleaning, washing, child-minding, cooking, food preparation and entertainment being examples of activities which could be provided for through the market place.

Some have argued that the commodification of home work 'reduced the scope of (and women's control over) what went on inside it' (Women and Geography Study Group, 1984). To a certain extent this was true though, to the degree that working-class women could afford such assistance, it was no doubt viewed as desirable in terms of any time it freed up. The centrality of the home would in many respects appear to have sharpened over the period. As a concept and an active process 'the home' became a more pronounced social and physical reality for both middle and working classes. It became an ever more active force in gender relations consolidating distinctions between work and non-work and their gender associations. With regard to status the home was crucial to the ways in which individuals could distinguish and demarcate themselves from others and in the rapidly changing world of the eighteenth and nineteenth centuries this was increasingly important. While such tendencies can cross-cut class boundaries the recognition by workers of the benefits of an adequate home acted to strengthen their resolve to act as a class (just as the acquisition of substantial property, whether possessions or actual dwellings, must have given the middle classes something to defend).

In the twentieth century, the tendencies towards privatism and individualism have become more pronounced with the home playing an active and enhanced role. In the face of globalised economies, concentration and centralisation, and mass production, the home stands as a polar opposite conveying both the image and reality of individual control and action. In Britain, rising homelessness and deteriorating housing conditions for a significant portion of the population stand in acute contrast to the established image of the Englishman's home as castle. In the nineteenth century, middle-class paternalism and working class self-help allowed many to secure the base they had been searching for whether as tenants or owners though in reality it was only in the twentieth century that the really dramatic changes occurred in housing conditions. However, that struggle for improvement does indicate the importance of the home to individuals. Moreover, by being actively fought for and achieved the home has increasingly become both a reality as a physical and social arena and as an important constitutive force with regard to social relations between people themselves and broader social groupings. This examination of the home through time indicates the ways in which the home itself has been constituted and the part it plays in expressing and influencing the changing shape of society.

Acknowledgments

I am grateful for comments made by Peter Saunders and Nigel Thrift on an earlier draft of this paper and for the points raised by individuals at various seminars. In no respects are they responsible for the errors which remain – these are mine alone.

Notes

1 Work is continuing on a larger study of the home which will cover the period 1700 to 1985.

2 As Davidoff and Hall (1983) note lady is a class–gender concept.

3 In developing this argument there is potential disagreement with MacKenzie and Rose (1983). They argue that the (working-class) family was effectively destroyed in the early years of industrial capitalism and that it was saved, in part through the creation of the separate sphere, the home – an outcome of both working-class struggle and middle-class paternalism. Part of the divergence arises from their focus on the working-class family and the concern here with both the middle and working classes.

4 It is interesting how the concept of 'running a home' became consolidated in this period.

5 It certainly reoccurs with frequency in numerous reports, e.g. *State of Large Towns and Populous Districts*, 1885, Appendix 16.

6 Of course for the middle-classes the servant was the source, sometimes the only source, of awareness about working-class life (see Wohl, 1968; McBride, 1978; Davidoff, 1979 and Summers 1979).

7 There was certainly plenty of guidance. See Kerr's list of what constitutes an appropriate home (Burnett, 1978, 190).

8 Not least they had a considerable impact on gender relations. Suburbs became 'female', transport and work 'male'; see MacKenzie and Rose (1983).

Part Two
The Twentieth Century

• 7 •

Introduction: *The geography of late twentieth-century class formation* • *NIGEL THRIFT*

Britain in the late twentieth century is a more difficult form of capitalist society to describe and analyse than the Britain of the mid-nineteenth century (see Chapter 2). British society is larger (with a population that has more than doubled since 1851) and institutionally far more complex. The lines of determination between relations of production and class formation are accordingly more likely to be indirect. Certainly the heroic age of class struggle has been replaced by a more prosaic age of class dealignment.

The capitalist *economy* has changed substantially in form. The core of capital now consists of a depersonalised set of large multinational corporations: (1) spanning many different economic activities (Urry, 1981; Taylor and Thrift, 1982; Salaman, 1981); (2) engaging in extensive planning and product and market research in the face of the generally much reduced turnover time of capital; and (3) becoming more and more flexible in their approach to profit-making (Cooke and Morgan, 1985). Such a form of capitalism has involved the development of a large workforce of clerks, managers and other associated bureaucrats, all with appropriate educational qualifications. Basic manufacturing has been encircled by a vast service economy some parts of which are recognisably a continuation of nineteenth century themes (such as the City of London), other parts of which (such as many business services and various state-related services) are a twentieth-century phenomenon. (See Abercrombie and Urry, 1983, for an extended discussion of the significance of these developments.)

These changes have meant the growth of a large and effective *middle class* or, more accurately perhaps, a set of middle classes. It is no surprise, then, that nearly all recent Marxist accounts of class structure have revolved around the theoretical and practical problems generated by the middle class. It is possible to note a number of reactions to the problem of the middle class in the later phases of capitalism. The first is to effectively deny its existence as a separate class. There is a working class, there is a petty bourgeoisie, there is a bourgeoisie just as in Marx's time. All that has happened is that these classes' content has been revised (e.g. the orthodox French Communist Party line of the 1960s and early 1970s). The second reaction is to correlate the middle class with a new petty bourgeoisie based on functions like the ownership of intellectual skills, unproductive wage labour or income earned over and above the value of labour-power (e.g. Poulantzas, 1973, 1975; Urry, 1973). A third reaction is to argue for the existence of a completely 'new middle class' or 'professional managerial class' consisting of highly educated wage labour (Mallet, 1975; Ehrenreich and Ehrenreich, 1979; Walker, 1979; Gouldner, 1979). Abercrombie and Urry (1983) have taken this thesis further by identifying a 'service class' of top managers, professionals and bureaucrats, functionaries of capital (not capitalists) who rely on their credentials to generate power (see Renner, 1953; Gould, 1980; Goldthorpe, 1982 and the discussion below). They also point to a whole series of routine clerical workers who, over time, have become deskilled and are now, for all effects and purposes, members of the working class.

Finally, the middle class can be theorized as occupying a *contradictory* class relation between the working class and bourgeoisie, being both exploiter and exploited (Carchedi, 1977). In Wright's (1978, 1979b, 1980) original formulation there are three main possible contradictory locations; between bourgeoisie and working class (managers and supervisors), between bourgeoisie and petit bourgeoisie (small employers) and between petit bourgeoisie and working class (semi-autonomous wage earners). In the later (1985) formulation a much more complex typology is adopted which underlines the importance of contradictory class locations as intersections of exploitation relations (Roemer, 1982):

There will therefore tend to be some positions which are exploiting along one dimension of exploitation relations, while on another are exploited. Highly skilled wage-earners (e.g. professionals) in capitalism are a good example: they are capitalistically exploited because they lack assets in capital and yet are skill exploiters. Such positions are what are typically referred to as the 'new middle class' of a given class system (Wright, 1985, p. 87).

One of the reasons for the rise of the middle class (and especially its professional component) has been the enormous expansion of the *state* and state apparatuses. The late twentieth-century welfare state is a vast network of institutions, compared to its nineteenth-century forebear. There are the various economic institutions including the Bank of England and the other nationalised industries. More particularly, there are the extensive institutions of health, law and education. Together, these institutions form an important nexus of socialisation – the state has clearly taken over many of the reproductive functions formerly carried out within civil society (Offe, 1984a). In addition, these institutions provide a collective focus for consumption (Castells, 1977; Saunders, 1981). An important point to note about these state apparatuses is that they operate at many spatial scales from the national through the regional to the local (Saunders, 1985). Of late, of course, the degree of state intervention in society has been declining but it is still possibly too early to mark this as a definitive, long-lasting trend (but see Offe, 1984a).

In the sphere of *civil society*, gender divisions are still strong but they have been lessening. Many households now rely on two incomes; 43 per cent of women now go out to work, although much of this work is still part-time and is crowded into the less well-paid occupations. However, ethnic divisions have possibly become much stronger than in the mid-nineteenth century when the most significant ethnic group was the Irish. Now with the advent of immigrants from a number of countries British civil society is more ethnically diverse but these ethnic groups tend to be disproportionately grouped in the working class. Households have continued their function as sites of production. There is evidence to suggest that, since the nineteenth century, outworking has continued to be an important source of income for many working-class households and may actually be on the increase at present (e.g. Mitter, 1986). In addition, households are still providing much of the means of their own subsistence but with the help of time-saving technology (Gershuny, 1978, 1985; Pahl, 1984). Households are becoming markedly more diverse in their structure. The 'standard' nuclear family of two adults and two children is decreasing both absolutely and as a proportion of all households while single parent and single person households are increasing rapidly at the same time. Thus the average size of the household decreased from 3.09 people in 1961 to 2.64 people in 1983 (Central Statistical Office, 1985). There are numerous reasons for these changes, of which the most important are divorce (in 1961 there were only 25 000 divorced people not remarried in the population of Great Britain; by 1983 the figure had increased to 1 655 000 (Central Statistical Office, 1985)), later marriage and childbearing and a population with more old people in it as a result of increased survival rates. An important point to note about British civil society is that it has become much more consumption-oriented than in the mid-nineteenth century. Some commentators have gone so far as to suggest that 'we may see developing in British society a major new fault line drawn not on the basis of class (ownership of means of production) but on the basis of sectoral alignment (ownership of means of consumption) (Saunders, 1984, p. 213). Whilst this statement may prove to be something of an exaggeration (Harloe, 1984; Dunleavy and Husbands, 1985) there is no doubt that patterns of household consumption have become important determinants of social change (see below).

The *space* of late twentieth-century Britain is being shaped in three ways. First, it is becoming a more and more concentrated space. Most large cities have expanded well beyond their official limits and have coalesced. One result is that there is now little difference between most 'urban' and 'rural' areas (with the exception of a few very remote areas). Many 'rural' areas, as a result of middle-class urbanisation of the countryside, have become middle-class suburbs with more or less trees and fields forming the Laura Ashley backdrop. This process of concentration has, of course, been a direct result of the enormous strides made since the nineteenth century in telecommunications and transport technologies. Britain has shrunk in terms of time distance and few places are now significantly far apart from other places, at least for those with the ability to pay to use the technologies. To a large extent places have, as a result, become decontextualised. Quite similar modes of experience and association are available to a large proportion of the British population, no matter where they live (Meyrowitz, 1985) and influences on action (especially information) of a more remote kind may be just as important as local influences. Second, and directly following on from the first point, many spaces in Britain are now artificially created milieux predicated not just on relations of production but also relations of consumption. The spread of the shopping mall and the fortress housing estate may not have gone as far as in the United States but still many milieux are effectively spatially interchangeable. A middle-class housing estate in Bristol may differ only in detail from a middle-class housing estate in Reading or Manchester. (Of course, in all this there are still many working-class ghettos in which, because of income, time distance is a considerable constraint.) Finally, the use of British space is now characterised by much greater flexibility. The evolution of flexibility within corporations, involving a bewildering array of strategies that can be used to turn a profit, has had important spatial effects which, in aggregate, mean that places are created and used up more quickly for the purposes of production or consumption. The decreasing turnover time of capital and the rapid recycling of space have become ever more closely linked (Harvey, 1985) with the result that local communities are more open to disruptions (whether as a result of the opening up of new production and consumption facilities or the closing down of old ones) than ever before.

The class character of late twentieth-century Britain is less easy to comprehend than that of the mid-nineteenth century because of all the factors mentioned above and no doubt many others as well. In sum, the British economy, state and civil society are all more complex.

What does seem clear is that it is no longer sufficient to describe the class character of late twentieth-century Britain as made up of a network of local production cultures integrated within the production and reproduction of capital. This does not mean that local production cultures no longer exist. A number of working-class cultures built around single industries can still be found, although many are currently in their death throes. But the problem is that the nature of places has changed in such a way as to diminish (not negate) the explanatory power of an approach based on the uneven development of production cultures. First, and most obviously, places are more likely to be middle class in character, clustered around service employment for the state or private capital and not direct factory production. Thus:

> Most women and, increasingly, most men will not spend most of their lives working full-time in capitalist enterprises producing mainly material commodities. [There are] . . . political and social consequences of the fact that the majority of people will not work full-time in such enterprises and for many people capitalism will be *indirectly* experienced as something *affecting* their experiences within the sphere of circulation (Urry, 1985a, p. 14, author emphasis).

Second, and following on from this point, *consumption* issues have become more important in the class constitution of places. There are good grounds for suggesting that as the volume of consumer goods available and the amount of time available to consume them has increased (although this is a hesitant and uneven process; see Table 7.1) so cultures based upon consumption have become more common. Indeed there is every reason to believe that consumption cultures have become an important determinant of class formation (e.g. Clarke and Critcher, 1985). This may mean that we should 'allow social relations of reproduction or cultural production to become the basis for specifying certain classes. This would certainly constitute a major reconstruction of the Marxist concept of class, but perhaps it is a necessary reconstruction' (Wright, 1985, n.28, pp. 60–1). Bourdieu (1984) has perhaps gone furthest in specifying what such a reconstruction might look like. (Other attempts, such as Aglietta's (1979) 'mode of consumption' are dangerously reductionist). Third, it may be that consumption issues are now the most crucial determinant of local politics, issues like the environment, education, taxation, quality of life, and so on. The 'dual politics' thesis has it that the politics of consumption is now more important at the local scale than class politics although class politics (the politics of production) are still important at the regional and national scales (see Table 7.2). Whilst this thesis can be disputed on a number of grounds (see below and Urry, 1985; Saunders, 1986) it still points to a number of significant

Table 7.1: Leisure time in minutes per average day in Britain for people aged 25–45 (1937, 1961 and 1975)

	Middle class	*Working class*
Employed men, with children		
1937	263	233
1961	250	245
1975	281	301
Employed men, no children		
1937	317	268
1961	251	284
1975	290	307
Non-employed women, with children		
1937	346	175
1961	272	292
1975	312	354

Source: Gershuny, 1985, p. 156

Table 7.2: The dual politics thesis

	Politics of production	*Politics of consumption*
Social base	Class interests	Consumption sector interest
Mode of interest mediation	Corporatist	Competitive
Level of intervention	Central state	Local state
Dominant ideology	Rights of private property	Rights of citizenship
Appropriate state theory	Instrumentalism (class theories)	Pluralism (interest group theories)

Source: Saunders, 1986

new developments. Fourth, as a general tendency, capitalist industry has in any case become much less tied to particular places as a result of technological change and what competitive advantages are offered by particular places now often revolve around the differences in quality and quantity of their labour supply (Storper and Walker, 1983). This tendency has been strengthened by the evolution of the multiplant form of corporate organisation whose relations of production are often intra-firm rather than intra-place (which is not to say that intra-place relations of production are no longer important). Thus many places now represent, in so far as they are linked to capitalist industry at all, nothing more than a supply of potential or actual labour power. Finally, places have become much more difficult to fence off as distinctive in their class mores because of the homogenising shifts in the space of Britain mentioned above coupled with the fact that the modern state reaches into all places. Urry (1984, p. 55) sums up the net effect of these changes so:

> International capital has been transformed first, through an increasing spatial indifference, and second, by the functionalising of its different global operations. Potential plants are often relatively small (even if part of massive multinationals) and capital will be relatively indifferent to where they are located. Hence labour-power assumes a particular importance as to location – and this includes differences in cost, skill, control, and reproduction. Provided there is or could be sufficient labour in a 'rural' area then expansion may well take place in that (greenfield) site rather than in alternative urban areas. Cities have become relatively less distinct areas, by-passed by various circuits of capital and of labour-power. Civil society is thus extended and, as a result of private transport, typical spatial constraints upon local civil societies are transcended. Individual subjects can increasingly choose where their labour-power is to be reproduced, in cities, towns, or 'rural' areas.

But, as Urry goes on to point out, precisely because places have become more diffuse and interchangeable labour pools, so what separates them from other labour pools has, in some senses, become more important. The game is to attract footloose capital so that even minimal local differences in the profile of labour supply (and to an extent, therefore, in class structure) can loom large in this situation.

Urry (1981; 1984; Abercrombie and Urry, 1983) suggests that, ignoring ethnic differences, there are four chief 'local' class structures that typify Britain today:

(1) large national or multinational corporations as the dominant employers – small service class – large number of deskilled white collar workers – large working class, either male or female, depending on supposed skill level – large informal economy.
(2) state as the dominant employer – large service class – large number of white collar workers – declining working class – high employment of women.
(3) traditional small firms as the dominant employers – large petty bourgeois sector – small service class – large male working class – lowish female employment.
(4) private service sector firms as the dominant employees – large service class – large number of deskilled white collar workers, both with high female component – smallish working class.

What has become clear is that the uneven development model is no longer completely adequate to the task of explaining class formation in space. Relations of consumption must now be set alongside relations of production. Places can no longer be seen as discrete social entities; class organisation within them is irretrievably tied to organisation in other places through national and regional levels of organisation and the state. Clearly, the task of explanation is considerably more complex.

It is no surprise, then, that accounts of class formation in space increasingly stress the importance of local civil society rather than just local class structure. Within this general trend a whole series of avenues of research have been opened up. For example, the study of local labour markets is addressed (as a way to study how the social division of labour interacts with class in particular places) (e.g. Cooke, 1982 a and b; Giddens and MacKenzie, 1982; Bradley, 1984, 1985). Again, general 'ethnographic' studies detailing local class consciousness have become popular (e.g. Thrift, 1986). And, of course, the importance of gender is now consistently (and properly) stressed (e.g.

Lancaster Regionalism Group, 1985). Perhaps the major gap in research consists of studies attempting to understand how different spatial scales of class organisation intermesh with one another to give a class particular strengths and weaknesses in particular arenas of conflict (Harris, 1983). Class capacity remains something of a mystery.

The example of the British service class will help to throw some light on these and other issues.

The British service class

The concept of the service class (or 'salariat') originates with the Austro-Marxist, Renner. In his original book, published in 1953, Renner (1978) isolated three main components of the service class: employees in public (i.e. state) service (civil servants and other officials); employees in private economic service (business administrators, managers, technical experts, and so on) and employees in social services (what Renner calls 'distributive agents of welfare'). Renner argues that the service class can be distinguished from other classes on two main grounds. First, the service class does not share in ownership of the means of production but its members can still be separated from the working class because their labour is non-productive. They are not sources of surplus but rather they constitute a charge on the surplus value which is directly or indirectly extracted from the working class. Second, the service class employment relationship is not a straightforward wage-labour contract, as with the working class. It is based upon a salary which implies relative security of employment, prospects for promotion and, most important of all, 'trust' that the employee will carry out his or her job, signified by the award of a measure of autonomy and discretion.

The idea of the service class has since been developed by, amongst others, Dahrendorf (1969), Gould (1980), Goldthorpe (1982; Goldthorpe, Llewellyn and Payne, 1980; Goldthorpe and Payne, 1986) and Urry (1981, 1984, 1985; Abercrombie and Urry, 1983). There are also clear lines of connection to the work of Johnson on the professions (1977a,b, 1982), the Ehrenreichs on the 'professional managerial class' (Ehrenreich and Ehrenreich, 1979) and even Wright's (1985) discussion of the possession of credentials. Broadly speaking each of these authors adds to basic relations of production that typify the service class other market relations and relations of reproduction. In other words, in the case of the service class at least, class relations are not only constructed through the social relations of production. Currently the literature suggests that the service class has been formed by at least four main processes. These are:

(1) As in Renner's original formulation, the service class consists of unproductive wage labourers. This is not a pejorative description. This situation has arisen because there has been a vast growth of unproductive labour in all capitalist economies in the shape of the expansion of services employment and the state (see above), as a result of the intertwining of capitalist development with an increasing specialisation of the social division of labour (Walker, 1985a, b).

(2) The service class, as in Renner's formulation of the employment relation, has a degree of autonomy and discretion in the way its members operate at work. In late twentieth-century capitalist societies, with their complex division of labour, authority must increasingly be delegated (the managerial function) and specialist knowledge must increasingly be drawn upon (the professional function). Thus, the service class has a good 'work situation' (Lockwood, 1958).

(3) The service class operates within a primary labour market characterised by high incomes, a degree of job security, geographical mobility, and opportunities for promotion. This is the result of the growth of the large and complex bureaucracies of corporations and the state. Thus, the service class has a good 'market situation' (Lockwood, 1958).

(4) The service class is predicated on the growth in importance of educational credentials which both make its labour more attractive and, to a degree, allow it to close off access to its work and market situations through the use of professions, examinations and other social mechanisms.

The service class of managers and professionals is formed by these four processes coming together. It is a compositely rather than a uniquely determined class, based upon a number of different social processes *and* the way that these processes have both defined and been defined by struggle with other classes.

The capacity of the service class to fight for its own interests comes from four main sources. First of all, there is the simple observation that it is growing rapidly rather than declining in size as a result of developments in the division of labour and other arenas. Second, there is the fact that the service class has disproportionate access to resources, economic and otherwise, on which it can draw to maintain its connectedness. Third, members of the service class are more mobile and so can gain access more easily to one another than can members of the other classes. And, fourth, the connectedness of other social classes has been weakened. The capitalist class has been weakened by 'depersonalisation' and 'internationalisation' (although the service class still depends upon its dictates) while the working class has been eroded by its shrinking numbers and its inability to gain a hold on the burgeoning division of labour.

Clearly, there are a number of objections to the service class thesis (see, for example, the critique in Crompton and Jones, 1984). There is a substantial boundary problem in deciding where the service class ends and a white collar 'clerical' middle class begins. There is a problem in deciding how a process of deskilling might apply at the lower boundary of the class. There is a problem in identifying clear class interests. There is a problem in demonstrating a redistribution of income from other classes (but see Urry, 1985a). And so on. It is doubtful whether objections like these can be countered except by concrete studies of the service class in action over time.

In the description of the current condition of the service class in Britain that follows, the class is taken to be represented, when official figures are cited, by Social Classes I (professional occupations) and II (intermediate occupations) and by Socio-Economic Groups 1, 2 and 13 (employers and managers) and 3 and 4 (professionals) (see Office of Population Censuses and Surveys, 1980). Both of these sets of figures have disadvantages. First, they exaggerate the size of the service class by including certain employees who should be placed in other classes (but see Scase and Goffee, 1982). Second, they must be used with extreme caution in making temporal comparisons because of the changes made in the definition of the classes or groups over time. Third, they are strongly gender-biased and exclude unwaged people (Dunleavy and Husbands, 1985). And, fourth, they equate class solely with occupation. These very considerable disadvantages are offset by the fact that the official figures form the most generally accessible (and in some cases the only) sources of data.

In Britain, the service class has been expanding rapidly, most particularly as a result of the general rise in employment in service industries. Service employment expanded rapidly during the 1970s

Table 7.3: Employed population by sector, 1971 and 1981

Sector	*1971* No. employed	*% total employed*	*1981* No. employed	*% total employed*
Agriculture	633 990	2.69	514 100	2.26
Mining, Energy, Utilities Transport[(a)]	2 319 250	9.84	2 204 290	9.71
Manufacturing	8 137 060	34.54	6 192 490	27.28
Construction	1 668 610	7.08	1 605 030	7.07
Services	10 812 400	45.85	12 188 020	53.68

Notes:
[(a)] Some of the activities often included within the service sector in employment figures are included in this sector in census figures.
Source: Owen and Green, 1985, p. 2, from the Census of Population.

and into the 1980s (Table 7.3). For example during the decade from 1971 to 1981 the share of the total employed population accounted for by manufacturing fell from 35.54 per cent to 27.28 per cent while the share of the total employed population accounted for by services increased from 45.85 per cent to 53.68 per cent (Table 7.4). These trends have continued since 1981. However, aggregate figures

Table 7.4: Socio-economic structure of service class in manufacturing and services only, 1971 and 1981[a]

Manufacturing	1971 *No. of employees*	*Proportion of total employees (per cent)*	1981 *No. of employees*	*Proportion of total employees (per cent)*	1971–81 change *Absolute*	*Percentage*
Manufacturing						
Employers and Managers	533 550	6.56	627 390	10.14	94 380	+3.58
Professionals	251 050	3.09	231 290	3.79	−19 760	+0.65
Services						
Employees and Managers	1 341 680	12.42	1 679 050	13.78	337 370	+1.36
Professionals	504 920	4.67	567 470	4.66	62 550	−0.01

Notes:
[(a)] Some of the change in absolute and proportional figures is the result of changes in the classification of Socio-economic Groups from 1971 to 1981
Source: Owen and Green, 1984, p. 4, from the Census of Population

showing increases in service employment conceal important intra-sectoral variations (Table 7.5). For example, in the services sector transport and more recently government employment have declined, but these falls in employment have been more than balanced by increases in employment in the so-called 'producer services' (banking and finance, business services and real estate), in private health care

Table 7.5: Employees in employment, service-industry activities, Great Britain 1974–84

Service-industry activity	*1974*[a]	%	*1984*	%	*Change per annum (%)*
Wholesale distribution	811.8	6.8	913.2	7.0	1.25
Dealing in scrap, etc.	15.6	0.13	20.6	0.16	3.20
Commission exports	16.6	0.14	18.2	0.14	0.96
Retail distribution	2047.9	17.0	2090.5	16.0	0.21
Hotels and catering	808.2	6.7	916.0	7.0	1.33
Repair of consumer goods and vehicles	179.6	1.5	208.1	1.6	1.59
Railways	195.4	1.6	157.4	1.2	−1.96
Other inland transport	467.2	3.9	390.3	3.0	−1.65
Sea transport	84.3	0.7	45.9	0.4	−4.55
Air transport	47.0	0.4	42.0	0.3	−1.06
Services to transport	116.6	1.0	94.0	0.7	−1.94
Miscellaneous transport and storage	120.8	1.1	146.8	1.1	2.15
Postal services and telecommunications	434.2	3.6	421.5	3.2	−0.29
Banking and finance	392.3	3.3	508.3	3.9	2.96
Business services	704.7	5.9	916.3	7.0	3.00
Renting of movables, owning and dealing in real estate	173.5	1.4	144.8	1.5	1.23
Public admin. and defence	1636.5	13.6	1546.0	11.8	−0.55
Sanitary services	228.1	1.9	295.3	2.3	2.95
Education	1450.5	12.1	1564.0	11.9	2.65
Research and development	111.9	0.9	127.4	0.9	1.39
Medical and other health services	1027.5	8.6	1291.8	9.9	2.57
Other services	376.6	3.1	610.7	4.7	6.21
Recreational and cultural services	375.1	3.1	405.5	3.1	0.81
Personal services	191.6	1.6	172.7	1.3	−0.99
	12013.5	100.07	13047.3	100.1	0.90

Note:
[a] Thousands

Source: *Employment Gazette Historical Supplement*, No. 1, August 1984

and in 'other services' (Daniels, 1985; Daniels and Thrift, 1986).

These changes, signifying as they do new restructurings of capital and the continued development of the social division of labour, have been sufficient to guarantee a general expansion in white collar occupations, and especially service class occupations, continuing a trend active since at least 1911 (Routh, 1980). Thus, the number of non-manual service sector employees increased from 6 726 790 in 1971 to 7 843 500 in 1981 and the number of non-manual employees in the manufacturing sector declined only very slowly, from 2 242 140 in 1971 to 1 963 480 in 1981. (Meanwhile, of course, manual manufacturing jobs declined precipitately.)

Much of this increase in non-manual employees is undoubtedly the result of the general growth in part-time work in the 1970s and 1980s but even so, as shown in Table 7.5, there was a general proportional (and in some cases absolute) increase in service class occupations whether measured by Socio-Economic Group or social class (Table 7.6). It is important to note that the table also shows that this increase in service-class occupations was not confined to the service industries. In manufacturing industry, managers increased from 1971 to 1981, although professionals declined slightly.

Table 7.6: Persons in employment by social class in Great Britain, all sectors, 1981[a]

Social class	*Number (thousands)*	*per cent*
Service class – Professional (I)	93	4.06
Service class – Intermediate (II)	514	22.43
Skilled (non-manual) (III(N))	531	23.17
Skilled (manual) (III(M))	558	24.35
Partly-skilled (IV)	414	18.06
Unskilled (V)	137	5.98
Armed forces/unclassified	45	1.95
Total	2 292	100.00

Notes:
(a) 1971 figures are not given in this table because of general changes between the 1971 and 1981 classification
Source: Beacham, 1984, p. 7 after Census of Population

One of the implications of the continuation of growth in the size of the service class in the 1970s and 1980s has been consistently noted by Goldthorpe (1982; Goldthorpe, Llewellyn and Payne, 1980; Goldthorpe and Payne, 1986). This is that the service class has been 'forced' to

Table 7.7: Inter-class recruitment of men, aged 20–64, into service class positions in England only, 1972

	% of parents who held service class positions
Class	
Service	31
Routine non-manual	10
Petty bourgeoisie	11
Farmers	3
Working class	46

Source: Goldthorpe, 1982, p. 173.

take in a sizeable proportion of mainly men but also some women from other classes (Table 7.7). This recruitment could be interpreted as an 'invasion from below'. However it is important to underline the fact that when occupational changes are taken into account, so-called 'relative mobility' rates have stayed constant. Relative chances of access to service class positions are much the same as they have always been (Heath, 1981).

Further, certain social groups have been and still are relatively more excluded from the service-class. Women, in particular, are under-represented in service-class occupations (Table 7.8), even given that current occupational schemata tend to be biased against the clusters of occupations in which women predominate (Dunleavy and Husbands,

Table 7.8: Social class by gender in Great Britain, 1971 and 1981 (%)

Social class	Men		Women	
	1971	1981	1971	1981
Service class – Professional (I)	4.6	6.0	0.6	1.1
Service class – Intermediate (II)	18.7	23.2	16.1	21.2
Skilled (non-manual) (III(N))	12.6	11.9	38.4	40.1
Skilled (manual) (III(M))	37.0	35.1	10.3	8.2
Partly skilled (IV)	17.2	16.0	26.0	21.2
Unskilled (V)	7.5	5.2	7.1	7.1
Armed forces/unskilled	2.4	2.5	1.5	1.2
Total	100.0	99.9	100.0	100.1

Source: Beacham, 1984, p. 9 after Census of Population

1985). When women are included in service class occupations their earnings tend to be less, as well (Foord, 1984; Martin and Roberts, 1984). However there are some signs that this situation is changing – more women are being recruited into the professions (see Crompton and Sanderson, 1986) as well as into traditional female service-class occupations in education, health and welfare. Various ethnic groups are also strongly under-represented in service-class occupations and, like women, their incomes tend to be lower when they do attain membership (Table 7.9).

Table 7.9: Ethnic groups in different socio-economic groups in Great Britain, 1981 (%)

	White	*West Indian/ Guyanese*	*Indian/Pakistani/ Bangladeshi*
Males			
Service class – Professionals	6	2	8
Service class – Employees and managers	16	4	12
Intermediate	18	7	14
Skilled manual	38	49	35
Semi-skilled manual	16	27	25
Unskilled manual	5	11	6
Females			
Service class – Professionals	1	0	3
Service class – Employees and managers	7	2	4
Intermediate	53	50	41
Skilled manual	7	4	13
Semi-skilled manual	23	34	35
Unskilled manual	8	8	3

Source: Urry, 1985, p. 67, after Labour Force Survey

The growth in the numbers of the service class in recent years (and before) has not only been a result of shifts in the economy. Other processes have fuelled its growth as well and in particular the strength it has gained through the related factors of boosted income, favourable access to educational opportunity and provision of a common consumption-oriented lifestyle. First, the service class has been able to differentiate itself from other classes by the sheer weight of its economic resources, (and especially since 1979 when a new middle-class welfare state based upon redistribution of income to the middle class was introduced). Table 7.10 shows one indication of this fact.

ble 7.10: The distribution of income between classes (based upon head of usehold's occupation)[a]

ss	*Bottom 10%*	*9th 10%*	*8th 10%*	*7th 10%*	*6th 10%*	*5th 10%*	*4th 10%*	*3rd 10%*	*2nd 10%*	*Top 10%*
vice class	0.2	0.5	2.4	4.3	6.0	7.5	13.0	17.2	21.2	27.7
er non-manual	1.8	3.7	6.9	9.4	10.1	12.4	14.0	13.8	13.6	14.2
nual	2.3	4.0	8.2	12.2	14.5	15.3	13.2	12.8	10.5	6.9

s:
Table does not include retired or unemployed who occupy most of the lower deciles
ce: Urry, 1985, p. 65

Second, the service class has been able to maintain its access to educational qualifications very effectively indeed:

> the Nuffield researchers (Goldthorpe, Llewellyn and Payne, 1980; Halsey, Heath and Ridge, 1980) concluded that 'school inequalities of opportunity have been remarkably stable'; they endorsed Tawney's comment, originally made in 1931, that the 'hereditary curse upon English education is its organisation upon lines of social class'. Halsey, Heath and Ridge (1980) show that the gap in educational opportunity between the service class and the working class is dramatic; so that by the minimum school leaving age three quarters of the working class had left school, while three quarters of the service class stayed on. Yet this applies of course to a relatively tiny proportion of working class boys (less than one in 40 passed one 'A' level in the sample) (Urry, 1985, p. 69).

Third, service-class members have been able to maintain a relatively homogeneous lifestyle based upon conspicuous (but tasteful) consumption (Table 7.11). As Pahl (1966, p. 273) put it 'choice is a way of life'.

The lifestyle of the service class is clear enough. It consists of owner-occupiers living in highly self-serviced homes. That time-saving gadgets abound is no surprise. Service-class work hours tend to be longer than for other classes if work taken home is counted in. Leisure consists of various activities. Television is watched less in service-class households than in other classes (in 1985 exactly 12 hours per week less than in working-class households) and the hours saved are used in other ways, including those concerned with displaying choices that demonstrate what Bourdieu (1984) called the 'cultural nobility' of the service class (helped, of course, by the fact that the service class has the income to indulge these choices) (Table 7.12).

Table 7.11: Indicators of service class consumption culture in Great Britain, 1982, based on sample

Socio-economic group	*Owner-occupiers (by head of household) (%)*	*House with central heating (by head of household (%)*	*Covered by private medical insurance (by person) (%)*	*Smokers (by person) (%)*	*Ownership of two cars (by head of household (%)*	*Ownership of dishwasher (by head of household (%)*
Service class – professionals	89	87	24	21	37	19
Service class – employers and managers	86	83	19	29	36	15
Intermediate non-manual	87	75	} 10	} 30	22	5
Junior non-manual	63	67			16	2
Skilled manual	56	59	3	40	16	2
Semi-skilled manual	35	44	2	41	7	1
Unskilled manual	35	44	3	45	2	1
Economically inactive heads	43	51	–	–	3	1
Great Britain	56	60	7	35	14	5

Source: Office of Population Census and Surveys, 1984

Table 7.12: Participation in selected social and cultural activities in previous four weeks by socio-economic group, 1983 (%)

	Professional, employees and managers	*Intermediate and junior non-manual*	*Skilled manual*	*Semi-skilled and unskilled manual*
Open air outings				
Seaside	9	9	6	6
Country	5	3	2	2
Parks	4	5	3	3
Entertainment				
Going to cinema	9	10	5	4
Visiting historic buildings	13	11	6	5
Going to theatre/opera/ballet	8	7	2	2
Going to museums/art galleries	5	4	2	2
Going out for a meal	61	51	34	27
Going out for a drink	56	55	61	50
Dancing	10	13	9	9
Home				
Listening to records/tapes	69	70	60	54
Gardening	58	47	46	39
Needlework/Knitting	14	42	11	30
Home repairs/DIY	55	35	45	27
Reading books	68	70	44	45

Source: Central Statistical Office, 1985, p. 149

Two important points need to be noted here concerning the consumption-based lifestyle of the service class. First of all, this lifestyle is based upon interchangeable locations, signified by, for example, the increase in housing estates and out-of-town hypermarkets and shopping malls, and born out of the high geographical mobility of the service class. Second, the consumption lifestyle has, of course, wrought changes in the nature of capital. The service class constitutes an opulent and growing market. Thus there is a distinctive structure of building provision (Ball, 1983) for the service class, a whole set of distinctive niches for consumer goods and financial services, and so on. Manufacturing, service and construction industries have all become more and more geared to the needs of the service class as it has grown so that, in part, the service class feeds on itself.

The service class does not just form as a result of common economic, social and cultural characteristics, although in the case of the service class these characteristics undoubtedly give it a head start. In particular, they give it a fairly homogeneous class consciousness, based on shared values, and well described by Deverson and Lindsay (1975, p. 212):

> Successful middle class people do not, as a rule, question their motives for working hard, striving to achieve a comfortable life style, encouraging their children to be successful, and filling in their time with profitable activity. They have established a very definite way of life which puts them above most of the population and gives them society's assurance that they are doing the right thing. They are to be envied, even looked up to, by the majority who have not made it.
>
> They are wealthy enough to achieve a comfortable status in life, but not rich enough to be considered immoral. Only three in our sample had inherited wealth, only one mentioned the stock exchange as a source of income, and there were no evil property developers, mail-order sharks or other rough dealers. Most of them had reached their positions through a combination of intelligence, hard work, self-confidence and a dedication to duty. They are controlled, reasonable and honest; their success is seen as a result of these good qualities and they feel they deserve what they have – the nice houses, the good salaries and the respect of others.

In line with their lifestyle, members of the service class tend to emphasise a degree of stability and order, expressed in issues like their attitude to heritage and the environment (Wright, 1985; Lowe and Goyder, 1983). These are the values of 'deep England' (Thrift, 1983), based upon the 'rural' historical imagery revealed in country kitchens and Laura Ashley fabrics.

All this said, clearly political action (broadly defined) is a necessary condition for the formation of social classes. Certain class interests have to be protected or attained. But there are barriers in the way of coherent service-class political action. In particular, it is difficult for the service class to define common class interests because it tends to be politically highly fragmented. For example, there are no distinctive service-class political institutions (although the advent of the SDP/ Liberal Alliance may eventually change this situation). In addition, service-class political organisations have to compete with other class organisations formed earlier on which have well-established modes of organisation (Abercrombie and Urry, 1983).

Of course, this does not mean that the service class has no distinctive political allegiances. In discussing service-class politics, two important observations need to be made. First, the size of the service-class electorate has been growing in line with the general expansion of service class occupations (Table 7.13). Second, quite clearly the

Table 7.13: Class composition of the electorate, 1964 and 1973 (%)

	1964	*1983*
Service class	18	27
Routine non-manual	18	24
Petty bourgeoisie	7	8
Foremen and technicians	10	7
Working class	47	34
Total	100	100

Source: Heath, Jowell and Curtice, 1985, p. 36, based on sample survey

Table 7.14: Voting according to class, 1983 General Election (%)

	Conservative	*Labour*	*Alliance*	*Others*	*Total*
Service class	54	14	31	1	100
Routine non-manual	46	25	27	2	100
Petty bourgeoisie	71	12	17	0	100
Foremen and technicians	48	26	25	1	100
Working class	30	49	20	1	100

Source: Heath, Jowell and Curtice, 1985, p. 20, based on sample survey

service class is a conservative class in its political allegiances. At the national level, few of its votes go to the Labour Party. Most go to the Conservatives and the Alliance (Table 7.14).

It has been widely argued that the class base of politics has declined since the 1966 General Election, that Britain has experienced a period of 'class dealignment' (Sarlvik and Crewe, 1983) in which voters no longer support their 'natural' class party to the extent that they used to. The problem, of course, lies in identifying to what extent electoral misfortune is the result of bad political strategies followed by the losing party (or parties) and to what extent it is the result of a real shift in class voting patterns. Needless to say the debate here is long and crucially dependent upon the measures of class voting used, the adequacy of class classifications, and the choice of an electoral base year at which dealignment is supposed to have set in. To the extent that class dealignment has taken place (and that extent is disputed; contrast, for example, Dunleavy and Husbands, 1985 with Heath, Jowell and Curtice, 1985) then a number of interrelated processes can be identified that contribute to it. Three stand out, however.

The first of the processes contributing to class dealignment results from the changing shape of the British class structure. Specifically, it is the rise of the service class which has had the most effect:

There is little evidence that class differences have withered away or that the classes have changed their character, but there can be no question that the shape of the class structure has been gradually changing throughout the post-war period.

The implications of the two claims are very different. If class dealignment has occurred, the implication is that the political parties should stop appealing to voters' class interests. If classes have become fragmented and lack the distinctiveness they once had, class issues will be less potent sources of votes.

But if, on the other hand, as we suggest the class structure has simply changed shape, the implication is that class interests persist. Parties must therefore continue to appeal to them, since they remain fundamentals of electoral choice. For a party to abandon class appeals is to run the risk of losing the class votes that it still has (and in Labour's case a majority of its votes still come from the working class). According to this view, Labour faces a particular dilemma. Its class base is shrinking, but it dare not abandon it for it has nowhere better to seek votes. Equally, all is not rosy for the Conservative party since, although the (service class) is expanding it has to compete with two other parties, the Liberal and Social Democratic parties which are also relatively strong in the (service class) (Heath, Jowell and Curtice, 1985, p. 36).

A second process contributing to class dealignment that is often identified consists of the replacement of class allegiances by other sectoral cleavages based upon both production (and especially state and non-state employment) and consumption (and especially individual or collective consumption). The service class can be expected to be particularly affected by consumption cleavages, given that:

people's consumption locations are not influenced solely or simply by their class positions. Rather it is the combination of their class position and other social characteristics – such as their urban and regional environment, stage in the life cycle, household position, the time period when they entered the housing market, ability to gain access to state subsidies – all of these other factors are also involved in how people consume goods and services. The basic reality of class structured access to consumption is not in question. Yet neither are consumption positions simply corollaries of class (Dunleavy and Husbands, 1985, p. 139).

Dunleavy and Husbands (1985) suggest that exposure, and especially cumulative exposure, to consumption sectors like home ownership, household access to a car, family use of private medical care, past or present use of private schooling, and so on all increase the probability that a voter will favour the party that favours a growth in a particular consumption sector to which she has become committed. Clearly such an approach has particular relevance to the voting behaviour of the service class (Table 7.15).

Table 7.15: Voting in the 1983 General Election by social class and consumption sector (%)

Social class	*Number of private consumption sectors*	*Labour*	*Conservative*	*Alliance*	*Conservative lead over Labour*
Employers/ petit bourgeoisie	Two	16	59	25	+43
	Three or more	0	88	12	+88
Controllers of labour (service class)	One or none	31	44	25	+36
	Two	17	54	30	+84
	Three or more	6	70	34	+66
Non-manual workers	None	37	47	16	+10
	One	21	50	29	+29
	Two	17	48	37	+31
	Three or more	10	51	39	+41
Manual workers	None	57	21	21	−36
	One	47	24	29	−23
	Two	38	36	26	−2
	Three or more	23	40	37	+17

Source: Dunleavy and Husbands, 1985, p. 142

Perhaps the most extreme view of the consumption sector explanation is provided by Saunders (1981; 1984; Cawson and Saunders, 1983) who suggests that, because consumption is 'constrained but not determined by production' (Saunders, 1984, p. 207), there is no necessary alignment between class and consumption. Instead each consumption sector produces its own band of interest groups who organise and struggle around a single consumption issue rather than in any concentrated or developing way. In Saunders's 'dual state' depiction (see above), then, consumption issues are handled by local governments in the context of hundreds of local political arenas. Perhaps Dunleavy and Husbands (1985, p. 139) viewpoint is appropriate to cite here. In their view:

recent trends do not suggest . . . the displacement of class politics by issue-specific, micro-social mobilisations. Instead, the extent to which any single consumption process affects alignment reflects primarily two factors; the degree of fragmentation of the electorate around the line of cleavage involved; and the importance of the issue area both in terms of its objective economic implications for people and in terms of how dominant ideological messages present the issues involved.

Most debate on the political importance of consumption sectors has focused on housing tenure and has ranged from those who countenance housing tenure as a determinant of political action by the middle class (e.g. Pratt, 1982; Thorns, 1981; Dunleavy and Husbands, 1985) to those who don't (e.g. Ball, 1983; Heath, Jowell and Curtice, 1985). In the heat of this debate other consumption sectors tend to have been neglected. One important set of consumption issues which have been shown to inspire service-class political activities are those 'conservation' issues revolving around national heritage and the environment. The service class is very much involved in these issues which appeal both to its general ideology of an unchanging and green England (Wright, 1985) and the need to defend the 'positional goods' of old masonry and countryside (Hirsch, 1977) against newcomers. First of all, it is heavily represented in various of the heritage and environmental groups (Table 7.16). Second, service-class members tend to take on the leadership of heritage and environmental groups, whatever the class complexion of the group concerned, because of their social background and skills. Take the case of environmental groups:

The social composition of voluntary organisations is an important determinant of the kinds of skills and knowledge they command . . . environmental groups have a largely middle- and upper-middle class membership. From this section of the population they attract a high proportion of professional people with

Table 7.16: Social composition of three environmental groups (by head of household) (%)

	Bedfordshire and Huntingdon Naturalists Trust (1980)	*National Trust (1973)*	*Royal Society for the Protection of Birds (1979)*
Managerial and professional (service class)	78	72	25
Technical and clerical	9	24	41
Skilled manual	11	3	20
Unskilled manual	2	1	14

Source: Lowe and Goyder, 1983, p. 10

authority. A survey of Yorkshire amenity groups found that 62 per cent of them all, and 74 per cent of those in urban areas, could call on more than six different professional skills from among the following: teacher, architect, historian, lawyer, financier, planner, surveyor, estate agent, journalist, archaeologist, youth leader and forester. Similarly, a summary of amenity societies in Kent revealed that most societies included amongst their members at least one architect, nearly half had a lawyer, 15 per cent a surveyor and 12 per cent a planner (Lowe and Goyder, 1983, p. 91).

Service-class members with the same knowledge and background as their counterparts in local and national government are more easily able to gain trust and cooperation than other class members. In many cases, the result is that service class members can force their class interests through those of opposing classes. Thus:

studies of rural Suffolk have shown that environmental protection favours middle class residents, farmers and landowners, but acts against working class interests particularly in restricting employment and housing opportunities and public amenities. Ferris (1982) in his case study of environmental involvement in the Barnsbury area of Islington, has shown how a well endowed environmental group can pursue interests which are at odds with the interests of the majority of the area's residents. The main achievement of the Barnsbury Association, founded in 1964 by a group of newly arrived young professionals in a traditional working-class area of private rented accommodation lay in 'the way they gained official acceptance of what they defined as the major problems facing the area'. Their aims of enhancing the environment of recently improved housing, and changing the policy for the area from redevelopment to the improvement of older houses, and their successful promotion of a traffic management scheme were, Ferris suggests, irrelevant or even counter to the interests of the majority, for whom standards of housing were more important than general amenity (Lowe and Goyder, 1983, p. 102).

A third process contributing to class dealignment is the changing nature of local political cultures. Johnston (1985, p. 295) puts it thus:

The parties which have dominated English politics for the last half century – Conservative and Labour – have developed not simply social changes within the electorate (whereby certain classes support one party and others support the second) but *socio-spatial cleavages*, with members of particular classes varying in their degree of support for a particular party according to its importance in the local political, social and economic milieu. Thus labour gets its strongest support from the working class, on a national basis, but its support from all classes varies spatially – being greatest in those areas where working class voters are most numerous and where labour has traditionally been strong (in the area as a whole, and not just the constituency). Similarly, the Conservative Party gains most votes from the middle class nationally, but obtains its strongest support, from all classes, in constituencies and areas where middle class milieux dominate. The Liberal Party has no firm class base (nor does its new ally, the SDP); it has made electoral inroads in certain areas – often on a pragmatic, *ad hoc* basis, at by-elections and via local government election successes – and then has built on this support, establishing some spatial, if not socio-spatial, continuity of voting strength.

In this depiction, service class political action is both national and local. Interestingly, however, Heath, Howell and Curtice (1985) suggest that the nature of the local milieux of the service class makes much less difference to the voting pattern of its members than for other classes, perhaps because their life chances are much less affected by the places through which they live, because of service class association with bureaucracies and their high rates of geographical mobility.

Johnston's mention of the milieux of the service class leads conveniently to the discussion of service class geography. The geography of the service class is important because the members of the service class tend to be particularly active in shaping the places in which they live in their image. Everywhere in Britain, as the service class expands, it is shaping places to suit its lifestyle.

The geography of the British service class is fairly straightforward, at least in outline. Most importantly of all, it connects to the geography of service industry (Figure 7.1). To summarise, for a century and more the geography of the service industry has been consistently biased toward the 'South' (which can be defined as the South East, South West and East Anglia), and most especially the South East (Lee, 1984). This is no particular surprise. The South East contains many high level services. It has the City of London (Thrift, 1986), the bulk of large corporate headquarters (Goddard and Smith, 1977) and associated producer service firms (Dunning and Norman, 1983), the chief arms of government, the major part of research and development effort (Howells, 1984), and it is central to national and international communication networks. It also has a good proportion of lower level services like transport, retailing and distribution, riding on the back of the South East's population size and wealth. Over the last twenty years or so this complex of service activities has spilled over the boundaries of the South East into parts of the South West and East Anglia, partly as a result of office decentralisation (especially in the producer service sector), partly as a result of the growth of high

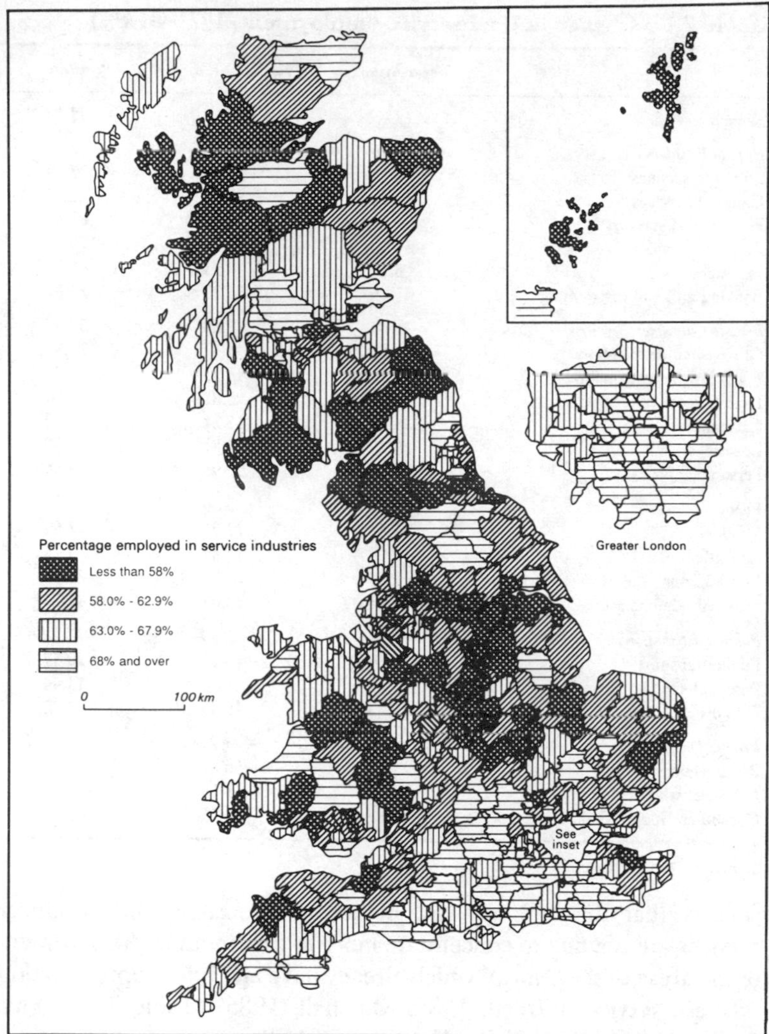

Figure 7.1 The location of service employment: services employment as a percentage of total employment, 1981
Source: Beacham, 1984

technology manufacturing industry, and partly as a result of consumer services like retailing following the market (Massey, 1984; Boddy, Lovering and Basset, 1986).

What is perhaps more surprising is that the evidence seems to

Table 7.17: Change in total service employment, 1971–81 (%)

	Great Britain	*Tyne and Wear*	*Berkshire*
Services	*13.45*	*7.86*	*31.09*
Private Producer Services	*33.00*	*42.29*	*84.96*
Strategic services	4.11	71.16	127.63
Contract services	47.02	51.43	67.72
Professional services	38.74	19.02	81.66
Property services	58.90	123.88	170.02
Insurance	8.79	8.54	61.19
Banking and Bill discounting	35.20	36.32	24.37
Private Consumer Services	*18.03*	*12.84*	*34.82*
Other retail distribution	3.84	4.42	22.36
Food/Drink distribution	−3.50	−13.95	7.99
High Street services	14.49	5.81	31.84
Catering	30.04	16.21	74.40
Leisure	28.20	29.81	−15.30
Personal services	76.35	93.96	185.54
Public Services	*13.69*	*9.00*	*11.73*
Medical	32.63	27.72	32.59
Education	19.03	−2.47	9.99
Local administration	−11.03	−11.71	−22.80
National administration	4.61	28.03	41.74
Public Distribution	*−9.74*	*−9.50*	*−12.28*
Public transport	−16.39	−10.20	−29.57
Post/Telecom.	−1.03	1.64	−14.44
Utilities	−8.34	−15.45	12.82
Private Distribution	*1.79*	*−23.70*	*61.63*
Road/Sea transport	−25.28	−56.81	−19.29
Industrial wholesaling	16.82	1.15	124.35
Consumer Goods wholesaling	11.87	−11.85	48.89

Source: Green, 1985, p. 14

suggest that the high growth, higher level services like producer services are tending to concentrate more in the South to the detriment of the areas of the 'North' which already have an under-representation of these services (Green, 1985; Marshall, 1985) (Table 7.17). This finding has to be coupled with others including:

(1) the fact that Northern areas tend to be more reliant on state service employment which is now being cut back (Massey, 1984);
(2) the fact that, although there was an evening out of the spatial distribution between 1971 and 1981, still the South has benefited most from the increase in female part-time jobs (Centre for Urban and Regional Development Studies, 1984); and
(3) men employed in the North tend to be concentrated in the

declining service industries (Green, 1985). Thus, the overall picture is one of North–South polarisation of the service industries, with the South increasingly favoured.

This is not, of course, to claim that every place in the South is gaining service employment and every place in the North is losing it. There are always exceptions to any rule. Townsend (1986), for example, in a study of Britain over the 1978 to 1981 period, finds examples of urban centres displaying service employment growth in the North as well as the South. However, what seems certain from this study is that the most rapid service employment growth in Britain in this period was in what Townsend calls 'freestanding' (that is, outside the influence of major conurbations) service towns, centres like Exeter, Guildford, Reading, Bath and Oxford – and most of these centres were in the South (Table 7.18).

At this point, it would be possible to represent the changes in the distribution of the service class as a direct and unequivocal reflection of the changes in the location of service industry (and certain manufacturing sectors, as well). This would be an error of the gravest kind. There is no direct line of causality between the geography of production and the geography of the service class, with the service class blindly and loyally following on the location of industry. This is not just because the state and civil society (whether at national or local levels) intervene in the links between production and class, although clearly they do and their interventions are important. It is also because the service class has its own causal powers which can influence the location of industry. Six examples of how these powers operate will suffice to make this point. First of all, as capital has become depersonalised, so managers and professionals have increasingly come to decide where manufacturing or service industry locates. It is no surprise, then, to find a bias to the kind of environments the service class prefers in these location decisions, given obvious constraints. The same point applies, of course, to location decisions made by members of the service class employed by the various state apparatuses. Second, as the service class pool of labour becomes concentrated in particular places, so employers must go to those places to find labour – a mutually reinforcing process. Third, the service-class labour market is of much greater spatial extent than the labour markets of other classes (see Coombes, Green and Owen, 1985), given the propensity of its members for long distance commuting, their greater mobility (partly a function of working in upper reaches of the hierarchies of

Table 7.18: Areas of increasing service sector employment in Great Britain, 1978–81

Service sector category of employment	Percentage of TTWA's[a] showing net increase 1978–81 in each region[b]											Total changes in the TTWA/s	Total change 1971–1 (%)	(%)	Leading cases, TWWA by ranked chi-squared values
	SE	EA	SW	EM	WM	YH	NW	NO	WA	SC	Total[c]				
Insurance, banking and finance	13	6	17	9	8	9	8	7	10	13	303	123,800	114,000	9.6	Stevenage, Ripon, Northwich, Milton Keynes
Producer services	13	8	15	8	6	10	8	6	11	15	272	207,500	155,900	4.3	Swindon, Basingstoke, Chester
Medical and dental services	15	5	17	8	8	9	8	7	8	15	282	113,100	92,000	7.2	Braintree, St. Helens, Clacton, Yeovil

Source: Townsend, 1986, pp. 536–674

Notes

[a] TTWA, Department of Employment Travel to work area as defined in 1978

[b] SE South East, EA East Anglia, SW South West, EM East Midlands, WM West Midlands, YH Yorkshire Humberside, NW North West, NO north, WA Wales, SC Scotland

[c] Total number of TTWAs, 380

national and international organisations) and their greater sophistication in job search coupled with more and better sources of job information. Thus, service class members have much greater choice than members of other classes over jobs (and over where to live) (Pahl, 1966) which means that employers must be more willing to respond to these preferences. Fourth, the kind of environments necessary to reproduce the labour of the service class and most especially 'good' schools are more likely to be found in particular places which, again, in a mutually reinforcing process, become more and more attractive to service-class members and so to their employers. It is no surprise, then, that the South has a disproportionate number of people with higher education qualifications. Fifth, the kind of designer–consumer environments within which the service class finds consumption satisfaction and cultural sustenance are more likely to be found in particular places, are more likely to attract more service-class residential preferences, and so are more likely to attract employers. Sixth, the existence of these consumer environments provides a powerful locational determinant (in the shape of a market) for many of the service industries, especially those providing direct customer services like retailing, restaurants and so on. It would be possible to go on but the point is made. There is no way of reading off the geography of the service class directly from the geography of production. At the same time this is by no means to suggest that the two are not related. Rather the connections are complex (and even when spatial distributions do coalesce this may be a demonstration of equifinality with different causes producing the same result).

In the light of these comments what, then, is the spatial distribution of the service class? A fairly detailed summary can be given, filtered through the Centre for Urban and Regional Development Studies classification of local labour market areas (Table 7.19). The service class is clearly over-represented in the South of England where the majority of its jobs are located (although everywhere the service class tends to be unevenly distributed compared with the distribution of other classes (Owen and Green, 1985)). There is some evidence to suggest that in the South, and in the South East in particular, the share of the service class has been increasing for some time (Pinch and Williams, 1983). More recently, in Berkshire, for example, between 1971 and 1981 there was a relative increase in the service class amongst employees in services to add to the existing over-representation of the class in that county. Meanwhile in areas in the North of the country like Tyne and Wear the service class was relatively declining

Table 7.19: The CURDS classification of local labour market areas[a]

Class	*Title*	*No.*	*Places*
1	London dominant	1	London
2	Conurbation dominants	5	Birmingham, Glasgow, Liverpool, Manchester, Newcastle-upon-Tyne
3	Provincial dominants	5	Bristol, Edinburgh, Nottingham Leeds, Sheffield
4	Subregional dominants	9	Brighton, Blackburn, Cardiff, Coventry, Middlesbrough, Newport, Portsmouth, Preston, Swansea
5	London subdominant cities	7	e.g. Southend
6	London subdominant towns	23	e.g. Maidenhead
7	Conurbation subdominant cities	13	e.g. Motherwell
8	Conurbation subdominant towns	22	e.g. Northwich
9	Smaller northern subdominant	24	e.g. Rugby
10	Southern freestanding cities	12	e.g. Norwich, *Plymouth*
11	Northern freestanding cities	13	e.g. Derby
12	Southern service towns	22	e.g. Canterbury, *Winchester*
13	Southern commercial towns	14	e.g. Trowbridge
14	Southern manufacturing towns	13	e.g. Wellingborough
15	Northern service towns	12	e.g. Llandudno
16	Northern commercial towns	19	e.g. Hereford
17	Northern manufacturing towns	14	e.g. Scunthorpe
18	Southern rural areas	19	e.g. Penzance
19	Northern rural areas	34	e.g. Penrith

Notes:
(a) The main dimensions of this classification are as follows:
(1) a regional dimension between North and South along the line between the Severn Estuary and Lincolnshire;
(2) an urban–rural dimension, separating out places as cities, towns, or rural areas according to population size with London treated as a category on its own. The other main regional centres are termed Dominants and are subdivided into Conurbation, Provincial or Regional Dominants;
(3) a division which distinguishes between LLMA's forming part of the wider Metropolitan Region served by a dominant (termed sub-dominant) or laying beyond the region's influence (termed freestanding);
(4) an industrial structure dimension attributed only to freestanding towns categorised as service, commercial or manufacturing, according to the importance of service employment.

Source: Centre for Urban and Regional Development Studies, 1983, see also Coombes *et al.*, 1982[a]

(Green, 1985) (Table 7.20).

Within this general North–South split, the service class has been 'decentralising' from the major urban cores faster than the other classes into the suburban and rural areas of Britain (the so-called 'outer city') (Herington, 1984). This process has been going on for quite some time (see, for example, Pinch and Williams, 1983, on the 1961 to 1971 period). This rapid 'decentralisation' is partly the result

Table 7.20: Change in resident services employees by socio-economic group, 1971–81 (%)

Area	*Service class: Employers & managers*	*Professionals*	*Intermediate non-manual*	*Junior non-manual*	*Skilled manual*	*Semi-skilled manual*	*Unskilled manual*
Tyne and Wear LLMAs							
	0.73	−0.04	2.95	−3.57	−0.34	0.83	−0.45
South Shields	−1.69	−1.00	0.49	−3.16	0.88	4.06	0.56
Sunderland	0.55	−0.67	2.13	−3.73	−0.54	2.61	0.05
Berkshire LLMAs							
Bracknell	3.10	0.13	2.69	1.58	−0.56	−1.33	−1.79
Maidenhead	2.80	0.71	2.13	−1.88	0.61	−4.05	−0.43
Newbury	5.47	0.02	0.70	5.06	−3.03	−3.46	−3.34
Reading	2.74	0.43	2.30	−0.65	−0.72	−1.36	−1.45
Slough	2.27	−0.36	1.09	1.95	0.03	−1.24	−1.81
Great Britain	1.36	−0.01	2.99	−2.25	−0.55	0.17	−0.85

Sources: Census of Population. Green, 1985, p. 29.

Table 7.21: Location quotients, showing over- and under-representation of socio-economic groups employed in manufacturing and services, 1971–81: according to CULPS 19-fold classification of LLMAS.

LLMA Class	Socio-Economic group 1971							1981						
	Employers and managers	Professional workers	Intermediate non-manual	Junior non-manual	Foreman and skilled manual	Semi-skilled manual and personal service	Unskilled manual	Employers and managers	Professional workers	Intermediate non-manual	Junior non-manual	Foreman and skilled manual	Semi-skilled manual and Personal Service	Unskilled manual
Manufacturing														
1. London	1.423	1.153	1.173	1.348	0.861	0.908	0.730	1.358	1.031	1.230	1.362	0.838	0.847	0.766
2. Conurbation Dominants	0.876	0.820	0.859	0.990	0.987	1.085	1.108	0.848	0.811	0.876	0.973	1.019	1.080	1.209
3. Provincial Dominants	0.968	0.915	0.944	1.027	1.066	0.936	0.945	0.967	1.023	0.969	1.053	1.035	0.967	0.935
4. Subregional Dominants	0.827	1.063	1.087	0.925	1.026	1.027	1.043	0.849	1.203	1.130	0.961	1.022	0.993	1.054
5. London Subdom. Cities	1.450	1.632	1.349	1.178	0.926	0.824	0.753	1.422	1.607	1.452	1.216	0.857	0.789	0.695
6. London Subdom. Towns	1.547	1.926	1.458	1.240	0.896	0.793	0.656	1.526	1.682	1.236	1.267	0.850	0.760	0.636
7. Con urb. Subdom. Cities	0.829	0.882	0.837	0.877	1.034	1.087	1.118	0.843	0.817	0.753	0.887	1.038	1.135	1.126
8. Con urb. Subdom. Towns	0.835	0.986	0.906	0.899	0.968	1.096	1.296	0.880	0.993	0.911	0.902	0.994	1.103	1.202
9. Smaller N. Subdoms.	0.697	0.835	0.900	0.793	1.044	1.107	1.262	0.717	0.774	0.836	0.801	1.049	1.196	1.200
10. S. Freestanding Cities	0.964	1.060	0.965	0.985	1.067	0.979	0.726	1.026	1.004	1.089	0.971	1.026	0.993	0.770
11. N. Freestanding Cities	0.796	1.728	0.861	0.832	1.077	1.032	1.262	0.328	0.787	0.896	0.854	1.111	1.020	1.227
12. S. Service Towns	1.251	1.035	0.988	1.011	0.981	0.959	0.773	1.164	1.110	1.009	0.971	0.985	0.932	0.802
13. S. Commercial Towns	0.984	1.022	1.227	1.074	0.995	0.949	0.899	1.027	1.122	1.063	1.028	0.970	0.998	0.874
14. S. Manufacturing Towns	0.911	1.159	1.156	1.021	1.096	0.881	0.802	1.052	1.331	1.189	1.055	1.009	0.918	0.735
15. N. Service Towns	1.151	0.887	1.003	0.909	1.034	0.984	0.933	1.054	0.861	0.822	0.921	1.064	0.962	0.963
16. N. Commercial Towns	0.823	0.888	0.935	0.843	1.093	0.994	1.153	0.843	0.842	0.882	0.866	1.113	0.996	1.204
17. N. Manufacturing Towns	0.673	0.744	0.863	0.703	1.018	1.156	1.452	0.713	0.859	0.869	0.785	1.046	1.175	1.289
18. S. Rural Areas	1.036	0.871	0.960	0.886	1.058	0.978	0.904	1.119	0.814	0.801	0.826	1.039	1.020	0.896
19. N. Rural Areas	1.062	0.690	0.873	0.731	1.043	1.024	1.164	0.994	0.732	0.722	0.756	1.087	1.017	1.120

Services														
1. London	1.049	1.219	0.959	1.154	0.872	0.860	0.926	1.101	1.243	0.974	1.104	0.876	0.897	0.844
2. Conurbation Dominants	0.917	0.941	1.029	1.105	0.970	0.978	1.165	0.864	0.967	1.019	1.055	0.978	1.097	1.183
3. Provincial Dominants	0.947	1.081	1.047	1.020	1.024	0.984	1.104	0.923	1.109	1.044	1.026	1.020	1.009	1.094
4. Subregional Dominants	0.995	0.381	1.022	0.979	0.981	0.998	1.037	0.942	0.946	1.050	0.979	1.005	1.004	0.063
5. London Subdom. Cities	1.058	1.480	1.007	0.970	1.015	0.879	0.845	1.137	1.165	0.951	1.045	0.968	0.801	0.746
6. London Subdom. Towns	0.156	1.401	1.092	0.937	0.948	0.996	0.795	1.247	1.350	1.031	1.010	0.936	0.843	0.749
7. Conurb. Subdom. Cities	1.039	0.568	1.028	1.043	1.033	0.936	1.039	0.960	0.784	1.022	1.018	1.064	1.055	1.101
8. Conurb. Subdom. Towns	0.994	0.562	1.034	0.980	1.054	1.042	1.039	0.976	0.863	1.056	0.961	1.071	1.057	1.125
9. Smaller N. Subdoms.	0.962	0.703	1.057	0.943	1.078	1.068	1.195	0.927	0.657	1.038	0.964	1.075	1.097	1.298
10. S. Freestanding Cities	0.937	1.042	0.962	0.917	1.062	1.054	0.941	0.972	1.060	0.957	0.978	1.042	0.976	0.906
11. N. Freestanding Cities	0.932	0.779	1.024	0.973	1.021	1.107	1.132	0.907	0.770	1.003	0.984	1.034	1.113	1.173
12. S. Service Towns	1.149	0.901	0.939	0.906	0.993	1.118	0.807	1.112	0.920	0.978	0.925	0.994	1.004	0.863
13. S. Commercial Towns	0.897	0.853	0.981	0.852	1.067	1.062	0.941	0.947	0.904	0.962	0.915	1.058	0.970	0.950
14. S. Manufacturing Towns	0.875	0.828	0.967	0.830	1.083	1.034	0.924	0.934	0.939	0.936	0.938	1.086	0.911	0.990
15. N. Service Towns	1.068	0.884	0.970	0.908	1.077	1.145	1.014	1.045	0.909	1.034	0.911	0.978	1.133	0.950
16. N. Commercial Towns	1.024	0.937	1.022	0.913	1.092	1.103	1.069	0.990	0.796	1.072	0.918	1.022	1.069	1.143
17. N. Manufacturing Towns	0.918	0.660	1.083	0.892	1.175	1.116	1.156	0.900	0.672	1.058	0.921	1.126	1.120	1.248
18. S. Rural Areas	0.966	0.838	0.825	0.765	1.188	1.101	0.858	0.987	0.910	0.829	0.823	1.178	0.984	0.804
19. N. Rural Areas	1.000	0.958	0.917	0.774	1.105	1.199	0.957	0.963	0.898	0.948	0.834	1.091	1.158	0.987

Source: Owen and Green, 1985, pp. 13–141.

of the growth of service class jobs in these areas, and partly the result of service class residential preferences – the two are linked. More recent evidence makes it possible to be precise about the chief locations of service class growth. This evidence shows that the service class has become more prominent in towns outside London which have a small town residential environment but are still within commuting distance of the capital, in freestanding cities like Norwich, in service towns like Canterbury and in villages in rural areas (Table 7.21). These are generally places with considerable and growing service industry employment, and relatively small populations. At the same time, it is vitally important to remember that most of the service class do not live in those places; the majority of the class still live in the major conurbations, either in the suburbs or in 'gentrified' inner city areas (see Smith and Williams, 1986).

However the direction of service-class growth into these smaller, more rural areas is important; it demonstrates local labour market growth, it signals ideal service class residential preferences and it also illustrates the impact of the service class on places, on geography. More than any other class below it, the service class has the mobility to choose where to live (as Pahl (1966, p. 260) put it, 'the people to whom place means least, have a way of life in which choice of living place is very important') and, quite often, more capacity than other classes below it to influence how its choices of residence function and look. The final part of this section, therefore, examines two of these places, and the impacts of the service class within them.

From the leafy suburbs of upper-middle-class London, through the London commuter belt towns like Bishop's Stortford or Saffron Walden, to the cathedral towns like Exeter or Salisbury to the small rural villages of the type made famous by Pahl, the service class lives in a series of milieux bent towards tasteful consumption. These are the designer civil societies, the consumption cultures. In them, the consumption-cum-reproduction preferences of the service class are made particularly clear. There are the 'good schools' (Figure 7.2). There are service class icons like BMWs or Audis in some driveways. There are the modern shop fronts, injected into the restored buildings (Figure 7.3):

> Evocative and ancient though the buildings may be from the first floor up, the shop frontages in the market towns and cities are very definitely 1980s. The weekly and traditional markets for the farming hinterlands may still exist, but it is the Sainsburys, Burtons, Bootses, W. H. Smiths and Currys that now

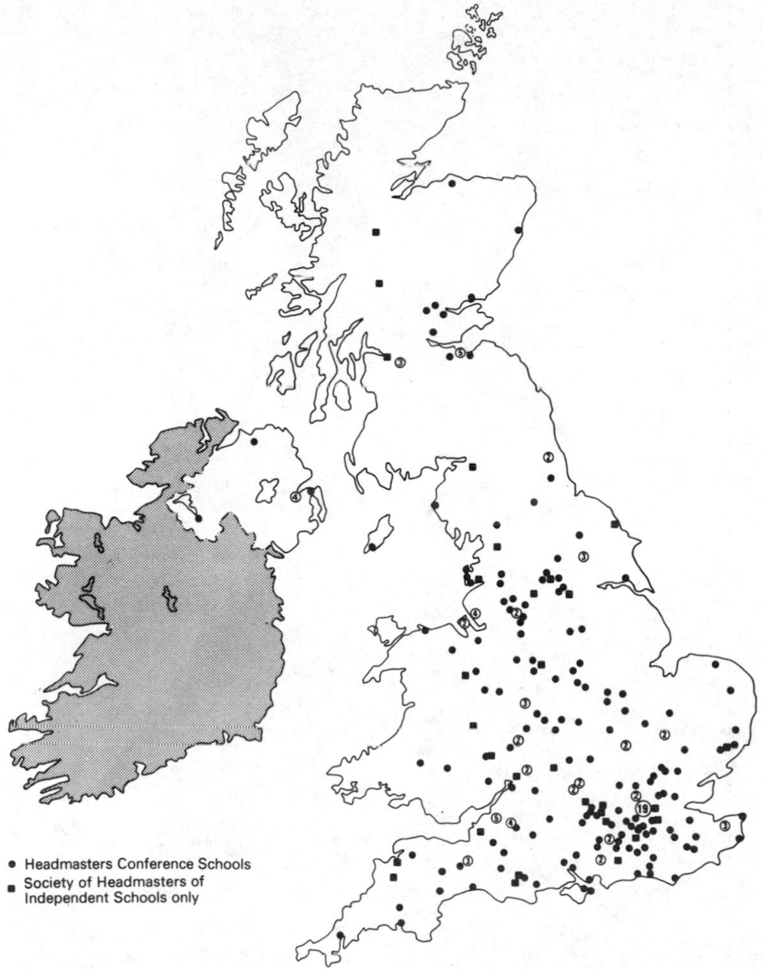

Figure 7.2 The location of public schools belonging to the Headmasters Conference and the Society of Headmasters of Independent Schools (Note: Where schools belong to both organisations they have been assigned to the Headmasters Conference)
Source: Burnet, 1985

dominate high street commercial life. . . . Interspersed with them, too, are retail businesses that clearly illustrate recent social shifts and the changing aspirations of a new rural clientele. Specialist fashion shops such as Country Casuals – selling chic, fashionable rusticism – are testaments to a new prosperity and spending power (Beresford and Stephen, 1986, p. 24).

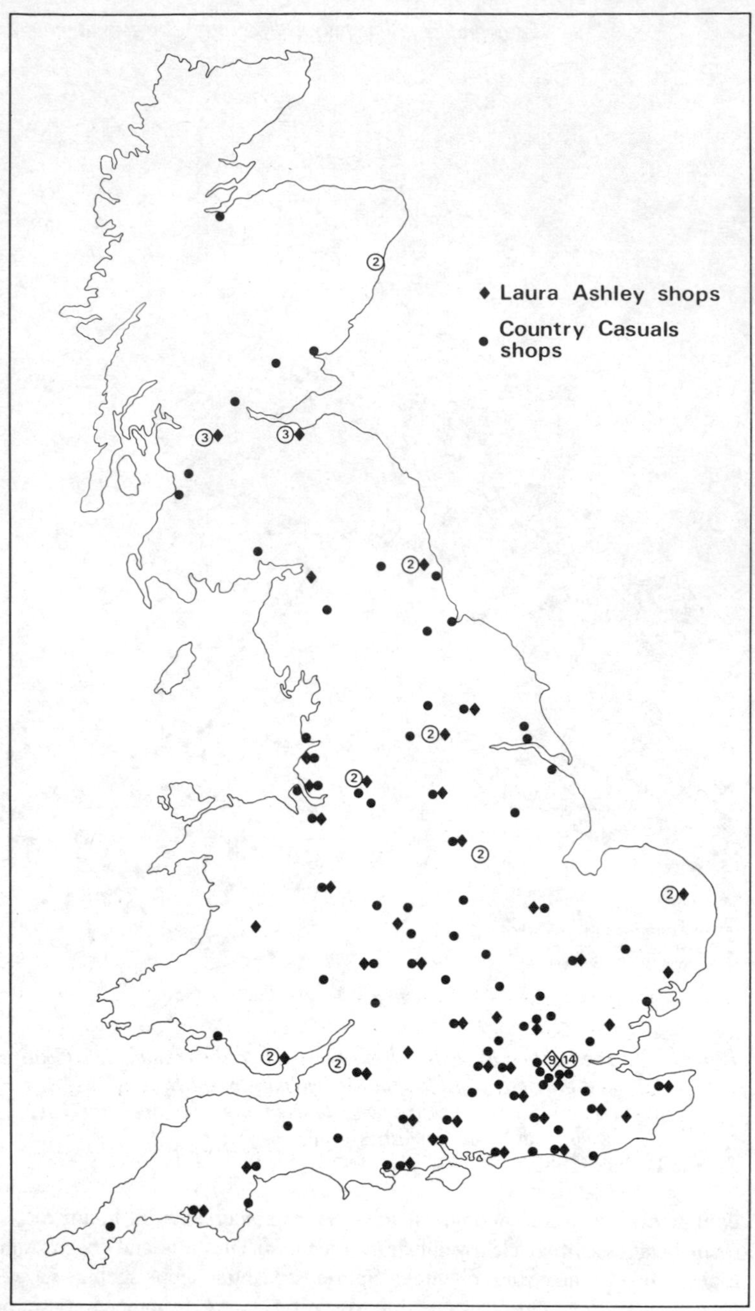

Figure 7.3 The location of key service class retail outlets
Source: Retail Directory, 1986

Most significant of all, perhaps, but generally unsung by academics (except for Young and Willmott, 1973 and Deverson and Lindsay, 1975), there are the housing estates. The housing estate is of crucial importance to service class Britain. It provides a service class labour pool for employers. It provides a degree of place interchangeability for mobile service class members. It provides a range of housing to suit the service class life cycle (increasingly segmented by the construction industry and ranging from the starter homes so popular in the 1970s, to the legions of tightly packed Barratt and Wimpey semi-detached and detached houses still going up all over the country to the increasingly important up-market houses satisfying the post-war baby boomers now trading up (usually arranged in closes of six to ten houses, with features like double garages, en suite bathrooms and numerous vernacular touches) to the boom sector of country cottage style retirement homes'. And the housing estate provides a reinforcing environment for service class consciousness. Order, routine. You are what you see.

Winchester

Of the successful local labour markets in Britain in the 1970s (and into the 1980s) Winchester, with its population of 36 000 in 1981, was the most successful (Champion and Green, 1985) (Figure 7.4). Winchester's economy, at least in the context of a generalised recession, has boomed. It has (and has had for several years) the lowest unemployment rate in Britain. It was the only place in the country where unemployment actually fell between 1971 and 1981. This was mainly because of the fastest growth of jobs in Britain from 1971 to 1981, including an 84 per cent increase in service employment. By 1981 more than 80 per cent of Winchester's jobs were in the service sector (Champion and Green, 1985).

Winchester's economy is based upon three main groups of workers. First of all, there are the London commuters, working outside the town but bringing much of their salaries back to spend in the local economy. These are the senior civil servants, the insurance assessors, the workers in the City of London. Second, there are the group of workers who live in and around Winchester and who operate within the context of a fairly stable and diverse set of local employers – a

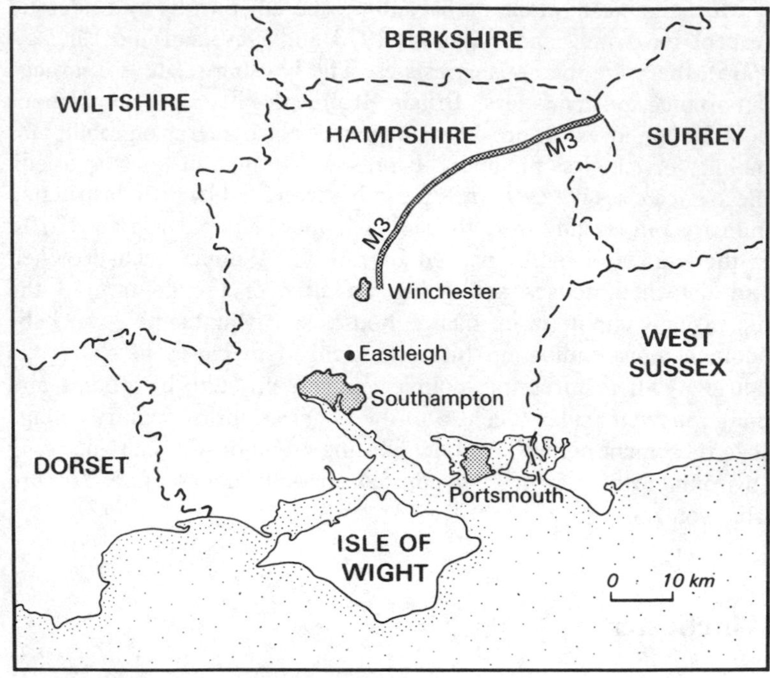

Figure 7.4 Locations in Hampshire mentioned in the text

government sector, including the Hampshire county and city councils, the Army and the prison, an education sector that includes Winchester College (a private school), a health sector, a fairly dynamic manufacturing sector industry, taking in Plessey, IBM, and various small computer engineering and software companies, a large local retail and consumer service sector (building societies and local banks, the shops, the quality restaurants, the wine bars), even the Cathedral. Finally, there are the workers who come into the city to work from outside it, mainly from places like Southampton and Eastleigh, who spend a proportion of their wages in the local economy.

Thus the city offers more than the usual number of service class jobs to service class workers. These workers' numbers are bolstered by the presence of the London commuters and a good proportion of retired people, formerly in the service class. Winchester is a service class haven (Table 7.22), acting as both a pool of educated labour

Table 7.22: Winchester in 1981[a]

Population	*Winchester* 35 664	*Great Britain* –
Social class of head of household (%)[b]		
I	8.3	4.5
II	25.7	18.8
III (N)	10.0	9.1
III (M)	18.7	26.2
IV	10.6	12.2
V	3.5	4.1
Service employment (%)	75.3	56.7
Retired persons (%)	19.8	17.7
Households with two or more cars (%)	18.3	15.5
Population with higher educational qualifications degree or equivalent (%)		
Male	24.2	13.7
Female	17.9	12.2
Proportion of households in owner occupation (%)	52.4	55.7

Notes:
(a) Based on 10 per cent sample and so results must be used with caution.
(b) Percentage does not sum to 100 because armed forces, retired and unwaged are not included.
Source: Office of Population Censuses and Surveys, 1984a

(more than a quarter of the population have a degree or similar qualification) and a node constructed to consume high incomes, a function which is boosted by the many tourists who visit every year. The signs are everywhere – in the emphasis on heritage (old buildings like the Guildhall are being carefully restored), in the bijou pedestrianised shopping centre, in the kind of shops to be found, in the 56 sports clubs. This is a consumption culture:

Winchester's affluence is mainly understated, tucked discreetly behind Georgian facades, betrayed by the clues of English class: quilted green jackets, flannel shirts, silk scarves and sensible shoes, although the yuppies have arrived. 'Can we have a bottle of champagne and a kir' called out a young man in pinstripes, taking his lunch at Mr. Pitkin's wine bar.

Paul Bennett, an advertising executive in his early thirties who drives a BMW, said 'The standard of living is high, and people are ambitious. It's pleasant to look at and has a London mentality. I like hanging about successful people' (Chesshyre, 1986, p. 60).

But growth has brought its problems. First, there is a labour shortage for certain kinds of jobs. 'For Michael Musselwhite at Comsult (a computer company), [the biggest problem] was (and still is) to find new staff. So far this year his company has spent £700 on advertising for sales staff, but without success' (Beresford and Stephen, 1986, p. 28). Second, and related to the first point, housing prices are very high primarily because of a chronic housing shortage. Annual house price rises have averaged between 15 and 20 per cent. A three-bedroomed terrace house sells within a week for upwards of £45,000 (Beresford and Stephen, 1986). No wonder there are fifteen building societies in the main street (extra building societies are being discouraged) as well as a clutch of estate agents. Third, and again related, Winchester has become *de facto* a positional good. The politics of the city are therefore becoming biased towards dealing with the problem of growth (whether in the form of more employment or more housing or more offices). In particular, there is the familiar service class politics bent towards preventing growth that would spoil the town's 'character', entailing an appeal to the eternal values of heritage and self-interest at the same time. The problem of growth has become even more pressing since the M3 opened in 1985:

> David Cowan, chief executive of the local council, will tell you that his planning department is continuously fighting off development proposals. He himself, he says, has been approached by cabinet ministers' brothers on behalf of sizeable companies offering 500 jobs to the area – 'but we just can't take them'. The extra housing is simply not available (Beresford and Stephen, 1986, p. 24).

In effect:

> the city council has . . . hoisted 'keep out' signs round Winchester. While most councils would go on bended knee for any enterprise on their patch, Mr. Cowan said: 'Winchester looks good on the letterhead and executives love to live here. We have the honesty and the duty to say we can't cope. Imagine what the community would do to us if we were to allow a multi-storey car park near the Cathedral' (Chesshyre, 1986, p. 60).

The Plymouth commuter-shed

The service class has not only been increasing its presence in service towns like Winchester. Many of the rural areas of Britain, especially those in the commuter-sheds of large towns and cities, have been extensively settled by the service class since Pahl (1965) first identified the influx in the 1960s (see subsequent work by, for example, Redford,

1970; Ambrose, 1974; Connell, 1974, 1978; Newby *et al.*, 1978; Lewis and Maund, 1979, reviewed in Philips and Williams, 1984; Pacione, 1980). The commuter-shed of Plymouth provides some fine examples of this process (Figure 7.5). For a considerable time the area has been becoming more oriented towards the service class (Table 7.23). There are a number of reasons for this phenomenon. First the increase in car ownership amongst the service class and the upgrading of the A38 and other major roads in the area have made commuting more and more feasible. Second, there has been a general increase in service employment in the area and especially employment in financial, business and professional and scientific services (a complicating factor in the area is employment in the Army and at the Plymouth Dockyards) (Table 7.24). Service class employment has kept up during the recession, even though Plymouth has been badly hit; unemployment in Plymouth was above the national average in 1985 at more than 15

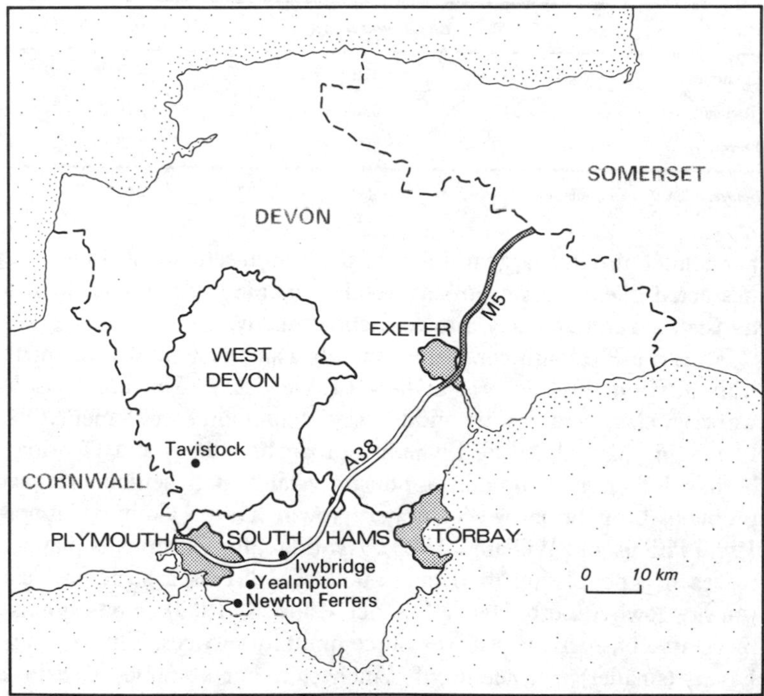

Figure 7.5 Locations in Devon mentioned in the text

Table 7.23: Changes in social class in two districts bordering Plymouth, 1951 and 1981 (%)[a]

Social class	*West Devon*		*South Hams*	
	1951	*1981*	*1951*	*1981*
Service class – Professional (I)	5	6	5	4
Service class – Intermediate (II)	25	39	19	33
Skilled (III)	40	39	46	57
Partly skilled (IV)	22	12	19	4
Unskilled (V)	8	4	10	2

Notes:
(a) the West Devon and South Hams districts only approximate a part of the Plymouth commuter-shed. Part of the South Hams district is also in the commuter-shed of Torbay. The Cornish side of the Plymouth commuter-shed has been omitted. This area remains generally less service class in character.
Source: Grafton, 1983, p. 74[a]

Table 7.24: Service-sector employment in Devon, 1971–81

Place	*Employment change*	*% change 1971–81*
Plymouth	1 970	3
Torbay	2 630	10
Devon	45 800	23

Source: Census of Population

per cent. Third, the large number of small rural settlements in the area has acted like a magnet to service-class members, enabling them to translate a rural ideology into residential reality.

Thus the Plymouth commuter-shed boasts a system of settlements with different class characteristics (Table 7.25). The area has its working class and lower middle class commuter settlements like Plympton (just inside the Plymouth urban boundary) and Ivybridge, both with their massed ranks of housing estates. Both settlements have problems brought on by accelerated growth (Devon County Council, 1983; Philips and Williams, 1983). Ivybridge, for example, is planned to reach a population of over 12 000 by 1991 as a structure plan priority town (South Hams District Council, 1983). Consequently there are considerable stresses on community services. The area also has its (smaller) equivalents of Winchester. For example, Tavistock, with a population of about 9000 people, has a high service class component. It is an historic rural market town which, over the last thirty

Table 7.25: Some centres in the Plymouth commuter-shed, 1981

	Population	Social class of head of household[a b] (per cent)						Service employment %	Retired persons %	Households with two or more cars %	Economically active population employed outside district of residence %	Population with higher educational qualifications (degree or equivalent) %		Proportion of households owner occupation %
		I	II	III (N)	III (M)	IV	V					Male	Female	
Plymouth	242,560	3.3	14.0	9.1	25.9	10.2	3.9	68.6	17.6	10.7	–	9.0	10.4	54.7
Tavistock	8,798	6.1	24.9	7.1	19.5	7.5	2.2	71.5	22.1	18.8	–	17.6	12.2	74.7
Ivybridge	5,649	3.4	29.5	16.0	18.3	5.9	2.5	77.7	11.7	19.4	46	16.4	14.8	78.8
Wembury	1,975	12.5	25.5	12.0	18.2	7.8	2.1	70.1	18.5	29.5	60	31.2	22.7	64.5
Newton Ferrers and Noss Mayo	1,666	14.5	43.0	1.2	9.1	0.6	5.5	69.4	27.2	31.9	58	30.4	37.5	70.7
Modbury	–	–	–	–	–	–	–	–	–	–	24	–	–	–
Yealmpton	–	4.5	18.3	9.1	26.2	12.2	4.1	56.7	17.7	15.5	–	13.7	12.2	55.7

Notes

[a] Based on ten per cent sample and so results must be used with caution. For example, according to small area statistics service class representation is higher in Ivybridge, Yealmpton and Newton Ferrers.

[b] Percentage does not sum to 100 because armed forces, retired and unwaged are not included.

Source: Office of Population Censures and Surveys, 1984b

years, has experienced an influx of service class members commuting to Plymouth (or taking local employment), as well as retirees. The town's environment is in keeping with its social mix. The shopping centre is compact and it is to be kept this way as 'a shopping area characterised by small-scale traditional and specialist shops' (West Devon Borough Council, 1983, p. 10). Housing estates are, with some exceptions, small and select. As might be expected one of the major themes in the town's politics is the problem of growth. Conservation is a major issue (the central area of the town is an Outstanding Conservation Area) and there is clear evidence of a decision to keep more growth out. A new Gateway supermarket built in the town centre caused particular frictions. Finally, the Plymouth commuter-shed area is sprinkled with small rural settlements. As in many other similar situations around large conurbations, the process of service class invasion of these settlements is highly variable. As Bradley (1985, p. 51) puts it, 'the local social structures of village England are currently extremely diverse'. But some of the villages in the Plymouth commuter-shed have over time become almost entirely service class (and retirement) areas via the twin processes of rural 'gentrification' and the building of small housing estates. In certain villages like Newton Ferrers and Noss Mayo, more than three-quarters of the employed workforce belong to the service class. Villages like Wembury, Yealmpton and Modbury also have high service class representations (Grafton, 1983). Other classes are kept out of these villages by tight planning controls and the high house prices.

Discussion

These two sketches only scratch at the surface of local variation in service class social structures. Given space limitations, this is inevitable. But clearly there is a potentially enormous research agenda to be addressed. There is, for example, the problem of how to deal with conflict between the service class and other social classes. In what arenas is this conflict chiefly played out and at what spatial scales? (Harris, 1983; Urry, 1983). Then there is the related problem of class consciousness. How, for example, is it possible to deal with Wright's (1985, p. 237) vision of the colliding perceptual worlds of the service class gentrifier and the black working class resident of inner city London?

> People live in different worlds, even though they share the same locality: there is no single community or quarter. What is pleasantly 'old' for one person is decayed and broken for another. Just as a person with money has a different experience of shopping in the area than someone with almost none, a white homeowner is likely to have a different experience of the police (the considerate homebeat officer who comes round to commiserate after yet another stereo or colour television has been stolen) than a black person – houseowner or not. Likewise if I read the *Guardian* or the *Times* and can substantially determine my own relations to the borough, then maybe I don't actually need to read the *Hackney Gazette*. Those stories of daily misery and violent horror can stay local to someone else's paper, together with the job advertisements (although, of course, I'll keep a close eye on the rising house prices).

These and other issues require more research. There is a long way to go before it can even begin to be said that the geography of service class formation has been satisfactorily investigated.

• 8 •

The growth of scientific management: *transformations in class structure and class struggle*[1]

• *JOHN URRY*

1 Introduction

It is customary in debates on scientific management to examine fairly directly what its consequences were for labour, and in particular whether it resulted in its deskilling. In this chapter, however, I shall argue that this is too narrow a focus and that there are further aspects which also demand attention. First, the development of new systems of management was not something which was simply inevitable, resulting either from technological imperatives or from the accumulation of capital. In particular, such developments could only result where it was possible for 'management' to wrest control away in part *from* 'capital'. Hence, there is involved here a crucially important 'class struggle' between management and capital, a struggle whose conditions and consequences have been underexamined. Scientific management could only develop, at least initially, where there were relatively few constraints upon the 'causal powers' of management being realised; and this is by no means simply a question of the strength of labour and *its* ability to resist managerial prerogatives. Second, since the resulting forms of management are not inscribed within the 'economy' it is necessary to explain their particular features. In general it is necessary to show why there was departure from the pattern of direct coercion; and also to see the resulting forms as effectively unintended, resulting from the particular patterns of constraint and struggle characterising different sectors within different national economies. Third, the development of scientific management produces a number of further effects, to increase the size and power of the 'intermediate' classes, to expand the professions, to enlarge systems of higher education and to enhance credentialism. Moreover, these are not effects which affect labour merely through 'deskilling'. Rather the heightened powers of such intermediate classes effect a further separation of mental from manual labour, increase the importance of credentials and hence of *access* to education, weaken the power of labour to develop its own autonomous practices and institutions, and enlarge the 'horizontal' disaggregation of civil society. Thus, not only may labour be weakened through 'deskilling' (and this is a justly controversial issue), but also through some important overall shifts in the balance of class forces which transform the structures within which class relations are generated. In particular, this process is most developed within the USA – the weakness of labour directly resulting from the strength of the intermediate classes which has followed from the power of management to scientise forms of capitalist control.

In the following section I shall consider the development of scientific management in the USA. I shall not elaborate the details of the various systems of management which were proposed, nor analyse the degree to which F. W. Taylor was responsible for the changes made. My main objective will be to demonstrate the conditions of struggle under which such changes could be introduced in the years just before, during and just after the First World War. In the third section, I shall detail some of the consequences of that development especially through consideration of the engineering profession, the growth of college education, and the expanded powers of the 'service class'. In the concluding section, I shall draw some contrasts with development in Britain and suggest that the contrasting trajectories of social struggle and development within Britain and the USA stem from the particular patterns of managerial change in the two countries in the first thirty or forty years of this century. The USA, which in many respects is the archetypal 'capitalist' society, is that with the strongest 'service class' and where labour is weakest. Its class relations are exactly the opposite of what, given conventional argument, one would expect. This has to be explained by examining the patterns of constraint and struggle surrounding the degree, speed and forms of the restructuring of capital. In other words, there has been a 'managerial revolution' especially in the USA – but its importance lies not in the consequences of whether there is a 'soulful' corporation pursuing the maximisation of growth rather than profits. Rather its importance lies in the transformation of class relations and the realisation in part at least of the powers of the 'service class'.

2 The development of management in the USA

It is now a commonplace to note that the growth of the factory had a profound effect in changing people's work habits and experiences. There was some shift from an orientation to task towards an orientation to time (Thompson, 1967). However, it is also clear that the growth of the factory did not result in a direct increase in the social control that capital exercised over labour. What Marx called the 'real subsumption' of the labourer was not simply brought about by the factory system. There is widespread evidence that prior to the development of 'scientific management' in its various forms, the labourer was not generally placed under conditions of real subsumption by *capital* (on the USA, see Brody, 1980). There were three alternative bases of control: first, that exercised by skilled craft workers – as Nelson (1975, p. 4) says: 'the factory of 1880 (in the USA) remained a congeries of craftsmen's shops rather than an integrated plant' (see also Braverman, 1974 and Montgomery, 1979); second, that effected by 'foremen' especially through 'driving' the workers via authoritarian rule and physical compulsion (see Nelson, 1975, ch. 3 on the 'Foreman's Empire'); and third, that produced through 'internal contracting' by which contractors hired and fired their own employees, set their wages, disciplined them and determined the production methods to be used (Clawson, 1980; Littler, 1978, 1982b; and Stark, 1980). There was of course great variation between different industries and areas as to which of these different forms of control were found; and indeed there were often a combination of such forms within a single enterprise. Littler (1982b) suggests that internal contracting was important in the period up to 1914 in the following industries: iron and steel, foundries, coal, engineering, armaments, arsenals, potteries, glass, newspaper printing and clothing (see also Clawson, 1980). Internal contracting was more common in the traditional industrial areas on the East Coast, and was often structured along lines of ethnic division as waves of immigrants settled in the

USA beginning in the East (Littler, 1982b; Buttrick, 1952 and Sofer 1970). It was also in certain cases such as clothing structured along lines of gender division (see Benenson, 1982). Finally, as Clawson (1980) points out, inside-contracting was an importantly non-bureaucratic form of control since the contractor did production work as well as supervision, there were no set qualifications, no levels of authority, essentially no written documents or files were kept, and there were no codified rules (or very few rules). There were two implications: first, that the class position of such contractors was that of a 'contradictory class location' (Clawson, 1980, p. 90. See also, more generally, Wright, 1978); and second, that for the growth of 'management' and hence of managerial bureaucracies, this power of the inside contractor would have to be substantially broken (see Stone, 1974, and Montgomery, 1979, on how this constituted a form of 'workers control').

It was a basic premise of all such systems of control in nineteenth-century America that workers knew more than anyone else about how to do the detailed work and that they possessed the knowledge relating to the relevant labour process. Capitalist control was effected but only indirectly. It rested upon the power of skilled workers and/or foremen and/or inside contractors, who exercised dictatorial control over labour, often of a patriarchal and/or racist form. Control was overwhelmingly 'personalistic' rather than bureaucratic. In general, then, as Hobsbawm (1964, p. 297) argues, nineteenth-century capitalism operated 'not so much by directly subordinating large bodies of workers to employers, but by subcontracting exploitation and management'. Within about thirty years, however, much of this was to change in the USA. In the following discussion of the emergence of scientific management, I shall consider what it was that transformed the American social structure. In the mid-nineteenth century there were no middle managers in the USA; while the number of 'administrative employees' within American industry increased 4.5 times between 1899 and 1929, from 7.7 per cent to 18 per cent of total employment (Chandler, 1980; Bendix, 1956). The growth of 'management' and what I elsewhere term the 'socialisation of unproductive labour', (Abercrombie and Urry, 1983, ch. 6), occurred in the USA because of a struggle waged in part against both labour *and* against capital. It is necessary to explain how and why this struggle was successful. Why was it that in at least parts of the USA labour lost its monopoly on the knowledge of the day-to-day organisation of work, and why did the form of capitalist control which had persisted during the nineteenth-century collapse? Part of my approach here will be to try to examine the issue posed by Stark (1980, p. 101) when he says of the growth of management that 'the occupants of the new positions did not simply "fill in" a set of "empty places" created by forces completely divorced from their own activity, but actually participated, within a constellation of struggling classes, in the creation of these positions themselves'. In particular, the development of a large-scale management involved overcoming two particular forms of resistance: on the one hand, from the workforce itself especially from the skilled craftsmen; and on the other hand, from the owners and existing managers who believed that 'scientific' management was an unnecessary and dangerous expense.

I will now briefly describe some of the main aspects of Taylorism before analysing these conditions of struggle under which 'management' and the 'service class' emerged in the first quarter of this century in the USA.

Taylor (1947) realised that workers controlled the details of their work, and thus, so long as workers knew more than their managers, then management would have to cajole the workers to co-operate. This could be clearly seen in relationship to piecework. Since management did not know how long in fact it took to do each piece of work, it was rational for workers to engage in 'systematic soldiering' and hence to restrict output. Taylor realised that the only long-term solution to this from the viewpoint of capital was to devise a new system of capitalist control that would overcome the rational tendency for workers to restrict output. And this could only be achieved by transforming the very form of knowledge possessed by workers. In particular, it was necessary to create the separate category of 'management', which had until then enjoyed only a somewhat protean existence, based upon a necessary 'mental revolution' (Person, 1929, p. 9).

According to Taylor, the first stage in this process was for the management to learn what its workers already knew. 'The Managers assume . . . the burden of gathering together all of the traditional knowledge, which in the past has been possessed by the workmen' (Taylor, 1947, p. 36. See also Littler, 1978). The second stage for Taylor was for the management to 'take over all of the work for which they are better fitted than the workman; almost every act of the workman should be preceded by various preparatory acts' of the management (Taylor, 1947, p. 38). As a result there would have to be an enormous growth in the bureaucratisation of industry since Taylor advocated the creation of a 'planning room' where there should be a concentration of the 'brain-work' which had been removed from the shop floor. Thus, in the third stage of the process, management had to specify in advance precisely what each worker was required to do. And, although these tasks might have been similar to those which had been previously done, they were now to be determined within the 'planning room', or more generally within the bureaucratic structure. Taylor refers to the almost equal division of the actual work of the establishment between the workman, on the one hand, and the management, on the other. Under the old system, practically the whole problem was left to the workman, while under scientific management there were two divisions, and one of these divisions was deliberately handed over to the side of the management (Person, 1929). The Taylor system, then, involved an enormous expansion in what Taylor himself called 'non-producers'.

This new form of control was necessary because of the deskilling of the labour process which is entailed in scientific management. There are a number of different aspects here: the maximised fragmentation of work into their simplest constituents; the divorce of planning and execution; the separation of indirect and direct labour; the minimisation of skill requirements and job-learning time; and the employment of scientific 'planning' to co-ordinate the entire process of production (Littler, 1982b, 1978; Urwick, 1929; Taylor, 1947; Copley, 1923).

There is much controversy as to the degree to which Taylorian scientific management was to be found in American industry by, say, 1920. Overall it seems that the fully-fledged system was only implemented in about 140 enterprises and these were primarily concentrated in small-scale precision production industries mainly located in the northeastern States (Palmer, 1975; Nadworny, 1955; Nelson, 1975). However, Montgomery argues that, considered much more generally, the basic principles of scientific management had been very widely accepted by the 1920s. These principles included the centralised planning and integrating of the successive stages of production; the systematic analysis of each distinct operation; the detailed instruction and supervision of each worker in the performance of each discrete task; and the designing of wage payments to induce workers to do what they were told (see Montgomery, 1979; Littler, 1982b).

The following were the main conditions which facilitated the growth of scientific management in the USA, as a consequence of which there was the development of a new class, the 'service class', which had profound effects on the *structure* of American society.

(1) *Technological* changes which outstripped the capacity of craftsmen trained in traditional techniques to organise production in the way they had in the past (Brody, 1980). Particularly important effects of such technological innovations were upon the organization of the railways which increasingly required more elaborate systems of control to manage the enormous extensions of the rail system (Chandler, 1980). Other technological innovations of importance included the development of continuous process methods in certain refining, distilling, chemical and food processing industries; of undercutting machinery in the coal industry; and a little later of mass production techniques in both metalmaking and metalworking industries (see Brody, 1980; Chandler, 1980).

(2) *Growth* in the size of both enterprises and plants in the period after 1865. Especially important here was the vertical integration of different components of production, distribution, marketing, so that by 1900 there were high concentration levels in many industries (see Herman, 1981; Chandler, 1980 and Person, 1929). Also by 1900 plants employing thousands rather than hundreds of workers were fairly common (there were 1500); by 1914, such plants accounted for 18 per cent of all manufacturing employment (Herman, 1981; Littler, 1982b).

(3) Declining rate of profit from the 1880s and widespread pattern of *mergers* (Nelson, 1959; Edwards, 1979; Littler, 1982b). This was especially marked between 1898–1902, and transformed many industries from a competitive to an oligopolistic pattern. Between 1896 and 1905 the hundred largest corporations quadrupled in size and controlled 40 per cent of American manufacturing industry by 1905 (Nelson, 1959; Chandler, 1980, p. 23; Brody, 1980, p. 8).

(4) Dramatic expansion of *immigration* into the USA, especially from 1897 onwards. Immigrants were normally single males, often illiterate, coming from southern and eastern Europe and working in the old industrial areas of the northeast. By 1913 over half of the workers in many industries were immigrants (for example, 58 per cent in iron and steel, 72 per cent in cotton textiles, 83 per

cent in clothing, etc. (Nelson 1975; Noble, 1979; Montgomery, 1979). Such immigration produced:

(a) extraordinarily high turnover rates amongst semi- and unskilled workers. Schlichter concluded in 1913 that the average labour turnover was 100 per cent per annum (Schlichter, 1919; Littler, 1982b);

(b) a wide social gap between the worker and the management, enabling the latter to treat the former as an object of supposedly 'scientific' study, based on appropriate racial stereotypes (Nelson, 1975; Node, 1979; Littler, 1982b);

(c) continuous problems for management of adapting the illiterate, unskilled, 'prefactory' labour force to industrial conditions – as Noble says:

> Living in terms of their own cultural heritage, which they sustained and which sustained them in a strange and hostile environment, the new immigrants defied ready absorption into the industrial process (Noble, 1979, p. 58).

(d) ethnic segregation of neighbourhoods which distanced the immigrant workers especially from the skilled, until after the First World War at least, a tendency which was also reinforced by the associations and community associations of the immigrants which were often organised into secret societies (Bodimar, 1977; Brody, 1980; Beneuson, 1982);

(e) readily available strikebreakers which caused the failure of strikes in textiles, mining, iron and steel, railways and so on. Foner argues that:

> Often there was a simultaneous process: the moment it appeared that a union was being formed and a strike prepared, the employers would introduce machinery and import unskilled labour to operate the machines (Foner, 1955, p. 17);

(f) segregation and fragmentation of the labour force into primary and secondary components, where in the case of the latter the skill and knowledge required for labour was embodied within the socio-technical organization of the factory and not within the mainly immigrant workers themselves (Montgomery, 1979).

(5) The growing strength of the *working class* movement, especially from the 1894 Pullman strike up to the 'holocaust' of 1919 and the perceived need to deal with this (Foner, 1955; Dubofsky, 1983; Montgomery, 1979). Adams writes:

> Regardless of cause, geographic location, type of industry or ethnic grouping, turbulence in industrial relations flared all over the United States. It rocked large cities and small towns, manufacturing areas and agrarian communities. Industrialization had outdistanced American social attitudes and institutions. In many cases this led to a collapse of civil authority, to near anarchy and to military rule . . . Americans on the eve of World War I lived in an age of industrial violence (Adams, 1966, p. 228; and see Noble, 1979, pp. 56–7. For details of strikes in the USA from 1877 onwards see Brech, 1972).

This is further indicated both by the exceptional growth in trade union membership which rose from under 500 000 in 1897 to over five million in 1920, and by the emergence of political socialism as an effective presence during this period up to 1920 or so (see Dubofsky, 1983; Brody, 1980).

(6) The impact of the *First World War*, which had a number of effects: a marked increase in union membership and strikes (see Dubofsky, 1983; Stark, 1980); an extension of scientific management to government enterprises, especially the arsenals (Haber, 1964); extension of state contracts for an enormous volume of *standardised* products which greatly facilitated the introduction of machinery and systematic management techniques (Stark, 1980); increases in managerial and white-collar employment (so much so that the term 'white-collar' derives from the wartime period (Haber, 1964)); and a more cooperative managerial ideology which laid greater emphasis upon the virtues of work and on a limited degree of worker consultation since labour-organizations were clearly set to stay (see Bendix, 1956; Haber, 1964; Stark, 1980).

(7) The growth in the numbers and influence of *industrial engineers* (although this is partly an effect as we shall see). Already by 1900 engineering was the largest profession in the USA (except for teachers), and in the next thirty years it multiplied five-fold, particularly in the areas of electrical and chemical engineering. Engineers were overwhelmingly male, three-quarters had middle class professional social origins, they generally had a college education, and most became managers within large corporations

(Noble, 1979; Layton, 1971). There was a symbiotic process – the monopolization of 'scientific engineering' by professional engineers was the reverse side of the monopolization of such engineers by the large science-based corporations. Noble (1979, p. 43) summarises:

> the big corporations, because of their control over patents, had combined their capacity to command the industrial application of science with their exclusive legal right to do so. The industrial corporation as it emerged as the locus of modern technology in America, became at the same time the habitat of the professional engineer.

Noble demonstrates that the profession of modern engineering was from the very beginning in the USA (1860s onwards) integrated with that of corporate capital, even to the extent of attempting to foster appropriate working practices and social habits among the labour force.

Three important consequences stemmed from this organization of professional engineers within the USA. First, they in part produced the divorce between mental and manual labour itself and thus enlarged the size effectivity and ultimately the differentiation of mental workers as we shall see. The engineering profession itself increased from 7000 in 1880 to 136 000 in 1920 (Stark, 1980). Secondly, as Noble (1979, p. 168) argues:

> In emphasising the role of formal education as a vital aspect of their professional identity, they (professional engineers) at the same time laid the groundwork for the education-based occupational stratification of twentieth-century corporate America.

The existence of a relatively small but increasingly wealthy and powerful grouping served to exacerbate the demand for substantial opportunities to acquire such positions, in other words, it was argued that there should be much more widely diffused educational opportunities especially to obtain a college degree. The demand for mass higher education helped both to produce a reserve army of qualified mental workers and to escalate the level of qualifications appropriate for any particular place within the social division of labour. And thirdly, the engineers provided a model of how education and industry were to be integrated over the course of the twentieth century as one occupation after another sought to strengthen its market-power by connecting together the production of knowledge with the production of the producers via the modern university.

(8) The growth of *progressivism* during the period 1890–1920. This was a broad multiclass movement of intellectuals, politicians, professionals, farmers and small-scale capitalists who exposed the limitations of the democratic system (with arguments for the referendum, for example), who argued for increased government intervention in the economy, who sought to improve the provision of housing, social services and welfare, and to promote the growth of efficiency through the use of science (Kolko, 1963, Haber, 1964; Palmer, 1975). The development of the movement for efficiency had a number of aspects: personally, it emphasised hard work and denigrated feeling and emotion; mechanically, it involved estimating and maximising the energy input–output ratio of a machine; financially, it implied the calculation and optimising the commercial effectiveness of the enterprise, and sociologically, it signified the pursuit of social harmony among all components of the society and leadership by the most competent. One important sphere within which Progressive thinking was applied was in the development of systematic management, by F. W. Taylor, the founder of 'scientific management', the Gilbreths and their time-and-motion studies, C. Barth who introduced the slide rule to the shopfloor, C. B. Thompson whose speeches and articles served to popularise the new creed of efficiency, as well as various cost-accountants and production controllers (see Palmer, 1975; Haber, 1964; Litterer, 1963; Littler, 1982b). Haber well summarises the Progressive character of Taylor's system:

> He proposed a neat, understandable world in the factory, an organization of men whose acts would be planned, coordinated, and controlled under continuous expert direction. His system had some of the inevitableness and objectivity of science and technology. A Taylor plant became one of those places where an important segment of the American intelligentsia saw the future – and saw it worked (Haber, 1964, p. xi).

One important feature of the movement for scientific management was that it was fairly self-consciously organised. The viewpoint was represented particularly in the *Engineering Magazine* and the *Transactions of the American Society of Mechanical Engineers* and various organisations were formed, such as the 'Efficiency Society', the 'Taylor Society' and the 'Society for the Promotion of Scientific Management' (Palmer, 1975; Copley, 1923). Crucial meetings were held especially that in 1903 when Taylor read his paper on 'Shop Management' to the

'American Society of Mechanical Engineers'. And although the 'movement' was characterised by considerable discussion (for example, over the importance of 'motion' studies), by 1912 and the hearings in Congress, there was widespread public awareness and some acceptance of the broad objectives of the new class of 'management' (Nadworny, 1955).

I shall now consider some aspects of the emergence of this class; in particular that it was located as a 'class-in-struggle' conflicting with both labour *and* capital; and that to succeed it had undermined resistance from both the workforce and from capitalists and existing foremen and managers who generally believed that a growth in 'scientific' management was an unnecessary expense that would undermine their own prerogatives (Nelson, 1975; Clawson, 1980; Stark, 1980; Abercrombie and Urry, 1983). I will consider firstly the resistance of labour to the growth of scientific management.

This can be initially examined by reference to Braverman's *Labour and Monopoly Capital* (Braverman, 1974). In this book he argues that the development of scientific management involves the separation of conception and execution, the former coming to reside with capital, the latter with labour. However, as Burawoy argues, this is not strictly speaking correct:

> Rather than a separation of conception and execution, we find a separation of workers' conception and management's conception, of workers' knowledge and management's knowledge (Burawoy, 1978, p. 277).

Partly as a consequence, he argues, workers showed great ingenuity in opposing, outwitting, and defeating the agents of scientific management, before, during and after the 'appropriation of knowledge'. However, up to about 1910 there was in fact relatively little union opposition to 'scientific management', partly because it had not been introduced into strongly unionised plants; while for the next ten years or so there was widespread opposition. This came initially through the AFL which was particularly important in attempting to protect the 'secrets of the craft' (Nadworny, 1955). Sam Gompers well realised how scientific management would 'reduce the number of skilled workers to the barest minimum', and the costs for labour were strongly emphasised in Professor Hoxie's report on scientific management prepared for the US Commission on Industrial Relations (Nadworny, 1955). Apart from the opposition at the Watertown Arsenal, perhaps the most impressive opposition of labour to new forms of management was to be seen in the Illinois Central and Harriman lines Railroad Carmen's strike which lasted for nearly four years and involved about 30 000 workers (see Aitken, 1960; Palmer, 1975). The carmen maintained an extraordinarily determined opposition to the transformation of their skilled trades which resulted from the attempt to introduce piece work and bonus systems, speed-ups, and time and motion studies. In the course of the strike 533 strikers were jailed, 91 per cent of strikers were forced to move to cheaper housing, and 16 men committed suicide.

However, for all the sustained and militant opposition of some groups of craftworkers to scientific management, such workers were generally unwilling to develop broad-based industrial alliances with semi- and unskilled workers, especially immigrants, blacks or women workers. Benenson (1982) suggests that where the very earliest industrial unions were established, these were to be found in industries where skilled workers were not threatened by displacement by the less skilled as in coal and garment-making. The organisation of labour during this period was not then simply the result of craft workers responding to the degradation of skill (as in Braverman's analysis) but was much more varied, geographically, industrially and historically, and involved differing and complex alliances or workers, not only struggling against specific 'deskilling' but much more generally over the forms of control, both within the workplace and the community (for details see Foner, 1955; Palmer, 1975).

By 1919–20 the opposition of labour to scientific management had partly subsided, although as Palmer (1975) points out this was much more true of the official union leadership than of all groups of workers. This stemmed from a number of conditions. First, there were various semi-corporatist arrangements established in wartime which ensured, as Person (1929, p. 20) put it, 'labor's interest in good management and increased productivity'. Second, there was the more conciliatory and accommodating attitude of the engineers themselves. Thus, in 1917, C. B. Thompson (1917, p. 267) argued that 'scientific managers have been freely advised to recognize more fully the necessity of cooperation with the unions'. And third, after 1919 and the next years when up to 20 per cent of the American labour force went on strike, labour was decimated in the early 1920s. One and a half million members were lost and the AFL advocated a new doctrine of labour–management cooperation (Brody, 1980).

I will now consider scientific management's other struggle, from capital and existing management. The starting point here is to recognise Burawoy's claim that 'one cannot *assume* the existence of a cohesive managerial and capitalist class that automatically recognises its true interests' (Burawoy, 1978). Indeed, the very growth of 'scientific management' in the USA in a sense reflects not so much the strength of capital and its ability to deskill labour but rather its relative weakness, in particular to prevent the appropriation of effective economic possession by a new class of 'managers'.

This opposition was well recognised at the time – C. B. Thompson (1917) described scientific management as a 'veritable storm-centre', while H. Person (1929) talked of the general reluctance of most managements to undertake theoretically 'revolutionary improvements' rather than to continue existing opportunistic practices which were according to Litterer (1963, p. 370), 'increasingly chaotic, confused and wasteful'. Taylor himself stated in his testimony in 1912 to the *Special House Committee to Investigate the Taylor and Other Systems Of Shop Management* that:

> nine-tenths of our trouble has been to "bring" those on the management's side to do their fair share of the work and only one-tenth of our trouble has come on the workman's side. Invariably we find very great opposition on the part of those on the management's side to do their new duties (Taylor, 1947, p. 43).

This is confirmed in Nelson's survey of 29 Taylorised plants where he found that opposition came both from foremen and supervisors and more generally from management; Nelson concludes that 'the experts encountered more opposition from managers than workers' (Nelson, 1975, p. 75). For example:

> Gantt encountered serious opposition from the management at the Sayles Bleachery and Joseph Bancroft & Sons, and less formidable problems at the Canadian Pacific shops; Bart antagonized his employers at the S. L. Moore Company and lost the confidence of the Yale & Towne officers; Gilbreth alienated the managers of the Herrmann, Aukam Company; C. B. Thompson complained bitterly of the opposition he encountered from the supervisors at the Eaton, Crane & Pike Company; Cooke reported a similar experience at Forbes Lithograph; Sanford Thompson noted the suspicions of the managers at Eastern Manufacturing; Evans faced substantial opposition from certain superiors and many foremen; and the experts who worked at the Pimpton Press and Lewis Manufacturing Company found Kendall, Taylor's friend and admirer, a highly critical observer of their work (Noble, 1979, p. 75).

One reason for the opposition of existing management was that Taylor

(1947, p. 31) attempted, as he put it, to substitute 'exact scientific investigation and knowledge for the old individual judgement or opinion, either of the workman or the boss'. This involved giving considerable autonomy to the industrial engineer. Layton (1971, p. 139) argues that the effect was that: 'Taylor has opened the possibility of an independent role for engineers in an area in which their position had been that of bureaucratic subordinates'. The more general significance of this conflict for the overall structure of American society will be explored in the next section.

3 Management, the 'service class' and the structure of American society

The first and most evident consequence of the development of scientific management, or more generally of complex managerial hierarchies, was to produce a substantial change in the occupational structure in the USA. This was not merely a question of the growth in the number of engineers, although they did increase from 7000 in 1880 in 136 000 in 1920. But it involved more general changes, firstly, in the structure of American manufacturing industry, as summarised below:

Table 8.1: Administrative/production employees in American manufacturing industry, 1899–1929

	Administrative employees (excludes owners and top executives)	*Production employees*	*Ratio A/P (%)*
1899	348 000	4 496 000	7.7
1909	750 000	6 256 000	12.0
1923	1 280 000	8 187 000	15.6
1929	1 496 000	8 361 000	17.9

Source: Bendix (1956, p. 214)

Secondly, already by 1900 a third of the labour force were employed in the tertiary sector of industry (services) and this increased to almost one-half by 1930, mainly at the expense of primary industry (agriculture/mining/quarrying); see below.

Table 8.2: Sectoral distribution of the American labour force, 1900–30

	Employment in different industrial sectors (%)		
	Primary industry	*Secondary industry*	*Tertiary industry*
1900	37.6	30.1	32.3
1910	31.6	31.6	36.8
1920	27.4	34.4	38.2
1930	22.0	31.1	46.9

Source: Sabole (1975, p. 9)

Thirdly, more generally there was an overall growth in what Burris (1980) and others term the 'new middle class'.

Table 8.3: New middle class positions in the US labour force, 1900–30

	1900	*1910*	*1920*	*1930*
Total (000s)	1,605	2,536	3,785	5,314
Proportion of Labour Force	6%	7.3%	9.5%	11.3%
Sector (proportions of Labour Force)				
Private	3.7%	5.0%	6.8%	8.0%
State	2.3%	2.3%	2.7%	3.0%

Source: Adapted from Burns, 1980; Blau and Duncan, 1967

The first point to note about these figures is that by comparison with the other major industrialised societies there was an extremely rapid and marked growth both of engineers and related administrative workers within manufacturing industry, and of a more general 'new middle class' within the first thirty years of this century. This growth was not something inscribed within the logic of capitalist accumulation in general or of American capitalist accumulation. It can be seen as the growth of a 'service class', a class which in a sense inserted itself within American society and although serving capital, it did so in part on its own terms. The USA then saw the first and most systematic growth of a new class, the 'service class', which was something achieved at the expense of existing capital and labour. As a consequence of this insertion it transformed American society in quite fundamental ways; it led to the substantial realisation of its causal powers. I will now briefly detail what some of these transforming consequences were.

Noble (1979) has most effectively shown how the growth of engineers, of scientific managers, was something crucially linked with the development of corporate capital. Particularly important were the innovations involved in the growth of the chemicals and electrical industries which formed the vanguard of modern technology in the USA. Their development in turn fostered the gradual 'electrification' and 'chemicalisation' of older, craft-based industries which thus rapidly acquired 'scientistic' features, partly through the recruitment of chemical and electrical engineers (Noble, 1979). This led to the growth of technical education, which was well-summarised by Professor J. B. Turner's call to replace the 'laborious thinkers' produced by the classical colleges by the 'thinking labourers' necessary for industry (Noble, 1979; Layton, 1971–1974). The emergent, technically trained, electrical and chemical engineers were predominantly employed within large corporations and promotion mainly consisted of movement within the corporation into management. Professional advancement consisted of promotion within the corporate hierarchies of the science-based industries. These professional engineers were particularly significant in effecting a number of major changes in the USA in the period 1860–1930: standardising weights and measurements, modernising patent-law in favour of science-based industrial corporations, developing large industrial research laboratories with a heightened division of labour, integrating industrial and university-based research, ensuring an appropriate industry-based curriculum within the dramatically expanding university system, and encouraging the general development of modern management and related techniques (Noble, 1979).

Three particular consequences need to be explored. First, the development of engineers/managers helped to weld science and technology into the growing corporate structure and this had the effect of further separating engineers/managers off from the directly productive workers. This was partly because their growth served to generate an 'ideology of technical expertise' which then served other occupations as they systematised their cognitive categories and developed new organizational forms in, as Stark (1980, p. 118) puts it, 'their attempts to define and maintain their privileged position over and against the working class and struggled to increase their autonomy from the capitalist class in the schools, the universities, and the state' (see also Burrage, 1972; Larson, 1977). The engineers thus provided a model of how education and industry were to be integrated over the course of the twentieth century as one occupation after another sought to strengthen their market-power by connecting together the production of knowledge with the production of the producers via the modern university. Schools of business administration had already been established, the first, the Wharton School of Finance and Commerce in 1881, with others at Berkeley and Chicago following in 1898, at Dartmouth and New York University in 1900, and at Harvard as early as 1908 (Touraine, 1974). There was a structural linkage effected between two sets of elements, specific bodies of theoretical knowledge, on the one hand, and markets for skilled services or labour, on the other hand (see Larson, 1980). Thus higher education became the means for bringing about professionalisation and for the substantial transformation of the restructuring of social inequality. As Noble puts it, 'the integration of formal education into the industrial structure weakened the traditional link between work experience and advancement, driving a wedge between managers and managed and separating the two by the college campus' (Noble, 1979). He goes on to note that in emphasising the role of formal education as a vital aspect of their professional identity engineers at the same time lay the foundations for the educationally-based system of occupational stratification that characterises the USA. Thus the very process of professionalisation contributed to the restructuring of the patterning of social inequality, to a system based on the salience of occupation, to legitimation via achievement of socially recognised expertise, and to a heightened concentration upon education and the possession of credentials (Noble, 1979; Abercrombie and Urry, 1983; Wiebe, 1967; Disco, 1979).

This set of developments led to an extraordinary expansion of higher education in the half century after 1880. By 1930 the USA possessed more institutions of higher education than France possessed academic personnel and its university and college population was ten times larger than the secondary school population in France (Debray, 1981, Mulhern, 1981). It would also seem plausible to suggest that this especially large increase in both the size of the middle classes and of the mobility into them in the USA (Kocka, 1980) was an important factor in preventing the development of strong work, market and political divisions between such employees and the working class in this period. Kocka (1980, p. 117) talks of the 'indistinctness and relative insignificance of the collar line in industry', although it should be noted that he attributes this to the lack of bureaucratic and corporate structures in pre-industrial America (compared particularly with Germany up to 1933).

One important reason for the development of a large number of occupations all pursuing a similar programme of professionalisation via the university was that the development of industrial engineering had raised but left unanswered a whole series of questions and issues concerned with the nature of work and the worker. Bendix (1956, p. 288) summarises:

> When Taylor and his followers proposed that the selection and training of workers be put on a scientific basis, they opened the way not to the promotion of industrial harmony on the basis of scientific findings, but to the involvement of industrialists in intellectual debates for which their training and interests had not prepared them.

During especially the 1920s and 1930s a large-scale debate developed as to what workers were really like and how they could be appropriately motivated. A resulting battery of tests and testers emerged so as to investigate their typical attitudes and aptitudes. This was associated with the more general bureaucratisation of industry and the realisation by management that the exercise of control would ideally involve the elaboration of rules, the delegation of authority, and specialisation of administrative functions and the development of complex systems of personnel investigation and management (Bendix, 1956; Baritz, 1960). Each of these developments presupposed new occupations, especially various branches of organisational psychology and sociology, which literally became in Baritz's term 'servants of power' and which copied the professionalisation strategy employed by the industrial engineers (see Baritz, 1960; Nelson, 1975; Church, 1964). And this was part of a general movement which Wiebe (1967, p. 113) well summarises:

> the specialized needs of an urban-industrial system came as a godsend to a middle stratum in the cities. Identification by way of their skills gave them the deference of their neighbours while opening natural avenues into the nation at large. Increasingly formal entry requirements into their occupations protected their prestige through exclusiveness.

He also points out that each of these groups, making up a 'service class', appeared first in the older, larger and more industrially developed cities in the Northeast. Wiebe (1967, p. 160) talks of the development of 'an aggressive, optimistic, new middle class' sweeping all before it from about 1900 onwards. This was then reflected in a further development of the 'helping professions', a process which should not be seen as simply one which involved responding to certain clearly defined 'social needs' (Bledstein, 1976; Wiebe, 1967). Nor though should such professions be seen as purely autonomous since as Lasch (1977, p. 17) argues we should not ignore 'the connection between the rise of modern professionalism and the rise of professional management'; or more critically 'American professionalism has been corrupted by the managerial capitalism with which it is so closely allied'. Lasch points out the considerable similarities between the appropriation of knowledge, centralisation and deskilling in the industrial and in the non-industrial spheres of social activity. An exceptionally powerful and wide-ranging 'service class' developed in the USA and its emergence not merely weakened labour in the sphere of work but within most areas of social and political life.

4 Conclusion

I have therefore shown that the development of scientific management' represented the initial part of the process by which the resources and capacities of the 'service class' developed in the USA. I have in particular suggested that scientific management was not something inscribed in the nature of capitalist relations of production but has to be specifically struggled for. Indeed, far from scientific management being something that would be introduced unless resisted, it is rather the case that such innovations would *not* be introduced unless they are very specifically struggled for and *and* unless undoubtedly widespread opposition can be effectively neutralised. Hence, although (a) such developments are broadly 'functional' for capital, and (b) it is functionally necessary for labour to be controlled by capital, it does *not* follow that such functions explain either the growth of, or the persistence of, scientific management as a form by which capital controls labour. In particular, it is necessary to investigate the industrial and spatial variations involved in order to explain how and why struggles to 'scientise' management were only variably successful, and in general were less successful in Britain than in the USA, Germany and Japan. Hence, in order to explain just why managerial change was particularly developed in the USA, it is necessary to show why the existing social forces were unable to prevent change, whereas in the UK they were so able.

Littler (1982a) in criticising the 'Ambrit' fallacy maintains that scientific management was introduced into parts of American industry before the First World War during a period of economic expansion; in Britain by contrast scientific management, where it was introduced, occurred later, in the 1920s and 1930s during a period of profound economic depression. Furthermore, the 'rationalisation' of work was not something which affected all industries to anything like the same degree. In the USA we have already seen that the transformations of the metal-working, electrical and chemical industries were particularly important. In Britain, the movement to scientific management primarily affected the food, drink, tobacco, chemical and textile industries, and involved innovations under the direction of the Bedaux consultancy firm (Littler, 1982a, 1982b). Overall the Bedaux system seems to have been a way of speeding up the work done with little consideration being paid to other aspects of good and efficient management (Brown, 1935). Moreover, scientific management was introduced considerably later in Britain than in other European societies (Maier, 1979).

Thus, apparently similar capitalist societies are constituted quite differently, with diverse sets of interrelationships between the constitutive social entities. One such social entity with very significant 'causal powers' is that of the service class. These powers are to restructure capitalist societies so as to maximise the divorce between conception and execution and to ensure the elaboration of highly differentiated and specific structures within which knowledge and science can be maximally developed. They are thus to deskill productive labourers and to maximise the educational requirements of places within the social division of labour. This implies the minimising of non-educational/non-achievement criteria for recruitment to such places; and the maximising of the income and resources devoted to education and science, and more generally to the sphere of 'reproduction'. The service class will thus possess powers to enlarge the state structures by which they can organise and 'service' private capitalist enterprises.

Furthermore, the degree to which such powers are realised depends upon not only its mutually antagonistic relations with other classes (especially capital and labour), but also its constitutive forms of intra-class organisation and interconnectedness. The realisation of the powers of the service class depends upon both establishing and sustaining a multiplicity of appropriate 'collectivities-in-struggle'. Stark (1980, p. 119) summarises:

In attempting to defend their claims to technical expertise or to maintain the currency value of their certified degrees, the members of these new occupations stand not with one foot in the working class and one foot in the capitalist class but with one foot in a professional association and one foot in a bureaucratic (corporate or state) organization. The constellation of relations of conflict and alliance between these associations and other organizations arising from work, community, and political life must be the object of study in the analysis of class relations in the current period.

It is this which I have tried to examine in this chapter; namely the growth of scientific management and the resulting transformations of the social structure due to the development of the 'service class', particularly in the USA.

Note

1 I am grateful for the comments of Scott Lash, Mary Rose and Mike Savage, all from the University of Lancaster.

• 9 •

Knowing your place: *Class, politics and ethnicity in Chicago and Birmingham 1890–1983* • *DENNIS SMITH*

1 Dynamics of capitalist democracy

I want to explore the part played by ideas of place and ethnicity in the working of capitalist democracy in Britain and the United States. For example, I am interested in the different ways that the feeling of attachment to a place and the sense of membership within an ethnic group are expressed in the political sphere. Also, how do these factors influence the management of class relationships? However, before analysing in more detail the significance of place and ethnicity I want to explain why Chicago and Birmingham are appropriate cities upon which to focus a comparative and historical investigation of this kind.

In the 1890s few people needed reminding that Britain was a very well-established industrial capitalist nation. Equally notorious was the fact that the United States of America was a thorough-going political democracy. It was more startling to be told that some American cities had become the scene of business enterprise on a scale which belittled previous human efforts, or to be informed that in some British cities popular government had been achieved to a degree which put the rest of that country to shame. These were the messages brought back by Julian Ralph, the energetic roving reporter from New York, following his visits to Birmingham (in 1890) and Chicago (in 1893).

In Birmingham, Ralph found:

a city that builds its own street railroads, makes and sells its own gas, collects and sells its water supply, raises and sells a great part of the food of its inhabitants, provides them with a free museum, art gallery, and art school, gives them swimming and Turkish baths at less than cost, and interests a larger proportion of its people in responsibility for and management of its affairs than any city in the United Kingdom, if not the world. It is, above all else, a business city, run by business men on business principles (1890, p. 99).

Chicago also struck Ralph as a property-owning democracy energised by vigorous commercial activity. He was told that 'the clerks and small tradesmen who live in thousands of . . . pretty little boxes are the owners of their homes'. He marvelled at the public open spaces, such as Lincoln Park, which are 'literally for the use of the people that own them' (Ralph, 1893, pp. 54, 55). Connected by rail to a market of some thirty million people, Chicago was a 'rapid and business-like city':

The speed with which cattle are killed and pigs turned into slabs of salt pork has amazed the world, but it is only the ignorant portion thereof that does not know that the celerity at the stockyards is merely an effort of the butchers to keep up with the rest of the town (Ralph, 1893, p. 49).

Ralph may have been blind to slums, suffering and cynicism in both cities but the main point here is that in the 1890s Birmingham and Chicago could plausibly be presented as successful prototypes of modern capitalist democracy.

By contrast, in the early 1980s, each city is a widely-cited example of the misery and disappointment that capitalism may produce in advanced industrial societies. During the recession years of 1979–80 the Mid-West experienced the largest regional downswing in the United States. The industrial sectors which were hit the hardest – iron and steel, fabricated metals, electrical machinery, and non-electrical machinery – account for over half of the manufacturing employment in the Chicago area. Birmingham has shared in a drastic decline in the economic fortunes of the West Midlands. In 1974 the average wages of manual workers in that region placed them at the head of a league table containing ten regions in the United Kingdom. By 1983 they had fallen to eighth position. A painful consequence is that levels of poverty and unemployment have risen considerably in both cities (Haider, 1982; *Guardian*, 2 January 1984).

Not surprisingly, some sharp political turbulence has occurred in the last few years. In 1982 a new Conservative administration led by

Neville Bosworth was elected in Birmingham with a determined policy of 'privatising' a wide range of council services. The following year Harold Washington became Chicago's first black Democratic mayor after the roughest election in that city for a long time. The regimes headed by Bosworth and Washington have two characteristics in common. Each of them came to power expressing fundamental criticisms of the way capitalist democracy was operating (in Birmingham and Chicago, respectively) and each has subsequently encountered deep-rooted opposition from vested interests entrenched in the existing system.

In view of the facts just outlined, Birmingham and Chicago seem good places to explore the workings of capitalist democracy in Britain and the United states. By 'democracy' I mean a political order in which widespread bargaining occurs throughout the population, institutionalised in part through political parties and partly expressed through elections on the basis of an extensive suffrage. The outcomes of these bargaining processes have an important regulating effect on the behaviour of governments, legitimising certain activities and making others politically imprudent. The term 'capitalist' implies that social relations are to a great extent regulated and/or legitimised in terms of market principles of supply and demand and the pursuit of profit. It also assumes the existence of a thriving and politically influential class of large property owners (and managers) whose power is to a significant extent sustained by their dominating position in the market, not least as purchasers of labour.

Chicago and Birmingham are not supposed to be 'typical' of American and British society (any more than New York and London would be, or New Orleans and Belfast). However, the ways in which these two 'second cities' have developed during the past century has shaped the experience of several million people in both societies. No comparative study of capitalist democracy in Britain and the United States can ignore evidence specific to Birmingham and Chicago (see also Smith, 1982).

I want to argue that feelings about place and ethnicity play an important part in managing a conflict within capitalist democracies between two principles of legitimacy based, respectively, upon the promise of fulfilment and the promise of security. Capitalism offers fulfilment – satisfaction of the urge for possession (including 'self-possession') and an associated sense of self-justification.[1] However, there is an implicit understanding that the potential degree of fulfilment is greater, the more you are prepared to take risks. Democracy offers security – guaranteed rights to welfare, respect and a voice within a larger collectivity. In this case, it has to be accepted that the degree of security is greater to the extent that these rights embody a workable compromise between the conflicting aspirations held by different members of the collectivity. Stated in this way, the conflict takes the form of a contradiction: the promise of fulfilment depends upon forgoing a degree of security; the promise of security depends upon limiting your ambitions for fulfilment.

In order to contain the potential conflict between the promise of fulfilment and the promise of security it is necessary for a capitalist democracy to reconcile the urge to possess and the desire to be a recognised member of a community. Feelings of attachment to specific places are relevant in this context. The sense of possession over a place may not depend upon having full legal ownership. In the sphere of residence and the 'social management' of specific territories, day-to-day control may be exercised by people who are not the formal owners. Nevertheless, in a capitalist society possession as 'private property' remains the ideal.

In the relationship between people and places, two forms of 'belonging' are relevant. Places 'belong' to people – but people also 'belong' to places by virtue of their attachment to communities whose sense of identity is bound up with specific localities. The sense of attachment to a place is most strongly felt when the two forms of belonging – a relationship of possession and a relationship of membership – coincide for a group or individual. To quote the famous song, the working-class Glaswegian enjoying a companionable drink on a Saturday night can sing not only 'I belong to Glasgow' but also 'Glasgow belongs to me'. It is significant that he declares his allegiance to his city rather than his class, a point to which I shall return.

In some well-known cases, one or both of these forms of belonging may be very weakly experienced. For example, strong communal bonds may sustain a group culture which expresses no strong sense of attachment to the group's current location. This may engender (in some minorities, for example) a collective feeling of being entrapped in a Babylonian captivity. Another combination of forms of belonging may be found among some 'privatised' families in the 'affluent' working class. In this case, a strong sense of territorial possession (say, among owner-occupiers on a private housing estate) may be combined with weak communal bonds.

Conflict between the desire for strong communal bonds and the urge to possess – between the principles of community and property – may take a more serious form. Some of the implications of this were already being considered in the mid-nineteenth century when it was still unclear how the potentialities of capitalism and democracy would work themselves out in urban industrial societies. The community to which democratic ideology conventionally refers is 'the people'. However, the stability of capitalist institutions, including private property, may be threatened if 'the people' are commonly defined with reference to their position in the market or the mode of production: as 'the people' in opposition to their 'exploiters', as the labouring (or unemployed) masses confronting the propertied ruling class.

The possibility of reconciling the potentially conflicting principles of community and property is an implicit concern of two great mid-nineteenth century bourgeois works published in 1848 and 1843 respectively: *The Communist Manifesto* and *A Christmas Carol*.[2] Each is directed at a wide reading public and presents a very serious message in terms which ordinary men and women may understand. In a sense, both are ghost stories of enormous power. Karl Marx and Fredrick Engels begin by declaring that 'A spectre is haunting Europe – the spectre of Communism'. In their book they describe the processes whereby the propertyless labouring population within the capitalist system becomes increasingly cohesive. The proletariat, which has been 'an incoherent mass scattered over the whole country', is becoming united: 'it becomes concentrated in greater masses, its strength grows, and it feels its strength more'. Increasingly, the labouring class acquires the capacity to act on a communal basis. As its sinews grow and its consciousness develops, the proletariat becomes capable of engaging in struggle against the capitalist class and, ultimately, against the capitalist system itself (Marx and Engels, n.d.).

The proletarian movement is 'the self-conscious, independent movement of the immense majority', accompanied by 'a portion of the bourgeois ideologists, who have raised themselves to the level of comprehending theoretically the historical movement as a whole'. A fusing of the principles of property and community is achieved in part through a transformation of proletarian consciousness. The great final act is 'the abolition of bourgeois property' as a consequence of which 'capital is converted into common property, into the property of all members of the society'. It belongs to all those who themselves belong to the national (ultimately, the international) community (Marx and Engels, n.d.).

According to Marx and Engels, 'the bourgeoisie . . . produces . . . its own gravediggers. Its fall and the victory of the proletariat are equally inevitable' (Marx and Engels, n.d., p. 71). Is the overthrow of capitalism and the bourgeoisie at the hands of the working class indeed an unavoidable destiny? That issue lies just below the surface in *A Christmas Carol*. When Ebenezer Scrooge is shown his own future grave by the Ghost of Christmas Yet To Come, the hope of avoiding an unpleasant fate is uppermost in his mind: 'Are these [he asks] the shadows of the things that Will be, or are they the shadows of the things that May be only?' (Dickens, n.d., p. 80). No answer comes. An earlier spectre shows him 'two children – wretched, abject, frightful, hideous, miserable', whose plight is due to the greed of Scrooge and his fellows:

> This boy is Ignorance. This girl is Want. Beware them both, and all of their degree; but most of all beware this boy, for on his brow I see that written which is Doom, unless the writing be erased. (Dickens, n.d., p. 65).

The message of *A Christmas Carol* is that a transformation in the consciousness of capitalists like Scrooge is their best hope of avoiding doom. At the beginning of the story Scrooge excludes others from his wealth and excludes himself from their communal life. By the end of the tale he has had a very severe fright and changes his life completely. He shares his property, and enters into community, with those upon whose labour and compliance he depends for his very survival. Within this parable, as in *The Communist Manifesto*, community and property are reconciled – but with very different consequences for the class structure. It is noteworthy that Dickens closely relates the final, 'happy' class relationship between himself and the Cratchits to the institutions of the family and the city (in this case London). The hierarchy of class is invested with the warmth of paternalism and with civic pride:

> Scrooge was better than his word. He did it all, and infinitely more; and to Tiny Tim, who did NOT die, he was a second father. He became as good a friend, as good a master, and as good a man, as the good old city knew, or any good old city, town, or borough, in the good old world (Dickens, n.d., p. 88).

So far, I have argued that a sense of attachment to place is strongest when it expresses both the urge for possession and the influence of strong communal bonds. I have also argued that the bonds and divisions associated with property ownership and community membership frequently intersect in contradictory ways and that this may occur in a manner which threatens the stability of a given capitalist order. By implication, strong feelings of attachment to place may have a tendency to reinforce 'stabilising' tendencies within capitalist democracies. However, as a general proposition that would still beg a large number of questions. It will be necessary to examine not just place but, rather, the interplay between place, social class, political party and ethnicity in the development of Chicago and Birmingham. I can anticipate the argument slightly in one respect by making the obvious point that in both Britain and the United States the democratic political orders which have developed place great stress upon national and ethnic affiliations. In both cases, this fact has contributed to a weakening of the disruptive potential of class divisions generated in the sphere of property relations.

In the second part of this paper I am going to present the broad outlines of the division of labour and mode of production in the two cities, indicating the trajectories of their rise and fall within the capitalist order over the past century. The third section is devoted to a description of some similarities and differences between the cities over the same period with respect to class consciousness, the party system and ethnic relations. In the fourth section I analyse the significance of place and ethnicity for class relations and the political order in Birmingham and Chicago. In the final section I discuss the implications of my analysis for some aspects of the development of capitalist democracy as exemplified in the two cities over the past three decades.

2 Rise and fall

Chicago, with its population of three million people, is three times the size of Birmingham. Nevertheless, the atmosphere of the Metropolis of the Mid-West has some resemblances to that of the Capital of the West Midlands. In the early 1980s Peter Jenkins, writing in the *Guardian*, described Birmingham in this way:

> Some people don't like the city centre but I do. It reminds me of Chicago although that is to flatter it architecturally . . . I like the violent irregularity of the skyline, the brash mixture of old and new, and the confident equation of wealth and concrete (*Guardian*, 12 February 1981, p. 17).

In fact, both cities manage to look brash and staid at the same time. In better days their factories provided profits for capitalists and good wages for skilled workers. Now, large steel plants (in Chicago) and car factories (in Birmingham) are idle or on short time. Manufacturing jobs are being lost from each city as firms close down or find better sites in the suburbs or in other towns. The proportion of the city population in need of public services (welfare, pensions, health care and so on) has tended to increase while the tax base has been eroded (*Sunday Times*, 27 February 1983; *Chicago Sun-Times*, 18 July 1982).

In the past, Birmingham's prosperity has been based upon its wide diversity of local trades, especially in 'metal-bashing' and engineering. Since the turn of the century, the production of motor vehicles, especially in the large works at Longbridge, has become increasingly important to the local economy. By the 1950s, between one-fifth and a quarter of Birmingham's capital and labour was tied up, directly or indirectly, in motor production (Sutcliffe and Smith, 1974). Since the 1960s there has been a tendency for employment in the manufacturing sector to decline in favour of service industries (City of Birmingham, 1973). However, during the post-war period there has been no major change in the structure of an industrial sector which in 1951 was described as being 'more broadly based than that of any city of equivalent size in the world' (Wise, 1951).

In the course of the past century, the emphasis within Chicago's economy has shifted from processes related to agriculture, such as the production of the McCormick Reaper, to the manufacture of a very wide range of industrial products. Metropolitan Chicago is, for example, the nation's leading producer of radios, television sets, telephone equipment, electrical machinery and household appliances (Cutler, 1982). The area has been recently described as having 'one of the most diversified and best balanced economies in the nation' (Cutler, 1982, p. 165). Chicago's workers are less dependent than those in Birmingham on a few large employers. For example, the top ten employers in the Chicago area account for only a third of the total workforce. Only half of the largest private employers are manufacturers.

Both cities have benefited from their central locations in relation to regional and national economies. The influence of this factor has been felt especially strongly in Chicago. Its inhabitants have tended to look down upon New York as a rather out-dated and effete would-be rival. By contrast, in the West Midlands London is felt as a powerful presence whose dominance is sullenly resented. Birmingham has New

Street Station, Spaghetti Junction, an airport and the National Exhibition Centre but it would be foolish to pretend that they could compete, in national and international importance, with O'Hare Airport, the McCormick Place Exposition Center and Lake Calumet Harbor.

So far, I may have given the impression that Birmingham is a kind of 'Chicago writ small'. However, the two cities have arrived at their apparently rather similar situations in the early 1980s by very different routes. For example, during the half century following the end of the First World War Birmingham was a city of rising prosperity in a society whose global economic and political power was falling. In the same period Chicago was a city experiencing a gradual decline within a society whose global power was increasing. The steadily rising trajectory of Birmingham's prosperity could be traced back to at least the eighteenth century whereas Chicago had burst upon the scene in a spectacular way in the decades following the American Civil War. In 1833, when about 150 000 people were living in Birmingham, Chicago had a population of some 350 souls. Bears were being killed on the fringes of what is now the Loop (or central business district) (Cutler, 1982, p. 19). From this standing start Chicago's population overtook that of Birmingham during the 1870s.

Chicago's rocket-like surge in population and wealth could not be maintained. Between the two world wars the city's inhabitants had to come to terms with the fact that the local impetus for growth was falling away. 'Hungry money' found its way to areas like California and (later) the South-West rather than Illinois. Techniques had to be learned by local politicians and businessmen to ensure that the fall back to earth was not too precipitous and disruptive. Birmingham's rise was, by comparison, more gradual and sedate as well as more sustained. While Chicago suffered, Birmingham sailed through the Depression of the 1930s with relatively little difficulty. However, during the past decade the economic climate in the West Midlands has deteriorated to an unprecedented degree. The arc of Birmingham's rise and fall may turn out to be a mirror image of Chicago's path. Chicago rose like a rocket and has glided slowly downwards. Birmingham ascended much more gradually but is experiencing a very sharp decline for which local experience offers no preparation whatsoever. These different trajectories have had profound implications for the development of Chicago's Democratic organisation and Birmingham's Labour movement, as I argue later.

3 Ethnicity, politics and class

If we turn more directly to the issues of ethnicity (including race), politics and class, then we meet once again the pattern of medium-term similarities which may hide longer-term differences between the ways in which the two cities have developed. From the viewpoint of 1984, the last quarter of a century appears to present a common profile in Birmingham and Chicago in a number of respects. For example, during the late 1950s and early 1960s, Birmingham – along with places like Luton – acquired a reputation as the heartland of working-class affluence. Wage earners seemed to care most of all about their own domestic living standards and to be casting their votes, as pragmatic householders, according to that criterion. Consciousness of class solidarity – as Labour opposed to Capital – appeared to be very weak. In the early 1960s, Graham Turner (1964) argued that these attitudes had deep roots:

> For decades, workers from all over Britain have been trekking to the car cities. . . . These are men who are prepared to up stakes, to take risks, to cast themselves hopefully into new environments.
>
> What was at first one slender rift in the traditional class structure is growing wider with the years, for car workers have been more affluent and for longer than almost any other major group in British industry. Now, in each motor metropolis, you will find (if you scratch the surface gently) the beginnings of a blue-collar middle-class after the American pattern (Turner, 1964, pp. 103–4).

Between 1959 and 1966 Birmingham's Labour Council was controlled by Harry Watton whose regime could certainly not be described as radically socialist. In 1963 he made Birmingham the first Labour-controlled authority to abolish the general rate subsidy to housing. Watton's strategy has been described as being 'to placate the Conservative municipal voter in the hope that he would not go to the polls, (Sutcliffe, 1978, p. 174). According to the Midlands correspondent of the *Statist*:

> For eight years Birmingham was a municipal dictatorship. The strong man was Alderman Harry Watton, leader of the majority Labour group. During that time nothing of importance was done by the city council which he did not personally approve. No important project of his was ever defeated. He made running the council virtually a full-time job, combining it with private semi-

retirement and part-time lecturing in craft printing. Living a modest life in one of the city's twilight suburbs, he sacrificed private prosperity for satisfaction of another kind. You could call it the reward of public service, or you could call it the glow of power. Probably, as Watton claims, it was a bit of both. But for eight heady years he was Birmingham; what he said went (*Statist*, 6 January 1967, p. 15).

The tone and content of that passage would be very familiar to Chicagoans. Watton's regime in Birmingham coincided, more or less, with the epoch of Richard Daley's greatest influence as Mayor of Chicago, a post he held between 1955 and 1976. Daley lived modestly in Bridgeport. This is a relatively poor, Irish-controlled neighbourhood about four miles south-west of the Loop. Milton Rakove describes Daley's political approach as follows:

Daley's philosophy of the role of government, which dominates his behaviour as mayor of Chicago, is a complex potpourri of his Catholicism, his pragmatism, his conservatism, his liberalism, his pull-yourselves-up-by-your-bootstraps outlook, his fealty to democracy, his respect for ability and authority, his admiration of the symbols of power and glory, his acceptance of the values of the status quo, and an Edward Burkeian rejection of violent change (Rakove, 1975, p. 22).

It should not be necessary to add that for several years Daley was Chicago; what he said went.

The retirement of Watton and the death of Daley have been followed by much more difficult times for both the Birmingham Labour Party and the Democratic machine in Chicago. In part, these difficulties have been tied up with the handling of racial and ethnic questions which have played an important part in the politics of both cities throughout the last quarter of a century. These questions advanced very rapidly up the political agenda during the middle and late 1960s. In Chicago there was widespread rioting by the black population. In Birmingham Enoch Powell made a speech protesting about coloured immigration which made him a popular hero amongst the local (and, to some extent, the national) population (Lewis, 1979).

Once more, I have to emphasise that Birmingham is not just 'Chicago writ small'. Taking the last century as a whole, ethnicity, politics and class have related to each other in very different ways in the two cities. For example, the Irish have done less well as a group in Birmingham than they have in Chicago. Between 1933 and 1976 Chicago's mayors were all born of Irish descent in Bridgeport. By contrast, the most important arena of ethnic hostility in Birmingham before the 1950s was that of relations between the English majority and the Irish minority. Irish workers and their families had been the butt of 'no-popery' riots as early as 1867. A century later, the Irish were becoming less visible as a residence group. They were moving out of the central wards and middle ring of Birmingham and dispersing into the suburban outer ring. Nevertheless, the politics of Anglo-Irish relations continue to leave their deep marks on Birmingham. In 1886 they were produced by Joseph Chamberlain's split with Gladstone over Irish Home Rule. More recently, Irish bombs have done the work (Cutler, 1982; Reynolds, 1964; Rex and Moore, 1967; Sutcliffe and Smith, 1974).

By the end of the 1960s a new demographic pattern was clearly visible, mainly as an effect of New Commonwealth immigration from the Caribbean, the Indian sub-continent and East Africa. The 1971 Census showed that a band of 'Inner-city' wards contained a relatively high proportion of residents whose parents had both been born in the New Commonwealth. Typical figures were Sparkhill 24.5 per cent, Sparkbrook 30 per cent, Deritend 27 per cent, Small Heath 21 per cent, Saltley 17 per cent, Newtown 16.6 per cent, Aston 30 per cent, Handsworth 32.5 per cent, Soho 48 per cent and Sandwell 20 per cent. These areas included private housing of a low standard and some old council housing estates. By contrast, in the suburbs – including a number of newer council housing estates – the proportion of Asians and West Indians among the population was very much smaller: for example, Yardley 0.7 per cent, Longbridge 1.08 per cent, Erdington, 1.6 per cent. Within the city as a whole, the white population remained overwhelmingly preponderant. In the late 1970s 'immigrants constituted about one in ten of the economically active population in Birmingham' (Rex and Tomlinson, 1979, pp. 76, 110).

Asian and West Indian political activists had to come to terms with a political system dominated by two parties which are identified nationally with institutions (the trade unions, the City) generally assumed to be promoting the interests of sections of the indigenous working class and large property owners. In their research on the Handsworth district of Birmingham in the mid-1970s, John Rex and Sally Tomlinson found that West Indians and Asians tended to prefer Labour to Conservative candidates although among the latter there was also a substantial Conservative vote. Asian workers' associations and related ethnic organisations negotiated with politically influential groups both inside and outside the Labour movement. Amongst West Indians, a great deal of political activity was outside both the Labour Party and the trade unions. To a great extent it was concerned with fostering a 'revolutionary black consciousness' which 'had effectively displaced simple working-class consciousness amongst West Indians in Handsworth'. At the same time, they found some evidence that the National Front was getting support from among the white population (Rex and Tomlinson, 1979).

West Indians and Asians in Birmingham face the problem of finding a way into or around a political order which was not shaped with their interests in mind. By contrast, the Democratic machine in Chicago built up its power from the 1930s by responding to the needs of ethnic minorities who felt 'left out'. Control of City Hall was 'rented' from the people by exploiting an elaborate system of ward bosses and precinct captains in the neighbourhood. Demands from below were aggregated and partially satisfied. On polling day the Democratic vote was duly delivered (Gosnell, 1937; Guterbock, 1980).

Chicago's growth in the late nineteenth and early twentieth century had fed upon and stimulated several waves of European migration. After the Irish invasion of the 1840s and 1850s came the Germans and the Scandinavians. During the half-century before national immigration controls were imposed in 1927 Chicago also sucked in thousands of people from Southern and Eastern Europe. Earlier immigrant groups, who were becoming increasingly 'Americanised', tended to move away from the city centre, vacating territory for the newcomers. The sons and daughters of these new arrivals would later beat the same track towards the suburbs. At the height of the influx, Chicago was the third-largest Irish, Polish, Swedish and Jewish city in the world, the second-largest Czech city and the largest Lithuanian city (Cutler, 1982; D'A Jones and Holli, 1981).

America's own black people began to come in from the South in very large numbers at about the time of the First World War. They congregated in a 'black belt' which expanded over several decades until it covered large areas of the South and West sides of the city, which became highly segregated. The blacks voted Democrat, too, although they remained very low down in the pecking order of Chicago politics. More recently, many people from Central and South America have come to Chicago. The Hispanic population in the city amounted to about 14 per cent in 1980 and is very rapidly increasing. These latest arrivals are in some respects similar to Birmingham's newcomers, since they are both dark-skinned and foreign-born. The 'Latinos' are being assimilated into Chicago's machine politics with great rapidity. Their leaders played an important part in the campaigns leading up to Harold Washington's election victory in 1983 (Clayton and Drake, 1946; Spear, 1967; Wilson, 1965; *Chicago Defender* 11 January 1983).

So far, I have suggested that Birmingham's politics are characterised by a relatively low degree of 'traditional' working-class solidarity and a persisting inability to sympathise with the particular needs expressed by ethnic minorities. I have also suggested that Chicago's politics are practically devoid of class consciousness and much more sensitive to the demands of ethnic minorities. That is accurate as far as it goes. However, the interplay between class, ethnicity and politics will have to be discussed further, taking into account the highly-charged awareness of 'place' which enters into these relationships in the two cities.

4 Knowing your place

The Birmingham described by Julian Ralph in 1890 contains more obvious evidence of the work of Scrooge's ghosts than of the spectre haunting Europe. At that date, the Unionist regime headed by Joseph Chamberlain was gradually moving towards the Conservative Party to establish a political union of large property owners and their associates. Unionist rule in Birmingham drew upon the powerful ideological support of a paternalist civic tradition – clothed in democratic dress and christened 'municipal socialism' – which had been established over the past two decades. The themes of property and community were united in an emphasis upon the city as a collectivity managing its resources on behalf of its members. Municipal affairs, it was asserted, were carefully and generously guided by the city's most substantial citizens.

Ralph found that 'A succession of public-spirited men' had held political power, 'always having the community in mind as a thing to be worked for'. Mayors had been chosen 'from the active classes – merchants, manufacturers, shopkeepers, or professional men'. He was happy to report that 'No socialist has ever been elected to the Council.' John Thackray Bunce, a very influential local newspaperman, was presumably well aware of the desirability from his point of view, of outflanking movements from below. Ralph reported Bunce's opinion that the voters of Birmingham were 'the owners of a magnificent estate and lucrative industrial undertakings'. They were participating in the truest form of cooperation – a real socialism, self-imposed, self-governed, conducted with the assent and by the efforts of a united community, and conducing to the equal advantage of all its members' (Ralph, 1980, p. 111).

Half a century later, much of this municipal ideology remained intact. Sir Charles Petrie explicitly linked it with the career of the Chamberlain family. In *The Chamberlain Tradition*, published in 1938, he pointed out that when Neville Chamberlain became Lord Mayor of Birmingham at the time of the First World War he was following seven relatives into that office (Petrie, 1938). Petrie writes of Neville's father, Joseph:

> No man in modern times has done more to raise the standard of municipal life, for he rightly believed that local government could only succeed if the natural leaders of the people participated fully in their obligations. . . . 'We have seen in the United States of America how the withdrawal of men of character and of ability from all concern and interest in local work has depreciated the standard of public morality. . . . In our local parliament we want men of the highest ability and culture to keep alive, by their own examples and in their own persons, a love of knowledge and the appreciation of the highest intellectual requirements. On the other hand, it is absolutely necessary that we should remain in close sympathy and relationship with the mass of the people, whose daily needs and common wants should find fitting and frequent expression in our midst (Petrie, 1938, p. 54).

The classic statement of Birmingham's 'civic gospel' had been made by George Dawson, an eminent local minister, in 1866:

> A great town exists to discharge towards the people of that town the duties that a great nation exists to discharge towards the people of that nation; . . . a great town is a solemn organism through which should flow, and in which should be shaped all the highest, loftiest, and truest ends of man's intellectual and moral nature (Dale, 1898, p. 101).

Running through this passage is an emphasis on moral standards and spiritual uplift rather than practical welfare. This might be expected at the opening of a library. However, the point is that the supposed unity of community and property – of security anf fulfilment – was a difficult myth to sustain. Birmingham's city fathers built impressive Law Courts and fine educational institutions but they were less responsive to the popular demand for greatly improved working-class housing

(Smith, 1982). In practice, welfare was neglected in favour of the invitation to moral fulfilment. Between the two world wars the Unionist administration was highly vulnerable on this issue to criticism from the nascent Labour movement.

Dawson's words would have been meaningless to most Chicagoans, at that time or since. A more appropriate assertion in their case would have been: 'the neighbourhood is a kind of town which provides its inhabitants with collective security'. Mayor 'Big Bill' Thompson's description of Chicago as 'a wide open city' has applied for much of the past century (Clayton and Drake, 1946). Nelson Algren's verdict on 'Hustlertown' in 1951 is as follows:

> You can belong to New Orleans. You can belong to Boston or San Francisco. You might conceivably – however clandestinely – belong to Philadelphia. But you can't belong to Chicago. . . . For it isn't so much a city as it is a draft hustler's junction in which to hustle awhile and move on out of the draft. That's why the boys and girls grow up and get out. Forever fancying some world-city right out of the books wherein some great common purpose lends meaning to their lives. As no brokers' portage ever can (Algren, 1951, p. 83).

Algren has an obvious affection for Chicago as a place (in this he is not an untypical Chicagoan) but it is not couched in terms of a sense of either possession or community. He found that 'Chicago divided your heart. Leaving you loving the joint for keeps. Yet knowing it can never love you' (Algren, 1951, pp. 30–1).

In fact, the bonds of belonging were focused at a different level. As Mike Royko puts it, until at least the 1950s Chicago was made up of 'neighbourhood-towns' within larger 'ethnic-states': 'To the north of the Loop was Germany. To the northwest Poland. To the west were Italy and Israel. To the southwest were Bohemia and Lithuania. And to the South was Ireland.' You could always tell where you were even with your eyes closed, by the smells, sounds and 'by whether a stranger hit you over the head with a rock' (Royko, 1971, p. 30). For many people all they needed, including a job in a factory or store, could be found within the neighbourhood. There were many good reasons to:

> stay close to home and in your own neighbourhood-town and ethnic state. Go that way, past the viaduct, and the wops will jump you, or chase you into Jew town. Go the other way, beyond the park, and the Polacks would stomp on you. Cross those streetcar tracks, and the Micks will shower you with Irish confetti from the brickyards. And who can tell what the niggers might do?
>
> But in the neighbourhood you were safe. At least if you did not cross

beyond, say, to the other side of the school. While it might be part of your ethnic state, it was still the edge of another neighbourhood, and their gang was just as mean as your gang (Royko, 1971, p. 32).

In the light of my analysis at the beginning of this paper, this brief comparison between the city (in Birmingham) as an arena of fulfilment and the neighbourhood (in Chicago) as a sphere of security suggests an interpretation of some important dynamics of capitalist democracy in Birmingham and Chicago during the twentieth century. Birmingham's paternalistic civic tradition failed to provide substantial benefits to the city's poorer inhabitants, especially in the sphere of housing conditions (see, for example, Green, 1973; Woods, 1978; Englander, 1981). The gradually increasing importance of the local Labour Party between the wars, culminating in the victory of 1945, may be understood in this light (Hastings, 1959; Rolf, 1983). Birmingham's Labour administrations in the post-war period encouraged – and initially benefited from – an increase in the proportion of the local blue-collar population who were well-housed and relatively affluent. They did not overthrow the 'civic gospel' but broadened its compass and made it their own. As Anthony Howard wrote in the latter phase of the regime of Harry Watton:

Labour has . . . moved in and appropriated to itself the Chamberlain inheritance. . . . The mere fact of being in power has inevitably given it a tremendous advantage in terms of identification with municipal achievement and social improvement. But more than that: if there is a political heir of Joseph Chamberlain in Birmingham today, he sits on the Labour benches in the Council Chamber and not on the Tory ones (*New Statesman*, 7 August 1964, p. 170).

In Birmingham, the symbols of collective spiritual fulfilment – public monuments, libraries, law courts – were insufficient to stem a powerful tide in the direction of increased material security for the working class. This was achieved by largely collective means, notably the Labour Party and the trade unions, although the benefits were consumed in a relatively 'privatised' form. By contrast, in Chicago the benefits of collective security within the ethnic neighbourhood failed to meet a powerful demand among many inhabitants for the individual material and spiritual fulfilment promised in 'the American Dream'. Pursuit of this fulfilment, implicit in the idea of being 'a free American', could not take a collective form. Instead, it meant moving out to a more prosperous and respectable neighbourhood and eventually finding a home in the suburbs. Ironically, many of the suburban grand-children of those who resided in the ethnic-states experience a great thirst for the last experience of 'community'. They may alleviate this thirst by making return trips to the 'old' neighbourhoods or by maintaining formal allegiance to the parental church.[3]

How do these differences between Birmingham and Chicago relate to the significance of ethnicity and race for class and politics? For several decades, the survival of the Democratic machine has to a great extent depended on incorporating newly-important ethnic groups into its institutions and ensuring that conflicts amongst different constituencies do not become too disruptive. As is well known, in Chicago's politics the rhetoric of ethnicity and 'the American way' is predominant and class divisions are relatively insignificant factors in consciousness or organisation. A more important constraint on the functioning of machine politics is the situation of black Americans. They have not followed the typical 'ethnic career' of conversion from being 'foreign' to being emancipated, individualistic American citizens, passing through the half-way house of 'hyphenated' Americanism in the ethnic neighbourhood. The blacks have been American from the beginning, long imbued with the ideals of 'the American Dream'. However, unlike refugees from European autocracies, the Blacks were for several generations 'unfree Americans'. The stigma of slavery has bitten deep into the consciousness of all concerned, producing an ideological contradiction associated with 'being American' which cannot be resolved with comfort: either 'the American Dream' is a palpable fraud since not all Americans may pursue it on equal terms; or blacks are 'not really American' (for recent discussion, see Fox-Genovese and Genovese, 1983). Whenever the racial issue arises, as it frequently does in Chicago's politics, then 'being American' becomes a troubled state. I will return to this issue later.

Ethnic and racial factors have entered into the politics of Birmingham in a very different way. 'Being American' encompasses a very wide variety of ethnic identities within which no single one is clearly superior. Chicago has been called 'the most American of cities' (for example, Algren 1951). By contrast, Birmingham is a thoroughly English city. Unlike 'being American', 'being English' does not encompass a variety of ethnic identities. It is itself a specific ethnic identity. The American city of Chicago has throughout its history included several different ethnic neighbourhoods. The English city of Birmingham is, by contrast, just one place within an ethnic territory whose boundaries are national. It is tempting to say that the equivalent term to 'American' is 'British' except that in the latter sphere the single ethnic element of Englishness is overwhelmingly predominant and the territorial boundaries of 'the British' in, say, 1914 referred to an Empire which has now largely ceased to exist. 'Britishness' does not have the potential for 'soaking up' practically all ethnicities which is characteristic of the American equivalent. Rather, 'the British' have encompassed a limited range of ethnic identities ordered in a clear status hierarchy with the English at the top, followed by the Scots, Welsh and those inhabitants of the Empire who derive from Britain, and finally – as a kind of embarrassed afterthought implied by the latter-day ideology of Empire (later Commonwealth) – the indigenous peoples of the Empire. How or if the Irish fit in has, of course, always been a problem.

Two implications of this discussion are as follows: first, the ethnicity of the English, being ordered on a national basis rather than in terms of the neighbourhood as in Chicago, encompasses class relationships instead of fragmenting them and making them invisible; and second, the ideology of 'being British' derives from a conception of the British Empire as both a union of English-speaking peoples linked by ties of 'kith and kin' to Britain and a system for administering the 'lesser breeds' as part of 'the white man's burden'.

An American witness from the early part of the century provides appropriate evidence at this point. In *England and the English from an American Point of View*, which appeared in 1909, Price Collier noted 'The homogeneity of the people, and the resulting good feeling and fairness on both sides; the wholeness of the nation . . . (and) the interlacing of the classes, which result in the sturdiest sort of patriotism. . .'. Collier was amused by the snobbishness of servants but added: 'Above all things, do not forget the most important factor of all – they are all English, they are all of the same race as their masters. This explains, if not everything, almost everything' (Collier, 1909, p. 6).

Englishness was not a condition that denied the existence of class differences. Instead, it subsumed them within a shared ethnicity sometimes identified in terms of 'national character' or 'good form'. Such sentiments had political force as was demonstrated, in a minor way, by an incident during the municipal contest in Handsworth in 1913. Norman Tiptaft, the Socialist candidate, accused his Tory opponent of representing 'vested interests' who were preventing Birmingham from being 'a healthier city, a better city, a more humane city'. As a reply, the Conservative candidate merely issued a short letter whose main point was that Tiptaft's accusations had been 'unmanly, un-English and unfair'. I should add that Tiptaft's campaign was nearly successful. He lost by only two hundred votes (Tiptaft, 1954). This incident suggests another general observation. Being English meant belonging to a class system (as it still does) – but Englishness is able to change in subtle ways as class relationships are themselves transformed.

Frank Fox, an Australian observer writing in the early 1920s, described the English method of colonial rule as follows:

> The Englishman – the superbly arrogant Englishman . . . desires none of the accidental and external signs of greatness. It for him suffices if he has the real power. . . . In ruling the blind heathen, more fussy people fail because they wish to 'set him right', to induce the barbarian to become as they are. The Englishman does not wish to set people right. He is right; that suffices. It is not possible for inferior races ever to be like him; it is better to let them wallow (Fox, 1923, p. 6).

It was, of course, not 'the done thing' to 'wallow' with 'them', which is why, when as a young man Neville Chamberlain went to the West Indies on behalf of the family business he needed, in the words of Sir Charles Petrie, 'all his family courage'. Chamberlain and his wife found that 'no house was ready for them [and] they were compelled to take up their residence in a newly built negro hut' (Petrie, 1938). Petrie's propagandist work presents much indirect evidence that imperialist attitudes were powerfully reinforced in Birmingham by 'the Chamberlain tradition'. Petrie was proud to report that the Chamberlains had 'always been English through and through' and that a previous biographer had 'been unable to trace one drop of foreign blood in them'. Neville had 'The Empire . . . in his blood'. His 'patriotism was born in Birmingham and developed across the sea' (Petrie, 1938, pp. 17, 29).

Paradoxically, the other face of imperialism was parochialism. Indifference to other ethnic groups shaded into ignorance of them. Parochialism has been strengthened with the loss of the Empire. While contempt for other ethnic groups remains a powerful feeling amongst the English, there is much less widespread willingness to accept responsibility for or obligations towards 'lesser breeds'. In these circumstances, the term 'British' even begins to appear to some as a liability, allowing 'foreigners' to claim consideration in 'our' communities and carve out their own enclaves in 'our' space.

5 From place to space

My argument so far, setting aside reservations and refinements, is as follows:

(a) In capitalist democracies such as Britain and the United States there is a potential conflict between the promise of fulfilment and the promise of security which is related to the co-existence of the principles of property and community as bases of the social order. By the mid-nineteenth century, capitalist property relations had become threatened by the possibility that a propertyless working class would become the major element within the 'democratic community'. Among the factors weakening the likelihood of such a polarisation were feelings of attachment to place and of membership within ethnic groups;

(b) In late nineteenth-century Birmingham, an ideological fusion of the principles of property and community occurred through the representation of the political elite of Birmingham as the ministers of a 'civic gospel', the managers of 'municipal socialism'.

However, between the two world wars the leaders of Birmingham's working class exploited a widespread feeling that the existing unionist town council was failing to provide sufficient material security for the working population. In the post-war period Labour administrations in Birmingham strengthened the association between the city government and the welfare of working people. During the same period, affluent working-class families, whose improved living conditions were in part won by collectivist means, became increasingly 'privatised'. By contrast, in Chicago a sense of possession and of community membership were both focused upon the ethnic neighbourhood at least until the 1950s. However, the conditions of collective security were not the same as those conducive to individual fulfilment. Pursuit of the American Dream meant leaving the ethnic community behind. By contrast with their counterparts in Birmingham, mobile Chicagoans who had won self-advancement by individualistic means commonly felt a hankering for an idealised version of the old ethnic neighbourhood.

(c) In Birmingham, 'Englishness' implies membership of a nationwide ethnic group; in Chicago ethnicity typically identifies one you with a particular area within the city. In Birmingham, ethnicity has encompassed class relations and has undergone subtle alteration as these relations have been transformed; in Chicago, ethnicity obscures class relationships and tends to take rigid forms. 'Englishness' legitimises (in the opinion of much of the population) a relatively guilt-free rejection of other ethnicities, from (say) Calais outwards, especially if they are perceived as a threat to the material security of the English. By contrast, American blacks are subject not to guilt-free rejection but to guilt-ridden hatred. Their presence is perceived to endanger the successful pursuit of fulfilment in terms of the American Dream.

In this final section of the paper, I want to argue that the political significance of attachment to place has recently decreased in Birmingham and Chicago. In its stead, there is a greater emphasis upon competition for ethnic (or racial) space. The relevant distinction between urban 'places' and urban 'spaces' is as follows. 'Places' are replete with well-established human associations deriving from the fact that particular communities frequent or reside in them. 'Spaces' are areas perceived in terms of their *potential* for being acquired or occupied by members of either your own or some other potentially threatening group or category. Crudely, 'places' are 'full' and 'fixed', stable arenas; 'spaces' are 'potential voids', 'possible threats', areas that have to be feared, secured or fled. The shift from a politics of place to a politics of space is encouraged by the weakening of territorially-based communal bonds in the city. It is also fostered by a tendency to retreat into the privatised household and by the strengthening of feelings of vulnerability arising in the course of the pursuit of fulfilment or security.

Enough has been written recently about 'fear in the inner city' and '*angst* in the suburbs' to make it unnecessary to dwell on the apparent strength of the feelings which find expression in quotations like the following:

The big question in my mind is how long I'll be able to sit comfortably here – in this neighbourhood . . . I dread the thought that me and my family will find ourselves swimming in some kind of blood bath (53-year-old white house painter).

Lots of people have come from slum areas here, there is general rowdyism and too many coloureds (44-year-old unemployed white van driver).

The green areas have been turned into rubbish pits and dog runs and the white people would like to see the coloureds go (70-year-old retired machinist) (Terkel, 1970, pp. 152–3; Rex and Tomlinson, 1979, p. 154).

The first person was speaking in Chicago in the early 1960s, the second and third were in Birmingham in the mid 1970s. I want to concentrate upon important differences between the contexts within which such feelings have been strengthened. In each city the context has been shaped by the dialectic between place, ethnicity, politics and class over recent decades. Some specific comparisons will be helpful.

I have already suggested that Chicago's Hispanic population – being dark-skinned, foreign-born and recent arrivals – are the closest equivalent in that city to the Asian and West Indian communities in Birmingham. There is some evidence that the recent mayoral campaign in Chicago gave a massive boost to the registration of voters in Hispanic areas. In the Democratic primary, the Hispanic vote for Washington was 12 798 but in the election shortly afterwards this figure rose to 43 082 (Preston, 1983). Although such a judgement can only be speculative and impressionistic, it seems likely that Hispanic voters and leaders will penetrate further and faster into Chicago's political system than Asians or West Indians into Birmingham's.

If the above comparison is a valid one – if the Hispanic minority in Chicago may be compared with Birmingham's black minorities – which group in Birmingham may be contrasted with Chicago's huge black population, constituting forty per cent of that city's inhabitants in 1980? (Preston 1982). In fact, it would be a useful exercise to compare the progress of Chicago's (mainly 'working-class') black population with that of Birmingham's (mainly white) working-class population. Their different fates have been closely bound up with the development of the Chicago Democratic organisation and the Birmingham Labour movement, respectively.

Conditions favouring the organisation of the work-force, politically and industrially, on the basis of class solidarity have always been weak in Birmingham. During and after the 1930s, the upward gradient of local prosperity meant that there were pickings to be had by workers and their families if they applied pressure on employers and councillors. However, the success achieved by the Labour leadership did not owe much to strong class feeling. It owed more to the weakness of resistance from above, especially after the virtual collapse of Conservative organisation in Birmingham during the war (for a recent discussion, see Rolf, 1983). The causes of that collapse are still not entirely clear. However, Birmingham's Labour Council, which held unbroken power from 1952 to 1966, followed a programme whose underlying logic was that the 'civic gospel' should be transformed from myth into reality. One achievement to which this programme contributed was that between 1945 and 1967 82 000 permanent dwellings were built in the city, 60 000 by the Council itself (Newton, 1976). In the quarter century after the end of the war the slum-ridden centre of Birmingham was completely transformed.

Paradoxically, having 'come into its inheritance', so to speak, the Birmingham Labour leadership presided over the dissolution of the very conditions which gave the 'civic gospel' substance. To put it crudely, by helping to give the working class good living conditions, Labour politicians undermined an important basis of their own political support. Home occupiers, worried about the cost of holidays, cars and re-decorating, began to complain about the level of the rates. Furthermore, the legitimacy of the 'civic gospel' had been strongest when the relationship between the municipal elite and the citizenry was reinforced by the deference owed to gentlemen and employers. A Labour Council seeking the support of unionised voters earning good incomes could not draw upon those cultural resources. In any case, the census taken at the end of the 1960s revealed a very high level of employment outside the unskilled and semi-skilled manual sector. Rex and Tomlinson comment:'It seems fair to say . . . that nearly every second Brummie might be classified in Marxist terms as *petit bourgeois*' (Rex and Tomlinson, 1979; also important, Hindess, 1971).

During its years in the wilderness, the Birmingham Conservative Party underwent a profound change. Its consequences soon became clear upon the party's return to office. In 1970, *The Economist* reported as follows:

> Critics have called present-day Birmingham Tories 'poujadist'. They argue it has become a party of little men of white-collar managers, retailers, small businessmen and shopkeepers, more concerned to turn local government into a profit-making business than to uphold the Chamberlain municipal legacy. . . . Alderman Griffiths [the local Conservative leader] . . . believes that the council has only a limited function. It should 'only do the things for people that they cannot do for themselves'. Otherwise, it must be 'self-effacing'. Already much of Labour's municipalisation programme has been dismantled. Council restaurants have been sold to private enterprise. Direct labour activities have been run down. But the Tories have also rejected much of their old civic gospel. Ironically, but also symbolically, they are selling the freehold property around Corporation Street, acquired by Joe Chamberlain in the 1870s for city redevelopment, to private developers (*The Economist*, 7 February 1970, p. 24).

On 6 May 1982, Alderman Griffiths' successor, Neville Bosworth, led the Birmingham Conservative Party to victory on an even more radical programme. His party's object was to reduce the Council's wage bill by 'privatising' a wide range of services – including refuse collection, housing management, school meals, the architects' and solicitors' departments, swimming baths, other leisure services and the maintenance of parks and recreation grounds – which had until then been provided 'on the rates'. Apart from the local Labour Party, one of the new administration's keenest opponents was the National Association of Local Government Officers who clearly had a great deal at stake (*Guardian*, 21 February 1983, 27 August 1982).

In both philosophy and practise, the Bosworth regime is deeply hostile to the 'civic gospel' and committed to reforming the system of capitalist democracy at the local level. In some respects, however, this approach represents not 'a new beginning' but a culmination of the tendencies that I have just outlined. Over the past two or three decades the political significance of Birmingham as a place commanding strong attachments has greatly declined. There is very little life left in the myth that the act of voting is an expression of community membership. Council business is not widely regarded as a process of managing the collective assets of the community. Instead, the Council finds itself having to mediate between competing neighbourhood-based interests within the city (council-estate dwellers, mortgage holders, members of various ethnic groups and so on) while public spending is perceived as a direct liability on the pockets of residents and employers rather than an indirect servicing of assets.

In these circumstances, the trajectory of Birmingham's rise and relative decline over the past few decades – described in the second section of this paper – takes on particular significance. As I have suggested, the long-run tendency for prosperity to increase, combined with the powerful effect of the Chamberlain tradition, meant that a strong working-class tradition embedded in defensive institutions did not develop in Birmingham. During the past decade, Birmingham's work force has had to face up to an unprecedented collapse in local employment prospects and business activity. It has neither a 'civic gospel' nor deep-embedded class institutions from which it can draw sustenance. However, the shell of ethnicity remains. This, at least, provides English workers with inalienable claims to group membership. In a climate of deep anxiety, there are very strong and obvious temptations to exclude 'outsiders' from the 'spaces' occupied by ethnic 'insiders'.

It is worth noticing that one of the consequences of the most recent Conservative victory in Birmingham is that supposedly 'neutral' functions of local public administration have become increasingly embroiled in political controversy. Officials concerned with, for example, housing and planning have been helping to manage relations between ethnic groups on a city-wide basis for several years. In Chicago, this task has been handled by the machine. It is difficult to be sure how important the contribution has been that Birmingham's local government officials have made to the containment of conflict. Nor is it clear what the consequences would be if the management of relations among different ethnic groups were to be left largely to residents in the neighbourhoods of Birmingham.

The decentralised situation just imagined actually existed, in some respects at least, in inter-war Chicago. Anton Cermak built up the fortunes of the Democratic organisation during the late 1920s and early 1930s. He did it on the basis of a carefully constructed coalition of Chicago's ethnic groups, forged in negotiation with leaders at the precinct and ward levels. To some extent, Cermak exploited the hostility of recent arrivals from Europe to the Irish (as 'top dogs') and to the blacks. However, his successor, Edward Kelly, presided over a great improvement in relations among the three groups mentioned. The Democratic machine became predominant in Chicago, aided by funds released under New Deal legislation. William Dawson emerged as the political leader of the Blacks who populated huge tracts of the South Side of the city. Dawson and his associates provided the link between the white Democratic machine and the black Democratic 'sub-machine'. In many respects, the machine was loosely-jointed before Daley came to power. In its structure it reflected the fact that the centre of gravity in the political sphere was close to the neighbourhood grassroots (or sidewalks). The key political fixers were men belonging to an 'alley-fighting' tradition, men still well represented in the 1980s, for example by politicians such as Edward Vrdolyak, the Croatian boss of the Tenth ward in South Chicago (Allswang, 1971; Cayton and Drake, 1946; Wilson, 1965; Kornblum, 1974).

Richard J. Daley was able, for a considerable period, to centralise a great deal of the machine's power in his own person. Under his *aegis*, the image and fabric of Chicago, especially its centre, were reconstructed with a degree of energy and a flair for publicity which recall the age of Chamberlain in Birmingham. In Daley's opinion, Chicago was 'the only city in the history of the civilization of the world that is well on the way to solving its urban problems, (Rakove, 1975). During his reign of two decades from the mid-1950s he rebuilt much of the Loop. He also poured capital into expressways, public transport, lake front development and the Chicago Circle campus of the University of Illinois. A huge sculpture by Picasso was installed in the Plaza of the Civic Center (Rakove, 1975; Royko, 1971).

However, the contrast between the city centre and elsewhere was (and still is) horrific. One of Daley's political opponents pointed out:

> Get off the subway anywhere in the central business area and you won't find a broken sidewalk. Get off the subway almost anywhere else, and you will . . . [in Chicago's ghettos] the segregation and oppression of Chicago's blacks in housing, jobs, schooling, and the quality of community life are crucial deterrents to general community improvement of any kind. . . . Under the Daley system of tight control . . . the party has to try to overrun, dominate or starve every significant citizens' committee and community organization, especially in the ghetto (Rakove, 1975).

Daley's influence helped to shift power and resources away from the neighbourhoods (particularly the black neighbourhoods) and towards the centre. However, although it put on a cleaner public face, the ethos of the machine did not change. It would be implausible to argue that Daley either wished, or had the means, to substitute a powerful 'civic gospel' for the strong attachments to local 'ethnic-states' which had characterised the Chicago of his youth and early manhood. Nevertheless, during his regime the undermining of the latter began to accelerate. To some extent, that was a consequence of the growing movement of second and third generation 'white ethnics' out towards the suburbs. To some extent, also, it reflected the relative weakness of neighbourhood organisation among the blacks who were becoming an ever-growing proportion of Chicago's population.

During the 1960s, as is well known, black riots and protests and the campaigning activities of groups such as the Woodlawn Organisation had the effect of making 'the race issue' at least as important in Chicago as disputes among different white ethnic groups. By 1965, James Q. Wilson (1965, p. v) was able to write: 'race is a public issue in a way it never was before [in Chicago]. Newspapers and television, city council and school board debates, business and civic association meetings resound with an explicit discussion of concrete race issues which once would have been alluded to obliquely, if at all'. Up until that time, Chicago's blacks had looked upon the local political system in a way rather similar to that of the Birmingham working class in the early part of the twentieth century: acquiescence in its demands was sweetened by the promise it offered of earthly fulfilment and security but the hard school of experience taught you not to expect to get much in practice from that source. During the 1970s Chicago's black leadership began to take independent initiatives, just as Birmingham's working-class leadership had begun to strike out on its own in the late 1930s. In both cases, these initiatives were aided by a weakening of competence and authority in the dominant political establishment: the death of Daley in 1975 was responsible in one case, the disruptive effects of the Second World War in the other. The object in each case was the same: to make the system keep its promises.

The extent to which the politics of racial space have displaced the politics of ethnic place in Chicago is shown by the following fact. In 1983, when Harold Washington, a mild-mannered and rather grandfatherly black politician, won the Democratic mayoral primary by an unexpected fluke, the votes of the vast majority of the city's white Democrats were given at the subsequent election to his Jewish Republican opponent. Only the threat of a black mayor could have produced this effect among Chicago's heavily Catholic population. Washington won by a narrow margin and very quickly faced resistance from a thoroughly recalcitrant city council. It is still too soon to discern the outlines of some future state of political equilibrium in terms of which Chicago may be governed. However, it seems at least possible that eventually a black machine will predominate in Chicago, perhaps in coalition with Hispanic groups, and that white ethnic enclaves will have to bargain with a black political establishment. The victory of Chicago's blacks may well have a conservative effect in so far as it arises out of a strong positive commitment to the existing political order and its ideology. However, this conservative attitude to the system will hardly be a guarantee of social peace if the system's failure to keep its promises is perceived as flowing from obstruction by hostile whites.

In this paper I have argued that attachments to places (neighbourhoods, cities) have important effects in that they help to contain certain conflicts and shape specific processes occuring within capitalist democracies. I have contrasted some of the consequences which have resulted from the focusing of such attachments in the political sphere at the city level in Birmingham and at the level of the neighbourhood in Chicago. In the post-war period, these political arrangements have been transformed in both cities, in one case as a result of the political and industrial successes of Birmingham's Labour movement, in the other case as a consequence (in part) of Mayor Daley. A transition from a politics of place to a politics of ethnic or racial space has occurred in both cities, but not in the same way. In Chicago it has occurred without major changes in the established political order or its ideology. These have shaped and continue to shape the perceptions and ambitions of blacks and whites within the city. It may be anticipated that if the promises of capitalist democracy are inadequately realised, the blame will be cast upon individuals or groups within the system rather than upon the system itself.

By contrast, between the mid-1960s and early 1980s the fundamental principles of capitalist democracy espoused within local government in Birmingham (and, incidentally, at the national level) underwent a profound alteration. Although the Conservative and Labour parties continued to have important differences, the centre ground of politics shifted decisively away from the 'civic gospel', away from the assumption that the citizenry's welfare and contentment were public responsibilities exercised by local government. It moved towards the ethos of 'privatisation' towards the view that the state should be 'self-effacing' and only do for people what they cannot do for themselves. I would suggest that such a drastic reordering of assumptions has been possible because of the nature of English ethnicity. A speculative list of relevant ethnic characteristics might include: a deep-ingrained resistance to assimilation with other ethnic cultures, a high degree of sensitivity to variations in the English class structure, and an unwillingness to be introspective. However, the main point is that whereas in Chicago failures by capitalist democracy to keep its promises are blamed upon 'actors', in Birmingham they are blamed upon the 'system' itself. In other words, if the 'system' is not performing well, then the 'system' must be changed. After all, there's nothing wrong with *us*, is there?

Acknowledgments

I am very grateful to Colin Bell and Val Riddell, both of whom have made valuable comments on this paper.

Notes

1 By 'self-possession' I mean the experience of being to a great extent responsible for your own fate.
2 *A Christmas Carol* was subsequently reprinted in *Christmas Books*, published in 1852. My references are to the edition of the latter published by Thomas Nelson, n.d. References to *The Communist Manifesto* are taken from the reproduction of Samuel Moore's translation in 1888 of the original German text, published by the Foreign Languages Publishing House, Moscow, n.d.
3 This is a composite and over-simplified characterisation of some essential parts of a complex and diverse pattern. See for example, Kornblum (1974), Holli and D'A Jones (1977); D'A Jones and Holli (1981); Hunter (1974); Suttles (1968) and Hansen (1982).
4 For a relatively pessimistic view with respect to the political opportunities open to Chicago's Hispanic population, published before the Washington Campaign, see Belenchia (1982).

• 10 •

Spatial development processes: *organized or disorganized?* •

PHILIP COOKE

1 Introduction

If the 1960s were characterized by relatively stable patterns of economic development, broadening of welfare state services and political settlement between the contending class organizations, the 1980s are indisputably characterised by their reverse. Not only has development, as measured by output and employment indices slowed, it has declined absolutely and relatively in some advanced economies, such as the UK, declined absolutely in many less-developed countries such as Mexico, Chile or Tunisia, yet continued to rise at an accelerating pace in newly industrializing countries such as South Korea, Singapore and Taiwan (Belassa, 1984). Welfare spending is in retreat under monetarist hegemony in the advanced countries as structural crisis imposes limits upon growth (Offe, 1984a). And to the extent that there really was a definable class settlement in the post-war UK, USA and continental European countries this has either broken down completely, as in Thatcher's Britain, or received severe though perhaps, as yet, not debilitating shocks in certain northern European countries. To employ the language of a long-established Germanic analytical tradition, the 1960s probably marked the high water mark of 'Organised Capitalism' while the 1980s signify the onset of 'Disorganised Capitalism' (Urry, 1985b; Offe, 1984b; Urry and Lash, 1986).

While there are important questions to be raised about the validity of broad-sweep, long-range theorizations such as these, which despite their conceptual superiority to such theories as 'Industrial Society' and 'Post-Industrial Society' nevertheless share their time-scale, and may well run the risk of appearing somewhat archaic shortly after coming to fruition (Giddens, 1979a), it is clear that some rather dramatic changes in the pace and direction of economic and social change have occurred over the past two decades. Many of these are picked up by theorists of the 'Disorganized Capitalism' school. In this chapter I want to focus mainly upon those which have a socio-spatial dimension. I wish to do this as the prelude to a discussion of the nature of the spatial development process under capitalism, emphasizing certain organizational features of that process which are often swamped by economic analysis of the same process. This I do in the second section of the chapter. Then I want to go on to consider the relationship between spatial development and certain imperatives of the restructuring of economic relationships, focusing particularly upon the nature and role of technology in the development process – this is the third section of the chapter. Then, in the last two sections I want to examine some recent evidence of socio-spatial processes drawn from an overview of restructuring in Britain during the past twenty years or so, focusing on the paradigmatic relationship of space and technology in economic change, and pointing up some of the key features of the spatial development planning process.

2 Organized and disorganized capitalism

The clearest statement of the distinctions between these two forms of capitalism is presented by Urry (1985). In terms of time-scale, the organized phase begins in the late nineteenth century with the ending of the Long Depression that occurred in the developed economies of that time. The pace and scale of organization varied from country to country but all had in common the following features. Industrial and financial capital concentrated, centralized and became more bureaucratized. A scientific stratum grew to service capital; employers and trade unions organized collectively and exerted pressure on the state, which itself grew and promoted national interests rigorously both internally and externally, especially in the form of imperialism.

In spatial terms, concentration produced distinctive spatial divisions of labour, regions tended to be sector-specific with extractive and heavy-industries predominant amongst those that were most organized. Regional economies were labour-intensive and supported large industrial cities which serviced them financially and commercially. Collective organizations of capital and labour were themselves regionally organized and regions tended to form direct trading links with markets overseas, especially colonial ones, as sub-imperial industrial metropoles. Regional representation within national politics was strong and distinctive.

The 'disorganized capitalism' thesis is that these structures had been transformed in the advanced economies by the period between the mid-1960s and early 1980s. In summary form the general and spatial features of this phase are as follows. Concentration and centralization have transcended national boundaries as the world economy has grown. White-collar work, especially that of the scientific/professional stratum has exploded whereas traditional blue-collar occupations have been eroded through a combination of deindustrialization and automation. Corporatist forms of interest mediation have become vulnerable or have broken down at the level of the nation-state; increasingly wage-bargaining is becoming localised. Multinational firms are no longer easily regulated by the state, and have 'capitalised' the Third World, a process involving the 'de-capitalisation' of manufacturing in the advanced world. Class politics are in decline and are being augmented by internationalist social movements pursuing issue-based political goals.

Spatial change involves the removal of regional economic distinctiveness and a greater reliance everywhere on service-dominated labour markets. Plant sizes have peaked in employment terms and there have been sizeable shifts of productive output and employment from metropolitan to small urban and rural locations. Population density decline in cities is associated with a decline in their tax-base combined with a failure by the state to take a leading role in the replacement of fixed investment in the urban fabric (the Inner City problem). Much of the labour-intensive employment base of cities and older regions has either disappeared permanently or been exported to low labour-cost countries now participating in the 'new international division of labour'.

Disorganization derives from the breakdown of old modes of state regulation of the economy, the openness of world trade in credit and commodities and the global scope and development of multinational enterprise. Moreover, this has coincided with a profound restructuring of the world economy consequent upon the long period of economic crisis experienced in the West with the ending of the post-war boom in the late 1960s/early 1970s. In most Western societies the spread of the state's involvement in economic and everyday life has been turned back; there is a profound disaffection with the capacity of the state to remedy market-failure and a widespread ideology to the effect that state intervention and expenditure are responsible for the inflationary surge which weakened the Western economies in the 1960s and 1970s. The leading economic philosophy of the moment rests on the injunction that salvation relies on a return to market principles and a weakening of the social-democratic faith in planning.

There are two criticisms that can be advanced of these formulations. The first concerns the characterisation of the 'organized' phase as being ineluctably one in which capital concentration and centralization predominated. Clearly, it would be foolish to argue that this did not occur but it is far from being a ubiquitous tendency. In some advanced economies such as Italy and France but not Germany the domestic market for mass-produced goods remained small, and in most, mass-production was closely tied to export markets. The rest of production was often the province of small and medium, non-corporate organization. Moreover state regulation was not as pronounced as is implied by the 'organized capitalism' thesis because of economically liberal regimes, and the political weight of small agricultural interests and of small-scale capital. Furthermore, the impact of organized labour upon capital or the state, outside a few concentrated industries should not be overstated – the regionalized system of labour organization in France and America, but, again, not Germany, for example, reduced labour's perception of the need to organize industrially or represent its interests through the state. This is not to say that 'organized' characteristics did not emerge, at some points, notably during and after the interwar Great Depression and in France and Italy after the war, but that they were by no means permanent features of the economic order (Piore and Sabel, 1984).

This tension between the leading edge of concentrated mass-production, tied often to a centralized finance system and the rather overshadowed, but nevertheless important, smaller, craft-led sector of industry and localized services had spatial connotations too. New regional mixures arose in areas where extractive and heavy industry had yet to make inroads, such as the West Midlands for motor vehicles and electrical engineering or outer London for vehicles and domestic appliances in Britain; Paris and Bavaria for the same new industries in France and Germany; and the mid-West and California in the USA. However, the individual companies responsible for production in such sectors did not concentrate at the same rate even in single countries – the contrast between Ford and GM being a vivid illustration – and in Europe, where the 'GM path of amalgamation' predominated, full concentration was not achieved in some cases until the end of the 'organized capitalist' phase in the late 1960s. By then, many of the industries which *are* good examples of 'organized capitalism', coal, steel and chemicals had lost political and economic power to the new consumer sectors, and had long been in a condition of employment, though not always output, decline. A further feature of the industries of the third technological revolution (Mandel, 1975) is that they were, and remain, heavily dependent for componentry upon the small-to-medium sized company sector, were normally subject to seasonal fluctuations in the market which casualized the workforce to an unusual extent, and possibly as a result were often quite late in accepting uionization of the workforce.

So, the criticism here is not that there are no common features of 'organized capitalism' to be found across some sectors and many advanced economies from the 1880s to the 1960s, but that the universality of these features is over-stated. The organization of capital, the relationship between finance and industrial capital, their relationship to the state and to labour varied over time and space, both internationally and inter-regionally. Moreover, although mass-production became the dominant ideological tendency, or *technological paradigm*, it was far from the only, or necessarily major form of production, either of goods or services. Indeed in both employment and output terms mass-production in large corporations remained the junior partner in the period under consideration, such that even in the 1970s in the home of mass production, the USA, 70 per cent of engineering production came from small firms in small production runs (Piore and Sabel, 1984).

The second line of criticism concerns the degree to which contemporary capitalism can be considered 'disorganized'. While it is certainly true that the introduction of floating exchange rates in the early 1970s destabilized the fixed currencies of the major trading nations and made international transactions a more hazardous business, by the 1980s finance capital had re-equipped, especially through the application of new technology to speed up the rate at which trading-information could be acquired, and its capacity to 'read the market' is now vastly enhanced. Even when a highly de-stabilizing crisis such as that surrounding the less developed country debt-burdens of the 1980s emerged, international banks were able very quickly to relieve the crisis by re-scheduling loans and restructuring debts. In other words, world finance may well operate in a more uncertain environment now than hitherto, but that hardly adds up to disorganization.

Moving to the industrial sphere, the argument is rather similar in the sense that multinational corporations, especially the very largest of these, seem relatively little affected by the gales of economic recession, have the capacity to restructure functionally and over space and are penetrating ever-deeper into the under-capitalized world, including the state socialist countries as market places or production platforms. Clearly, many Western corporations have had a shock, particularly from the competitive surge in numerous producer and consumer goods sectors from Japanese corporations. However, competition for markets (including labour markets) has seen even the largest Western multinationals such as GM or Ford adjusting their strategies, absorbing important lessons in product-quality, work organization and, not least, relationships with the galaxies of small-to-medium sized sub-contractors on which they depend, in order to re-assert their competitive position in the world and domestic market place.

It is important not to view this process as controlled in any strategic or centralised manner on an inter-corporate basis as Smith (1986a) notes with reference to British Leyland:

> In view of the fact that the management of BL had to undergo a long and costly process of learning it would be misleading to describe the restructuring of the company as being a deliberate and well-ordered national or local manifestation of a process orchestrated by and/or on behalf of 'international capitalism' (Smith, 1986a; see also Bardou *et al.*, 1982; Bhaskar, 1980).

The 'disorganized capitalism' thesis might well agree with this but the key question is whether as a result of the widespread restructuring that has occurred in a rather 'bunched' fashion over the past two decades, over most industrial and financial sectors, disorder or a new order has emerged.

Spatially speaking, there are growing signs that a new order is emerging both on a world scale, and more evidently on an inter-regional scale, especially in the UK. Looking at the world-scale first, let us take two important manufacturing sectors, and then briefly look at an interrelated set of service sectors – producer services.

(i) Motor vehicles

Motor vehicles production is an important element of the world economy, in many respects a harbinger of new production techniques, labour relations and forms of international economic integration. It has passed through three phases of development, each with its centre of gravity in a different continent. The first was the achievement of mass-production by American producers in the first decade of the twentieth century, the result of a complex of product and process innovations, and managerial differentiation leading to new forms of market penetration such as segmentation, annual replacement and so on. Notwithstanding the dependence of mass-production upon sub-contracting relations, the world followed suit and sought to replicate the new technological paradigm. The 'American Plan' was ultimately embraced in Europe in the post-1945 period although individual nations pursued different paths and a diversity of products resulted.

European recovery heralded the second phase, and its temporary hegemony was built on the diversity of its products. The small car penetrated a segment of the US market neglected by home producers, forcing US producers to respond in kind under the impetus of the energy shocks of the 1970s. As this occurred, European producers moved up-market and opened up a new luxury market segment in the US. In the 1970s Europe was easily the world's greatest source of motor vehicles and its greatest exporter. Once again, the leader was being emulated and overtaken, driven by the dynamic of competition.

Out of this phase of the development of the industry a new leader in a new continent emerged – Japan. Initially protected by tariff barriers and dependent on licensing European technology, Japan adapted US and European technology and management practice, building massively upon the dualistic nature of the production relations characteristic of mass-production, with its raft of small suppliers keeping it afloat, to create a new synthesis. Quality control and intensified subcontracting gave the Japanese a price and quality edge which makes them now the world's leading vehicle exporter and probable world leader in output in the mid-1980s.

So the world order has changed, not without serious local disruptions, with competition providing the motive force for such shifts. Productivity, price, quality, distribution, parts, servicing and so on are key elements in the competitive, but, to the extent that it involves emulation, relatively orderly, struggle for domination. In the process, other parts of the world space-economy have been integrated in new ways. Mexico has become a major supplier of componentry for the US car industry, though not a major assembler of vehicles. Elsewhere in Latin America, Brazil and Argentina achieved full production with less than 95 per cent local content as a result of earlier investments by Germany and the US. In Asia, India, Taiwan and South Korea are substantial producers though tied technologically to Japan, and in the Indian case to the UK to some extent. The picture, therefore, is of increasing world economic integration and the *reorganization* of spatial production relations, at a rapid pace, without undue signs of disorganization, precisely because of the power of multinational enterprise (Jones and Womack, 1985).

(ii) Microelectronics

Much of the same pattern is discernible in the most internationalized sector of all – microelectronics. Intense competition has produced a number of locational shifts on a world scale. The one-way flow of US investment into Western Europe has been complemented by a lesser flow from Japan in the same direction and an increased flow by both into the US. The peripheral parts of Western Europe have become important offshore locations for US and Japanese investors to penetrate European and Middle-Eastern markets. US and Japanese capital has established significant production centres in the Newly Industrialized Pacific countries of Asia, some of the more advanced of which have developed integrated producer-user complexes (Lin, 1985). Low-skill assembly-only work has moved to less developed industrialising countries in Asia and the Caribbean. Competition between, primarily, the US and Japan is forging a new economic order amongst diverse countries in terms of their market-standing, skill-levels, local entrepreneurship and labour-cost advantages. The labour-cost variable is decreasing in importance as automation grows in the production process, but foreign direct investment is not being withdrawn from NIC locations because of the emergence of substantial markets for finished products, especially personal computers, in those countries.

This ordering process even extends to the differentiation of functions within what were originally offshore 'export platforms'. Thus Taiwan and South Korea are becoming world export leaders in computer terminals and monitors, Singapore concentrates on supplying disk drives while Taiwan, South Korea and Hong Kong are expanding as exporters of finished personal computers. Meanwhile, R & D, marketing and testing, along with a considerable amount of basic production remains in the innovation complexes of the US, Japan and Western Europe, with Japan the leader in standard componentry, the US and Western Europe stronger in the production of special components (Ernst, 1985).

(iii) Producer services

Internationalization of producer services has become more important as the internationalization of manufacturing has itself burgeoned. The real estate, accounting, legal, consulting and insurance services required by banks and industrial corporations can be supplied cheaply and effectively by means of large corporations sub-contracting such requirements out to specialist companies who themselves become internationalized in the process (Daniels & Thrift, 1985). Until relatively recently much of the activity of such companies focused on the domestic market, but by the 1980s world competition for the international producer services market had brought about a transformation in company practice. Following and slightly modifying Reed's (1983) analysis the new world order now consists of the following:

(i) Supranational Centres – London, New York;
(ii) Supernational Centres – e.g. Frankfurt, Paris, Zurich, Tokyo;
(iii) International Centres – e.g. Brussels, Chicago, Hong Kong, Sao Paulo;
(iv) World Regional Centres – e.g. Los Angeles, Milan, Montreal, Seoul.

The first category deals in the full range of international services – commodity exchange, currency clearing, securities dealing, specialist services (insurance, legal, accountancy, etc.); the remaining categories either specialise more in some than others, or serve a more restricted part of the globe (Thrift, 1986).

Thus, it is reasonably clear from the foregoing discussion that three features have emerged from the undoubted break in the pattern and organization of world capitalism over the past two decades. First, international competition for expanding markets and market niches has led corporations, and even much smaller companies (see Frobel *et. al.*, 1980) to engage in production as well as trading activities in wholly new areas of the world in order to gain market advantage. Secondly, the emergence of new producers, imitating, synthesizing and emulating the performance of lead-countries who were first to innovate in manufacturing or service sector activities has brought a significant spatial restructuring of the world economy – the rise of the Pacific Basin, relative decline in the older industrialised economies. But, thirdly, such change, rapid as it is, seems capable of producing not a disordered melange, but new specialisms, a marked degree of hierarchy and a relatively well defined new economic order based upon the financial and technical power of successful competitors.

Such characteristics, now being mapped out on a world scale, are also replicated in the internal space-economies of particular countries. In the UK there is now a relatively well-established hierarchy of financial and technical power whose apex is in London and the South East where corporate financial and manufacturing headquarters, research and marketing facilities predominate. In the semi-periphery of Britain are to be found a mixture of restructured, established manufacturing industry, regional consumer and producer services and some new industries in the computer and defence sectors of the economy. And on the periphery we find the branches of London and overseas-headquartered companies, de-industrialized localities and proportionally large numbers of public-sector service workers. This too, is a reasonably well-ordered hierarchical system of financial and technological power, replicated in comparable, though not identical, ways in other advanced, national space-economies (Lipietz, 1985; Soja, 1985; Massey, 1984).

3 Spatial paradigms: the re-ordering process

In a recent critique of Massey's (1984) industrial restructuring thesis as applied to the re-organization of the space-economy, that is, the thesis that spatial divisions of labour derive from the overlaying of historic rounds of investment (and disinvestment) upon specific local space economies, Warde (1986) has pointed to what he sees as three difficulties with this 'geological metaphor'. First, he argues, the 'transformation rules' which govern the deposition of layers of investment in space are not specified. Second, the connection between sequences of restructuring and particular social class effects is unclear. And third, the range of local social effects other than those having to do with social class is inadequately explored.

Without necessarily solving these problems, attempts can be made to address them, in part, from the foregoing discussion of organized and disorganized capitalism. With respect, first of all, to the question of the 'transformation rules' which are followed as the spatial development process proceeds it is important first to consider the appropriateness of the concept 'rules'. If one rejects a deterministic explanation of social process it needs saying at the outset that any 'rules' which may be followed are likely to be rather different from those drivers observe when motoring along a busy highway. They may only be identifiable post hoc, rather in the way that Smith (1986) referred to the British Leyland experience in the 1980s, as distinct from being available in recipe form ready to be applied. Nevertheless, the idea that capitalists behave intentionally in their investment and disinvestment decisions is clearly a reasonable one, and one which warrants exploration.

Inevitably, decision rules of the kind we are concerned with here take a hierarchical form. In the first instance, in a capitalist economy, what, in Marxian terms, is referred to as 'the law of value' has to be observed if a company is to survive and be in a position to develop. Even in a socialist economy with finite sources of surplus there has to be, as there indeed is, a method for allocating resources in the least wasteful manner – linear programming is widely used in the Soviet planning system, for example (Nove, 1983). Similarly, in those parts of the capitalist economy – state services, for example – not normally subject to the law of value, questions of 'value for money' arise when resources become limited, as UK residents are only too aware. So, the first rule is fairly straightforward: it is that outputs should at least balance, preferably exceed and continue exceeding at an increasing rate, inputs measured in cost terms.

However, countries differ culturally in the ways such rules are specified. Japanese capital has longer time horizons over which profitability may be measured on capital advanced than British or American companies. Different political regimes can render their producers artificially profitable by the imposition of tariff barriers, again Japan is a case in point, and the wave of protectionist legislation in the West in the 1980s is also significant.

A second rule is that of competition – between countries of whatever political stripe – and within capitalist countries. The rule – defeat the opposition in the marketplace – clearly underpinned much of the discussion of the earlier part of this paper, and is a crucial motivating force in the economic development process. While on the face of it being a process which ought to lead to chaos and disorganization, it appears from contemporary experience to be one which can fairly rapidly lead to the emergence of new ordering processes, the dynamism for the further re-adjusting of those orders, and their refinement into hierarchical sets of social and spatial relationships.

The third and last macro-rule to be discussed here concerns technology. In the contemporary period of restructuring, this factor, set within the context of the two rules discussed above, is the principal dynamic of economic change. To understand this, it is helpful to introduce the concept of 'technological paradigm' (Dosi, 1983; Soete and Dosi, 1983). The concept is useful in specifying change in the *nature* of competition. Development occurs as participants strengthen or weaken due to their capacity to implement managerial and technological 'breakthroughs' of a transformative kind, i.e. their ability to impose a new technological paradigm, just as the American car industry did in the 1900s, the European in the 1970s, and the Japanese in the 1980s. Each emergent technological paradigm threatens the existing technological trajectory which, in turn, may fight back – steam ships leading to better and faster sailing ships; Concorde leading to Jumbo Jets – and defeat it or not, as the case may be.

Clearly, the technological paradigm concept is a complex unity of ideological, social and political factors as well as technological ones. The manner in which new paradigms defeat old ones will vary but certain ingredients are essential. Take the rise of the Japanese motor industry:

(i) Political factors such as the loss of a war, the imposition of Western democratic structures, and the will of government to revive the Japanese economy by prioritising the development of key industrial sectors, including cars, and planning the financial and policy frameworks appropriate to achieving this over a lengthy period, were crucial.

(ii) Ideological factors such as national disgrace, a recognition of the necessity for co-operation – to the extent that labour conflicts, often bloody, were never allowed to swing the balance of class forces away from corporatist–paternalist domination, and a hostility to direct foreign intervention, played their part.

(iii) Technological factors such as the adoption and adaptation of American management philosophy and European technology, placed in the context of (i) and (ii) resulted in an efficient, high quality, low price system of production based on 'just-in-time' inventories and 'total quality control' of the product which out-competed the US and Europe in the small car market, especially following the oil crises of 1973 and 1979 (Schonberger, 1982).

(iv) Market factors then signal warnings to competitors who may seek to revive the old paradigm by over-producing and seeking to cheapen the price, or as in this case, continuing to lose market share, and taking the 'if you can't beat 'em, join 'em' developmental route. Thus Japanese production and management methods are being directly or indirectly inserted into Western production culture either through direct investment or imitation, and the new technological paradigm has triumphed over the old (White and Trevor, 1983).

Now, what is often overlooked in accounts such as that just given, is that technological paradigms have spatial connotations, and that to the extent that the content of these spatial connotations consists of different though complementary elements to those of technological paradigms, then one may reasonably speak of the transformation rules of the spatial development process taking the form of *spatial paradigms*.

Within the macro-rules of value, competition and technology, there are what might be termed middle-range rules which firms can adopt to respond to new technological paradigms. Those were clearly enunciated by Massey and Meegan (1982) as

(a) rationalisation – i.e. reducing the labour force;
(b) intensification – i.e. speeding up the labour process;
(c) technological change – i.e. automating production processes.

These need not be thought of as exhaustive of the restructuring rules available to companies – for example, changes in management practices, changes in ownership relations such as joint ventures, and changes in relations with suppliers, can be added as significant forms of restructuring in response to a new technological paradigm. Nevertheless, the three middle-range rules noted above are useful in analysing changing relationships between firms and the labour they employ. And once this relationship is considered, questions of a socio-spatial nature enter the argument in important ways. Moreover, once these elements are introduced, the role of the state, especially with regard to its spatial planning function becomes an integral element of the re-ordering process. This can be referred to as the development of a new spatial paradigm.

4 Social paradigms: ordering 'de-maturity'

In this section I will try to address the two other criticisms made by Warde (1985, 1986) of Massey's (1984) 'geological metaphor'; namely, the lack of a clear analysis of the relationships between restructuring sequences and, first, specific social class effects and, second, specific non-class social effects. The critique is that Massey's consideration of the impact of inward investment on different spatial class formations (specifically Cornwall and South Wales) is descriptively valuable but inadequately explained. Its value lies in its demonstration of the manner in which the arrival of new industry undermined classic proletarian bases of identification in heavy-industrial South Wales while, paradoxically, helping to form the basis for collective working class organization in Cornwall where such a class-base had either been long-eroded by the loss of its industry's competitive edge in minerals, or never truly coalesced into a class force because of its dispersion, isolation and existence in a more deferential, agricultural social setting. With respect to non-class social effects, such as those of gender or ethnicity the critique is comparable and even though an explanation as to why new industry often employs women in former heavy industry areas is offered by Massey, that is cheap labour, this does not capture, for example, the undoubted sectoral variation in female activity rates in new industries in declining regions. Moreover, other non-class questions are not explored.

These points constitute a substantial agenda of research questions for those engaged in socio-spatial studies over the next few years. All that will be attempted here is to point to some possibly important factors that should be taken into account in undertaking such studies.

If we go back to consider the key factors underlying the emergence of new technological paradigms and their possible spatial correlates, then the law of value in a competitive world-system fuelled, in part, by technological change clearly creates certain pressures upon labour as well as capital. Most notably, pressure will be exerted upon the qualitative and quantitative content of labour in the production process. I am dealing here with the Marxian distinction between 'dead' and 'living' labour. The purchase of the latter implies two things; first, that the factor of subjectivity in labour power content remains valued by the purchaser, perhaps, for example, because of the elements of creativity, skill and flexibility which it embodies. Second, that such subjectivity has not yet been embodied in technology ('dead' labour) is signified by the probability that if it had, it would clearly be in the interest of labour purchasers to invest in the technology. 'Dead' labour does not associate in trade unions, for example.

Because of the competitive demand for companies to raise productivity to maintain profitability, the Marxian insight that capital has a long-run tendency to expel 'living' labour from the production process by continually raising the technical composition of capital (Fine and Harris, 1979) is borne out, especially in the contemporary period which is one associated with the crisis of a technological paradigm shift. Neo-Schumpeterians such as Freeman and Soete (1985) refer to the period we are currently passing through as one of 'revolutionary' as distinct from 'radical' or 'incremental' technical change. At present there is, as always, a contradiction in the capital/labour relation between the desire, on the one hand, to invest in new 'smart' technology which enables greater productivity gains to be achieved through automation, robotization and so on, resulting in substantial job-loss, and, on the other hand, a desire to exploit the subjective element of 'living' labour to the full in the form of greater flexibility in work practices and management systems. The resolution of this contradiction is having profound social effects, some of which have spatial effects too.

Perhaps the clearest way to exemplify the manner in which wide-ranging economic restructuring, of the kind being considered in this chapter, creates relatively ordered socio-spatial relations out of the social disorder that appears to attend technological paradigm shift is to contrast two post-war periods of restructuring. The first of these occurred during the 1960s and early 1970s, the second has been developing through the 1980s.

The first restructuring period is associated, politically, with the Labour governments' commitment to modernization of British industry. It was a period when the UK was gearing up for an initially abortive attempt to join the European Economic Community, in a context of loss of empire and the first signs of revived market penetration from competitors whose economies had been devasted by the Second World War. The competitors in question, especially Japan and the German Federal Republic, had in important ways followed the American pattern of mass-production of standardised products aimed at volume markets in consumer goods. The UK response was politically-led along similar lines. The Industrial Reorganization Corporation was set up to encourage mergers and takeovers which would enhance economies of scale, productivity deals were agreed with trade unions, redeployment of workers took place from old declining industries to newer ones, regional assistance helped redeployment to some extent, but more importantly, it assisted capital to shift production to new plants where new kinds of worker could be employed. This is the restructuring of which Massey (1984) writes. It was associated with a degree of social convergence over space as unemployment and income levels evened out a little between classes and regions (Urry, 1985; Massey, 1985), there was a marked degree of feminisation of the labour market with regions where female activity rates had been low catching up, and there was some de-skilling of work as craft-jobs were replaced in many industries by new labour-saving technology.

Importantly, this earlier period of restructuring was associated with the principle that regions with a high representation of members of the working class should themselves be modernised, enabling that class to reproduce itself albeit in modified form *in situ*. This was made possible by the co-incidence of a restructuring process which, although driven primarily by the need to reduce the overall amount of 'living' labour in production, nevertheless remained, by contemporary standards, relatively labour-intensive. The places which benefitted least from this process were the older industrial conurbations, the manufacturing base of which in old, medium-sized and inefficient plants, was sacrificed to the construction of a new spatial division of labour. Inner-city areas were particularly negatively affected by these changes. They lost mostly male jobs in mechanical and electrical engineering, and, perhaps because these consumer industries (especially the latter) were experiencing the competitive squeeze most, these were the industries where low-paid jobs for women increased in greatest numbers in the regions. These jobs were overwhelmingly in the lowest, operator, grades.

The present period of restructuring is very different in its socio-spatial effects from the earlier one. To begin with, it is predicated on the failure of the previous round of restructuring to modernise the UK economy in the right way. It has now become clear that investment in technical change aimed at making labour-cost savings alone has mainly had the effect of putting the UK in price-sensitive competition with newly emergent industrial economies in southeast Asia and elsewhere, a competition which can scarcely be won due to the labour cost advantages enjoyed by such countries. The real competitive game is non-price competition, based on product quality, innovativeness and value for money. Getting into this game means giving political priority to changing large parts of the UK's industrial culture because it requires the adoption of quality-control criteria which both government and UK industry perceive as best achieved by 'dead' rather than 'living' labour. Moreover, the consumer, confronted with choice from more technologically advanced countries, now demands a more differentiated product than the standardised car or TV set of yesteryear. Areas, and social classes in them, associated with the older forms of product and production process are now seen as something of a drain on the capacity of firms to engage fully in the new competitive contest.

This problem has been referred to as one associated with the *maturity of the general environment* (Camagni, 1985). It is emphatically not simply a physical environmental phenomenon but rather something which:

> refers to the condition of many old established, highly urbanised and diversified urban areas which are suffering from a general maturity of the economic and environmental structure: physical congestion, high land rents and labour costs, union aggressiveness and high social resistance to change, bureaucratisation of industrial and management practices (Camagni, 1985).

In such regions and urban concentrations, locational advantage is lost to newer locational settings. Often, tertiary sector employment continues to grow quite rapidly, especially for women, but cannot offset manufacturing job loss. It is the problem being faced by the North American 'Snow-belt', many larger UK cities, not least London, and older industrial regions of Europe such as Wallonia, Lombardy and the Ruhr. In stereotypical terms it is the socio-spatial expression of what is sometimes known as 'the crisis of Fordism' (Lipietz, 1984).

Such locations are not necessarily being entirely vacated by capital in the 1980s. Rather there are signs of a restructuring which is jettisoning much of the low-skill operative labour – often female – taken on by manufacturing industry a decade or two earlier, and its replacement by new technology. For example, in the UK engineering industry there was a 43 per cent fall in operator staff between 1978 and 1984 compared with a 36 per cent increase of professional engineers, scientists and technologists (Cooke and Morgan, 1985). It may be presumed that, to the extent that the earlier restructuring brought mainly operator jobs to problem regions, the latter will have been hit disproportionately by the job-shedding aspects of the contemporary restructuring, but are unlikely to have benefitted greatly from the upsurge in demand for highly qualified labour. There is limited evidence (Morris, 1976) that some peripheralized plants increasingly use their low-skill labour as a casualised, semi-employed reserve brought in on a short-term contract basis. This practice, which used to be the norm in core engineering factories before trade unionization became strong in the post-war years, is also being resorted to in highly competitive sectors such as motor vehicle manufacture (Smith, 1986a).

Weaker unions, new technologies which enable flexible management and manufacturing systems and require flexible work and labour market practices from lower order employees, consumer demand for less stereotyped products, the need to get away from *mature* social formations, the diminished need for 'living' labour with ordinary skills combined with the growing demand for creative, highly qualified labour adapted to the newly flexible production environments, are all working to re-organize the social composition of those in work and the characteristics of those out of work. The latter, by and large, have skills which have become redundant, the former are increasingly bifurcated into a well-paid middle- to upper-middle professional service class and a working class rump dipping in some contexts into 'waged poverty' as the variable demand for variable capital (i.e. labour-power) makes its impact on the local labour market.

Such changes as these are clearly complex, differentiated by industrial sector and by geographical space. Economic revitalization is often to be found taking place in regions which do not display a mature general environment. The problem of the mature socio-spatial formations is to 'de-mature' (Abernathy, Clark and Kantrow, 1983) through environmental rejuvenation and new firm formation in which older social practices such as robust collective organization by workers are weakened. In barest outline these are some of the social class, and non-class social, forms entailed in the re-ordering process associated with technological and spatial paradigm shift. They include, importantly, the expansion and contraction with associated occupational differentiation of operative workforces; the tendency towards driving out of 'living' labour from the production process but the absorbing of increasing amounts of subjectively autonomous living labour into the conceptual and control sides of that process; the breaking up of class conscious pools of employed workers as technical change renders Fordist structures out-dated; and the selective incorporation, dis-incorporation and re-incorporation of workers along gender, age, and, probably, ethnic lines as the rules of the competitive struggle and the relative strengths and weaknesses of organised labour in different spatial locations change, particularly in an era of rapid technological transformation.

5 State planning and spatial paradigms

In liberal democracies the interests of capital and labour are represented in the political process. Over time the balance may tip away from the interests of capital sufficiently for the labour interest to be able to be expressed in clear policy forms, but, for the national state in question to remain capitalist this balance may not be allowed to shift so far in favour of labour for the interest of capital to be completely neglected. What occurs is a process of *transmutation* of interests such that capitals' interest in maintaining its capacity to accumulate is assisted in ways that also, in the short-term, at least, enable the interests of labour too to be furthered (Cooke, 1983). In what follows I will talk solely of industrial capital and industrial labour to try to illustrate the micro-rules of spatial transformation whereby socio-spatial relations enter a new spatial paradigm as capital enters its new technological paradigm.

For illustrative purposes I will discuss changes in the UK space-economy in the 1960s and 1980s, highlighting the role of state-planning in the process.

Recognition in the 1960s that the UK was losing market-share in numerous manufacturing sectors to overseas competitors led to a move within the state to establish quasi-autonomous economic planning machinery (National Economic Development Office) modelled in part on the perceived success of French indicative planning. An ideology of 'modernization' through state intervention in the macro-management of industrial development was accepted by both the main political parties and the higher echelons of the state buraucracy, and underpinned changes in the functional and spatial organization of British industry. The key to 'modernization' was perceived as lying in the achievement of labour – productivity gains through economies of scale bought by investment (mergers, takeovers) in mass-production. The aim was to improve UK standing in volume markets for the standardised products mass-production could yield. At this time, the involvement of labour in strategic thinking about modernisation was echoed in the manner in which firms delegated shopfloor authority to union stewards who became privileged mediators in the sphere of factory industrial relations.

Modernization required spatial restructuring too. The spatial planning machinery was overhauled in the 1960s in ways which assisted the industrial modernization process. At the regional level a substantial boost was given to peripheral regions by the extension of assisted area status to localities suffering from the decline of Victorian industries. Regional aid was a political demand from the labour side, resisted initially by capital, but later embraced, for example by the Confederation of British Industry, in the light of the significant aids to capital embodied within the legislation. Even though aids to labour were also included these were short-lived. Regional policy is thus a good example of the political transmutation of demands from divergent interests – 'bringing work to workers' and helping firms to modernize simultaneously. At the city level, there was also a strong modernizing ideology at work, though favouring disproportionately the interests of commercial and financial capital. A great wave of city-centre rebuilding, with associated residential redevelopment cleared much old, smaller industry from city centres, industry de-centralized to the peripheral regions, and later to semi-peripheral growth towns beyond the conurbations. Industry found new, cheap, often female labour pools in previously male-dominated industrial or agricultural labour markets, and was able to cut labour costs both by de-skilling the labour process and employing more women than hitherto.

Thus the technological paradigm and spatial paradigm rules coincided around *modernization*, *economies of scale*, *state development planning* (economic and spatial) and *decentralisation of production*. In retrospect, it is clear that this strategy was unsuccessful, mainly because, as has recently been noted, British manufacturing investment was devoted to cutting labour costs by introducing labour-saving machinery rather than to seeking innovative, quality-conscious, product and process designs such as those that competitor nations were developing (Cooke & Morgan, 1985). As Britain made inroads into the standardized markets, the Newly Industrialising Countries began to compete in ways Britain could never match – the technological and spatial paradigms had been realised too late.

In the 1980s, a new technological paradigm has taken root and with it, taking its own, though complementary form, has emerged a new spatial paradigm. The technological paradigm is still underpinned by an ideology of 'modernization', but the rules for its implementation have changed dramatically. In place of the faith in 'planning' is a revived faith in 'the market' as the key motive force. British industry is being urged to re-discover the entrepreneurial spirit, classically thought to be embodied in 'the small business'. Managerial ideology has turned away from the labour market and production rigidities inherent in the huge mass-production plants towards the medium-sized, flexible manufacturing plant buying in an increasing amount of its production content from sub-contractors. Standardized markets have become fragmented into a myriad of market segments as customer tastes have become more sophisticated. Unionisation is anathema to the new paradigm, indeed casualization of labour and the increased use of small, sub-contracting business, union-free and flexible, as in the Japanese model is becoming widespread. Moreover, the decentralization strategy of the 1960s is no longer the norm, rather re-concentration, often back to refurbished urban plants, even in the inner-city, perhaps in an Enterprise Zone is not unknown (Cooke, 1986).

The spatial paradigm is already present, enveloping the new technological paradigm rules of the 1980s. Regional assistance has been more than halved, many peripheral areas have lost regional aid status altogether. The days when regional development agencies constructed large advance factories have disappeared, now they construct small incubator units, and liaise with private capital to provide seed-corn for new enterprises. Unemployed workers from closed branch-plants in the periphery are enjoined to move to the prosperous metropolitan region, amongst those unemployed are many women now augmenting the redundancy statistics as closures and technological restructuring render their low labour costs superfluous. At the city and sub-regional levels, similar 'post-modernist' tendencies are apparent. Inner-city land is being recycled for up-market residential and small-business entrepreneurship while ethnic ghettoes remain residualised by the withdrawal of expenditure on the renewal of the urban fabric. Established ideological pillars such as Green Belt protection of the urban fringe, and the construction of new environments in New Towns are crumbling or have been consigned to the private sector. Meanwhile islands of growth in the favoured, semi-rural settings of the under-unionised Home Counties develop, often on a raft of hidden state subsidies from the Ministry of Defence procurement budget (Lovering, 1985). From the 'convergence' years of the 1960s when unemployment and social welfare indices showed a diminution of disparities between the rich and poor communities of Britain, we have moved into an era of socio-spatial polarization as enterpreneurship is rewarded and communality is penalized.

So the technological paradigm and spatial paradigm rules move into synchronization around *entrepreneurship, economies of scope, market-reliance* and *reconcentration of production*. In the process, class organization, in the sense of trade-union collectivism, is being attacked in most of its strongholds, gender-equalization is in retreat as opportunities for working women are eroded in full-time factory work in favour of part-time service work, and the efforts of localities are stifled by the centralization of political and public economic power in the higher reaches of the state.

Conclusions

In this chapter I have sought to argue three things. In the first place, I thought it important to address an important macro-theory of the changes taking place in contemporary capitalism. The theory postulates that capitalism entered a stable phase of organisation in the 1880s due to the concentration and centralization tendencies within the leading productive sectors of the time, their move towards mass-production, and the influence of the state both in regulating domestic trade and securing foreign markets through imperialism. This phase has now broken down such that capitalism can now be designated 'disorganized' as a result of the growth of multinational corporations, the lack of a supranational, regulating 'state', and the removal of the stabilizing force of the trade and currency agreements characteristic of the organised phase. While agreeing with many of the descriptive features of this theory, I found it overstated the material importance of concentration and centralization in the organized phase, and underestimated the capacity of international capitalism to restructure in a manner which results in new forms of order emerging.

In order to explain this ordering process I examined the motor vehicle, electronics and producer services industries and remarked that each displayed organizing principles which derived from the competitive process that is the fundamental dynamic of the capitalist world-system. In a subsequent discussion I identified a hierarchy of 'rules' by which the competitive dynamic is augmented. The law of value, competition, and technology are essential elements, with the latter taking on a fundamental importance in the contemporary period. In discussing technology further I referred to the concept of 'technological paradigm', a complex of ideological, social and political as well as technological factors which drives the system forward functionally and spatially in a reasonably orderly fashion. Finally, I introduced the concepts of 'social and spatial paradigms', a set of equally ideological, social and political constructs which complement the emergent technological paradigm with reference to assisting its general spatial conditions of production to come to fruition. It is the combination of the ascendency of new technological, social and spatial paradigms as conditioned by the law of value and the competitive ethic which drives the spatial development process under capitalism forward in a relatively orderly fashion.

Acknowledgments

This chapter was read in an earlier form at the Nordplan Seminar

'Ideology in Context' held at Sidney Sussex College, Cambridge University, December 1985. Thanks to Gunnar Olsson, Allan Pred, Derek Gregory and Nigel Thrift for comments; the responsibility for the chapter is mine alone.

• 11 •

The affluent homeowner: *labour-market position and the shaping of housing histories* • *RAY FORREST AND ALAN MURIE*

Introduction

The vigorous drive to further extend home-ownership has refuelled debates in Britain around the relationships between housing tenure and class and the links between residential and social segration. A polarity of positions can be identified. On the one hand there is the view that the potential for money gains through home ownership provides the material basis for a significant consumption cleavage between those who own their homes (or are in the process of buying) and those households who remain in the public and private rental sectors. Saunders (1984) in particular has argued that:

> privatization of welfare provisions is intensifying this cleavage to the point where sectoral alignments in regard to consumption may come to outweigh class alignments in respect of production, and that housing tenure remains the most important single aspect of such alignments (p. 203).

Private home-ownership, he suggests, provides not only financial advantage and security but personal identity and 'ontological security'. And Marshall *et al.* (1985) pursue a similar theme in suggesting that:

> One particularly important feature of consumption patterns which is of crucial importance in the formation of social identities is home ownership (p. 274).

In this sense the argument links to political and policy claims as to the innate desire for home ownership and to the theoretical arguments advanced by, for example, Giddens (1981) concerning the meaningless and alienating nature of modern ways of life. It is home ownership which provides 'the haven in the heartless world' (Lasch 1977).

An opposing, and equally caricatured position, is that traditional class divisions remain paramount and find new expression in the transformation of housing provision. Differentiation *within* home ownership, it is argued, creates a highly stratified housing market and common values, aspirations and material advantages cannot be assumed (see, for example, Gray, 1982; Forrest, 1983). Empirical research on marginal home owners (Karn *et al.*, 1985) and differential rates of capital gains (e.g. Thorns, 1981) and spatial variations in the privatization of council housing (Forrest and Murie, 1986) is mobilised to support this view.

These arguments link also to continuing preoccupations with the impact of home ownership on working-class consciousness and political affiliation (see, for example, Edel, 1982; Dunleavy, 1979; Heath *et al.*, 1985; Marshall *et al.*, 1985). Within both the academic and policy literature the assumption that home ownership is a pivotal element in the dominant ideology of privatism is pervasive, if debatable. Both Left and Right subscribe it seems to the corrosive effects of individual home ownership on socialist zeal. It is not clear, however, when this golden age of collectivist solidarity existed nor how the spread of home ownership is contributing to its erosion. In this context, the connections between social structures and the individual consciousness of actors has become the subject of intense theoretical debate with general agreement that our knowledge of structural change has outdistanced empirical work on individuals and households. The rather functionalist accounts of the relationships between home-ownership and capitalism which stressed its role in maintaining political docility and commodity consumption were important correctives to the voluntaristic accounts of housing choice and mobility (for a useful review see Duncan, 1981). But actors, and indeed the working class (however defined) tended to become relegated as passive recipients of dominant ideologies, helpless victims of structural forces and apparently irrelevant in the process of social change.

Debates within the housing field have now become enmeshed with a renewal of interest in local social structures and local labour markets. Whilst the Marxist inspired work of the 1970s mapped out the broad contours of social and economic change, it was recognised that recession and economic restructuring was mediated by specific local factors and that there was a geography of economic restructuring and social restratification which required more detailed empirical analysis (Massey, 1984). And an increasing empirical effort is concentrated on household surveys and more qualitative styles of research. The household is back in vogue and issues of lifestyle, life chances, social and residential mobility are high on the research agenda. The reaction against the social survey and more traditional forms of empirical research and the theoreticism of the 1970s has left us relatively ignorant of the way households and individuals have responded to and coped with the social and economic transformations of the last two decades. And feminist perspectives on the nature of home and work (Watson, 1985) and research on the informal economy and the domestic sphere (Pahl, 1985) have been important influences in this reorientation.

In some ways we can see a return to the concerns of much sociology of the fifties and sixties. Then attention was focused on the transformation of community and class through the expansion of public sector employment, a white-collar proletariat and new managerial élites. It was to some extent influenced by expectations of continuing and proliferating affluence. The context is now very different. The formal labour market is now conceptualised as a shrinking core of key workers enjoying relative prosperity and security. Outside this core, wage labour is insecure, low paid or non-existent. Living labour is now in excess supply. There is a new non-working class of long-term unemployed, young never-employed, working-class elderly and single parents progressively excluded from norms of social consumption and increasingly dependent on state benefits and services. It is this group which is being concentrated in council housing (Forrest and Murie, 1986). Less is known, however, about the broader social structure of home ownership and processes of differentiation and stratification within it. There is a need to take these debates forward and provide some new empirical input to the theoretical discussion. One approach is to provide more detailed accounts of the individual household's experience of the housing and labour markets.

The research

This chapter draws on a piece of research designed to explore aspects of social differentiation within the owner occupied sector through qualitative, in-depth interviews.

The research was concerned to reconstruct and compare the housing, employment and family histories of two groups of home owners. Interviews were taped and structured around a short written schedule. Key factors relating to family formation, housing and employment moves were recorded on the interview schedule providing the framework for analysis of the more detailed and free-flowing tape recorded discussion. Interviews ranged from two to five hours and generated highly detailed and lengthy transcriptions. The nature of the data obtained through this style of research presents problems in a paper of this length. There is not the room to present material in a form appropriate to the method and then offer a discussion or evaluation of it. On the other hand merely to assert conclusions from material which is 'too lengthy to be reproduced' would be unconvincing. The compromise is to summarise some features and focus on individual cases. But the process of doing this diminishes and even denies the argument for this type of research which rests upon the insights gained from wide ranging in-depth interviews and respondents' own accounts rather than research-imposed categories and quantification. The compromise, however, seems unavoidable. This chapter concentrates on the housing histories of home owners at the top end of the market, a group which has been relatively neglected in contemporary housing research. Research has focused on the housing conditions and experiences of those on the *periphery* of the housing and labour markets. The unemployed and those in low-paid and insecure employment have been associated with a shrinking council housing sector and sub-sectors of owner occupation and private rented accommodation (Karn *et al.*, 1985; Forrest and Muric, 1983). And more recent ethnographic and qualitative work on housing has concentrated on problem council estates (Parker, 1983) or the lower end of the owner occupied market (Holme, 1985; Wallman, 1984). Whilst weak bargaining power in the labour market has been argued to be part of the explanation for the reduced housing opportunities of those on the social and economic periphery, the position of those in the strongest bargaining position has not been explored. Implicitly, at least, it is assumed that the mass of households enter the housing market and negotiate movement within it under similar terms. Moreover, attempts to link the housing and labour markets have tended to be at the macro-level (i.e. patterns of social and spatial segregation; income/price correlates).

Differentiated patterns of access and opportunity in housing tend to be explained in terms of stages in the family life cycle, income trajectories or specific historical conditions of entry such as particular state policies, levels of inflation and movements of interest rates. Differences are seen as a matter of degree rather than of kind. To some extent this derives from a uni-dimensional view of the housing market with choice and constraint located at either end of the continuum.

This model assumes that those at the top end of the housing market experience the highest degree of choice. This chapter suggests that *core* workers in the labour market exercise choice in the housing market within a framework of job-determined constraints. These constraints are accompanied by a range of subsidies and benefits which are unavailable to the majority of households. As a consequence of their strong bargaining position as *core* workers in growth sectors of the economy it is suggested that this group's housing histories are shaped by quite distinctive processes which go beyond the simple fact that their direct incomes are relatively large. This connects with research on residential movement and mobility which was a focus of interest in the 1960s (see Murie, 1974, chapter 1). Job-related moves and geographical mobility were associated particularly with managerial élites. It was these middle class 'spiralists' (Watson, 1960) who had to uproot and pursue a nomadic career (Seeley *et al.*, 1963). Those early residential mobility studies were largely unconnected with sociological research on managerial élites and professionals. Moreover, significant changes have occurred in both the housing and labour markets since those earlier studies. Most notably in housing, home-ownership has expanded and access to housing is increasingly determined by price which is subject to considerable geographical variation. The widening gap between property values in the London area and elsewhere has posed particular problems of labour mobility.

More generally, contemporary debates in housing and our perception of the issues may be unduly influenced by a problem-oriented perspective where empirical investigation is concentrated at the bottom end of the housing market. Mirror images are then constructed for those households assumed to be 'without problems'. This approach runs the risk of overlooking the specific factors which may be at work in different segments of the housing market.

Expectations from the literature

In explaining the upper end of the owner-occupied market, what would the available literature lead us to expect? Detailed research on the affluent middle classes has been rather sparse over the last decade. Recent empirical research which has been carried out has tended to concentrate on differentiating forms of entrepreneurial activity and the implications for class analysis (e.g. Scase and Goffee, 1982). There was a considerable theoretical output on the middle strata in the 1970s but little of this was grounded in specific empirical research and paid little attention to ways of life or aspects of house and home (Walker, 1979; see Abercrombie and Urry (1983) for a general review). And in earlier work issues of housing and housing tenure did not figure prominently (see Raynor, 1969; for a general review) although Pahl's work on commuter villages did look at the transformations of local housing markets through the inmigration of managerial élites (Pahl, 1965b). Housing has been a peripheral consideration in the majority of such studies and there is little published work which locates the housing experiences of affluent households in broader accounts of housing market processes.

An interrogation of social survey data would indicate that those who buy expensive dwellings have high incomes and are drawn predominantly from professional and managerial groups. Eligibility 'rules' exclude other sections of the population. In this way there is often a simple connection made between current or previous economic circumstances (labour-market position) and residential differentiation.

A very different emphasis, however, can be built up from references to other factors influencing residential behaviour. For those more affluent households who are able to exercise choice some may choose not to maximise housing expenditure or status for various reasons. A range of considerations are involved in satisficing rather then optimising. Family life cycle factors, wealth, inheritance, inter-generational transfers (including gifts and loans) can all act to 'distort' the simple relationships between labour-market position and position in the owner-occupied market. Some of these factors can be highlighted by referring to the literature on residential choice and mobility (Murie, 1974). However, the implication of much of this literature is that the individual household is not the key unit of study. Rather than suggest that this view is misplaced or attempt to rehabilitate a focus on the household this article rests on a view that there is a need to draw on more qualitative research including studies of households and localities. This is desirable to provide one 'test' of theoretical arguments and interpretations established through other methods and to identify issues, which may ultimately be more extensively researched through such methods.

Because this article draws on in-depth household interviews it is instructive to identify some key themes emerging from a literature which refers to individual decisions and housing behaviour. For our purposes four 'expectations' can usefully be identified which relate to the top end of the market and households with choice in housing.

1 A major factor in household movement decisions is modification of housing space and other requirements. These housing-led moves may coincide with family-cycle progress. They will be most marked among those who have most choice in housing. Thus at the top end of the market we would expect to find a group of households who have taken advantage of their market situation to adjust their housing to changing needs. They will have participated in a series of housing-led moves in their progress to their present situation. (Rossi, 1980; Rossi and Shlay, 1982).
2 The top end of the market provides the goal for a group of households who actively manipulate the housing market to climb a housing ladder. These 'spiralists' make decisions about when to move and what to buy related to obtaining the best return through housing transactions.
3 As a variation on the housing ladder theme Farmer and Barrell (1981) have suggested that there is a group who channel their entrepreneurial energies into housing speculation rather than business activity.

> We have argued that the group from which small business proprietors are traditionally supposed to be drawn, those with some initial capital, a desire to increase it, and a taste for taking risks, will in general have been more sensible to continue to make their transfer earnings in their existing job and speculate in the housing market (p. 325).

The expectation would be that this group would rise to the top end of the housing market.

4 The characteristics of households at the top end of the market may be inferred by deduction from those who are disadvantaged. Thus, for example, various studies have identified age at marriage, age at birth of first child, number of children, number of wage earners, and marital breakdown as factors predisposing households to careers in rented housing. Early entry to home ownership, later marriage and childbirth are factors in home ownership pathways (see e.g. Payne and Payne, 1974). The implication is that those at the top end of the market are likely to have married later, had children later, had a longer period with two wage earners and entered home ownership early in their housing history.

The research area

Our interviews with home-owners at the top end of the market involved identifying a locality with expensive dwellings. We did not go through a sophisticated process of social area analysis or attempt to define an area of high status. We identified a high house-price area with assistance from local estate agents. The area identified is presented in advertisements as 'the ultimate address' and an 'exclusive residential area'. It is a leafy wooded suburb of Bristol. Two of the roads included are of large detached houses in large gardens (one-third of an acre or more). Most of these houses were built between the wars to high standards by a respected local builder. These are large houses with large rooms and five or more bedrooms. Most have been modernised to include new kitchens and two or more bathrooms and WCs. However, most retain some original features including wooden panelling on walls, original fireplaces and wooden parquet flooring. These properties are currently valued at between £100 000 and £150 000. Some interviews were also completed with households in newly-built properties on a site in the same locality. These are executive dwellings marketed at £80 000 or more. These valuations may appear modest by London standards but in the context of Bristol's house price structure they represent the élite end of the urban housing market. Unmodernised small terraced dwellings can still be acquired for £10 000–£15 000 and large tracts of owner occupied Victorian terraced properties in the South and East of Bristol are priced at around £20 000. There is some indication of a shortage of high status properties appropriate for family residences. Bristol has a large number of converted flats and houses tend to have modest gardens. Incoming executives from London wishing to avoid peripheral commuter villages can face long search times to find suitable properties. This was evident from this research and other recent studies of company moves (City of Bristol Planning Department, 1985). A housing shortage at the top end of the owner-occupied market may seem a novel social problem but should company decentralisation from London become more extensive a highly polarised price structure may develop in the city.

Small area statistics from the 1981 Census reveal that the area is exclusively owner-occupied. Of all households 57 per cent have three or fewer persons yet 86 per cent of dwellings have at least 7 rooms. The car is the exclusive mode of travel to work with 71 per cent of households owning at least two. Heads of household are all in social classes I or II (Registrar General's Classification) with the exception of those who are retired. Typically they are *employees* (84 per cent) in senior executive or administrative positions in the service sector or public administration (74 per cent).

The housing histories

Interviews were carried out with seventeen married couples (thirty-four persons) and one single elderly male. Housing histories were constructed separately for each of these adults.

None of the individuals involved had been owner-occupiers prior to marriage. Twenty of those interviewed had left their parental home at some time before marriage but none had been single-person owners. While this may reflect changing generational experience the individuals include a considerable number whose housing histories prior to marriage are set against a background of declining private renting and expanding owner-occupation among young single professionals and others. None of the individuals had lived in property rented from the public sector since they married or since they left home (and only four had as children). A striking feature in these histories was experiences of tied accommodation often linked to jobs, for example, in hospitals or in armed forces accommodation.

The majority of persons interviewed had moved directly into owner occupation at marriage but this did not always represent early entry to owner occupation in age terms. In addition some had interrupted histories in owner occupation and moved out into the rented sector for short periods. Only three married couples had moved six times in the owner-occupied market, only one had moved five times (three in a first marriage and two in a second). Three married couples and the one single person had owned four dwellings. The majority had moved three or fewer times as home-owners. Some had very extended histories of housing moves – but mostly in rented and tied accommodation.

There was considerable variation among the individuals interviewed in terms of age at marriage (or leaving the parental home). More than half had married before the age of 25. Nor was delayed family growth or long periods with two earners in the household a common feature.

All of the individuals concerned had had families. These were most commonly of two or three children. In only five marriages was there a period of four or more years between marriage and birth of the first child. It is apparent however that this group who have delayed family building include more of the youngest adults (and children) in the study.

There is another dimension which is also important – mobility and assistance with residential movement. Only seven of the individuals interviewed had parental homes in the Bristol region. Of these, two (a married couple) had a 'services career' involving moves to East Anglia, London, Leicester, Nottingham and Manchester. Of the remaining four households including a 'local' only one (two persons with Bristol childhoods) had spent their whole career in Bristol. The other three only made brief and short forays from Bristol (Dorset (twice), Exeter, Frampton Cotterell and Chipping Sodbury). The males in these four 'localist' households were currently all self-employed. Two were involved in long-established family firms in which the wives also worked. In the other two cases new businesses had been created by those in executive careers. In both of these cases wives had remunerative employment and in one case benefits from a separate family business. Only one other married couple had as localist a housing history. These were two 'immigrants' from the Far East establishing their own business in Bristol after periods of residence in

Croydon (M) and Bath (F). The remaining group of households had all moved long distances. The most complex service careers included periods abroad and in various locations in the UK. Non-service careers also included periods abroad. The housing histories with fewer moves were still likely to have been of the Edinburgh, Sussex, Bristol type and were job led. They were not local housing adjustment moves. For those moving more often the geography of moves was equally extended.

The key features of the housing histories of the individuals interviewed are presented in summary form in Table 11.1. The broad profile of this group sets them within the general description of spiralist cosmopolitans (Watson, 1960; Merton, 1968). With a few exceptions their orientation to Bristol is transient and instrumental. For some of the older households Bristol may prove to be their housing destination but by and large this has been determined by the dynamics of the labour market rather than any enduring allegiance to the area through long-established kinship links or social networks. Those with local connections and more localised housing histories tend to be owner managers of long-established family firms, the entrepreneurial middle class. The majority, however, are members of the established salaried middle class – 'administrators, managers, highly qualified scientists and employee professionals' (Scase and Goffee, 1982, p. 187). As Scase and Goffee observe, this group is distinguished from other less permanently structured members of the middle class through 'credentialism'. They possess not only highly marketable skills but academic, professional and technical qualifications (p. 186). They are, however, essentially employees whose social advancement and position is dependent upon saleable skills in the labour market rather than ownership of capital.

The executive's tale[1]

A fuller appreciation of the distinctive process at work in shaping the housing histories of the salaried middle class is provided by a fuller treatment of one individual. In this particular case the individual is now a senior executive in a multinational company. Case histories would never seek to claim representativeness or typicality. Their value lies in the sense of process conveyed although we have selected this particular case because it raises points which are common to the other interviews. What follows draws on interview transcripts and focuses on the housing movements in recent years of one individual male.

The respondent was born in Lancashire in 1946. He was an only child. His parents were owner-occupiers and his father worked in the insurance industry and his mother was a housewife. He (unlike most of those interviewed) lived at the same address throughout childhood and until marriage. When he was 16 he became an apprentice navigating officer and worked at sea for ten years. He married towards the end of this period and at this stage bought a house in Lancashire. The house was a new two-bedroomed bungalow for which they paid £4995 (1969):

I can remember we had to borrow £150 off my dad because we worked everything out and we got a mortgage from the Nationwide. They said they would give us a 90% mortgage, but of course it's 90% of what they value the property. The property was valued at £X00 less than the asking price and we had to borrow £150 off my dad. It was built by a firm called John Laing Construction, and it was a private house but it was built on land owned by the Duke of Westminster. The land itself was leasehold on something like 999 year lease at a ground rent of £10 per annum. We used to have to go to the Bailiff on the estate and hand over our money. On that estate lots of houses had been sold to the RAF and to the Police and you could walk out of your door at half-past-eight and all the RAF guys would be going to work and you felt as though you were in Married Quarters. And the houses on the estate varied – there were three bedroomed semis at about £4000 to three and four bedroomed detached houses which I think were about £7500. So there was a lot of variation on the estate. It turned out to be a huge development and about 15 builders went broke in developing it. And these RAF guys, depending on their rank, if you were a Corporal you were in a three bedroom semi, if you were a Wing Commander or a Captain you were in a four bedroom detached.

While living at this address his wife resigned her job and travelled with him at sea until she became pregnant. At this point he changed jobs to a land-based job with a multinational oil company. Initially he joined as a trainee and continued to live in Lancashire:

All of the moves from then on since have been company moves.

The first of these moves was at Harrogate. They bought a new three-bedroom detached house for just over £7000. Their previous house had been sold for £5400:

We had great trouble selling.

Table 11.1 Profiles of affluent home-owners

Interview Number	Age	Current Household Type	Age left parental home	Age first house purchased	Age at marriage	No. of homes since parental home	No. of homes	Years of marriage without children	No. of children	Job history	Present occupation	Occupation of father
1	58	2 persons	23	30	30	8	2	?	2	Medical Career	Disabled	Bank Cashier
2	54		17	26	26	10	2	?	2	Domestic	Domestic	Clergyman
3	49	With adult family	22	25	22	10*	6	3	3	Executive Career	Senior Executive	Skilled Engineer
4	47		20	23	20	10*	6	3	3	Secretarial	Domestic	Club Secretary
5	58	2 persons	24	24	24	9*	6	1	3	Executive Career	Senior Executive	Teacher
6	51		17	17	17	9*	6	1	3	Domestic	Domestic	Teacher
7	50	With adult family	24	24	24	4*	4	2	2	Executive/ S.E. Business	S.E. Dealer	Estate Agent
8	49		23	23	23	4*	4	2	2	Secretarial	P.T. Secretary	Shopkeeper
9	86	Single person	18	43	26	11	4	3	1	Banking Career	Retired	Plant Manager
10	40	3 gener-ations, including 2 young children	25	25	25	3*	3	8	2	Executive, S.E. Business	S.E. Business	Farmer
11	37		17	22	22	5	3	8	2	Medical Career	Deputy Nursing Officer	Civil Servant
12	53	4 school age children	18	30	29	18+	3	2	4	Professional Executive Career	Senior Executive	Engineer
13	48		19	25	24	11+	3	2	4	Domestic	Domestic	Civil Servant
14	67	2 persons	21	35	32	8+	1	3	3	Medical Career	Semi-retired	Civil Servant
15	66		22	34	31	7	1	3	3	Medical Career	Semi-retired	Jeweller (Self employed)

16	61	2 persons	35	36	35	3*	2	4	2	Family Firm	S.E. Business	Insurance Company
17	50		17	25	24	4+	2	4	2	Family Firm	P.T. Family Firm	Shop Manager
18	56	2 persons	21	40	23	20+	2	1	5	Services Career	Senior Executive	Skilled Engineer
19	57		22	41	24	20+	2	1	5	Domestic	Domestic	Accountant
20	45	3 school age	24	24	24	7	3	7	3	Architect/Family Firm	Family Firm	S.E. Ships Chandler
21	42	children	20	21	21	8	3	7	3	Secretarial/Family Firm	Family Firm	Company Director
22	42	1 young	23	23	23	5*	4	3	3	Family Firm	Managing Director	Company Manager
23	41	child	22	22	22	5*	4	3	3	Domestic	Domestic	Contractor
24	47	2 persons	19	32	19	10*	2	2	2	Services Career	Business Consultant	
25	47		19	32	19	10+*	2	2	2	Domestic	Domestic	Services
26	41	1 young	24	24	24	6	4	6	1	Banking Career	Regional Manager	Carpenter
27	42	child	25	25	25	5*	4	6	1	Domestic	Domestic	Tool Maker
28	42	3 young	26	26	26	6*	6	2	3	Executive Career	Senior Executive	Printing Manager
29	39	children	23	23	23	6*	6	2	3	Education Career	P.T. Teacher	Draughtsman
30	43	2 young children	19	31	31	6	2	2	2	Self-made Family Business	S.E. Businessman	Engineering Superintendent
31	34		18	22	22	4	2	2	2	Medical Career	Domestic	Carpenter
32	56	3 young	29	29*	29/43	7	5	2	3/5	Executive Career	Senior Executive	Bus Driver
33	40	children	21	30	28	5	2	2	3	Domestic	Domestic	Printer
34	47	? young	24	33	33	10	3	8	2	Professional Career	Civil Servant	Bank Manager
35	40	children	20	26	26	7	3	8	2	Domestic	Domestic	Clergyman Invalid

* Left home to marry

Notes:

(a) No. 32 was the only person to have married twice and to have been a home owner prior to first marriage.

The RAF standardised things, so that all the Flight Sergeants in the three bedroomed detached house all had the same colour curtains, all had the same furniture and even to the extent that the gates and garden sheds were graded according to rank. The higher your rank, the bigger your garden shed, you see. But they would all be positioned in identical positions in the gardens, so. . . .

I think it was generally accepted that it all kept the value down, but we didn't know at first.

But as the estate matured in that first year or two, it became more obvious.

When we moved from Lancashire to Harrogate they (the employer) covered all expenses arising from the estate agents' fees, solicitors' fees, and removal expenses.

There is actually a sort of a safety net to prevent you losing money on your property or not getting the full value for it, which we didn't know about in that first move. We were then new in the company and they didn't publicise it so we didn't get all we were entitled to in our first move.

One of the things we try to do in the firm is that we try to get the people to move themselves. If you say to Pickford's 'I am moving with Company X' whatever, the price goes up, so to ensure you keep the cost of the move down you have to do it as though it's a private move. But firms are now more open. We say to people that this is our personnel package and those are all the things we do to move you. In those days they didn't and they expected you to go along and say 'Look, I'm having problems selling the house' and they would say, they kick off by saying, when you put it on the market you give an agency sole agency, so if you then have difficulty in selling it you go to another agent and you put it up with two agents and we had to do that. We had to put it up with two agents and it actually went with no problems. In addition to that you, in those days, got an allowance which was equivalent to 10% of your salary as a payment for curtains etc. So nearly all your expenses were covered, plus an allowance for carpets, curtains.

And then we went to live in Nantwich. And we made a big leap in housing because we sold our house in Lancaster for £11 950, something like that and we bought a house for £17 995.

But at that time house prices were taking off (in the South East especially) and we in the company were having great difficulty in attracting into London the right calibre of people, so a thing called 'increased mortgage allowance' was introduced. I'll try and explain how it works. When you put the house on the market, you could sit and hope you would get the market value for the house. Or if you could not there was a fall-back situation. The fall-back situation was if you didn't sell within a couple of weeks or X number of months, you could go to the company and ask for the company to have the house valued. The company would then look in the yellow pages and employ two estate agents who would come round to your house and value it. The company would then take the mean of those two valuations and they would guarantee that price. With regard to the house in Harrogate, we hadn't sold it and we had got it with a couple of agents. Because we had already committed ourselves to the house in Nantwich and the move, we wanted to get out, so we asked the company to value the property. They valued the property at £11 200, which was considerably less than the amount of money we were asking for. We got notification of the company valuation one week and the next weekend we had an offer which was £11 995, which we accepted.

The company introduced this thing called increased mortgage allowance. They would say if you sold your house for £10 000 and you bought one for £15 000, we would say your mortgage went up by £5000. We would pay you an annual amount equivalent to the amount of mortgage you would pay on £5000, less your tax. That was paid annually for a period of four years, so we went from £11 995 to £18 000 but we didn't know about this allowance. So we did the move initially off our own bat with the allowances – all the expenses for solicitors, estate agents, removal expenses – the 10% had gone up to 15%. And we moved into this new house in Nantwich, and it was a great struggle and we had only been in it for about two months when the personnel guys said 'Please fill in this form because you've gone upmarket and we owe you. . . .' We didn't know it existed. Now if we'd known it did exist, we may have gone upmarket even more. I'm not saying we would, but we may have done.

This was brought in specifically because people were refusing to move into the South East.

The house in Nantwich was a newly-built four-bedroomed detached house:

We were in Nantwich for four years and then I was promoted again to the head office, which was in London, Waterloo, and this was 1979 and we had the three children by this time. And that was a great problem because house prices had escalated and there was very little for sale in the South East. It was an enormous area that we could choose from anyway, North London or South London, and it was terribly difficult because we had many, many trips down there to try and find something and it was a case of estate agents 'phoning us up in the North, saying 'There's a house just come up for sale, can you get down here today if possible'. It took us several months to find something and in the end we picked something in desperation and it was a bungalow which we said we would never have again, we had had a bungalow when we were first married and said we would never have another bungalow. But we did pick another one and it was right out in a very rural part of West Sussex, right out in a pine forest. We saw it on a lovely hot summer's day in July and we didn't see it again until we moved in in the middle of November and we were devastated. Very remote and. . .

I was going to work in Waterloo. We looked north of London but we didn't like it. We looked at places like Harpenden. As I was going to work in Waterloo logically I would travel into Waterloo on the train, so I then got British Rail maps and we hatched off areas round the main railway lines into Waterloo Station, which were either in walking distance of the station or driving distance. Then I got in touch with estate agents and worked my way out from London, saying 'How much are four bedroomed detached houses?' and when they said £150 000 that was another area we crossed off our list. So we moved ourselves further and further down the railway lines until we came to south of Horsham.

It was a Scandinavian house in a wood. But we also didn't expect to be there very long. We were told when I was going there that it would only be for a couple of years, but in fact it was less than that, it was only twenty months.

We sold that house in Nantwich for £43 000 and we bought the bungalow for £56 000. That was very difficult because it was when gazumping was going on. We saw the bungalow on the Saturday afternoon. We came down on numerous occasions. We had four days down and it was the last place we looked at on our way back up north. The lady who owned it was away on holiday so the agent took us round and we couldn't put an offer in. We then went away on holiday. We were on a holiday in South Wales, and I rang the estate agent from a call box to find out if we had got the bungalow because we had put an offer in of £56 000 with the estate agents. What we had been told was that the woman was coming back on the Saturday and she would open the offers on the Saturday. She actually came back on the Wednesday and was trying to play one person off against another. When I rang up the guy said somebody had offered £56 500 and I said I would match that offer – the company sponsors the move. In other words it is a guaranteed purchase, because she wouldn't get involved in a chain with the changing price situation, and it was accepted at £56 500.

Up to and including that move to Sussex, we had always picked an area that we liked and was convenient for working and a house that we liked. Obviously, having only four days to look, it was a compromise. But from then on when we were in Sussex, the children were in an awful school. It turned out to be a dreadful school, so from then on we have picked schools and then houses afterwards.

I then moved to a management post, near Liverpool, so that was very nice because that was a move which brought us back home. And at this stage our eldest son was ten coming up to his eleven plus.

So, the bungalow (had) cost us £56 500 and we spent £2 500 on it and we put it on the market, we had it valued by two people, it wasn't a company valuation but we got hold of two estate agents and said 'We're putting our house on the market, blah, blah' and they came and valued it for us. They valued it at £66 or £67 000.

This was 1979–1981 and in that period house prices in the South East had dropped in some parts and we were pretty pleased with that. So we put it on the market and it had always been our policy to move as quickly as we could, to tie in with schooling and so on. We didn't get anything so I had to go to the company and say 'It looks as though we are going to have to move before we sell the house' and they said 'Well, (one of the conditions of getting all this money off them if you like) if you do that you have to accept the guaranteed price'. So we then had to go and get two valuations from local people and the company then took the mean of those and one guy who actually valued it at £66 000 and another guy was going to value it at sixty, but by means of gentle persuasion we got him up to sixty-two, and so the company valued it at sixty-four.

(It was eventually sold at £59 000).

That was the first time in all these moves we ever had to fall back on the company's guaranteed price system.

That is the guaranteed price. Once you accept that the company will say 'Well, that was £64 000, put it on the market for £60 000.' The company would make up the difference. No matter what it's sold at, you get the guaranteed price. And they would then pay for the cost of the bridging loan.

And then we bought another bungalow, since we didn't like bungalows! This was a four year old four bedroom house costing £78 250.

The reason why we went for about £78 000 is that when we moved from Nantwich we had IMA (Increased Mortgage Allowance) from £5000 for the house from Harrogate to Nantwich, £43 000 to £56 000; £30 000 from Nantwich to Sussex and when we actually then moved up to the north, it finished the £5000. So then we had £12 000 to go on it, so we got that guaranteed price of £64 000. We then had the additional IMA available to us of £12 000 which took us up to £76 000, and we were looking at houses between £75–80 000. That was the range we were looking at, and we got this one for £78 250.

We had only been there three months when the firm decided to close the unit down, at the end of the first year. The company moved down to Taunton, but the rest of the family stayed in the North for another year because our son was going off to another school and we wanted him to have a year there before we came down.

They didn't sell the house immediately, but carried on living in it and the husband lived in a hotel for a period of time then at a pub for many months:

We didn't actually start looking for something until towards the end of that second, well Easter before the end of the two years, and that's when we put the house up for sale.

I started working in Taunton in October 1982 but I was still responsible for the unit I ran in the North until that closed at the end of February 1983. For a four or five month period I had dual responsibility for two places two hundred miles apart! So I did two days down here and three days in the north. Now there was no way physically or mentally I could get involved in the family house hunting, because of the workload. So I said whilst this was going on I can't do it. I also wanted to keep the eldest boy at the school he got into in the north for the first year, so it was agreed that I could travel then.

Schools had to be chosen first, because the only schools that his headmaster thought were equivalent (to the one he was attending) were the Cathedral and Bristol Grammar.

When we had moved into the north the eldest boy was ten, the second boy was eight and the little girl was not of school age. We knew the area. We knew good areas and bad areas for housing. We also knew the schools and we knew the best primary school and we went deliberately to the catchment area of the primary school which was also in the catchment area for the grammar school.

It was a state grammar school. Because the authorities still had secondary modern and grammar schools and the eleven plus selection, we deliberately went to live in the catchment areas of the two schools, because of the type of area it was. This may sound snobby, but the type of area it was parents very much wanted their children to get into the grammar school and therefore there was tremendous pressure on this particular primary school to keep up academic standards. Now, in sitting eleven plus we decided that we would get my eldest son to sit for a direct grant school. He was offered a place, full fees paid, so we put him into that school. That meant we had taken him out of the state education system and that was one of the reasons why we kept him at the school for a year. We felt he had worked so damned hard it would be unfair not to give him the year there. So then that's why, when I came to work in Taunton, the main criterion was, as we'd taken him out of the state education system, we had to keep him within the type of school he was at. Therefore, I started to look at the schools and you've got places like, there's a school in Wellington, there's a school in Tiverton and there are schools in Bristol. Private education is fine but some of them cost you a mint and I can't afford it, so in opting for the schools we realised that the comparable schools were QEH, the Cathedral School and the Grammar School at Bristol. That was one of the reasons that made us pick Bristol.

Now I should also say that by this time the children were getting very upset about all these moves. When he (the eldest) came here it was his fourth new school in four Septembers and it was getting very traumatic and when it came to picking a house we really more or less allowed them to pick the house. Now it sounds a bit silly, but they were extremely happy in the north and they had a lot of friends living locally and they wanted to move on to an estate where they felt they could make friends more easily and also when we came here there was very little choice. I mean in the north everything was selling, things were going overnight here and we ended up in the price range we were looking at with just two houses, this one – a new one – and one other which I think by the time we got to see it was under offer anyway. Well, I should say that we had a fairly small area to look at because I was having to commute and had to live near motorways and obviously couldn't travel through Bristol,. . .

We decided our son was going to the Cathedral School and, not knowing primary schools in the area, we asked the headmaster there which would be the best primary because the younger son by this time was ten and coming up to eleven plus age. Now he recommended the local school, so that was another reason why we chose this area.

In seeing a number of headmasters in Bristol I asked each of them which was the best preparatory school and which were the best state primary schools and each of them named the same schools. This problem of moving round at this rate, the schools become of paramount importance because we feel we disturb them so much we want to do the very best we can.

Well, whatever one thinks of the state education system, there is a degree of selectivity in a comprehensive system and the selectivity is basically the catchment area of the school. And if there is an advantage in moving, all right, you may go upmarket in housing terms, you have the other advantage you can get into a good catchment area. Now, we then got catchment areas sorted out and also with regards getting the second son into a prep. school, this area at that time was in the catchment area for the Grammar School. So it was April '83 that we came up to make a decision on the house and we went for a house up there (across the road). We saw it, brought the kids up at night, the kids said they liked it, we came back the next day to put a deposit on it.

Exactly the same house as this one only on the other side of the road.

And it had been sold in the morning. So in talking to the developers, they said they were building an identical house on this plot and through a very, very long period of protracted negotiation we bought this house. The builders built this house out of sequence of their development, especially for us. This was supposed to be the last house to be built and they turned round and they built this one before about five or six other houses. But we had to put a deposit down on this house for them to build it and my solicitor wouldn't let me put the deposit down until the builders had come up with a completion date and the builders wouldn't come up with a completion date until they had started it, and they wouldn't start it until they had the deposit. So we had a long string of negotiations and eventually I got a gentleman's agreement with the director. . .

With the house in the north, we were friendly with an estate agent and we got the estate agent to value it for us and he said we should get something like £86 000 for the house in the north. Then we put it on the market at £86 000 in May 1983 and it didn't sell. We reduced it to £85 000 and because it was becoming critical with the pressure for us to exchange contracts for the deposit of 10% of this house, we had to go for a company valuation. And the company said to me 'Name two estate agents to value it'. So I went along to our estate agents and said 'Who are the estate agents that put up the price of the property in this area?' They said 'so and so and so and so'. So we said we would get them to value ours. It was hilarious, you learn as the years go by. And the net result of that was that I got a guaranteed price of £84 000. (It was actually sold for £78 000).

This house we bought for £89 000. When we moved down here I had no more IMA to go. But at the same time, in the intervening period between us moving up north and moving down here, the company changed their policy over IMA because they suddenly realised it had been introduced to support people moving from cheap areas into more costly areas and yet everybody had used it to trade all round the country and go upmarket, so they said 'We've got to do something about this'. They produced a map where the country was divided up into areas, it would be the north west, the south west, Scotland and Northern Ireland, the north east, central London, another ring round London, presumably home counties and then the south. Each area was indexed and if you moved into the home counties I think the index was something like 1.5 so if you were moving from the north where the index was 1, to an area where the index was 1.5 then what you did, if you had your house valued at £50 000 you multiplied it by the index 1.5 and you had a maximum of £25 000, that was how they worked out the maximum levels of IMA that they would give you, but they would still not go above the £25 000 ceiling. Now, in moving down from the north west into Bristol the index was something like 0.5 or 0.2, so we did move into a more costly area but because we had already used up our £25 000 there was no more to play with. Now, because of the £12 000 IMA associated with the move from Nantwich into Sussex in 1979 and because the system works for seven years, that terminates in 1986 which means in 1986 we will have £12 000 IMA available to us and I could approach the company and say 'I moved at your behest, to a more expensive area'. This would mean we would then get IMA on the difference of the £84 000 to £89 000. But, as it is always possible that my next move could be into London, the decision we are faced with is, do we use it now or do we hang on to it?

In talking about the properties they bought over the period described, the respondent commented that they had always bought newish houses because they are easier to sell.

The other reason we buy a new house or we bought new houses, was that if you buy a new house on an estate everybody's in the same boat and it doesn't matter whether they've moved a quarter of a mile or two hundred miles they are to some degree in a new area. They are to some degree strange to it and therefore you tend to get usually a community spirit within the estate and it's easier to make friends that way. And the house in Sussex, although it wasn't that new itself, it was on the tiny little estate. The only time we have not lived on an estate is when we went into the north when it didn't matter. We were going into an area we knew, where we already had relatives. The rest of the time it's been one of the reasons why we have only really been looking at estates. Now another thing is, if you pick an estate and you pick one with four bedroomed houses, you assume, rightly or wrongly, that the families that occupy them are going to have children.

The main advantages of home ownership were identified as security. Some of the financial calculations involve anticipation of future moves at the behest of the employer.

One of the other things that I have always been conscious of, is that in being promoted back into the south east, you can significantly alter your quality of life. To give you an example, if we had put the boys into a school in Tiverton, we could have gone and lived six miles outside Tiverton and bought a house that was on the market at that time for about £90 000 which was everybody's idea . . . most people's dream house, it was a sixteenth century house that had six bedrooms and about four or five rooms beside, in about two acres of land. Now, if we bought that house, we would never have left it. And therefore, in picking the most expensive area, you don't get the same amount for your money and therefore it is relatively easier to move from a house like this. Even if it decreased in value to £108 000 it would be much easier to move from this house into something in the south east than it would have been from a house in the Wellington area, you know, where for £90 or £100 thousand pounds you get a mansion with shooting and fishing rights. And because there's this possibility of moving back into London, (I suppose because I must be driven to some degree by ambition) I've tried to ease the pain of that. We've always tried to maximise house values. We have gone upmarket as much as we possibly could each time we've moved. All right, we could have gone up a bit more when we moved down to the south east, taken advantage of IMA, but that was simply because there wasn't the house available, if there had been we would have gone up in value.

Also, because of the position I am in with the firm, when we moved up to the north I was entitled to an executive loan and we took the maximum amount of the executive loan and we also got a bigger mortgage than we actually needed for the house and we invested half that additional mortgage and all of my executive loan in a school fees plan, a capital plan for school fees. That takes care of one child's school fees for evermore and one for a period of time, but having got the kids into those schools, all the other bloody things that go with it. . . . Having had my mortgage and the kids' education, OK, means that we don't have very much spare money.

For instance, we don't go out, we just don't.

We don't go to the picture house, anything like that. And yet a lot of my colleagues have second houses becuse they've used the executive loan to buy a bungalow in Wales, or they have ocean-going yachts and all these sort of things. It's a matter of where you put your values. All we actually want is that my children realise their potential. So if their potential is one 'O' level, that's what I want them to do. If their potential is 9 'O' levels and an Oxbridge place, that's what I want them to get. I just believe, rightly or wrongly, that in the type of schools they go to they are more inclined to reach that potential because of the philosophy of the school.

The view from the top

What general conclusions can we begin to draw from the preceding sections? Given the nature of the research, certain caveats clearly apply. The empirical material is highly detailed but limited to a small group of households in a specific segment of the owner occupied market in Bristol. Moreover, the conclusions drawn and the specific emphases derive from our interpretation of material which cannot be easily represented in a short chapter. Nevertheless, in the absence of other contemporary material on more affluent home-owners it is the only information we have on this segment of the housing market. Moreover, the housing histories which were collected were never intended as oral histories in the sense of being self-standing and uncontaminated by the arguments and debates produced from entirely different sources and methodologies. We are confident that set within general debates on housing market processes and transformations in the labour market, the research provides sufficient basis for valid speculation on possible new lines of enquiry, the adequacy of existing frameworks of analysis and a modest corrective to bottom-up perspectives on the links between housing and employment.

It is appropriate to make a number of observations on the histories themselves. One is struck by the historically specific nature of the routes and trajectories. The housing histories of this group have been shaped by factors which would be non-existent or of considerably less significance for households entering the housing market today. They have been shaped by wartime, evacuation, periods of National Service and, for many, tied accommodation has been a prominent feature of their early housing experiences. They have moved through the housing market at times of rapid tenure change and experienced a relatively buoyant labour market and, not surprisingly, the housing histories are *male* dominated in the important sense of determining *when* moves occurred. The number of moves and their general location were almost exclusively associated with the job career of the male salary earner. After marriage, the pattern is one of male dominance (and probably prior to marriage depending on the occupation of the male parent). This may be more marked at the top end of the market where, by and large, the overriding consideration is the maintenance of the high earning-capacity of the male and where issues of size, space, status and the employment needs and possibilities of the female partner are unlikely to necessitate or justify housing moves. Various constraints were much more evident than might be expected. They were not the constraints which operate at the bottom end of the market but related to a determination to remain in a job career structure involving future moves, the need to maintain investment and to minimise family disruption. To a significant degree they were self-imposed constraints regarding the maintenance of a relatively high standard of living and a job position (reluctance to trade down). This was particularly notable for those who anticipated an eventual promotion to a London head office. For these households the need to maintain a high and accumulating housing investment was paramount if such a move were not to involve a considerable drop in housing standards. And perhaps contrary to expectations, those wishing to spend £100 000 or so in the Bristol housing market had very limited choice particularly if they were seeking an urban location rather than a period cottage in a commuter village. Some households in our group had lengthy search periods living in hotels or private renting until a suitable property came on the market. Housing costs in this period were generally met by the company.

From these housing histories, there is little confirmation of the expectation that a necessary condition for arriving at the top end of the housing market is late marriage or family growth, early entry to home ownership or regular moves to climb a housing ladder. Some of those at the top end of the market appear to have disregarded all of the evidence with which they might have conformed.

Consideration of house size, location and schooling are more apparent than appreciation in property value or accumulation through housing. It may be that this group are making sufficient in the labour market and business activity not to be preoccupied with accumulation through consumption related activities. There is no one who fits the Farmer and Barrell model of the housing market entrepreneur in this study. If they exist they are more likely to be found in housing locations where mobility and occupational careers are not paramount concerns. The evaluation of these housing histories does not, however, imply a reversion to 'everyone is different' or a 'complexity' of interacting factors. There are striking similarities between groups of individuals and some characteristics which connect them all. Some of these can be listed as follows: geographical mobility and lack of local connection; parents in white-collar, self-employed or skilled employment; higher education, post-school qualifying education; and entry to an occupation with a clear career structure.

A prominent feature of these housing histories (and a feature which is sometimes highlighted by contrast with households towards the bottom end of the owner-occupied market) is that their privileged housing position is not related to the relative autonomy of housing processes or housing/family strategies. Rather it is features of job career which emerge most strikingly. It is difficult to view housing histories of this owner group as demonstrating that where people live is significantly determined by conscious housing strategies or manipulation of the housing market to maximise wealth or shelter.

Those at the top end of the market are apparently drawn from a narrow range of jobs and fall into a limited number of job history categories. They do not encompass people in different economic situations some of whom have worked the housing system to greater advantage. But in what ways are job histories similar? The similarities rest principally in the job histories of husbands (and this no doubt says something about domestic relationships). In every case husbands' job histories have almost exclusively been either in successful family firms or have involved employment in a job with an established career structure with opportunities for promotion and incremental salary structures. These careers can be sub-divided. In the public sector they are medical or professional careers. The largest group, however, are in the private sector and are banking or executive careers. Among the executive careers there are some important differences. There are those who have remained with one company and those who have moved around; and there is an important group who entered business in senior executive positions after long careers in the armed forces – such careers are best regarded as training or qualifying stages in executive careers rather than involving 'career change'. In some cases executive careers have been followed by self-employment on the establishment of the new businesses. A notable feature of the careers of those employed in the private sector is that their jobs are in capital intensive or expanding multinational enterprises or in the banking and finance sectors.

Service careers (extending beyond minimum service in say, national service) involve tied accommodation at low rents. With increasing seniority the opportunities for saving and investment as well as cash sums on leaving, are important. Medical careers similarly involve cheap tied accommodation which combines with regional promotion and salary increase to facilitate leaping the lower rungs of any housing ladder. In these terms the conditions for achieving a place at the top end of the housing market are not just about income, but about sectors of the economy and career structures within firms.

The general picture which emerges is of a group of households for whom the prominent academic and policy debates in housing are of considerably less relevance. Core workers in the labour market, senior employees in the growth and high status sectors, may represent a housing élite where the issues of housing subsidy, accumulation, leakage and the activities of urban gatekeepers are qualitatively different.

As regards subsidies, the housing debate has been preoccupied with the relative size of state subsidies to the two principal tenures, home ownership and council housing. It is clear, however, that we need to develop a broader account of the subsidy structure recognising that employer related benefits may be of equal if not greater significance for some households. Titmuss (1958) for example, recognised long ago that welfare subsidies take on many forms and are not limited to the activities of government. Employer-related subsidies may include low interest loans, grants for fixtures, fittings, carpets, etc, moving allowances and payments for rent or hotel costs during search periods. They may involve substantial contributions to the increased cost of new housing through the kinds of complex schemes referred to earlier. The general point is that a group of households in the housing market are effectively cushioned from the vagaries of the market. For this group, movements in interest rates and the retention of mortgage interest tax relief may be of little significance. And there is little requirement to leak money from the housing system through over-borrowing or second mortgages when substantial indirect leakages occur through personnel policies. Why bother disguising a car loan as a house improvement loan when the company pays for improvements when you move in (and the car is provided anyway!)? And those various indirect housing subsidies are written off against tax within the company. The housing histories of senior executives are as likely to have been shaped by the policies and actions of personnel managers as urban managers. And processes of discrimination may operate within sectors and firms according to seniority, status, class and gender. Past work on the role and significance of urban managers in the allocation of housing resources took little account of employment factors. This was another consequence of the problem-oriented, bottom-up approach to housing issues where models of access and discrimination for the whole housing market tend to be extrapolated from research on marginal groups in home ownership and the rental tenures.

One response to this argument would be that although the range and extent of employer related subsidies may be substantial for some households, they are of little numerical significance in the overall scheme of things. Certainly the numbers of employees with access to low interest loans, movement allowances and other subsidies is empirically unknown at present (but see Salt, 1985). But in the absence of firm data it is not unreasonable to assume that such grants and subsidies are of some importance at the upper end of the housing market. Even if they apply to only a small percentage of households they would need to be included in any assessment of the regressive nature of housing subsidies. At present this debate focuses on the regressive nature of tax relief, with those in the higher tax bands benefiting disproportionately. The differential between those at the top and bottom ends of the owner occupied market may, however, be much greater – and the abolition or phasing out of mortgage interest tax relief could increase rather than reduce such differentials. Indeed, it is possible to envisage a situation where it is the middle income, middle strata of home owners who face the full market price of housing and have responsibility for their own repairs, maintenance and mobility. Subsidies and grants of quite different kinds would be concentrated at either end of the housing market. Direct state subsidies would be targeted on marginal groups in the residue of the council housing sector and on the fringes of home-ownership whilst a small core of senior employees in high status professions and the growth sectors enjoy a range of privileges unavailable to the majority of home-owners. Current analyses may seriously underestimate the degree of concentration of housing subsidy at the top end of the housing market.

This concentration of subsidy will have spatial as well as social dimensions. It will be most evident in localities with the greatest degree of concentration of financial institutions and the headquarters of multinational companies. It is thus liable to have a strong North/South dimension although pockets of privilege will exist in, for example, some smaller northern towns where a large building society may be a dominant employer. In general, however, it will be associated with the changing geography of corporate dominance and technocratic power identified by Massey (1983a) among others.

And just as Massey observes that this development has strong gender and class dimensions ('these jobs are almost all for graduates and almost all for men') so too subsidies and grants for housing relocation are liable to benefit disproportionately white, middle-class males. Some caution must, however, be exercised here given the general availability of low interest loans to employees in the banking and insurance sectors where significant numbers of females are employed in the lower echelons (see Boddy, Lovering and Bassett, 1986). Whilst those in the lower grade jobs in these sectors will not receive the range of benefits identified in this study, many will be paying considerably less than market interest rates.

Concluding comments

This consideration of the housing histories of core employees contributes to a more rounded view of the relationships between housing and employment. Those in the strongest positions are enabled to derive financial privileges outside the purview of conventional housing market analyses. This reaffirms the need to approach changes in the housing market from a more general concern with transformations in the labour market. In this paper we have concentrated on a small segment of the housing market. We have contrasted the bargaining position of core workers in this segment with the position of an expanding marginalised group of working-class, elderly, young, single-parent families and ethnic minorities. This leaves a large middle stratum (or strata) in which quite different processes may operate. The nature and strengths of the connections between housing and labour markets will vary between groups, localities and over time. For some the connections will be negative, taking the form of housing immobility, and entrapment through exclusion from the formal labour market. For others, housing histories may be shaped more by housing and family life cycle considerations – this may be particularly true where employment location is fixed (e.g. the self-employed; those with family businesses). And there is a small elite who do not need to deliver their labour power to a particular place at a particular time. This is not the group referred to in this paper. Those at the top end of the urban housing market in Bristol may be affluent and relatively privileged but they are not 'exotics' in the sense that they are by and large dependent upon earned incomes in multinationals, small businesses or in the professions.

What this implies for the broader debates referred to at the start of this paper is the need to escape from all-embracing tenure categories and develop a more detailed conceptualisation of the housing market. This involves, in particular, an acknowledgment of spatial and historical differentiation and the specific processes at work in different segments of the labour market which help shape the nature and meaning of home ownership for individual households. This implies the need to move beyond conventional approaches to housing market differentiation and develop more processual, sociologically based accounts of housing biographies. We cannot assume that there is a common housing ladder with shared lower rungs and different rates of progress. Neither can we assume that tenure labels convey common values, aspirations and experiences. Position in the labour market and specific labour processes will shape housing histories in distinctive ways. Moreover, it is not necessarily the case that the key to this distinctiveness is to be found in local social and economic structures. For the majority of households discussed in this chapter notions of local housing and labour markets are of little relevance. Rather they occupy and move in national, indeed international, space. It is a housing market with stations in parts of Cheltenham, Edinburgh, Chester, rural Sussex and so on – and it is an exclusive line with first class compartments only. But this is only one dimension of its distinctiveness. There are issues of culture and class and specific preoccupations, aspirations and constraints. Those factors may combine to form distinct housing practices (Franklin, 1986) or what Giddens (1986) has referred to as projects (see also Sartre, 1963). It is these aspects which we need to explore further to develop a more coherent account of the relationships between class, space and housing provision.

Acknowledgments

This paper draws on research funded by the Economic and Social Research Council. Since writing it a shorter version has appeared in *Sociological Review*.

Note

1 In order to preserve confidentiality some details in this account have been changed.

Bibliography

Abercrombie, N. and Urry, J. (1983), *Capital, Labour and the Middle Classes*, London, Allen & Unwin.

Abernathy, W., Clark, K. and Kantrow, A. (1983), *Industrial Renaissance, Producing a Competitive Future for America*, New York, Basic Books.

Abrams, P. (1982), *Historical Sociology*, Shepton Mallet, Open Books.

Abrams, P. and Wrigley, E.A. (eds) (1979), *Town in Societies. Essays in Economic History and Historical Sociology*, Cambridge University Press.

Adams, G. (1966), *Age of Industrial Violence 1910–15*, New York, Columbia University Press.

Aglietta, M. (1979), *A Theory of Capitalist Regulation*, London, New Left Books.

Agulhon, M. (1982), *The Republic in the Village. The People of the Var from the French Revolution to the Second Republic*, Cambridge University Press.

Aitken, H. G. J. (1960), *Taylorism at Watertown Arsenal*, Cambridge, Mass., Harvard University Press.

Alexander, S. (1979), 'Women's work in nineteenth century London: a study of the years 1820–50' in J. Mitchell and A. Oakley (eds), *The Rights and Wrongs of Women*, Harmondsworth, Middlesex, Penguin.

Algren, N. (1951), *Chicago – City on the Make*, Oakland, California, Angel Island Publications.

Allswang, J. M. (1971), *A House for all Peoples: Ethnic Politics in Chicago 1890–1936*, Lexington, Kentucky, University Press of Kentucky.

Ambrose, P. (1974), *The Quiet Revolution*, London, Chatto & Windus.

Aminzade, R. (1981), *Class, Politics and Early Industrial Capitalism: a Study of Mid-Nineteenth Century Toulouse*, Albany, State University of New York Press.

Anderson, M. (1971), *Family Structure in Nineteenth Century Lancashire*, Cambridge University Press.

Anderson, M. (1985), 'The emergence of the modern life cycle in Britain', *Social History*, vol. 10, pp. 69–87.

Anderson, P. (1975), *Lineages of the Absolutist State*, London, New Left Books.

Anderson, P. (1980), *Arguments within English Marxism*, London, New Left Books.

Anon. (1855), *Cornwall: Its Mines and Miners*, London, Longmans.

Armstrong, W. A. (1966), 'Social structures from early census returns' in E. A. Wrigley (ed.), *An Introduction to English Historical Demography*, London, Edward Arnold.

Armstrong, W. A. (1972), 'The use of information about occupation' in E. A. Wrigley (ed.), *Nineteenth-Century Society*, Cambridge University Press.

Armstrong, W. A. (1981), 'The trend of mortality in Carlisle between the 1780's and the 1840's: a demographic contribution to the standard of living debate', *Economic History Review*, 2nd series, vol. 29, pp. 94–114.

Ashby, M. (1961), *Joseph Ashby of Tysoe, 1859–1919*, Cambridge University Press.

Atkinson, R. F. (1978), *Knowledge and Explanation in History*, London.

Bagwell, P. S. (1970), *The Transport Revolution from 1770*, London, Batsford.

Baines, E. (1822), *Directory of Leeds*, Leeds.

Baines, E. (1839), 'Report upon the condition of the town of Leeds and its inhabitants', *Journal of the Royal Statistical Society*, Vol. 2, pp. 23–8.

Ball, M. (1983), *Housing Policy and Economic Power. The Political Economy of Owner Occupation*, London, Methuen.

Ball, N. (1979), 'Practical subjects in mid-Victorian elementary schools', *History of Education*, vol. 82, pp. 109–20.

Balmforth, O. (1910), *Huddersfield Industrial Society Limited Jubilee History*, Manchester University Press.

Banks, J. A. (1979), *Marxist Sociology in Action*, London.

Bardou, J. *et al.* (1982), *The Automobile Revolution: the Impact of an Industry*, Chapel Hill, University of North Carolina Press.

Baritz, L. (1960), *The Servants of Power*, Westport, Conn., Greenwood Press.

Barker-Benfield, G. J. (1976), *The Horrors of the Half-Known Life: Male Attitudes to Women and Sexuality in 19th Century America*, New York, Harper & Row.

Barnsby, J. G. (1971), 'The standard of living in the Black Country during the nineteenth century', *Economic History Review*, 2nd series, vol. 24, pp. 120–39.

Barton, D. B. (1967), *A History of Tin Mining and Smelting in Cornwall*, Truro, D. B. Barton.

Barton, R. M. (ed.) (1972), *Life in Cornwall, 1850–1875*, Truro, D. B. Barton.

Beacham, R. (1984), 'Economic activity: Britain's workforce 1971–81', *Population Trends*, no. 37, pp. 6–14.

Bechofer, F. and Elliott, B. (1976), 'Persistence and change: the petite bourgeoisie in industrial society', *European Journal of Sociology*, vol. 17, pp. 74–99.

Bedale, C. (1980), 'Property relations and housing policy: Oldham in the late nineteenth and early twentieth centuries' in J. Melling (ed.), *Housing, Social Policy and the State*, London, Croom Helm.

Bedarida, F. (1979), *A Social History of England 1851–1975*, London, Methuen.

Belassa, B. (1984), 'Adjustment policies in developing countries: a reassessment', *World Development*, vol. 12, pp. 955–72.

Belenchia, J. (1982), 'Latinos and Chicago politics', in S. K. Gove and L. H. Masotti (eds), *After Daley. Chicago Politics in Transition*, Urbana, University of Illinois Press.

Bell, D. (1973), *The Coming of Post-Industrial Society*, New York, Basic Books.

Bell, Mrs Hugh (1907), *At The Works: a Study of a Manufacturing Town*, London, Edward Arnold.

Bendix, R. (1956), *Work and Authority in Industry*, London, John Wiley.

Benenson, H. (1982), 'The reorganisation of the U.S. manufacturing industry and workers experience, 1880–1920: a review of bureaucracy and the labour process by Dan Clawson', *Insurgent Sociologist*, vol. 11, pp. 65–81.

Bennett, A. (1910), *Clayhanger*, London.

Beresford, M. W. (1979), 'Review of change in the town', *Journal of Historical Geography*, vol. 5, pp. 346–8.

Beresford, P. and Stephen, A. (1986), 'Getting it right in the shires', *Sunday Times Colour Magazine*, 26 January, pp. 20–8.

Berger, S. and Piore, M. J. (1980), *Dualism and Discontinuity in Industrial Societies*, Cambridge University Press.

Berle, A. A. (1960), *Power without Property*, New York, Harcourt Brace.

Berle, A. A. and Means, G. C. (1932), *The Modern Corporation and Private Property*, New York, Macmillan.

Bertaux, D. (ed.) (1982), *Biography and Society. The Life History Approach in the Social Sciences*, Beverly Hills, California, Sage.

Best, G. (1971), *Mid-Victorian Britain 1851–76*, London, Weidenfeld & Nicolson.

Bhaskar, K. (1980), *The Future of the World Automobile Industry*, London, Kogan Page.

Billinge, M. (1982) 'Reconstructing societies in the past: the collective biography of local communities', in A. R. H. Baker and M. Billinge (eds), *Period and Place: Research Methods in Historical Geography*, Cambridge University Press.

Bishop, A. and Smart, T. (eds) (1982), *Vera Brittain's War Diary, 1913–17 Chronicle of Youth*, London, Fontana.

Blau, P. M. (1977), *Inequality and Heterogeneity*, New York, Free Press.
Blau, P. and Duncan, O. D. (1967), *The American Occupational Structure*, New York, John Wiley.
Bleasdale, A. (1983), *Boys from the Blackstuff*, London, BBC.
Bledstein, B. J. (1976), *The Culture of Professionalism*, New York, Norton.
Bluestone, B. and Harrison, B. (1982), *Deindustrialising America*, New York, Basic Books.
Boddy, M., Lovering, J. and Bassett, K. (1986), *Sunbelt City? A Study of Economic Change in Britain's M4 Growth Corridor*, Oxford University Press.
Bodmar, J. (1977), *Immigrants and Industrialisation: Ethnicity in an American Mill Town 1870–1940*, Pittsburg University Press.
Bohstedt, J. (1982), *Riots and Community Politics in England and Wales 1790–1810*, Cambridge, Mass., Harvard University Press.
Bonner, H. S. (1895), *Charles Bradlaugh*, London.
Bourdieu, P. (1984), *Distinction: a Social Critique of the Judgement of Taste*, Cambridge, Mass., Harvard University Press.
Bozzoli, B. (1981), *The Political Nature of a Ruling Class: Capital and Ideology in South Africa, 1890–1933*, London, Routledge & Kegan Paul.
Bradbury, B. (1983), 'The fragmented family: family strategies in the face of death, illness and poverty, Montreal, 1860–1885', in J. Parr (ed.), *Childhood and the Family in Canadian History*, Toronto, McClelland & Stewart.
Bradley, T. (1984), 'Segmentation in local labour markets', in T. Bradley and P. Lowe (eds), *Locality and Rurality: Economy and Society in Rural Regions*, Norwich, Geo Books, pp. 65–90.
Bradley, T. (1985), 'Reworking the quiet revolution. Industrial and labour market restructuring in village England', *Sociologia Ruralis*, vol. 25, pp. 40–60.
Bramwell, W. (1984), 'Pubs and localised communities in mid-Victorian Birmingham', *Queen Mary College (University of London), Department of Geography Occasional Paper No. 22*.
Braverman, H. (1974), *Labour and Monopoly Capital*, New York, Monthly Review Press.
Brayshay, W. M. (1977), 'The demography of three west Cornwall mining communities, 1851–1871: society in decline'. Unpublished Ph.D. thesis, University of Exeter.
Brayshay, W. M. (1980), 'Depopulation and changing household structure in the mining communities of west Cornwall, 1851–71', *Local Population Studies*, vol. 25, pp. 26–41.
Brayshay, W. M. (1980, pers. comm.), Unpublished data on overseas birthplaces of Cornish mining families.
Brech, J. (1972), *Strike*, Boston, South End Press.
Brewer, I. (1986), 'A note on the changing status of the Registrar General's classification of occupations', *British Journal of Sociology*, vol. 37, pp. 131–40.

Briggs, A. (ed.) (1959), *Chartist Studies*, London, Macmillan.
Briggs, A. (1963), *Victorian Cities*, London, Odhams.
Briggs, A. (1974), 'The language of "Class" in early nineteenth century England', in M. Flinn and T. Smout (eds), *Essays in Social History*, Oxford, Clarendon Press.

British Parliamentary Papers (PP)

PP, 1852–3, LXXIX, *Census 1851, Population Great Britain: Religious Worship*.
PP, 1864, XXIV, *Commission Appointed to Enquire into the Condition of all Mines in Britain (not coal)*.
PP, 1866, LVII, *Return of the Several Parliamentary Cities and Boroughs in England and Wales, arranged in order to the proportion of electors belonging to the working classes on the Register.*
PP, 1876, XVII, *Report of H.M. Inspector of Mines for Devon and Cornwall (District No. 14)*.
PP, 1884, XIX, *Report of H.M. Inspector of Mines for Devon and Cornwall (District No. 14)*.
PP, 1884–5, XXX, *Royal Commission on the Housing of the Working Classes*.
PP, 1888, XXII, *Select Committee on Town Holdings*.
PP, 1889, XV, *Select Committee on Town Holdings*.
PP, 1890, LVII, *Return of Allotments and Smallholdings*.
PP, 1890–1, LXVIII, *Return of Average Number of Hours worked per week in Chief Trade Centres in various Industries in years 1850, 1860, 1870, 1880 and 1890*.
PP, 1890–1, LXXVIII, *Return of Rates of Wages in the Mines and Quarries in the United Kingdom*.
PP, 1890–1, XLI, *Royal Commission on Mining Royalties*.
PP, 1890–1, LXXVIII, *Return Relating to Minerals (Output 1860–1890)*.
PP, 1893–4, XX, *Reports of the H.M. Inspector for Mines for the South-Western district*.
PP, 1893–4, CV, *Census 1891 Vol II Registration Areas and Sanitary Districts*.
PP, 1894, XXIV, *Report of H.M. Inspector of Mines for the South-Western District (District No. 12)*.
PP, 1896, LXVII, *Return of the Number and Size of Agricultural Holdings in Great Britain in 1895*.
PP, 1899, LXIV, *South African Republic Report on Trade, Commerce and the Gold Mining Industry for 1897*.
PP, 1900, XIV, *Reports of H.M. Inspector of Mines for the South-Western District (District No. 12)*.

PP, 1903, XV, *Report of H.M. Inspector of Mines for the Southern District (District No. 12).*

PP, 1904, XIII, *Report of H.M. Inspector of Mines for the Southern District (District No. 12).*

PP, 1904, XIII, *Report on Health of Cornish Miners.*

PP, 1907, XIII, *Report of H.M. Inspector of Mines for the Southern District (District No. 12).*

PP, 1909, XXXIII, *Report of H.M. Inspector of Mines for the Southern District (District No. 12).*

PP, 1909, XLIII, *Royal Commission on the Poor Law and Relief of Distress Appendix, Vol. XVI. Report on the Relation of Industrial and Sanitary Conditions to Pauperism.*

PP, 1910, XLIII, *Report of H.M. Inspector of Mines for the Southern District (District No. 12).*

Brittain, V. (1933), *Testament of Youth*. London. (All references to 1979 edition).

Broad, R. and Fleming, S. (eds) (1981), *Nella Last's War. A Mother's Diary 1939–45.*

Brody, D. (1980), *Workers in Industrial America*, Oxford University Press.

Brook, R. (1968), *The Story of Huddersfield*, London, MacGibbon & Kee.

Brown, G. C. (1935), 'A.F.L. Report on the Bedaux System', *American Federationist*, vol. XLII, pp. 936–43.

Bryant, M. (1979), 'The unexpected revolution: a study in the history of the education of women and girls in the nineteenth century', *Studies in Education No. 10*, Institute of Education, University of London.

Burawoy, M. (1977), *Manufacturing Consent: Changes in the Labour Process under Monopoly Capitalism*, University of Chicago Press.

Burawoy, M. (1978), 'Towards a Marxist theory of the labour process: Braverman and beyond', *Politics and Society*, vol. 3–4, pp. 247–312.

Burawoy, M. (1983), 'Between the labour process and the state: the changing face of factory regimes under advanced capitalism', *American Sociological Review*, vol. 48, no. 5, pp. 587–605.

Burawoy, M. (1985), *The Politics of Production*, London, New Left Books.

Burgess, K. (1980), *The Challenge of Labour*, London, Croom Helm.

Burke, G. and Richardson, P. (1978), 'The profits of death: a comparative study of miners' phthisis in Cornwall and the Transvaal 1876–1918', *Journal of Southern African Studies*, vol. 4, no. 2, pp. 147–71.

Burnett, J. (1969), *A History of the Cost of Living*, Harmondsworth, Middlesex, Penguin.

Burnet, J. F. (1985), *Public and Preparatory Schools Yearbook 1985*, London, A. & C. Black.

Burnett, J. (1968), *Plenty and Want: a Social History of Diet in England from 1815 to the Present Day*, Harmondsworth, Middlesex, Penguin.

Burnett, J. (1969), *A History of the Cost of Living*, Harmondsworth, Middlesex, Penguin.

Burnett, J. (1974), *Useful Toil: Autobiographies of Working People from the 1820s to the 1920s*, London, Allen & Unwin.

Burnett, J. (1978), *The Social History of Housing, 1815–1970*, Newton Abbott, David & Charles.

Burnham, J. (1941), *The Managerial Revolution*, Harmondsworth, Middlesex, Penguin.

Burns, J. C. (1980), 'The automated office', in T. Forester (ed.), *The Microelectronics Revolution*, Oxford, Blackwell.

Burrage, M. (1972), 'Democracy and the mystery of the crafts', *Daedalus*, Fall, pp. 141–62.

Burris, V. (1980), 'Capital accumulation and the rise of the new middle class', *Review of Radical Political Economics*, vol. 12, pp. 17–34.

Buttrick, J. (1952), 'The inside contract system', *Journal of Economic History*, vol. 12, pp. 205–21.

Cage, R. A. (1983), 'The standard of living debate: Glasgow 1800–1850', *Journal of Economic History*, vol. 43, pp. 175–82.

Calder, J. (1977), *The Victorian Home*, London, Batsford.

Calhoun, C. J. (1980), 'Democracy, autocracy and intermediate associations in complex organisations', *Sociology*, vol. 14, pp. 345–61.

Calhoun, C. J. (1982), *The Question of Class Struggle: Social Foundations of Popular Protest in Industrializing England*, University of Chicago Press.

Calhoun, C. J. (1983a), 'The radicalism of tradition', *American Sociological Review*, vol. 88, pp. 886–914.

Calhoun, C. J. (1983b), 'Industrialisation and social radicalism', *Theory and Society*, vol. 12, pp. 485–504.

Calhoun, C. J. (1984), 'Class society, populist politics', *L-80: Demokratie und Sozialismus*.

Calvert, P. (1982), *The Concept of Class*, London, Hutchinson.

Camagni, R. (1985), 'Industrial robotics and the revitalisation of the Italian North-West', paper presented to an International Seminar on 'Technologies Nouvelles', Brussels, April.

Camborne Election Papers (1885), 'Some of the speeches of Lieutenant-Colonel Fludyer, President of Mr Conybeare's Election Committee', Camborne Public Library.

Campbell, A. (1978), 'Honourable men and degraded slaves', in R. Harrison (ed.), *Independent Collier. The Coal Miner as Archetypal Proletarian*, Brighton, Harvester.

Cannadine, D. (1980), *Lords and Landlords: the Aristocracy and the Towns, 1774–1967*, Leicester University Press.

Cannadine, D. (1982a), 'Residential differentiation in nineteenth century towns: from shapes on the ground to shapes in society' in J. H. Johnson and C. G. Pooley (eds), *The Structure of Nineteenth Century Cities*, London, Croom Helm.

Cannadine, D. (1982b), 'Urban history in the United Kingdom: the "Dyos phenomenon" and after', in D. J. Cannadine and D. Reeder (eds), *Exploring the Urban Past: Essays in Urban History by H. J. Dyos*, Cambridge University Press.

Cannadine, D. and Reeder, D. (eds) (1982), *Exploring the Urban Past: Essays in Urban History by H. J. Dyos*, Cambridge University Press.

Carchedi, G. (1977), *On the Economic Identification of Social Classes*, London, Routledge & Kegan Paul.

Castells, M. (1977), *The Urban Question: a Marxist Approach*, London, Edward Arnold.

Cawson, A. and Saunders, P. (1983), 'Corporatism, competitive politics and class struggle', in A. King (ed.), *Capital and Politics*, London, Routledge & Kegan Paul.

Cayton, H. R. and Drake, St. C. (1946), *Black Metropolis*, London, Jonathan Cape.

Central Statistical Office (1979), *Standard Industrial Classification Revised 1980*, London, HMSO.

Central Statistical Office (1985), *Social Trends No. 15*, London, HMSO.

Centre for Urban and Regional Development Studies (1983), 'Functional regions: definitions, applications, advantages', *University of Newcastle-upon-Tyne, Centre for Urban and Regional Development Studies, Fact Sheet 1.*

Centre for Urban and Regional Development Studies (1984), 'Part time employment, 1971–81', *University of Newcastle-upon-Tyne, Centre for Urban and Regional Development Studies, Fact Sheet 21.*

Chadwick, E. (1842), *Report on the Sanitary Condition of the Labouring Population of Great Britain*, London.

Chalkin, C. W. (1974), *The Provincial Towns of Georgian England: Study of the Building Process 1740–1820*, London, Edward Arnold.

Champion, A. G. and Green, A. E. (1985), 'In search of Britain's booming towns. An index of local economic performance for Britain', *University of Newcastle-upon-Tyne, Centre for Urban and Regional Development Studies, Discussion Paper 72.*

Chandler, A. D. (1980), 'The United States: seedbed of managerial capitalism' in A. D. Chandler and H. Daems (eds), *Managerial Hierarchies*, Cambridge, Mass., Harvard University Press.

Chapman, D. (1955), *The Home and Social Status*, London, Routledge & Kegan Paul.

Chapman, S. D. (1971), 'Working-class housing in Nottingham during the industrial revolution', in S. D. Chapman (ed.), *The History of Working-Class Housing*, Newton Abbot, David & Charles.

Checkland, S. G. (1964), *The Rise of Industrial Society in England 1815–1885*, London, Longmans.
Checkland, S. G. (1968), 'Towards a definition of urban history' in H. J. Dyos (ed.), *The Study of Urban History*, London, Edward Arnold.
Checkland, S. A. and Checkland, E. O. A. (eds) (1974), *The Poor Law Report of 1834*, Harmondsworth, Middlesex, Penguin.
Chesshyre, R. (1986), 'The going is good in Domesday city', *The Observer*, 23 March, p. 60.
Church, R. L. (1964), 'Economists as experts: the rise of an academic profession in the United States, 1870–1920', in L. Stone (ed.), *The University in Society Vol. II*, London, Oxford University Press.
City of Birmingham (1973), *A New Plan for the City*, Birmingham City Council.
City of Bristol Planning Department (1985), *Moving to Bristol*, Research Paper, City of Bristol Planning Department.
Clark, G. L. (1981), 'The employment relation and the spatial division of labour: a hypothesis', *Annals of the Association of American Geographers*, vol. 71, pp. 391–412.
Clark, P. (1983), *The English Alehouse. A Social History 1200–1830*, Harlow, Longmans.
Clark, P. and Slack, P. (1976), *English Towns in Transition 1500–1700*, Oxford University Press.
Clarke, J. and Critcher, C. (1985), *The Devil Makes Work. Leisure in Capitalist Britain*, London, Macmillan.
Clawson, D. (1980), *Bureaucracy and the Labour Process*, New York, Monthly Review Press.
Cleaver, H. (1979), *Reading Capital Politically*, Austin, University of Texas Press.
Cohen, G. A. (1978), *Karl Marx's Theory of History: a Defense*, Oxford University Press.
Collier, P. (1909), *England and the English from an American Point of View*, London, Duckworth.
Collings, J. (1906), *Land Reform: Occupying Ownership, Peasant Proprietary and Rural Education*, London, Longmans.
Collingwood, R. G. (1956), *The Idea of History*, Oxford University Press.
Collins, P. (1969), *Thomas Cooper, the Chartist. Byron and the Poets of the Poor*, Leicester University Press.
Connell, J. (1974), 'The metropolitan village: spatial processes in discontinuous suburbs', in J. H. Johnson (ed.), *Suburban Growth*, London, John Wiley.
Connell, J. (1978), *The End of Tradition. Country Life in Central Surrey*, London, Routledge & Kegan Paul.
Connell, R. W. and Irving, T. H. (1980), *Class Structure in Australian History*, Melbourne, Oxford University Press.
Connell, T. W. and Ward D. (eds) (1981), *A Modern History of Leeds*,

Manchester University Press.

Conway, D. (1982), 'Self-help housing, the commodity nature of housing and amelioration of the housing deficit: continuing the Turner-Burgess debate', *Antipode*, vol. 14, 2, pp. 40–6.

Cooke, P. (1982a), 'Class interests, regional restructuring and state formation in Wales', *International Journal of Urban and Regional Research*, vol. 16, pp. 187–204.

Cooke, P. (1982b), 'Class relations and uneven development in Wales' in G. Day (ed.), *Diversity and Decomposition in the Labour Market*, Farnborough, Gower Press.

Cooke, P. (1983a), 'Labour market discontinuity and spatial development', *Progress in Human Geography*, vol. 7, pp. 543–65.

Cooke, P. (1983b), 'Radical regions? Space, time and gender relations in Emilia, Provence and South Wales', *Progress in Planning*.

Cooke, P. (1983c), *Theories of Planning and Spatial Development*, London, Hutchinson.

Cooke, P. (1983d), 'Regional restructuring: class, politics and popular protest in South Wales', *Environment and Planning Society and Space*, Vol. 1, 265–86.

Cooke, P. (1985), 'Class practices as regional markers: a contribution to labour geography' in D. Gregory and J. Urry (eds), *Social Relations and Spatial Structures*, London, Macmillan.

Cooke, P. (ed.) (1986), *Global Restructuring, Local Response*, London, Economic and Social Research Council.

Cooke, P. and Morgan, K. (1985), 'Flexibility and the new restructuring. Locality and industry in the 1980's', *U.W.I.S.T. Papers in Planning Research*, no. 94.

Cooke Taylor, W. (1842), 'Notes on a tour in the manufacturing districts of Lancashire', reprinted in William Dodd, (1968), *The Factory System Illustrated*, New York, Biblio Distribution.

Coombes, M. G., Dixon, J. S., Goddard, J. B., Openshaw, S. and Taylor, P. J. (1982), 'Functional regions for the population centres of Great Britain' in D. T. Herbert and R. J. Johnston (eds), *Geography and the Urban Environment Volume 5*, Chichester, John Wiley.

Coombes, M. G., Green, A. E. and Owen, D. W. (1985), 'Local labour market areas for different social groups', *University of Newcastle-upon-Tyne, Centre for Urban and Regional Development Studies, Discussion Paper* 74.

Co-operative Congress (1895) *Handbook of the 27th Co-operative Congress: Huddersfield, June 1895*, Manchester.

Copley, F. B. (1923), *Frederick W. Taylor*, 2 vols, New York, Harper & Row.

Corfield, P. J. (1982), *The Impact of English Towns, 1700–1800*, Oxford University Press.

Corrigan, P. (ed.) (1980), *Capitalism, State Formation and Marxist Theory*, London, Quartet.

Cowlard, K. A. (1979), 'The identification of social class areas and their place in nineteenth-century urban development', *Transactions of the Institute of British Geographers, New Series*, vol. 4, pp. 239–57.

Crompton, R. and Jones, G. (1984), *White-Collar Proletariat. Deskilling and Gender in Clerical Work*, London, Macmillan.

Crompton, R. and Sanderson, K. (1986), 'Credentials and careers. Some implications of the increase in professional qualifications amongst women', *Sociology*, vol. 20, pp. 25–42.

Crossick, G. (1977), 'The emergence of the lower middle class in Britain: a discussion', in G. Crossick (ed.) *The Lower Middle Class in Britain, 1870–1914*, London, Croom Helm.

Crossick, G. (ed.) (1977), *The Lower Middle Class in Britain, 1870–1914*, London, Croom Helm.

Crossick, G. (1978), *An Artisan Elite in Victorian Society: Kentish London 1840–80*, London.

Crossick, G. (1983), 'Urban society and the petit bourgeoisie in nineteenth century Britain', in D. Fraser and A. Sutcliffe (eds), *The Pursuit of Urban History*, London, Edward Arnold.

Crump, W. (1931), 'The Leeds woollen industry, 1780–1820', *Thoresby Society Publications*, Vol. 32, pp. 23–48.

Curl, J. (1973), *Victorian Architecture: its Practical Aspects*, Newton Abbot, David & Charles.

Currie, R. and Hartwell, R. M. (1979), 'The making of the English working class?', *Economic History Review*, 2nd series, vol. 18, pp. 633–43.

Cutler, I. (1982), *Chicago: Metropolis of the Mid-West*, 3rd edn, Dubuque, Iowa, Kendall/Hunt.

Dahrendorf, R. (1959), *Class and Class Conflict in Industrial Society*, London, Routledge & Kegan Paul.

Dahrendorf, R. (1969), 'The service class', in T. Burns (ed.), *Industrial Man*, Harmondsworth, Penguin, 140–50.

D'A Jones and Holli, M. (eds) (1981), *Ethnic Chicago*, Grand Rapids, Michigan, William B. Eerdmans.

Dale, R. W. (1898), *The Life of R. W. Dale*, London.

Daniels, P. (1985), *The Service Industries*, London, Methuen.

Daniels, P. and Thrift, N. J. (1985), 'The geographies of the U.K. service sector: a survey', *Economic and Social Research Council Changing Urban and Regional System Working Paper* 1.

Daniels, S. J. (1980), 'Moral order and the industrial environment in the woollen textile districts of West Yorkshire 1780–1880', unpublished Ph.D. thesis, University of London.

Danto, A. C. (1965), *Analytical Philosophy of History*, Cambridge University Press.

Daunton, M. J. (1976), 'House-ownership from rate books', *Urban History Yearbook*, pp. 21–7.

Daunton, M. J. (1980), 'Review of "The Victorian City"', *Journal of Historical Geography*, vol. 6, pp. 332–3.

Daunton, M. (1983), *House and Home in the Victorian City: Working-Class Housing 1850–1914*, London, Arnold.

Davidoff, L. (1979), 'The separation of home and work? Landladies and lodgers in nineteenth and twentieth century England', in S. Burman (ed.), *Fit Work for Women*, London, Croom Helm.

Davidoff, L. (1983), 'Class and gender and Victorian England', in J. Newton, M. Ryan and J. Walkowitz (eds), *Sex and Class in Women's History*, London, Routledge & Kegan Paul.

Davidoff, L., L'Esperance, J. and Newby H. (1979), 'Landscape with figures: home and community in English Society', in J. Mitchell and A. Oakley (eds), *The Rights and Wrongs of Women*, Harmondsworth, Middlesex, Penguin.

Davidoff, L. and Hall, C. (1983), 'The architecture of public and private life: English middle-class society in a provincial town 1780–1850' in D. Fraser and A. Sutcliffe (eds), *The Pursuit of Urban History*, London, Edward Arnold.

Davidson, C. (1982), *A Woman's Work is Never Done. A History of Housework in the British Isles 1650–1950*, London, Chatto & Windus.

Davin, A. (1979), 'Mind that you do as you are told: reading books for Board school girls, 1870–1902', *Feminist Review*, vol. 3, p. 98.

Davison, G. (1978), *The Rise and Fall of Marvellous Melbourne*, Melbourne University Press.

Debray, R. (1981), *Teachers, Writers, Celebrities*, London, Verso.

Dennis, R. J. (ed.) (1979), 'The Victorian City', *Transactions Institute of British Geographers*, new series, vol. 4, pp. 125–319.

Dennis, R. J. (1980), 'Why study segregation? More thoughts on Victorian cities', *Area*, vol. 12, pp. 313–17.

Dennis, R. J. (1984), *English Industrial Cities in the Nineteenth Century: a Social Geography*, Cambridge University Press.

Deverson, J. and Lindsay, K. (1975), *Voices from the Middle Class. A Study of Families in Two London Suburbs*, London, Hutchinson.

Devon County Council (1983), *County Structure Plan. First Alteration 1981 Data Base*, Exeter, Devon County Council.

Dickens, C. (n.d.), *Christmas Books*, London, Nelson.

Dinwiddy, J. (1979), 'Luddism and politics in the northern counties', *Social History*, vol. 4, pp. 333–63.

Disco, C. (1979), 'Critical theory as an ideology of the new class', *Theory and Society*, vol. 8, pp. 159–214.

Dobb, M. (1963), *Studies in the Development of Capitalism*, New York, International Publishers.

Donnelly, F. K. (1976), 'Ideology and English working-class history: Edward Thompson and his critics', *Social History*, vol. 2, pp. 219–38.

Donnelly, F. K. and Baxter, J. L. (1975), 'Sheffield in the English revolutionary tradition, 1791–1820', *International Review of Social History*, vol. 20, pp. 389–423.

Dosi, G. (1983), 'Technological paradigms and technological trajectories: a suggested interpretation of the alternatives and direction of technical change', *Research Policy*, vol. 2.

Douglas, R. (1976), *Land, People and Politics: a History of the Land Question in the United Kingdom, 1878–1952*, New York, St. Martin's Press.

Dubofsky, M. (1983), 'Workers' movements in North America, 1873–1970, a preliminary analysis' in I. Wallerstein (ed.), *Labour in the World Social Structure*, Beverly Hills, Sage.

Duffin, L. (1978), 'Prisoners of progress: women and evolution', in L. Duffin and S. Delamont (eds), *The Nineteenth Century Woman: her Cultural and Physical World*, London, Croom Helm.

Duncan, N. (1981), 'Home ownership and social theory' in J. S. Duncan (ed.), *Housing and Identity: Cross-Cultural Perspectives*, London, Croom Helm.

Duncan, R. (1963), 'Case studies in emigration: Cornwall, Gloucestershire and New South Wales, 1877–1886', *Economic History Review*, 2nd series, vol. XVI, no. 2, pp. 272–89.

Duncan, S. S. (1987), 'What is locality?', in J. R. Peet and N. J. Thrift (eds), *The New Models in Geography*, London, Allen & Unwin.

Dunleavy, P. (1979), 'The urban basis of political alignment: social class, domestic property ownership and state intervention in consumption processes', *British Journal of Political Science*, vol. 9, pp. 409–43.

Dunleavy, P. and Husbands, C. T. (1985), *British Democracy at the Crossroads: Voting and Party Competition in the 1980's*, London, Allen & Unwin.

Dunnell, K. (1979), *Family Formation 1976*, London, HMSO.

Dunning, J. H. and Norman, G. (1983), 'The theory of the multinational enterprise: an application to multinational office location', *Environment and Planning A*, vol. 15, pp. 675–92.

Durkheim, E. (1893), *The Division of Labour in Society*, New York, The Free Press.

Dutton, R. (1954), *The Victorian House: Some Aspects of Nineteenth Century Taste and Manners*, London, Batsford.

Dyos, H. J. (1968), 'Agenda for urban historians', in H. J. Dyos (ed.), *The Study of Urban History*, London, Edward Arnold.

Dyos, H. J. (1982), 'Some historical recollections on the quality of urban life', in D. Cannadine and D. Reeder (eds), *Exploring the Urban Past. Essays in Urban History by H. J. Dyos*, Cambridge University Press.

Dyos, H. J. (1983), 'Urbanity and suburbanity', in D. J. Cannadine and D. Reeder (eds), *Exploring the Urban Past. Essays in Urban History by H. J. Dyos*, Cambridge University Press.

Eagleton, T. (1976), *Criticism and Ideology*, London, New Left Books.

Edel, M. (1982), 'Home ownership and working class unity', *International Journal of Urban and Regional Research*, vol. 6, pp. 205–22.
Edwards, R. (1979), *Contested Terrain*, London, Hutchinson.
Ehrenreich, B. and Ehrenreich, J. (1979), 'The professional–managerial class', in P. Walker (ed.), *Between Labour and Capital*, New York, Monthly Review Press, pp. 5–45.
Eisenstein, Z. R. (ed.) (1978), *Capitalist Patriarchy and the Case for Socialist Feminism*, New York, Monthly Review Press.
Elias, N. (1978), *The Civilizing Process. The History of Manners, Volume 1*, Oxford, Blackwell.
Engels, F. (1878), *Anti-Duhring: Herr Ehgen Duhring's Revolution in Science*, Moscow, Foreign Languages Publishing House, 1959.
Engels, F. (1880), 'Socialism: utopian and scientific', in L. Fleuer (ed.) (1959), *Marx and Engels: Basic Writings on Politics and Philosophy*, New York, Doubleday.
Engels, F. (1895), 'Introduction to K. Marx: the class struggles in France 1848–1850', in *Marx/Engels Selected Works*, vol. 1, pp. 186–210 (1969), Moscow, Progress Publications.
Engels, F. (1969), *The Condition of the Working Class in England*, London, Panther.
Englander, D. (1981), 'Tenants and politics: the Birmingham tenants' federation during and after the First World War', *Midland History*, vol. 6, pp. 124–41.
Englander, D. (1983), *Landlord and Tenant in Urban Britain, 1838–1918*, Oxford University Press.
Ernst, D. (1985), 'Automation and the worldwide restructuring of the electronics industry: strategic implications for developing countries', *World Development*, vol. 13, pp. 333–52.
Evans, M. (ed.) (1982), *The Women Question*, London, Fontana.
Evans, S. and Boyte, H. (1982), 'Schools for Acton', *Democracy*, vol. 2, pp. 55–65.

Farmer, M. and Barrell, R. (1981), 'Entrepreneurship and government policy: the case of the housing market', *Journal of Public Policy*, vol. 2, pp. 307–32.
Ferris, J. (1972), 'Participation in urban planning: the Barnsbury case', occasional papers in Social Administration, No. 48, Social Administration Research Trust.
Fine, B. and Harris, L. (1979), *Rereading Capital*, London, Macmillan.
Flandrin, J. (1979), *Families in Former Times: Kinship, Household and Sexuality*, Cambridge University Press.
Foner, P. S. (1955), *History of the Labour Movement in the United States*, vol. 2, New York, International Publishers.
Foord, J. (1984), 'New technology and new gender relations. Reorganisation in the service sector: the case of women's employment', *University of*

Newcastle-upon-Tyne, Centre for Urban and Regional Development Studies, Discussion Paper 58.

Forrest, R. (1983), 'The meaning of home ownership', *Environment and Planning D, Society and Space*, vol. 1, pp. 205–16.

Forrest, R. and Murie, A. (1983), 'Residualisation and council housing – aspects of the changing social relations of housing tenure', *Journal of Social Policy*, vol. 12, pp. 453–68.

Forrest, R. and Murie, A. (1986), 'Marginalisation and subsidized individualism: the sale of council houses in the restructuring of the British welfare state', *International Journal of Urban and Regional Research*, vol. 10, pp. 46–66.

Foster, J. (1968), 'Nineteenth century towns: a class dimension', in Dyos, H. J. (ed.) *The Study of Urban History*, London, Edward Arnold.

Foster, J. (1974), *Class Struggle and the Industrial Revolution. Early Industrial Capitalism in Three English Towns*, London, Weidenfeld & Nicolson.

Foster, J. (1976), 'Some comments on class struggle and the labour aristocracy, 1830–1860', *Social History*, vol. 3, pp. 357–66.

Foster, J. (1979), 'How imperial London preserved its slums', *International Journal of Urban and Regional Research*, vol. 3, pp. 93–114.

Fox, F. (1923), *The English, 1909–1911*, London, John Murray.

Fox-Genovese, E. and Genovese, E. D. (1983), *Fruits of Merchant Capital. Slavery and Bourgeois Property in the Rise and Expansion of Capitalism*, Oxford University Press.

Franklin, A. (1986) 'Owner occupation, Privatism and Ontological Security; a critical reformulation', SAUS, University of Bristol (mimeo).

Fraser, D. (1976), *Urban Politics in Victorian England. The Structure of Politics in Victorian Cities*, Leicester University Press.

Fraser, W. H. (1981), *The Coming of the Mass Market, 1850–1914*, London, Macmillan.

Freeman, C. and Soete, L. (1985), *Technical Change and Full Employment*, Oxford, Basil Blackwell.

Friedman, A. L. (1977), *Industry and Labour. Class Struggle at Work and Industrial Capitalism*, London, Macmillan.

Frith, S. (1977), 'Socialisation and rational schooling: elementary education in Leeds before 1870', in McCann, P. (ed.), *Popular Education and Socialisation in the Nineteenth Century*, London, Methuen.

Frobel, F., Heinrichs, T. and Kreye, O. (1980), *The New International Division of Labour*, Cambridge University Press.

Gadian, D. S. (1978), 'Class consciousness in Oldham and other north west industrial towns 1830–1850', *Historical Journal*, vol. 21, pp. 161–72.

Gardener, P. (1961), *The Nature of Historical Explanation*, Oxford University Press.

Gaskell, E. (1977), *Mary Barton. A Tale of Manchester Life*, London (first published in 1848).
Gauldie, E. (1974), *Cruel Habitations: a History of Working-Class Housing, 1790–1918*, London, Allen & Unwin.
Gershuny, J. (1978), *The Self-Service Economy*, London, Macmillan.
Gershuny, J. (1985), 'Economic development and change in the mode of provision of services', in N. Redclift and E. Mingione (eds), *Beyond Employment. Household, Gender and Subsistence*, Oxford, Blackwell.
Giddens, A. (1973), *The Class Structure of the Advanced Societies*, London, Hutchinson.
Giddens, A. (1979a), *Central Problems in Social Theory: Action, Structure and Contradiction in Social Analysis*, London, Macmillan.
Giddens, A. (1979b), 'Postscript', in *The Class Structure of the Advanced Societies*, 2nd edn, London, Hutchinson.
Giddens, A. (1981), *A Contemporary Critique of Historical Materialism Volume 1*, London, Macmillan.
Giddens, A. (1984), *The Constitution of Society. An Outline of the Theory of Structuration*, Cambridge, Polity Press.
Giddens, A. (1985) 'Time, Space and Regionalisation' in D. Gregory and J. Urry (eds), *Social Relations and Spatial Structures*, London, Macmillan.
Giddens, A. and MacKenzie, D. (eds) (1982), *Social Class and the Division of Labour. Essays in Honour of Ilya Neustadt*, Cambridge University Press.
Gilman, C. (1972), *The Home: Its Work and Influence*, Urbana, University of Illinois Press. (Reprint of 1903 version.)
Ginswick, J. (ed.) (1983), *Labour and the Poor in England and Wales 1849–1851: Volume 1, Lancashire, Cheshire, Yorkshire*, London.
Girouard, M. (1978), *Life in the English Country House*, New Haven, Yale University Press.
Gloag, J. (1962), *Victorian Taste: Some Social Aspects of Architectural and Industrial Design, 1820–1900*, London, Black.
Goddard, J. B. and Smith, I. J. (1977), 'Changes in corporate control in the British urban system, 1972–1977', *Environment and Planning A*, vol. 10, pp. 1073–84.
Godwin, G. (1972), *Town Swamps and Social Bridges*, Leicester University Press.
Goldthorpe, J. (1982), 'On the service class, its foundation and future', in A. Giddens and D. MacKenzie (eds), *Social Class and the Division of Labour*, Cambridge University Press.
Goldthorpe, J., Llewellyn, C. and Payne, C. (1980), *Social Mobility and Class Structure in Modern Britain*, Oxford, Clarendon Press.
Goldthorpe, J. and Lockwood, D. (1969), *The Affluent Working Class in the Class Structure*, Cambridge University Press.
Goldthorpe, J. and Payne, C. (1986), 'Trends in intergenerational class mobility in England and Wales, 1971–1983', *Sociology*, vol. 20, pp. 1–24.

Goodman, D. and Redclift, M. (1981), *From Peasant to Proletarian. Capitalist Development and Agrarian Transition*, Oxford, Blackwell.

Gorz, A. (1982), *Farewell to the Working Class. An Essay on Post-Industrial Socialism*, London, Pluto Press.

Gosnell, H. F. (1937), *Machine Politics. Chicago Model*, University of Chicago Press.

Gould, A. (1980), 'The salaried middle class in the corporatist welfare state', *Policy and Politics*, vol. 9, pp. 401–18.

Gouldner, A. W. (1979), *The Future of the Intellectuals and the Rise of the New Class*, London, Macmillan.

Gourvish, R. T. (1972), 'The cost of living in Glasgow in the early nineteenth century', *Economic History Review*, 2nd series, vol. 25, pp. 65–80.

Grafton, D. (1983), 'The Plymouth rural fringe', in M. Brayshay (ed.), Post-War Plymouth: Planning and Reconstruction, *South West Papers in Geography, Occasional Paper* 8, pp. 66–80.

Gray, F. (1982), 'Owner occupation and social relations', in S. Merrett with F. Gray, *Owner-occupation in Britain*, London, Routledge & Kegan Paul.

Gray, R. (1981), *The Aristocracy of Labour in Nineteenth-Century Britain, c. 1850–1914*, London, Macmillan.

Green, A. E. (1985), 'Recent trends in the service sector in Tyne and Wear and Berkshire', *University of Newcastle-upon-Tyne, Centre for Urban and Regional Development Studies, Discussion Paper* 71.

Green, C. (1973), 'Birmingham's politics 1983–1891: the local basis of change', *Midland History*, vol. 2, pp. 94–8.

Gregory, D. (1982), *Regional Transformation and Industrial Revolution: A Geography of the Yorkshire Woollen Industry*, Minneapolis, University of Minnesota Press.

Gregory, D. (1984), 'Contours of crisis? Sketches for a geography of class struggle in the early Industrial Revolution in England', in A. R. H. Baker and D. Gregory (eds), *Explorations in Historical Geography. Interpretative Essays*, Cambridge University Press.

Groh, D. (1979), 'Base processes and the problem of organisation', *Social History*, vol. 4, pp. 265–83.

Guterbock, T. M. (1980), *Machine Politics in Transition. Party and Community in Chicago*, University of Chicago Press.

Haber, S. (1964), *Efficiency and Uplift. Scientific Management in the Progressive Era, 1890–1929*, University of Chicago Press.

Haider, D. H. (1982), 'Capital budgeting and planning', in S. K. Gore and L. H. Masotti (eds), *After Daley. Chicago Politics in Transition*, Urbana, University of Illinois Press.

Hall, S. (1981), 'Notes on deconstructing the popular', in R. Samuel (ed.), *People's History and Socialist Theory*, London, Routledge & Kegan Paul.

Halsey, A. H., Heath, A. F. and Ridge, J. M. (1979), *Origins and Destinations*, Oxford University Press.

Hamburger, J. (1963), *James Mill and the Art of Revolution*, New Haven, Yale University Press.

Hamburger, J. (1965), *Intellectuals in Politics. John Stuart Mill and the Philosophical Radicals*, New Haven, Yale University Press.

Hamer, D. A. (ed.) (1971), 'Introduction to Joseph Chamberlain and others', *The Radical Programme*, Hassocks, Harvester Press.

Hansen, L. N. (1982), 'Suburban politics and the decline of the one-city party' in S. K. Gore and L. H. Masotti (eds), *After Daley: Chicago Politics in Transition*, Urbana, University of Illinois Press.

Hareven, T. K. (1982), *Family Time and Industrial Time: the Relationship Between Family and Work in a New England Industrial Community*, Cambridge University Press.

Harloe, M. (1984), 'Sector and class: a critical comment', *International Journal of Urban and Regional Research*, vol. 8, pp. 228–37.

Harris, R. (1983), 'Space and class: a critique of Urry', *International Journal of Urban and Regional Research*, vol. 7, pp. 115–21.

Harrison, J. F. C. (1959), 'Chartism in Leeds', in Briggs, A. (ed.), *Chartist Studies*, London, Macmillan.

Harrison, R. (ed.) (1978), *The Independent Collier. The Coal Miner as Archetypal Proletarian Reconsidered*, Brighton, Harvester.

Hartmann, H. (1979), 'The unhappy marriage of Marxism and feminism: towards a new union', *Capital and Class*, no. 3, pp. 45–72.

Harvey, D. (1982), *The Limits to Capital*, Oxford, Blackwell.

Harvey, D. (1985), *The Urbanization of Capital*, Oxford, Blackwell.

Hastings, R. P. (1959), *The Labour Movement in Birmingham, 1927–45*, M.A. Thesis, University of Birmingham.

Hayden, D. (1981), *The Grand Domestic Revolution*, Cambridge, Mass., MIT Press.

Headrick, D. R. (1981), *The Tools of Empire: Technology and European Imperialism in the Nineteenth Century*, Oxford University Press.

Heath, A. (1981), *Social Mobility*, London, Fontana.

Heath, A., Jowell, R. and Curtice, J. (1985), *How Britain Votes*, Oxford, Pergamon.

Heaton, (1920), *The Yorkshire Woollen and Worsted Industries*, University of Leeds.

Heaton, H. (1960), 'Economic change and growth', in J. P. T. Bury (ed.), *The New Cambridge Modern History*, vol. X, Cambridge University Press.

Held, D. (1980), *Introduction to Critical Theory. From Horkheimer to Habermas*, London, Hutchinson.

Henriques, J., Hollway, W., Urwin, C., Venn, C. and Walkerdine, V. (1984), *Changing the Subject. Psychology, Social Regulation and Subjectivity*, London, Methuen.

Herington, J. (1984), *The Outer City*, London, Harper & Row.
Herman, E. S. (1981), *Corporate Control, Corporate Power*, Cambridge University Press.
Hewitt, M. (1958), *Wives and Mothers in Victorian Industry*, London, Rockcliff.
Himmelfarb, G. (1977), 'Social history and moral imagination', in Q. Anderson (ed.), *Art, Politics and Will. Essays in Honour of Lionel Trilling*, New York (reprinted in Neale (1983)).
Hindess, B. (1971), *The Decline of Working Class Politics*, London, MacGibbon & Kee.
Hirsch, F. (1983), *Social Limits to Growth*, London, Routledge & Kegan Paul.
Hobkirk, C. P. (1968), *Huddersfield: Its History and Natural History*, Huddersfield.
Hobsbawm, E. J. (1964), *Labouring Men: Studies in the History of Labour*, London, Weidenfeld & Nicolson.
Hobsbawm, E. J. (1978), 'The communist party historians group', in M. Cornforth (ed.), *Rebels and Their Causes*, London, Lawrence & Wishart.
Hobsbawm, E. J. (1984), 'Artisan or labour aristocrat?', *Economic History Review*, vol. 37, pp. 355–72.
Hoggart, R. (1957), *The Uses of Literacy*, London, Chatto & Windus.
Holland, G. C. (1843), *The Vital Statistics of Sheffield*, Sheffield.
Holli, M. and D'A Jones (eds) (1977), *The Ethnic Frontier*, Grand Rapids, Michigan, William B. Eerdmans.
Hollis, P. (1970), *The Pauper Press*, Oxford University Press.
Holme, A. (1985), *Housing and Young Families in East London*, London, Routledge & Kegan Paul.
Holmes, R. S. and Armstrong, W. A. (1978), 'Social stratification', *Area*, vol. 10, pp. 126–8.
Hopkins, E. (1979), *A Social History of the English Working Classes 1815–1945*, London, Edward Arnold.
Hoskins, W. (1963), *Provincial England: Essays in Social and Economic History*, London, Macmillan.
Hovell, M. (1918), *The Chartist Movement*, Manchester.
Howells, J. L. R. (1984), 'The location of research and development: some observations and evidence for Britain', *Regional Studies*, vol. 18, pp. 13–29.
Hunt, P. (1980), *Gender and Class Consciousness*, London, Macmillan.
Hunter, A. (1974), *Symbolic Communities. The Persistence and Change of Chicago's Local Communities*, University of Chicago Press.

Inglis, F. (1982), *Radical Earnestness. English Social Theory 1850–1980*, Oxford, Martin Robertson.
Inquiry into Friendly and Benefit Societies (1871), *1st Report of the Commissioners, with Minutes and Appendix*, London.

Jackson, B. and Marsden, D. (1962), *Education and the Working Class*, London, Routledge & Kegan Paul.

Jackson, J. T. (1980), '19th century housing in Wigan and St. Helens', *Transactions of the Historical Societies of Lancashire and Cheshire*, vol. 129, pp. 125–43.

Jackson, J. T. (1982), 'Long-distance migrant workers in nineteenth century Britain: a case study of the St. Helens' glassmakers', *Transactions Historical Society of Lancashire and Cheshire*, vol. 131.

Jenkin, A. K. H. (1934), *Cornish Homes and Customs*, London, Bell.

Jenkin, A. K. H. (1962), *The Cornish Miner: an Account of his Life Above and Underground from Early times*, London, Allen & Unwin.

Jenkins, P. (1983), *The Making of a Ruling Class. The Glamorgan Gentry 1640–1790*, Cambridge University Press.

Jenkyns, R. (1980), *The Victorians and Ancient Greece*, Oxford University Press.

John, A. (1979), *By the Sweat of their Brow: Women Workers at Victorian Coal Mines*, London, Croom Helm.

Johnson, R. (1978), 'Edward Thompson, Eugene Genovese, and socialist–humanist history', *History Workshop Journal*, no. 6.

Johnson, R. (1982), 'Reading for the best Marx: history-making and historical abstraction', in C.C.C.S. (ed.), *Making Histories*, London, Hutchinson.

Johnson, T. (1977a), 'What is to be known. The structural determination of social class', *Economy and Society*, vol. 5, pp. 194–233.

Johnson, T. (1977b), 'The professions in the class structure', in R. Scase (ed.), *Industrial Society. Class, Cleavage and Control*, London, Allen & Unwin.

Johnson, T. (1982), 'The state and the professions: peculiarities of the British', in A. Giddens and D. MacKenzie (eds), *Social Class and the Division of Labour*, Cambridge University Press.

Johnston, R. J. (1985), *The Geography of English Politics. The 1983 General Election*, Beckenham, Kent, Croom Helm.

Johnston, R. J. (1986), 'The neighbourhood effect revisited: spatial science or political regionalism?', *Environment and Planning D. Society and Space*, vol. 4, pp. 1–26.

Jones, D. (1975), *Chartism and the Chartists*, London, Allen Lane.

Jones, D. and Womack, J. (1985), 'Developing countries and the future of the world automobile industry', *World Development*, vol. 13, pp. 393–408.

Jones, G. S. (1976), *Outcast London*, Harmondsworth, Penguin.

Joyce, P. (1975), 'The factory politics of Lancashire in the later nineteenth century', *Historical Journal*, vol. 18, pp. 525–53.

Joyce, P. (1980), *Work, Society and Politics: the Culture of the Factory in Later Victorian England*, Brighton, Harvester Press.

Judt, T. (1979), *Socialism in Provence 1871–1914. A Study in the Origins of the French Left*, Cambridge University Press.

Judt, T. (1985), *Marxism and the French Left: Studies on Labour and Politics in France 1830–1981*, Oxford, Clarendon Press.

Kantorowicz, E. H. (1957), *The King's Two Bodies*, Princeton, N.J., Princeton University Press.

Karn, V., Kemeny, J. and Williams, P. (1985), *Home Ownership in the Inner City – Salvation or Despair?*, Aldershot, Gower Press.

Katznelson, I. (1979), 'Community, capitalist development and the emergence of class', *Politics and Society*, vol. 9, pp. 203–38.

Kay, J. P. (1832), *The Moral and Physical Condition of the Working Classes*, London, Frank Cass (1970).

Keating, P. (1976), *Into Unknown England: Selections from the Social Explorers, 1866–1913*, Glasgow, Fontana.

Kitteringham, J. (1975), 'Country work girls in nineteenth century England', in R. Samuel (ed.), *Village Life and Labour*, London, Routledge & Kegan Paul.

Kocka, J. (1980), *White Collar Workers in America, 1890–1940*, London, Sage.

Kohl, J. G. (1844), *England, Wales and Scotland*, London.

Kolko, G. (1963), *The Triumph of Conservatism*, New York, Free Press.

Kornblum, W. (1974), *Blue Collar Community*, University of Chicago Press.

Kovalev, Y. D. (ed.) (1956), *An Anthology of Chartist Literature*, Moscow, Progress.

Krut, R. M. (1979), '"A quart into a pint pot": the white working class and the "housing shortage" in Johannesburg, 1896–1906', B. A. Hons. dissertation, University of Witwatersrand.

Lancaster Regionalism Group (1985), *Localities, Class and Gender*, London, Pion.

Land Enquiry Committee (1914), *The Land: The Report of the Land Enquiry Committee*, vol. ii (urban).

Langton, J. (1975), 'Residential patterns in pre-industrial cities: some case studies from seventeenth-century Britain', *Transactions of the Institute of British Geographers*, vol. 65, pp. 1–27.

Larson, M. S. (1977), *The Rise of Professionalism: a Sociological Analysis*, Berkeley, University of California Press.

Larson, M. S. (1980), 'Proletarianisation and educated labour', *Theory and Society*, vol. 9, pp. 131–75.

Lasch, C. (1977a), 'The siege of the family', *New York Review of Books* XXIV, pp. 15–18.

Lasch, C. (1977b), *Haven in a Heartless World*, New York, Basic Books.

Laslett, P. (1971), *The World We Have Lost*, London, Methuen.

Laslett, P. (1972a), 'Mean household size in England since the sixteenth century' in P. Laslett and R. Wall (eds), *Household and Family in Past Time*, Cambridge University Press.

Laslett, P. (1972b), 'Introduction: the history of the family' in P. Laslett and R. Wall (eds), *Household and Family in Past Time*, Cambridge University Press.

Laslett, P. (ed.) (1972c), *Household and Family in Past Time*, Cambridge University Press.

Lawton, R. (1978), 'Population and society 1730–1900', in R. A. Dodgshon and R. A. Butlin (eds), *An Historical Geography of England and Wales*, London, Academic Press.

Layton, E. (1971), *The Revolt of the Engineers*, Cleveland, Press of Case Western Reserve University.

Layton, E. (1974), 'The diffusion of scientific management and mass production from the U.S. in the twentieth century', *International Congress in the History of Science*, vol. 4, pp. 377–86.

Lee, C. H. (1984), 'The service sector, regional specialisation and economic growth in the Victorian economy', *Journal of Historical Geography*, vol. 10, pp. 139–55.

Lefebvre, H. (1976), *The Survival of Capitalism*, London, Allison & Busby.

Lenin, V. I. (1948), *Imperialism, the Highest Stage of Capitalism*, London, Lawrence & Wishart.

Lentz, C. (1982), 'The Lizard Museum, Cornwall', letter to *History Workshop Journal*, no. 13, pp. 187–8.

Levine, A. and Wright, E. O. (1980), 'Rationality and class struggle', *New Left Review*, no. 123, pp. 47–68.

Lewis, G. J. and Maund, D. J. (1979), 'Intra-community segregation: a case study in rural Hertfordshire', *Sociologia Ruralis*, vol. 19, pp. 135–47.

Lewis, G. W. (1907), *The Stannaries: a Study of the English Tin Miner*, Cambridge, Mass., Harvard University Press.

Lewis, R. (1979), *Enoch Powell – Principle in Politics*, London, Cassell.

Lin, V. (1985), 'Health, women's work and industrialisation: women workers in the semiconductor industry in Singapore and Malaysia', paper presented at the International Sociological Association Conference on 'Regional Impacts of the New International Division of Labour', Hong Kong, August.

Lindert, P. H. and Williamson, J. G. (1983), 'English workers' living standards during the Industrial Revolution: a new look', *Economic History Review*, 2nd series, vol. 34.

Lipietz, A. (1984), 'La mondialisation de la crise generale du Fordisme, 1967–1984', *Les Temps Modernes*, November.

Lipietz, A. (1985), 'Le national et le regional: quelle autonomie face a la crise capitaliste mondiale?', Paris, *CEPREMAP Paper* no. 8521.

Litterer, J. (1963), 'Systematic management: design for organisational recoupling in American manufacturing firms', *Business Historical Review*, vol. 37, pp. 369–91.

Littler, C. (1978), 'Understanding Taylorism', *British Journal of Sociology*, vol. 29, pp. 185–202.

Littler, C. (1982a), 'Deskilling and changing structures of control' in S. Wood (ed.), *The Degradation of Work*, London, Hutchinson.

Littler, C. (1982b), *The Development of the Labour Process in Capitalist Societies*, London, Heinemann.

Lloyd, T. and Simpson, M. (eds) (1977), *Middle-class Housing in Britain*, Newton Abbott, David & Charles.
Lockwood, D. (1958), *The Blackcoated Worker*, London, Allen & Unwin.
Lovering, J. (1985), 'Regional intervention, defence industries and the structuring of space in Britain: the case of Britain and South Wales', *Environment and Planning D. Society and Space*, vol. 3, pp. 85–108.
Lowe, P. and Goyder, J. (1983), *Environmental Groups in Politics*, London, Allen & Unwin.
Lukács, G. (1924), *History and Class Consciousness*, London, Merlin (1971).

McBride, T. (1978), '"As the twig is bent", the Victorian nanny', in Wohl, A. (ed.), *The Victorian Family*, London, Croom Helm.
McCarthy, T. (1970), *The Critical Theory of Jurgen Habermas*, London, Hutchinson.
McGregor, O. R. (1957), *Divorce in England*, London, Heinmann.
McIntyre, S. (1980), *Little Moscows. Communism and Working-Class Militancy in Inter-War Britain*, London, Croom Helm.
McKendrick, N. (1982), 'The consumer revolution of eighteenth century England', in N. McKendrick, J. Brewer and J. Plumb (eds), *The Birth of Consumer Society: the Commercialization of Eighteenth Century England*, London, Europa.
McKendrick, N., Brewer, J. and Plumb, J. (1982), *The Birth of Consumer Society: the Commercialization of Eighteenth Century England*, London, Europa.
MacKenzie, S. and Rose, D. (1983), 'Industrial change: the domestic economy and home life', in J. Anderson, S. S. Duncan and R. Hudson (eds), *Redundant Spaces in Cities and Regions*, London, Academic Press.
McLeod, H. (1974), *Class and Religion in the Late Victorian City*, London, Croom Helm.
Macleod, R. (1971), *Style and Society*, London, RIBA.
Maier, C. (1979), 'Between Taylorism and technocracy: European ideologies and the vision of industrial productivity in the 1920's, *Journal of Contemporary History*, vol. 21, pp. 27–61.
Malcolmson, R. W. (1981), *Life and Labour in England 1700–1780*, London, Hutchinson.
Mallett, S. (1975), *Essays on the New Working Class*, St. Louis, Missouri, Telos Press.
Mandel, E. (1975), *Late Capitalism*, London, New Left Books.
Marshall, G., Rose, D., Vogler, C. and Newby, H. (1985), 'Class, citizenship and distributional conflict in modern Britain', *British Journal of Sociology*, vol. 36.
Marshall, J. N. (1985), 'Research policy and review. Services in a post-industrial economy', *Environment and Planning A*, vol. 17, pp. 1155–67.
Martin, J. and Roberts, C. (1984), *Women's Employment. A Lifetime Perspective*, London, HMSO

Marwick, A. (1981), *Class: Image and Reality in Britain, France and the U.S.A. since 1930*, London, Collins.

Marx, K. (1850), 'The class struggles in France 1848–50', in D. Fernbach (ed.), *Surveys from Exile*, pp. 35–142 (1973), Harmondsworth, Middlesex, Penguin.

Marx, K. (1867), *Capital*, vol. I, London, Laurence & Wishart.

Marx, K. (1871), 'The Civil War in France', in R. Tucker (ed.), *The Marx–Engels Reader*, pp. 618–52, New York, Norton.

Marx, K. (1885), *Capital*, vol. II, London, Lawrence & Wishart.

Marx, K. (1894), *Capital*, vol. III, London, Lawrence & Wishart.

Marx, K. (1932), *The German Ideology*, Collected Works vol. 5, London, Lawrence & Wishart.

Marx, K. (1950), 'Preface to a contribution to the critique of political economy', in K. Marx, and F. Engels, *Selected Works*, London, Lawrence & Wishart.

Marx, K. (1970), *A Contribution to the Critique of Hegel's 'Philosophy of Right'*, (ed. J. O'Malley), Cambridge University Press.

Marx, K. (1976), *Capital*, vol. I, Harmondsworth, Penguin.

Marx, K. and Engels, F. (1848), 'Manifesto of the Communist Party', in *Collected Works*, vol. 6, London, Lawrence & Wishart (1976).

Marx, K. and Engels, F. (1950), *Selected Works. Volume 1*, London, Lawrence & Wishart.

Marx, K. and Engels, F. (1971), *Ireland and the Irish Question*, Moscow.

Marx, K. and Engels, F. (n.d.), *Manifesto of the Communist Party*, Moscow, Foreign Languages Publishing House.

Massey, D. (1983a), 'The shape of things to come', *Marxism Today*, April, pp. 18–27.

Massey, D. (1983b), 'Industrial restructuring as class restructuring: production decentralisation and local uniqueness', *Regional Studies*, vol. 17, pp. 73–89.

Massey, D. (1984), *Spatial Divisions of Labour. Social Structures and the Geography of Production*, London, Macmillan.

Massey, D. (1985), 'Geography and class', in D. Coates, G. Johnston and R. Bush (eds), *A Socialist Anatomy of Britain*, Cambridge, Polity Press.

Massey, D., and Meegan, R. (1982), *The Anatomy of Job Loss. The How, Why and Where of Employment Decline*, London, Methuen.

Mayhew, B. and Levinger, T. (1976), 'On the emergence of oligarchy in human interaction', *American Journal of Sociology*, vol. 81, pp. 1017–49.

Mayhew, H. (1862), *London Labour and the London Poor*, London.

Meillassoux, C. (1975), *Femmes, Greniers et Capitaux*, Paris, Maspero.

Mendels, F. F. (1972), 'Proto-industrialisation: the first phase of the industrialization process', *Journal of Economic History*, vol. 32, pp. 241–61.

Merton, R. K. (1968 edition), *Social Theory and Social Structure*, New York, The Free Press.

Meyrowitz, J. (1985), *No Sense of Place. The Impact of Electronic Media on Social Behaviour*, New York, Oxford University Press.
Michels, R. (1949), *Political Parties*, New York, Free Press.
Middleton, C. (1981), 'Peasants, patriarchy and the feudal mode of production in England: a Marxist appraisal: 1. Property and patriarchal relations within the peasantry, 2. Feudal lords and the subordination of peasant women', *Sociological Review*, vol. 29, pp. 105–35 and 137–54.
Mills, D. R. (1980), *Lord and Peasant in Nineteenth Century Britain*, London, Croom Helm.
Mingione, E. and Redclift, N. (eds) (1985), *Beyond Employment: Household, Gender, Subsistence*, Oxford, Blackwell.
Mitchell, B. and Deane, P. (1962), *British Historical Statistics*, Cambridge University Press.
Mitter, S. (1986), 'Industrial restructuring and manufacturing homework. Immigrant women in the U.K. clothing industry', *Capital and Class*, no. 27, pp. 37–80.
Mongomery, D. (1979), *Workers Control in America*, Cambridge University Press.
Morgan, K. and Sayer, A. (1985), 'A modern industry in a mature region: the remaking of management-labour relations', *International Journal of Urban and Regional Research*, vol. 9, pp. 383–404.
Morris, L. (1986), 'The changing structure of Hartlepool', in P. Cooke (ed.), *Global Restructuring, Local Response*, London, Economic and Social Research Council.
Morris, R. J. (1976), *Class and Class Consciousness in Victorian Britain*, London, Macmillan.
Morris, R. J. (1979), 'The middle class and the property cycle during the Industrial Revolution', in T. C. Smout (ed.), *The Search for Wealth and Stability*, London, Macmillan.
Morris, R. J. (1983a), 'The middle class and British towns and cities of the Industrial Revolution, 1780–1870', in D. Fraser and A. Sutcliffe (eds), *The Pursuit of Urban History*, London, Edward Arnold.
Morris, R. J. (1983b), 'Property titles and the use of British urban poll books for social analysis', *Urban History Yearbook, 1983*, Leicester University Press.
Mulhern, F. (1981a), *The Moment of Scrutiny*, London, New Left Books.
Mulhern, F. (1981b), '"Teachers, writers, celebrities", intelligentsias and their histories', *New Left Review*, no. 126, pp. 43–59.
Mumford, L. (1961), *The City in History*, London, Secker.
Murie, A. (1974), Household Movement and Housing Choice, University of Birmingham, *Centre for Urban and Regional Studies Occasional Paper 28.*
Musson, A. E. (1976), 'Class struggle and the labour aristocracy 1830–60', *Social History*, vol. 1, pp. 335–56.
Muthesius, S. (1982), *The English Terraced House*, London, Yale University Press.

Nadworny, M. J. (1955), *Scientific Management and the Unions 1900–1932*, Cambridge, Mass., Harvard University Press.

Neale, R. S. (1966), 'The standard of living 1780–1844: a regional and class study', *Economic History Review*, 2nd series, vol. 19, pp. 590–606.

Neale, R. S. (1968), 'Class and class consciousness in early nineteenth century England: three classes or five', *Victorian Studies*, vol. 12, pp. 4–32 (reprinted in Neale (1972)).

Neale, R. S. (1972), *Class and Ideology in the Nineteenth Century*, London.

Neale, R. S. (1981a), *Class in English History 1680–1850*, Oxford, Blackwell.

Neale, R. S. (1981b), *Bath 1680–1850: a Social History or a Valley of Pleasure yet a Sink of Iniquity*, London, Routledge & Kegan Paul.

Neale, R. S. (1981c), 'Theory and history: a note on the Anderson/Thompson debate', *Thesis Eleven*, vol. 2, pp. 23–9.

Neale, R. S. (1983), 'Afterword', in *History and Class: Essential Readings in Theory and Interpretation*, Oxford, Blackwell.

Neale, R. S. (ed.) (1983), *History and Class. Essential Readings in Theory and Interpretation*, Oxford, Blackwell.

Neale, R. S. (1984), 'Cultural materialisms: a critique', *Social History*, vol. 9.

Nelson, D. (1975), *Managers and Workers. Origins of the New Factory System in the United States, 1880–1920*, Madison, Wisconsin, University of Wisconsin Press.

Nelson, R. (1959), *The Merger Movement in American Industry 1895–1956*, Princeton, N.J., Princeton University Press.

Newby, H. (1982), *The State of Research into Social Stratification in Britain*, London, Social Science Research Council.

Newby, H., Bell, C., Rose, D. and Saunders, P. (1978), *Property, Paternalism and Power*, London, Hutchinson.

Newton, J. L., Ryan, M. P. and Walkowitz, J. R. (1983), *Sex and Class in Women's History*, London, Routledge & Kegan Paul.

Newton, K. (1976), *Second City Politics. Democratic Processes and Decision-Making in Birmingham*, Oxford, Clarendon Press.

Noble, D. (1979), *America by Design*, Oxford University Press.

Nove, A. (1983), *The Economics of Feasible Socialism*, London, Allen & Unwin.

Oddy, D. J. (1983), 'Urban famine in nineteenth century Britain: the effect of the Lancashire cotton famine on working-class diet and health', *Economic History Review*, 2nd series, vol. 36, pp. 68–86.

Offe, C. and Wiesenthal, H. (1980), 'Two logics of collective action', in M. Zeitlin (ed.), *Political Power and Social Theory. Volume 1*, Greenwich, Connecticut, J.A.I. Press, pp. 67–115.

Offe, C. (1984a), *The Contradictions of the Welfare State*, London, Hutchinson.

Offe, C. (1984b), *Disorganised Capitalism*, Cambridge, Polity Press.

Offer, A. (1981), *Property and Politics 1870–1914. Landownership, Law, Ideology and Urban Development in England*, Cambridge University Press.

Office of Population Censuses and Surveys (1980), *Classification of Occupations 1980*, London, HMSO.

Office of Population Censuses and Surveys (1984), *General Household Survey 1982*, London, HMSO.

Office of Population Censuses and Surveys (1984a), *Key Statistics for Urban Areas. The South East*, London, HMSO.

Office of Population Censuses and Surveys (1984b), *Key Statistics for Urban Areas. The South West and Wales*, London, HMSO.

Osborne, J. (1981), *A Better Class of Person. An Autobiography 1929–1956*, London, Faber.

Ossowski, S. (1963), *Class Structure in the Social Consciousness*, London, Routledge & Kegan Paul.

Owen, D. W. and Green, A. (1985), 'A comparison of the changing spatial distributions of socio-economic groups employed in manufacturing and services', *University of Newcastle-upon-Tyne, Centre for Urban and Regional Development Studies, Discussion Paper* 70.

Pacione, M. (1980), 'Quality of life in a metropolitan village', *Transactions, Institute of British Geographers, New Series*, vol. 5, pp. 185–206.

Pahl, R. E. (1965a), *Urbs in Rure*, Geographical Papers, no. 2, London, London School of Economics.

Pahl, R. E. (1965b), 'Class and community in English commuter villages', *Sociologia Ruralis*, vol. 5, pp. 5–23.

Pahl, R. E. (1966), 'The rural–urban continuum', *Sociologia Ruralis*, 6.

Pahl, R. E. (1984), *Divisions of Labour*, Oxford, Blackwell.

Palmer, B. (1975), 'Class, conception and conflict: the thrust for efficiency, managerial views of labour and the working class rebellion, 1903–22', *Review of Radical Political Economy*, vol. 7, pp. 31–49.

Parker, T. (1983), *The People of Providence*, London, Hutchinson.

Parkin, F. (1972), *Class, Inequality and Political Order*, London, Paladin.

Parkin, F. (1979), *Marxism and Class Theory. A Bourgeois Critique*, London, Tavistock.

Payne, J. and Payne, G. (1974), 'Housing pathways and stratification: a study of life chances in the housing market', *Journal of Social Policy*, vol. 6.

Pelling, H. (1967), *The Social Geography of British Elections*, London, Macmillan.

Perkin, H. (1957), 'The origins of the popular press', in *The Structured Crowd* (1981), Brighton, Sussex, Harvester.

Perkins, H. (1969), *The Origins of Modern English Society 1780–1880*, London, Routledge & Kegan Paul.

Person, H. (1929), *Scientific Management in American Industry. The Taylor Society*, New York, Harper.

Petrie, C. (1938), *The Chamberlain Tradition*, London, The 'Right' Book Club.

Philips, D. R. and Williams, A. M. (1983), 'Rural settlement policies and local authority housing: observations from a case study of South Hams, Devon', *Environment and Planning A*, vol. 15, pp. 429–570.

Philips, D. and Williams, A. (1984), *Rural Britain. A Social Geography*, Oxford, Blackwell.

Phillips, L. (1905), *Transvaal Problems: Some Notes on Current Policies*, London, John Murray.

Pike, D. (1967), *Paradise of Dissent, South Australia 1829–57*.

Pinch, S. and Williams, A. (1983), 'Social class change in British cities', in J. B. Goddard and A. G. Champion (eds), *The Urban and Regional Transformation of Britain*, London, Methuen.

Piore, M. and Sabel, C. (1984), *The Second Industrial Divide. Possibilities for Prosperity*, New York, Basic Books.

Pollard, S. (1957), 'The ethics of the Sheffield Outrages', *Transactions of the Hunter Archaeological Society*, vol. 7, pp. 118–39.

Pollard, S. (1959), *A History of Labour in Sheffield*, Liverpool University Press.

Pollard, S. (1971), *Trades Union Commission. Sheffield Outrages Inquiry*, 1867, pp. XXXII (reprinted with an introduction by S. Pollard).

Pooley, C. G. (1977), 'The residential segregation of migrant communities in mid-Victorian Liverpool', *Transactions, Institute of British Geographers*, new series, vol. 2, pp. 364–82.

Pooley, C. G. (1979), 'Residential mobility in the Victorian city', *Transactions, Institute of British Geographers*, new series, vol. 4, pp. 258–77.

Poor Law Commissioners (1837–38), *Fourth Annual Report* Appendix A, no. 1, Supplement no. 1, London.

Porter, G. R. (1847), *The Progress of the Nation in its Various Social and Economical Relations*.

Porter, R. (1982), *English Society in the Eighteenth Century*, Harmondsworth, Middlesex, Penguin.

Postgate, R. (1923), *The Builders' History*, London, National Federation of Building Trades Operatives.

Poulantzas, N. (1973), *Political Power and Social Classes*, London, New Left Books.

Poulantzas, N. (1975), *Classes in Contemporary Capitalism*, London, New Left Books.

Pratt, G. (1982), 'Class analysis and urban domestic property: a critical re-examination', *International Journal of Urban and Regional Research*, vol. 6, pp. 481–502.

Preston, M. (1982), 'Black politics in the post-Daley era', in S. K. Gore and L. H. Masotti (eds), *After Daley. Chicago Politics in Transition*, Urbana, University of Illinois Press.

Preston, M. (1983), 'Political mobilization of black Chicago: drafting a candidate', *Political Science*, vol. 26, pp. 486–8.

Preteceille, E. and Terrail, J. (1985), *Capitalism, Consumption and Needs*, Oxford, Blackwell.

Price, R. (1975), *The Economic Modernization of France 1730–1880*, New York, John Wiley.

Prothero, I. (1979), *Artisans and Politics in Early Nineteenth Century London: John Gast and his Times*, London, Methuen.

Przeworski, A. (1977), 'Proletariat into a class: the process of class formation from Karl Kautsky's The Class Struggle to recent controversies', *Politics and Society*, vol. 10, pp. 125–53.

Przeworski, A. (1980a), 'Material interests, class compromise and the transition to socialism', *Politics and Society*, vol. 10, pp. 125–53.

Przeworski, A. (1980b), 'Social democracy as a historical phenomenon', *New Left Review*, no. 122, pp. 27–58.

Przeworski, A. (1985), *Capitalism and Social Democracy*, Cambridge University Press.

Przeworski, A. and Wallerstein, M. (1982), 'The structure of class conflict in democratic capitalist societies', *American Political Science Review*, vol. 76, pp. 215–38.

Rajan, A. (1984), *New Technology and Employment in Insurance, Banking and Building Societies*, Institute of Manpower Studies/Gower Press.

Rakovè, M. (1975), *Don't Make Waves. Don't Back Losers*, Indiana University Press.

Ralph, J. (1890), 'The best-governed city in the world', *Harper's Monthly Magazine*, Vol. 81, pp. 99–110.

Ralph, J. (1893), 'An Easterner looks at a western city', in A. L. Strauss (1968), *The American City*, Chicago, Aldine.

Raynor, J. (1969), *The Middle Class*, London, Longmans.

Redclift, N. and Mingione, E. (eds) (1985), *Beyond Employment. Household, Gender and Subsistence*, Oxford, Blackwell.

Redford, E. (1970), *The New Villagers*, London, Frank Class.

Reed, H. C. (1983), 'Appraising corporate investment policy: a financial centre theory of foreign direct investment', in C. Kindleberger and D. Audretsch (eds), *The Multinational Corporation in the 1980's*, Cambridge, Mass., MIT Press.

Reeder, D. A. (1961), 'Politics of urban leaseholds in late Victorian England', *International Review of Social History*, vol. 6, pp. 413–30.

Reid, A. (1983), 'Intelligent artisans and aristocrats of labour: the essays of Thomas Wright', in J. Winter (ed.), *The Working Class in Modern British History. Essays in Honour of Henry Pelling*, Cambridge University Press.

Renner, K. (1978), 'The service class', in T. Bottomore and P. Goode (eds) *Austro-Marxism*, Oxford, Clarendon, 249–52.

Retail Directory (1986), *Retail Directory 1986*, London, Newman Books.

Rex, J. and Moore, R. (1967), *Race, Community and Conflict. A Study of Sparkbrook*, London, Oxford University Press.

Rex, J. and Tomlinson, S. (1979), *Colonial Immigrants in a British City*, London, Routledge & Kegan Paul.

Reynolds, S. (1964), 'Roman Catholicism', in W. B. Stephens (ed.), *A History of the County of Warwick: Vol. 7 – Birmingham*, London, Oxford University Press.

Rice, M. S. (1939), *Working-Class Wives*, London, Penguin.

Richards, E. (1974), 'Women in the British economy since about 1700: an interpretation', *History*, vol. 59, pp. 337–57.

Rimmer, W. (1967), 'The industrial profile of Leeds, 1740–1840', *Thoresby Society Publications*, vol. 50, pp. 130–57.

Roberts, R. (1971), *The Classic Slum*, Manchester University Press.

Robertson, J. A. S., Briggs, J. M. and Goodchild, A. (1982), *Structure and Employment Prospects of the Service Industries*, Department of Employment, Research Paper 20.

Roemer, J. (1982), *A General Theory of Exploitation and Class*, Cambridge, Mass., Harvard University Press.

Rogers, B. (1980), *The Domestication of Women: Discrimination in Developing Societies*, London/New York, Tavistock.

Rolf, D. (1983), 'Birmingham labour and the background to the 1945 general election', in A. Wright and R. Shackleton (eds), *Worlds of Labour. Essays in Birmingham Labour History*, University of Birmingham, Department of Extramural Studies in association with WEA (West Midlands District) and Birmingham Reference Library, Social Sciences Department, Birmingham.

Rose, D. (1984), 'Home-ownership, uneven development and industrial change in late nineteenth century Britain', unpublished D.Phil. thesis, University of Sussex.

Rose, S. A. (1986), 'Gender at work. Sex, class and industrial capitalism', *History Workshop*, no. 21, pp. 113–31.

Rossi, P. (1980), *Why Families Move*, 2nd edn, Beverly Hills, Sage.

Rossi, P. and Shlay, A. (1982), 'Residential mobility and public policy issues: "Why Families Move" revisited', *Journal of Social Issues*, vol. 3, pp. 21–34.

Routh, G. (1980), *Occupation and Pay in Great Britain*, London, Macmillan.

Rowe, J. (1953), *Cornwall in the Age of the Industrial Revolution*, Liverpool University Press.

Rowe, D. J. (1961), 'The People's Charter', *Past and Present*, vol. 36, pp. 73–86.

Rowse, A. L. (1942), *A Cornish Childhood*, London, Frederick Warne.

Royko, M. (1971), *Boss: Richard J. Daley of Chicago*, New York, New American Library.

Rubinstein, W. D. (1980), *Wealth and the Wealthy in the Modern World*, London, Croom Helm.

Rule, J. G. (1970), 'The tribute system and the weakness of trade unionism in the Cornish mines', *Bulletin of the Society for the Study of Labour History*, vol. 21, pp. 24–9.

Rule, J. G. (1971), 'Methodism and Chartism among the Cornish miners', *Bulletin of the Society for the Study of Labour History*, vol. 22, pp. 8–11.

Ruskin, J. (1865), *Sesame and Lilies*, London.

Sabole, Y., (1975), *The Service Industries*, Geneva, ILO.

Sachs, A. and Wilson, J. (1978), *Sexism and the Law: a Study of Male Beliefs and Legal Bias in Britain and the United States*, London, Martin Robertson.

Salaman, G. (1981), *Class and the Corporation*, London, Fontana.

Salt, J. (1985), 'Housing and labour migration'. Paper presented at a Conference on 'Housing and Labour Market Change', Parsifal College, London.

Samuel, R. (1977a), 'Workshop of the world. Steam power and technology in mid-Victorian Britain', *History Workshop*, no. 3, pp. 6–72.

Samuel, R. (1977b), 'Mineral workers', in R. Samuel (ed.), *Miners, Quarrymen and Saltworkers*, London, Routledge & Kegan Paul.

Samuel, R. (ed.) (1975), *Village Life and Labour*, London, Routledge & Kegan Paul.

Samuel, R. (ed.) (1981), *People's History and Socialist Theory*, London, Routledge & Kegan Paul.

Sarlvik, B. and Crewe, I. (1983), *Decade of Dealignment*, Cambridge University Press.

Sartre, J. P. (1963), *The Problem of Method*, London, Methuen.

Saunders, P. (1978), 'Domestic property and social class', *International Journal of Urban and Regional Research*, vol. 2, pp. 233–51.

Saunders, P. (1979), *Urban Politics. A Sociological Interpretation*, London, Hutchinson.

Saunders, P. (1981), *Social Theory and the Urban Question*, London, Hutchinson.

Saunders, P. (1984), 'Beyond housing classes: the sociological significance of private property rights and means of consumption', *International Journal of Urban and Regional Research*, vol. 8, pp. 202–27.

Saunders, P. (1985), 'The forgotten dimension of central–local relations: theorising the regional state', *Environment and Planning C. Government and Policy*, vol. 3, pp. 227–52.

Saunders, P. (1986), 'Reflections on the dual politics thesis: the argument, its origins and its critics', in M. Goldsmith (ed.), *Urban Political Theory and the Management of Fiscal Stress*, Farnborough, Hants, Gower Press.

Saunders, P. and Williams, P. (forthcoming), 'The constitution of the home', mimeo, available from the authors.

Saville, J. (ed.) (1974), *The Socialist Register 1974*, London, Merlin.

Scase, R. and Goffee, C. (1982), *The Entrepreneurial Middle Class*, London, Croom Helm.

Schlichter, S. H. (1919), *Turnover of Factory Labour*, New York, D. Appleton and Co.

Schonberger, R. (1982), *Japanese Manufacturing Techniques*, London, Macmillan.

Schreiner, O. (1883), *The Story of an African Farm.*

Scott, J. (1979), *Corporations, Classes and Capitalism*, London, Hutchinson.

Scott, J. (1982), *The Upper Classes. Property and Privilege in Britain*, London, Macmillan.

Seeley, J., Sim, R. and Loosley, E. (1963), *Crestwood Heights*, New York, John Wiley.

Select Committee (1940), *Report on the Health of Towns*, London.

Shaw, M. (1977), 'The ecology of social change: Wolverhampton 1851–71', *Transactions, Institute of British Geographers*, new series, vol. 2, pp. 332–48.

Shaw, M. (1979), 'Reconciling social and physical space: Wolverhampton 1871', *Transactions, Institute of British Geographers*, new series, vol. 4, pp. 192–213.

Simpson, M. A. and Lloyd, T. (eds) (1977), *Middle Class Housing in Britain*, Newton Abbot, David & Charles.

Singleton, F. (1970), *Industrial Revolution in Yorkshire*, Clapham, Yorkshire.

Slater, G. (1968), *The English Peasantry and the Enclosure of Common Fields*, New York, Kelley.

Smith, D. (1982), *Conflict and Compromise. Class Formation in English Society 1830–1914. A Comparative Study of Birmingham and Sheffield*, London, Routledge & Kegan Paul.

Smith, D. (1986a), 'Factory and community: the restructuring of South West Birmingham', in P. Cooke (ed.), *Global Restructuring, Local Response*, London, Economic and Social Research Council.

Smith, D. (1986b), 'Modern times: Thorstein Veblen and Chicago', *Theory, Culture and Society*, vol. 20.

Smith, F. B. (1973), *Radical Artisan. William James Linton 1812–97*, Manchester University Press.

Smith, N. and Williams, P. (eds) (1986), *Gentrification of the City*, London, Allen & Unwin.

Soete, L. and Dosi, G. (1983), *Technology and Employment in the Electronics Industry*, London, Frances Pinter.

Sofer, C., (1970), *Men in Mid-Career – a Study of British Managers and Technical Specialists*, Cambridge University Press.

Soja, E. W. (1985), 'Regions in context: spatiality, periodicity and historical geography of the regional question', *Environment and Planning D. Society and Space*, vol. 3, pp. 75–90.

Sokoloff, N. (1980), *Between Money and Love: The Dialectics of Women's Home and Market Work*, New York, Praeger.

South Hams District Council (1983), *Ivybridge District Plan*, Totnes, South Hams District Council.

Soyer, A. (1846), *The Gastronomic Regenerator*, London.

Spear, A. H. (1967), *Black Chicago: the Making of a Ghetto 1890–1920*, University of Chicago Press.

Springett, J. (1979), 'The mechanics of urban land development in Huddersfield, 1770–1911', unpublished Ph.D. thesis, University of Leeds.

Springett, J. (1982), 'Landowners and urban development: the Ramsden estate and nineteenth century Huddersfield', *Journal of Historical Geography*, vol. 8, pp. 129–44.

Stacey, M. and Price, M. (1981), *Women, Power and Politics*, London, Tavistock.

Stark, D. (1980), 'Class struggle and the transformation of the labour process', *Theory and Society*, vol. 9, pp. 89–130.

Stedman Jones, G. (1974), 'Working class culture and working class politics in London, 1870–1900: notes on the remarking of a working class', *Journal of Social History*, vol. 7, (reprinted in Stedman Jones, 1983).

Stedman Jones, G. (1975), 'Class struggle and the industrial revolution', *New Left Review*, no. 90 (reprinted in Stedman Jones, 1983).

Stedman Jones, G. (1976), *Outcast London: a Study in the Relationship Between Classes in Victorian Society*, Harmondsworth, Penguin.

Stedman Jones, G. (1982), 'The language of Chartism' in J. Epstein and D. Thompson (eds), *The Chartist Experience: Studies in Working Class Radicalism and Culture, 1830–1860*, London, Macmillan.

Stedman Jones, G. (1983), *Languages of Class. Studies in English Working Class History 1832–1932*, Cambridge University Press.

Steedman, C., Urwin, C. and Walkerdine, V. (eds) (1985), *Language, Gender and Childhood*, London, Routledge & Kegan Paul.

Stone, K. (1974), 'The origin of job structures in the steel industry', *Review of Radical Political Economy*, vol. 6, pp. 113–73.

Stone, L. (1977), *The Family, Sex and Marriage in England 1500–1800*, London, Weidenfeld & Nicolson.

Storch, R. D. (1977), 'The problem of working class leisure. Some roots of middle class reform in the industrial north 1825–1886', in A. P. Donajgrodski (ed.), *Social Control in Nineteenth Century Britain*, London, Croom Helm.

Storper, M. and Walker, R. (1983), 'The theory of labour and the theory of location', *International Journal of Urban and Regional Research*, vol. 7, pp. 1–44.

Sturt, G. (1912), cited in Burnett, J. (1978), *A Social History of Housing, 1815–1970*, Newton Abbot, David & Charles.

Summers, A. (1979), 'A home from home – women's philanthropic work in the nineteenth century', in Burman, S. (ed.), *Fit Work for Women*, London, Croom Helm.

Sutcliffe, A. (1974), *Multi-storey Living. The British Working Class Experience*, London, Croom Helm.

Sutcliffe, A. (1978), 'Harry Watton and Stan Yapp: contrasting styles of leadership in Labour-controlled Birmingham', in G. W. Jones and A. Norton (eds), *Political Leadership in Local Government*, University of Birmingham Institute of Local Government Studies.

Sutcliffe, A. and Smith, R. (1974), *Birmingham 1939–1970*, London, Oxford University Press.

Suttles, G. (1968), *The Social Order of the Slum. Ethnicity and Territory in the Inner City*, University of Chicago Press.

Sykes, D. F. E. (1898), *The History of Huddersfield and its Vicinity*, Huddersfield.

Tawney, R. (1931), *Equality*, London, Unwin.

Taylor, B. (1983), *Eve and the New Jerusalem*, London, Virago.

Taylor, F. W. (1947), *The Principles of Scientific Management*, New York, Harper.

Taylor, M. J. and Thrift, M. J. (eds) (1982), *The Geography of Multinationals*, London, Croom Helm.

Taylor, P. J. (1986), 'What a world-systems analysis of political parties might look like'. Paper presented to the Colston Symposium, Geography and Politics, University of Bristol, April, 1986.

Terkel, S. (1970), *Division Street, America*, Harmondsworth, Middlesex, Penguin.

Thale, M. (ed.) (1983), *Selections from the Papers of the London Corresponding Society, 1792–99*, Cambridge University Press.

Therborn, G. (1983), 'Problems of class analysis', in B. Matthews (ed.), *Marx: 100 Years On*, London, Lawrence & Wishart.

Thomis, M. (1976), *Responses to Industrialisation: The British Experience 1780–1850*, Newton Abbot, David & Charles.

Thompson, C. B. (1917), *The Theory and Practice of Scientific Management*, Boston, Houghton Mifflin.

Thompson, E. P. (1965), 'The peculiarities of the English', in *The Poverty of Theory and Other Essays*, New York, Monthly Review Press (1978).

Thompson, E. P. (1966), *The Making of the English Working Class*, New York, Vintage.

Thompson, E. P. (1967), 'Time, work-discipline and industrial capitalism', *Past and Present*, vol. 38, pp. 56–97.

Thompson, E. P. (1968), *The Making of the English Working Class*, Harmondsworth, Penguin (originally published in 1963).

Thompson, E. P. (1971), 'The moral economy of the English crowd in the eighteenth century', *Past and Present*, vol. 50, pp. 76–136.

Thompson, E. P. (1978), *The Poverty of Theory and Other Essays*, London, Merlin.

Thompson, E. P. (1979), 'Eighteenth century English society: class struggle without class', *Social History*, vol. 4, pp. 133–66.

Thompson, F. M. L. (1977), 'Hampstead, 1840–1914', in M. A. Simpson and

T. H. Lloyd (eds), *Middle Class Housing in Britain*, Newton Abbot, David & Charles.

Thompson, J. B. (1984), *Studies in the Theory of Ideology*, Cambridge, Polity Press.

Thompson, J. B. and Held, D. (1982), *Habermas. Critical Debates*, London, Macmillan.

Thompson, P. (1975), *The Edwardians. The Remaking of British Society*, London, Weidenfeld & Nicolson.

Thompson, P. (1978), *The Voice of the Past. Oral History*, Oxford University Press.

Thompson, P. (ed.) (1982), *Our Common History. The Transformation of Europe*, London, Pluto Press.

Thorns, D. (1981a), 'Owner occupation: its significance for wealth transfer and class formation', *Sociological Review*, vol. 29, pp. 705–28.

Thorns, D. (1981b), 'The implications of differential rates of capital gains from owner occupation for the formation and development of housing classes', *International Journal of Urban and Regional Research*, vol. 5, pp. 205–27.

Thrift, N. J. (1981), 'Owners time and own time: the making of a capitalist time consciousness', in A. R. Pred (ed.), *Space and time in Geography. Essays Dedicated to Torsten Hägerstrand*, Lund Studies in Geography, Series B, Human Geography no. 48.

Thrift, N. J. (1983), 'On the determination of social action in space and time', *Environment and Planning D. Society and Space*, vol. 1, pp. 23–57.

Thrift, N. J. (1985), 'Flies and germs. A geography of knowledge', in D. Gregory and J. Urry (eds), *Social Relations and Spatial Structures*, London, Macmillan.

Thrift, N. J. (1986a), 'Little games and big stories. Accounting for the practice of personality and politics in the 1945 General Election', in K. Hoggart and E. Kofman (eds), *Politics, Geography and Social Stratification*, Beckenham, Kent, Croom Helm.

Thrift, N. J. (1986b), 'The fixers: the urban geography of international commercial capital', in J. Henderson, M. Castells (eds), *The Regional Impacts of Global Restructuring*, Beverly Hills, California, Sage.

Tiptaft, N. (1954), *The Individualist*, Birmingham, Norman Tiptaft Ltd.

Titmuss, R. (1958), 'The social division of welfare', in *Essays on the Welfare State*, London, Allen & Unwin.

Todd, A. C. (1967), *The Cornish Miner in America*, Truro, D. B. Barton.

Touraine, A. (1974), *The Academic System in American Society*, New York, McGraw Hill.

Townsend, A. R. (1986), 'The location of employment growth after 1978: the surprising significance of dispersed centres', *Environment and Planning A*, vol. 18, pp. 529–45.

Turner, G. (1964), *The Car Makers*, Harmondsworth, Middlesex, Penguin.

Tyrrell, A. (1970), 'Class consciousness in early Victorian Britain: Samuel Smiles, Leeds politics and the self-help creed', *Journal of British Studies*, vol. 9, pp. 102–25.

Urry, J. (1973), 'Towards a structural theory of the middle class', *Acta Sociologia*, vol. 16, pp. 175–87.

Urry, J. (1981a), *The Anatomy of Capitalist Societies. The Economy, State and Civil Society*, London, Macmillan.

Urry, J. (1981b), 'Localities, regions and social class', *International Journal of Urban and Regional Research*, vol. 5, pp. 455–74.

Urry, J. (1983), 'Some notes on realism and the analysis of space', *International Journal of Urban and Regional Research*, vol. 7, pp. 122–7.

Urry, J. (1984), 'Capitalist restructuring, recomposition and the regions', in T. Bradley and P. Lowe (eds), *Locality and Rurality: Economy and Society in Rural Regions*, Norwich, Geo Books.

Urry, J. (1985a), 'The class structure', in D. Coates, G. Johnston and R. Bush (eds), *A Socialist Anatomy of Britain*, Cambridge, Polity Press.

Urry, J. (1985b), 'From organised to disorganised capitalism'. Paper presented at an International Sociological Association Conference on 'Industrial Restructuring, Social Change and the Locality', University of Sussex, April.

Urry, J. (1985c) 'Deindustrialisation, households and politics', in Lancaster Regionalism Group, *Localities, Class and Gender*, London, Pion.

Urry, J. and Lash, S. (1986), *The End of Organised Capitalism?*, Cambridge, Polity Press.

Urwick, L. (1929), *The Meaning of Rationalisation*, London, Nisbet.

Van Onselen, C. (1979), 'The world the mineowners made: social themes in the economic transformation of the Witwatersrand, 1886–1914', *Review*, vol. 3, pp. 289–302.

Vance, J. (1967), 'Housing the worker: determinative and contingent ties in nineteenth century Birmingham', *Economic Geography*, vol. 43, pp. 95–127.

Veness-Randle, A. R. (1979), 'The social-spatial lifecycle of a company town: Calumet, Michigan', unpublished M.A. thesis, Michigan State University.

Vincent, J. R. (1967), *Poll Books. How Victorians Voted*, London.

Walker, P. (ed.) (1979), *Between Capital and Labour*, New York, Monthly Review Press.

Walker, R. A. (1985a), 'Class, division of labour and employment in space', in D. Gregory and J. Urry (eds), *Social Relations and Spatial Structures*, London, Macmillan.

Walker, R. A. (1985b), 'Is there a service economy? The changing capitalist division of labour', *Science and Society*, vol. 69, pp. 42–83.

Waller, P. J. (1981), *Democracy and Sectarianism. A Political and Social History of Liverpool 1868–1939*, Liverpool University Press.

Walsh, W. H. (1967), *An Introduction to the Philosophy of History*, 3rd edn, London.
Wallerstein, I. (1980), *The Modern World System II*, London, Academic Press.
Wallman, S. (1984), *Eight London Households*, London, Tavistock.
Ward, D. (1978), 'The early Victorian city in England and America', in J. R. Gibson (ed.), *European Settlement and Development in North America*, University of Toronto Press.
Ward, D. (1980), 'Environs and neighbours in the "Two Nations": residential differentiation in mid-nineteenth century Leeds', *Journal of Historical Geography*, vol. 6, pp. 133–62.
Ward, J. T. (1973), *Chartism*, London.
Warde, A. (1985), 'Spatial change, politics and the division of labour', in D. Gregory and J. Urry (eds), *Social Relations and Spatial Structures*, London, Macmillan.
Warde, A. (1986), 'Some political effects of restructuring in Lancaster', in P. Cooke (ed.), *Global Restructuring, Local Response*, London, Economic and Social Research Council.
Watson, S. (1985), 'Shifting dichotomies – the restructuring of productive and reproductive relations', paper presented at a conference on Labour and Housing Market Change, Parsifal College, London, 12/13 December.
Watson, W. (1960), '*The managerial spiralist*', Twentieth Century Fund, New York.
Weaver, M. E. (1966), 'Industrial housing in West Cornwall', *Industrial Archaeology*, vol. 3, pp. 23–45.
Webb, R. K. (1955), *The British Working Class Reader, 1780–1848*, London, Allen & Unwin.
Weinbaum, G. and Bridges, A. (1978), 'The other side of the paycheck: monopoly capital and the structure of consumption', in Z. Eisenstein (ed.), *Capitalist Patriarchy and the Case for Socialist Feminism*, New York, Monthly Review Press.
Wertsch, J. V. (1985), *Vygotsky and the Social Formation of Mind*, Cambridge, Mass., Harvard University Press.
West Devon Borough Council (1983), *Tavistock and District Local Plan*, Okehampton, West Devon Borough Council.
White, J. (1980), *Rothschild Buildings. Life in an East End Tenement Block 1887–1920*, London, Routledge & Kegan Paul.
White, M. and Trevor, M. (1983), *Under Japanese Management. The Experience of British Workers*, London, Heinemann.
Whitehand, J. W. R. and Patten, J. (eds) (1977), 'Change in the town', *Transactions, Institute of British Geographers*, new series, vol. 2, pp. 257–416.
Wiebe, R. H. (1967), *The Search for Order*, London, Macmillan.
Williams, G. (1968), *The Chartists*, London.
Williams, K. (1981), *From Pauperism to Poverty*, London, Routledge & Kegan Paul.
Williams, P. (1986), 'Social relations, residential segregation and the home', in Hoggart, K. and Kofman, E. (eds), *Politics, Geography and Social*

Stratification, London, Croom Helm.
Williams, R. (1977), *Marxism and Literature*, Oxford University Press.
Williams, R. (1981), *Culture*, London, Fontana.
Williams, R. (1983), 'Culture', in D. McLennan (ed.), *Marx. The First 100 Years*, London, Lawrence & Wishart.
Williamson, B. (1982), *Class, Culture and Community: a Biographical Study of Social Change in Mining*, London, Routledge & Kegan Paul.
Williamson, J. G. (1983), 'Urban disamenities, dark satanic mills and the British standard of living debate,' *Journal of Economic History*, vol. 43.
Wilson, J. Q. (1965), *Negro Politics. The Search for Leadership*, New York, Free Press.
Wise, M. J. (1951), 'On the evolution of the jewellery and gun quarters in Birmingham', *Institute of British Geographers, Transactions and Papers*, vol. 15.
Wohl, A. (1968), 'The bitter cry of outcast London', *International Review of Social History*, vol. 13, pp. 188–245.
Wohl, A. S. (1977), *The Eternal Slum: Housing and Social Policy in Victorian London*, London, Edward Arnold.
Women and Geography Study Group (1984), *Geography and Gender*, London, Hutchinson.
Woods, R. (1978), 'Mortality and sanitary conditions in the "Best governed city in the world" – Birmingham 1870–1910', *Journal of Historical Geography*, vol. 4, pp. 35–56.
Wright, E. O. (1978), *Class, Crisis and the State*, London, New Left Books.
Wright, E. O. (1979a), 'The value controversy and social research', *New Left Review*, no. 116, pp. 53–82.
Wright, E. O. (1979b), *Class Structure and Income Determination*, New York, Academic Press.
Wright, E. O. (1980), 'Varieties of Marxist conceptions of class structure', *Politics and Society*, vol. 9, pp. 323–70.
Wright, E. O. (1985), *Classes*, London, Verso.
Wright, L. (1966), *Clean and Decent: the History of the Bathroom and the W.C.*, London, Routledge & Kegan Paul.
Wright, P. (1985), *On Living in an Old Country. The National Past in Contemporary Britain*, London, Verso.
Wyman, M. (1979), *Hard Rock Epic: Western Miners and the Industrial Revolution, 1860–1910*, Berkeley, University of California Press.

Yelling, J. A. (1978), 'Agriculture, 1500–1730', in R. A. Dodgshon and R. A. Butlin (eds), *A Historical Geography of England*, London, Academic Press.
Yeo, S. (1976), *Religion and Voluntary Societies in Crisis*, London, Croom Helm.
Young, M. and Willmott, P. (1973), *The Symmetrical Family. A Study of Work and Leisure in the London Region*, London, Routledge & Kegan Paul.
Youngson, A. J. (1966), *The Making of Classical Edinburgh*, Edinburgh University Press.

Index of Names

Notes: Alphabetical order is word by word, n = note(s), t = table.

Abercrombie and Urry (1983), 1, 9, 67n, 70n, 207–8, 214, 215, 226, 257, 265, 271, 275, 335
Abernathy, Clark, and Kantrow (1983), 324
Abrams (1982), 12
Adams (1966), 262
Aglietta (1979), 212
Agulhon (1982), 12
Aitken (1960), 266
Alexander (1979), 201
Algren (1951), 291, 293
Allswang (1971), 301
Ambrose (1974), 248–9
Aminzade (1981), 51
Anderson, M. (1985), 28
Anderson, P. (1975), 59
Anon. (1855), 113, 116, 119, 120, 131
Armstrong (1966, 1972), 83–4

Bagwell (1970), 28, 61, 62, 71n
Baines (1822), 42; (1859), 43
Ball, M. (1983), 225, 230
Ball, N. (1979), 174, 181
Balmforth (1910), 80
Bardou *et al.* (1982), 311
Baritz (1960), 272
Barker-Benfield (1976), 176
Barton, D.B. (1967), 131, 139, 145
Barton, R.M. (1972), 119, 120, 123, 124, 134, 135, 136, 139
Beacham (1984), 221t
Bedale (1980), 199
Bedarida (1979), 25
Beeton, Mrs, 175, 184
Belassa (1984), 306
Belenchia (1982), 305n
Bell, D. (1973), 3
Bell, Mrs Hugh, (1907), 199
Bendix (1956), 257, 262, 268t, 272
Benenson (1982), 257, 261, 266
Bennett (1910), 91–2
Beresford, M.W. (1979), 106n
Beresford, P. and Stephen (1986), 242–3, 248
Berger and Piore (1980), 3
Berle (1960), 70n
Berle and Means (1932), 70n
Bertaux (1982), 12
Best (1971), 27
Bhaskar (1980), 311
Billinge (1982), 78
Blau (1977), 72n
Blau and Duncan (1967), 269t
Bledstein (1976), 272–3
Bluestone and Harrison (1982), 71n
Boddy, Lovering, and Bassett (1986), 233, 357
Bodimar (1977), 261
Bohstedt (1982), 62
Bourdieu (1984), 17, 212, 223
Bozzoli (1981), 146
Bradbury (1983), 153n
Bradley (1984), 214; (1985), 214, 252
Braverman (1974), 256, 265
Brayshay (1977), 140; (1980), 109, 132, 135, 141, 147; (1980, pers. comm.), 140
Brech (1972), 262
Briggs (1963), 41; (1974), 164
British Parliamentary Papers (PP):
  PP, 1852–3, LXXIX, 107n
  PP, 1864, XXIV, 120, 124, 129, 130, 132, 138
  PP, 1866, LVII, 106n
  PP, 1876, XVII, 112, 132, 138
  PP, 1884, XIX, 118t, 132, 141
  PP, 1884–5, XXX, 116, 119, 125, 126, 127, 131, 138
  PP, 1888, XXII, 116, 122, 123, 125,

126, 127, 137, 138, 142, 143, 144–5, 152n
PP, 1889, XV, 116, 123
PP, 1890, LVII, 116, 117, 118t
PP, 1890–1, XLI, 117, 130, 136, 142, 145, 146
PP, 1890–1, LXVIII, 132
PP, 1890–1, LXXVIII, 130, 132
PP, 1891, LXXVIII, 146
PP, 1893–4, XX, 141
PP, 1893–4, CV, 117, 118t, 126
PP, 1894, XXIV, 131, 132
PP, 1896, LXVII, 116–17, 118, 119
PP, 1899, LXIV, 144
PP, 1900, XIV, 141
PP, 1901, XLIII, 147
PP, 1903, XV, 146
PP, 1904, XIII, 142, 148
PP, 1907, XIII, 142
PP, 1909, XXXIII, 142
PP, 1909, XLIII, 136, 145, 147, 148
PP, 1910, XLIII, 132
British Workingman, The, 180
Brody (1980), 256, 260, 261, 262, 266
Brook (1968), 101
Brown (1935), 274
Bryant (1979), 174, 175
Burawoy (1977), 8; (1978), 265, 266–7; (1983), 70n; (1985), 8
Burgess (1980), 186
Burke and Richardson (1978), 141, 142, 146–7, 148, 153n
Burnett (1968), 171; (1969), 119, 125, 133, 135, 164, 178, 197; (1974), 170–1, 178–9, 181; (1978), 161, 170–1, 173, 183, 186, 194, 195, 196, 197, 204n
Burnham (1941), 70n
Burns (1980), 269t
Burrage (1972), 270
Burris (1980), 269
Buttrick (1952), 256–7

Calder (1977), 174, 177, 183, 184
Calhoun, 20; (1980) 72n; (1982), 18, 19, 59; (1983a), 59; (1983b), 68n; (1984), 71n
Calvert (1982), 69n
Camagni (1985), 322
Camborne Election Papers (1885), 122, 152n
Cannadine (1980), 76, 192; (1982a), 74
Carchedi (1977), 208
Castells (1977), 209
Cawson and Saunders (1983), 229
Cayton and Drake (1946), 289, 291, 301
Central Statistical Office (1985), 210, 225t
Centre for Urban and Regional Development Studies, 237; (1983), 238t; (1984), 234
Chadwick (1842), 187, 188–9, 197–8
Chalkin (1974), 163, 169, 171
Champion and Green (1985), 245
Chandler (1980), 257, 260
Chapman, D. (1955), 195
Chapman, S.D. (1971), 171
Checkland (1964), 197
Checkland and Checkland (1974), 113, 136
Chesshyre (1986), 247, 248
Chicago Defender, 289
Chicago Sun-Times, 283
Church (1964), 272
City of Birmingham (1973), 283
City of Bristol Planning Department (1985), 338
Clark, G.L. (1981), 15
Clark, P. and Slack (1976), 162
Clarke and Critcher (1985), 212
Clawson (1980), 256, 257, 265
Cleaver (1979), 8
Cohen (1978), 70n
Collier (1909), 294
Collings (1906), 121, 122
Connell, J. (1974, 1978), 248–9
Connell, R.W. and Ward (1981), 42, 44, 44t
Conway (1982), 110
Cooke, 21; (1982a,b), 15, 214; (1983b), 17; (1983), 324; (1985), 15; (1986), 326
Cooke and Morgan (1985), 207, 323, 326
Cooke Taylor (1842), 177–8
Coombes *et al.* (1982), 238t
Coombes, Green, and Owen (1985), 235
Co-operative Congress (1895), 80
Copley (1923), 259, 264

Cornish Post and Mining News, 126, 141, 142–3, 144, 145, 146
Cowlard (1979), 84, 85, 105
Crompton and Jones (1984), 217
Crompton and Sanderson (1986), 222
Crossick (1977), 19, 75, 76; (1978), 75, 76, 96; (1983), 76
Crump (1931), 42
Curl (1973), 193
Cutler (1982), 283, 284, 287, 288

Dahrendorf (1959), 3; (1969), 215
D'A Jones and Holli (1981), 288, 305n
Dale (1898), 290
Daniels, P. (1985), 219–20
Daniels, P. and Thrift (1986), 219–20, 314
Daniels, S.J. (1980), 106n
Daunton (1976), 106n; (1980), 106n; (1983), 161, 191, 193, 199
Davidoff (1979), 204n
Davidoff *et al.* (1979), 155
Davidoff and Hall (1983), 169, 200
Davin (1979), 174, 181
Davison (1978), 158
Dawson, George, 290
Debray (1981), 271
Dennis, 20; (1979), 106n; (1980), 96; (1984), 84, 95, 96
Deverson and Lindsay (1975), 225–6, 245
Devon County Council (1983), 250
Dickens (n.d.), 280, 281
Dinwiddy (1979), 11
Disco (1979), 271
Dobb (1963), 112, 128–9
Donnelly and Baxter (1975), 11, 38
Dosi (1983), 317
Douglas (1976), 152n
Dubofsky (1983), 262
Duffin (1978), 175–6
Duncan, N. (1981), 331
Duncan, R. (1963), 140
Duncan, S.S. (1987), 17
Dunleavy (1979), 331
Dunleavy and Husbands (1985), 210, 217, 221–2, 227, 228–30
Dunning and Norman (1983), 232
Durkheim (1893), 69n
Dutton (1954), 193

Economist, The, 299
Edel (1982), 331
Edwards (1979), 260
Ehrenreich and Ehrenreich (1979), 208, 215
Engels, 30, 55–7, 185; (1878), 59; (1880), 55; (1895), 60; (1969), 187, 189
Englander (1981), 292
Ernst (1985), 314
Evans and Boyte (1982), 72n

Farmer and Barrell (1981), 336
Ferris (1972), 231
Fine and Harris (1979), 320
Flandrin (1979), 167, 168
Foner (1955), 261, 262, 266
Foord (1984), 222
Forrest, 21–2; (1983), 331
Forrest and Murie (1983), 333; (1986), 331, 332
Foster (1968), 77; (1974), 10, 11, 51, 68n, 73, 74–5, 77, 96; (1977a), 11; (1979), 8
Fox (1923), 295
Fox-Genovese and Genovese (1983), 293
Franklin (1986), 358
Fraser, D. (1976), 29, 45, 46, 50
Fraser, W.H. (1981), 28, 186
Freeman and Soete (1985), 320
Friedman (1977), 8
Frith (1977), 47
Frobel *et al.* (1980), 315

Gadian (1978), 79
Gaskell (1977), 76
Gauldie (1974), 119, 168, 171, 187, 197
Gershuny (1978), 209; (1985), 209, 212t
Giddens (1973), 3, 4, 10; (1979a), 307; (1979b), 4; (1981), 17, 20, 48, 156, 330–1; (1984), 17, 20; (1986), 358
Giddens and MacKenzie (1982), 214
Gilman (1903), 155
Ginswick (1983), 80
Girouard (1978), 193
Gloag (1962), 193
Goddard and Smith (1977), 232
Godwin (1972), 181

Goldthorpe (1982), 208, 215, 220, 221t
Goldthorpe, Llewellyn, and Payne (1980), 215, 220, 223
Goldthorpe and Payne (1986), 215, 220
Goodman and Redclift (1981), 110
Gosnell (1937), 288
Gould (1980), 208, 215
Gouldner (1979), 208
Grafton (1983), 250t, 252
Gray, F. (1982), 331
Gray, R. (1981), 74, 78
Green, A.E. (1985), 234–5, 237–8, 239t
Green, C. (1973), 292
Gregory (1982), 71n; (1984), 10, 16
Groh (1979), 8
Guardian, 277, 282
Guterbock (1980), 288

Haber (1964), 262, 264
Haider (1982), 277
Hall (1981), 133
Halsey, Heath, and Ridge (1980), 223
Hamer (1971), 121–2
Hansen (1982), 305n
Hardy, Thomas, 115
Hareven (1982), 12, 153n
Harloe (1984), 210
Harris (1983), 215, 252
Harrison (1959), 45; (1962), 45
Hartman (1979), 159
Harvey (1982), 13–14; (1985), 211
Hastings (1959), 292
Hayden (1981), 184
Headrick (1981), 68n
Heath (1981), 221
Heath, Jowell, and Curtice (1985), 227, 228, 230, 232, 331
Heaton (1920), 42
Heaton, H. (1960), 71n
Held (1980), 11
Henriques *et al.* (1984), 12
Herington (1984), 238
Herman (1981), 260
Hewitt (1958), 179–80
Hindess (1971), 299
Hobsbawm (1964), 74, 257; (1984), 31
Hoggart (1957), 95–6
Holland (1843), 39
Holli and D'A Jones (1977), 305n
Hollis (1970), 62
Holme (1985), 333
Holmes and Armstrong (1978), 84
Hopkins (1979), 188t
Hoskins (1963), 168
Howard, Anthony, 292
Howells (1984), 232
Hunt (1980), 159
Hunter (1974), 305n

Inglis (1982), 11
Inquiry into Friendly and Benefit Societies (1871), 200

Jackson (1980), 171; (1982), 86
Jenkin (1934), 115, 116; (1962), 112, 113, 114, 116, 119, 120, 125, 130, 131, 134–8
Jenkins, P. (1983), 12
Jenkins, Peter, 282
John (1979), 179
Johnson, T. (1977a,b, 1982), 215
Johnston (1985), 231–2; (1986), 20
Jones, D., and Womack (1985), 313
Jones, G.S. (1976), 126
Joyce (1975), 98; (1980), 8, 17, 79, 97
Judt (1979), 12, 17; (1985), 12

Kantorowicz (1957), 70n
Karn *et al.* (1985), 331, 333
Katznelson (1979), 53, 55, 58
Kautsky, Karl, 8
Kay (1832), 189, 190, 191
Keating (1976), 152n
Kitteringham (1975), 136
Kocka (1980), 271–2
Kohl (1844), 41
Kolko (1963), 264
Kornblum (1974), 301, 305n
Krut (1979), 144, 146

Lancaster Regionalism Group (1985), 214–15
Land Enquiry Committee (1914), 126
Langton (1975), 164, 169
Larson (1977), 270; (1980), 271
Lasch (1977a), 273; (1977b), 331
Laslett (1972a), 167
Lawton (1978), 28, 86
Layton (1971), 262, 268, 270; (1974), 270
Lee (1984), 27, 232

Lefebvre (1976), 160–1
Lenin, 10, 60
Lentz (1982), 113
Levine and Wright (1980), 71n
Lewis, G.J., and Maund (1979), 248–9
Lewis, G.W. (1907), 113, 129, 130, 131, 135
Lewis, R. (1979), 286
Lin (1985), 313
Lipietz (1984), 323; (1985), 315
Litterer (1963), 264, 267
Littler (1978), 256, 258; (1982a), 274; (1982b), 256–7, 259, 260, 261, 264, 274
Lloyd and Simpson (1977), 192
Lockwood (1958), 216
Lovering (1985), 327
Lowe and Goyder (1983), 226, 230–1
Lukács (1924), 67n

McBride (1978), 204n
McCarthy (1970), 11
McGregor (1957), 182
McIntyre (1980), 17
McKendrick (1982), 164
McKendrick, Brewer, and Plumb (1982), 164, 169
MacKenzie and Rose (1983), 161–2, 201, 202, 204n
MacLeod, H. (1974), 196
Maier (1979), 274
Malcolmson (1981), 164–5, 166
Mallett (1975), 208
Mandel (1975), 70n, 71n, 310
Marshall, G., *et al.* (1985), 330, 331
Marshall, J.N. (1985), 234
Martin and Roberts (1984), 222
Marx (1867), 68n, 69–70n; (1871), 58; (1885), 59, 68n; (1894), 71n; (1932), 68n; (1976), 114; *see also* Marx *in subject index*
Marx and Engels (1848), 52, 58–9, 60, 68n; (n.d.), 280–1
Massey, (1983a), 151, 152; (1983b), 110–1, 357; (1984), 15, 232–3, 234, 315, 316, 319, 321, 331–2; (1985), 321
Massey and Meegan (1982), 318
Mayhew, B., and Levinger (1976), 72n
Mayhew, H. (1862), 185, 197
Meillassoux (1975), 160
Mendels (1972), 30–1
Merton (1968), 340
Meyrowitz (1985), 18, 210
Michels (1949), 65
Middleton (1981), 166
Mills (1980), 125
Mingione and Redclift (1985), 21
Mitchell and Deane (1962), 34t
Mitter (1986), 209
Montgomery (1979), 256, 257, 259, 261–2
Morgan and Sayer (1985), 7
Morris, R.J. (1976), 10, 323; (1979), 74, 77–8, 169, 171; (1983a), 167, 169, 171; (1983b), 98
Mulhern (1981a,b), 271
Mumford (1961), 169–70
Murie, 21–2; (1974), 334, 336
Musson (1976), 11, 79–80
Muthesius (1982), 161–2, 183, 185, 186, 191

Nadworny (1955), 259, 265
Neale (1968), 46, 73, 78; (1981a) 11, 74; (1981b), 73; (1983a), 69n
Nelson, D. (1975), 256, 259, 260–1, 265, 267, 272
Nelson, R. (1959), 260
New Statesman, 292
Newby *et al.* (1978), 248–9
Newton, K. (1976), 299
Noble (1979), 260–1, 262, 263, 267, 270, 271
Node (1979), 261
Nove (1983), 316

Offe (1984a), 209, 306; (1984b), 306
Offe and Wiesenthal (1980), 9
Offer (1981), 122, 152n, 197, 198–9
Office of Population Censuses and Surveys (1980), 217; (1984), 224t; (1984b), 247t
Ossowski (1963), 2
Owen and Green (1985), 218t, 237

Pacione (1980), 248–9
Pahl (1965a), 248; (1965a,b), 335; (1966), 223, 237, 242; (1984), 21, 209, 332
Palmer (1975), 259, 264, 265–6
Parker (1983), 333

Parkin (1972), 3
Payne and Payne (1974), 337
Pelling (1967), 147, 151
Perkin (1957), 62; (1969), 68n, 69n, 72n
Person (1929), 258, 259, 260, 266, 267
Petrie (1938), 290, 295
Philips and Williams (1983), 250; (1984), 248–9
Phillips (1905), 144, 146
Pike (1967), 180
Pinch and Williams (1983), 237, 238
Piore and Sabel (1984), 309, 310
Pollard (1957), 37; (1959), 30, 31, 33t, 35, 37, 41; (1971), 36, 37–8
Pooley (1977, 1979), 73
Poor Law Commissioners (1837–8), 188
Porter, G.R. (1847), 39–40
Porter, R. (1982), 164, 171, 172
Postgate (1923), 63
Poulantzas (1973), 58, 59, 208; (1975), 208
Pratt (1982), 157, 230
Preston (1982), 298; (1983), 298
Price (1975), 71n
Prothero (1979), 49
Przeworski (1977), 7, 8, 57, 59–60, 61, 68n, 70–1n; (1980a,b), 72n; (1985), 8
Przeworski and Wallerstein (1982), 72n
Pugin, 196

Rakove (1975), 286, 301–2
Ralph (1890), 276–7, 289–90; (1893), 277
Raynor (1969), 335
Reach, 80
Redford (1970), 248–9
Reed (1983), 314
Reeder (1961), 121, 122
Reid (1983), 31
Renner (1978), 208, 215, 216
Rex and Moore (1967), 3, 157, 287
Rex and Tomlinson (1979), 287, 288, 297, 299
Reynolds (1964), 287
Richards (1974), 159, 166–7
Rimmer (1967), 41, 42, 43–4
Roberts (1971), 96
Roemer (1982), 208
Rogers (1980), 136, 147
Rolf (1983), 292, 298
Rose, D., 20; (1984), 112, 152n, 199, 201
Rose, S.A. (1986), 27–8
Rossi (1980), 336
Rossi and Shlay (1982), 336
Routh (1980), 220
Rowe (1953), 113, 114, 115, 131, 132, 134, 140, 147, 152n
Rowse (1942), 115, 142, 143
Royal Commission on the Health of Towns (1844, 1845), 186–7
Royal Commission on the Housing of the Working Classes, 126, 138
Royal Commission on the State of Large Towns and Populous Districts (1845), 190, 204n
Royal Cornwall Gazette, 126
Royko (1971), 291–2, 302
Rubinstein (1980), 12, 27
Rule (1970), 112, 129; (1971), 134–5
Ruskin (1865), 174

Sabole (1975), 269t
Sachs and Wilson (1978), 176
Salaman (1981), 207
Salt (1985), 356
Samuel (1975), 135; (1977a), 27; (1977b), 129, 130, 131
Sarlvik and Crewe (1983), 227
Sartre (1963), 358
Saunders (1978), 157; (1979), 3; (1981), 3, 209, 229; (1984), 154, 157, 210, 229, 330; (1985), 209; (1986), 212, 213t
Saunders and Williams (forthcoming), 17, 154, 155
Scase and Goffee (1982), 217, 335, 340
Schlichter (1919), 261
Schonberger (1982), 318
Schorsch (1980), 34
Scott (1979), 26–7, 70n
Seeley *et al.* (1963), 334
Select Committee on the Health of Towns (1840), 186, 190
Select Committee on the Regulation of Buildings and the Improvement of Boroughs (1842), 186–7
Select Committee on Town Holdings (1886–92), 122–3, 127

Shaw (1977, 1979), 73
Singleton (1970), 80, 81
Slater (1968), 114
Smith, D., 21; (1982), 18, 19, 32, 40, 51, 278, 290–1; (1986a), 311, 316, 323
Smith, N. and Williams (1986), 242
Soete and Dosi (1983), 317
Sofer (1970), 256–7
Soja (1985), 315
Sokoloff (1980), 159
South Hams District Council (1983), 250
Spear (1967), 289
Springett (1978), 82–3; (1979), 81, 83; (1982), 81
Stacey and Price (1981), 158, 174, 175, 176, 179
Stark (1980), 8, 9, 256, 258, 262, 263, 265, 270, 275
Statist, 285–6
Stedman Jones (1974), 48, 49; (1975), 11; (1982), 72n; (1983), 12
Steedman, Urwin, and Walkerdine (1985), 11
Stone, K. (1974), 257
Stone, L. (1977), 165–9, 173
Storch (1977), 32
Storper and Walker (1983), 15, 213
Sturt (1912), 166
Summers (1979), 204n
Sunday Times, 283
Sutcliffe (1978), 285
Sutcliffe and Smith (1974), 283, 287
Suttles (1968), 305n
Sykes (1898), 70, 81, 101

Tawney (1931), 223
Taylor, F.W., 255, 258–9, 264–5; (1947), 258–9, 267–8
Taylor, M.J., and Thrift (1982), 207
Taylor, P.J. (1986), 12
Terkel (1970), 297
Therborn (1983), 67n
Thomis (1976), 172–3
Thompson, C.B., 264; (1917), 266, 267
Thompson, E.P. (1965), 10, 11, 72n, 78; (1966), 78, 112; (1967), 35, 256; (1968), 8, 51; (1971), 37
Thompson, F.M.L. (1977), 76
Thompson, J.B. (1984), 11
Thompson, J.B. and Held (1982), 11
Thompson, P. (1975, 1982), 12
Thorns (1981a), 230; (1981b), 331
Thrift, 20, 21; (1981), 35; (1983), 11, 16, 226; (1985), 16; (1986a), 16, 214; (1986b), 232, 315
Tiptaft (1954), 294–5
Titmuss (1958), 355
Todd (1967), 109, 131, 140
Touraine (1974), 271
Townsend (1986), 235
Turner (1964), 285

Urry, 21; (1973), 208; (1981a), 15, 25–6, 207, 215; (1981b), 214; (1983), 252; (1984), 15, 213–14, 215; (1985a), 211, 212, 215, 219, 222t, 223, 223t, 321; (1985b), 306, 307, 321
Urry and Lash (1986), 306
Urwick (1929), 259

Van Onselen (1979), 146
Vance (1967), 169
Veness-Randle (1979), 140

Walker, P. (1979), 208, 335
Walker, R.A. (1985a), 6, 13, 15, 216; (1985b), 216
Wallman (1984), 333
Ward, D. (1978), 85; (1980), 47, 48, 84, 95–6
Warde (1985), 15, 319; (1986), 316, 319
Watson, S. (1985), 332
Watson, W. (1960), 334, 340
Weaver (1966), 116, 119
Webb (1955), 62
Weber, *see subject index*
Weinbaum and Bridges (1978), 158
Wertsch (1985), 11
West Briton, 137, 150
West Devon Borough Council (1983), 252
White, J. (1980), 12
White, M. and Trevor (1983), 318
White, W. (1870), 85–6, 87t
Whitehand and Patten (1977), 106n
Wiebe (1967), 271, 272–3
Williams, G. (1968), 38

Williams, P., 20–1; (1986), 17, 154
Williams, R. (1977), 110
Wilson (1965), 289, 301, 302
Wise (1951), 283
Wohl (1968), 204n; (1977), 197, 198; (1977), 189
Women and Geography Study Group (1984), 202
Woods (1978), 292
Wright, E.O., 3–4; (1978), 208, 257; (1979a), 2, 8; (1979b), 208; (1980), 70n, 208; (1985), 2–3, 4, 5, 7, 12, 208–9, 212, 215, 226, 252–3
Wright, L. (1966), 168–9
Wyman (1979), 153n

Yelling (1978), 114
Young and Willmott (1973), 245

Subject Index

accumulation, through home-ownership, 353, 355; *see also* capital accumulation
action, 6, 7; individual, 203; *see also* collective action
administrative employees, 257, 338
advertising, 157
affluence/wealth: and class, 2, 3, 8, 178; and the home, 186, 193; home-ownership, 156, 332, 335–7, 352–8; service class (Winchester), 247; working class (Birmingham), 285, 292, 296; *see also* prosperity
age, 337, 339
age groups, 17, 25–6, 174, 201
agency, 11–12, 15; collective, 58
agriculture/farming, 114, 178–9; Cornish, 109, 113–16, 120, 124–5, 135, 136, 148
Akroyd, Edward, 100
allotments, 121, 152n; in Cornwall, 123–4, 135, 137
'Ambrit' fallacy, 274
amenities: domestic, 157–8; public, 231
amenity groups, 231
America, *see* United States
American Dream, 292, 293, 296, 297
American Plan, 312
American Way, 293
Americanism, 293
architecture, *see* house design
Argentina: cars, 313
armaments, 34, 256
artisan élite, 74, 76; *see also* labour aristocracy
artisans, 185; Sheffield, 31–41, 49, 50
Asia: industry, 313, 322
Asians, in Birmingham, 287–8
association(s), 9, 25–6, 28, 53, 210; *see also* organisation(s)
attachment to place, 276, 279–82, 296; Birmingham and Chicago, 21, 289–93, 297, 300, 302, 303–4
attics, 196
authority, 3, 26; delegation of, 216, 272; *see also* control; domination
automation, 308, 313–14, 318, 320

Babbage, Charles, 55
back-to-backs, 31–2, 81, 171–2, 197
Barnsbury Association, 231
banks/banking, 163–4, 311; employees, 219–20, 354–5, 357
bargaining: housing market, 357; politics, 278; wages, 308
Bath, 73, 163
baths/bathing, 193, 194
bay windows, 195–6
Bedaux system, 274
belonging, 279, 291–2; *see also* attachment to place
Berkshire, 237
Bessemer, 34
Birmingham, 21, 163, 276–8, 282–304; home-owners, 199, 200, 299
Blackburn, 199
Blacks, in Chicago, 288, 293, 297, 298, 301, 302–3, 304
Blaenau Festiniog, 199
blue-collar workers, 285, 292, 308
Bosworth, Neville, 277–8, 300
bourgeoisie: seventeenth to eighteenth century, 165, 167; nineteenth century, 51, 52, 54, 57, 60, 280–1; in Cornwall, 123, 128; in Oldham, 73, 74–5; twentieth century, 208; *see also* middle class(es); petty bourgeoisie
Bradford, 46, 77–8
Brazil: cars, 313
Bristol, 163, 337–8
British Empire, 294, 295, 321
British Leyland, 311, 316
Britishness, 293–4, 295
building/construction: eighteenth century, 164, 171; nineteenth century,

121, 186, 189–90, 192, 193, 197; in Cornwall, 109, 110, 114, 116, 119–20, 123, 124, 126, 127; in Huddersfield, 81; in Leeds, 41; twentieth century, 225, 245, 325, 326–7; *see also* housing
building societies, 75, 192, 199–200, 248; employees, 357; *see also* mortgages
Bunce, John Thackeray, 289–90
bureaucracy-bureaucrats, 58, 207, 208, 216, 307; housing, 21; scientific management, 257, 259, 272, 275; voting, 232
business administration, 215, 271
business organisations, 6
business services, 207, 219–20
businessmen, 84–6, 92, 101; *see also* small businesses

Camborne, 109, 113, 114, 117, 119, 122–7, 134, 143, 150–1
capital: commercial, 325; converted, 280–1; corporate, 263, 270; depersonalised, 235; financial, 307, 310, 325; industrial, 307, 310, 323, 324; restructured, 21, 213–14, 220, 225
capital accumulation, 26, 51, 55, 324; scientific management, 254, 269
capital and labour, 3, 5, 6, 8, 9, 14, 26, 55, 202; nineteenth century, 112, 185, 256–7, 280–1; twentieth century, 273, 285, 320, 324–7
capital and management (service class), 254, 265, 266–7, 269, 274
capital concentration and centralisation, 307, 308, 309–10
capital gains/money gains, 330, 331
capital investment, *see* investment
capitalisation, 308
capitalism/capitalist societies, xiii; historical geography, 13–14; model, 25–7; nineteenth century, 27–9; twentieth century, 207–15, 306–28; *see also* Marx/Marxist theory
capitalism: corporate, 6; industrial, 34; managerial, 273; organised/ disorganised, 21, 306–15, 327–8
capitalist class, 2, 4, 9; nineteenth century, 27, 34, 44; twentieth century, 217; *see also* capital and labour
capitalist democracy, *see* democracy
Cardiff, 106n, 199
careers, and housing, 21–2, 35
cars: ownership, 208–9, 249, 338; production, 283, 285, 312, 313
casual labour, 198, 310, 323, 326
cellars, 187, 195, 196
centralisation, 273, 307, 308, 309, 327, 328; *see also* concentration; decentralisation
Cermak, Anton, 301
charity, 27, 176, 181–2
Chartism, 56, 63, 64, 72n, 79; Leeds, 45–6, 49; Sheffield, 40, 49
chemical engineering, 262, 270
chemicals industry, 260, 270, 274, 310
Chicago, 21, 276, 277, 278, 282–3, 284–5, 286, 288–9, 291–3, 296–8, 301–4
child-bearing/childbirth, 175; and housing, 210, 337, 339, 351
child-minding, 185, 202
child-rearing, 159; eighteenth century, 166, 167; nineteenth century, 173, 177, 181, 184, 201
children, employment of, 171, 179, 181, 185, 191; in Cornwall, 120, 131–2, 136, 147; in Huddersfield, 91; in Wakefield, 84
choice: employment, 213, 235–7; housing, *see* residential choice
Church, 165–6
church attendance and membership, 77, 101–5, 199, 293
circulation, 25, 71n, 211
cities, 13, 48, 58; nineteenth century, 28, 29, 49–50, 75–6, 186, 191, 281; twentieth century, 210, 213, 303, 308, 325, 327; *see also* inner cities; towns 'civic gospel', 290, 292, 296, 298–9, 300, 304
civil society, 15, 20–1, 25–6; nineteenth century, 20, 27–9; twentieth century, 21, 209–10, 213, 235, 255; *see also* households
class(es), definition of, 2–4, 51, 53–4, 78–9, 105–6
class analysis, 4–12; and geography, 12–19
class awareness, 10

class capacity/connectedness, 5–6, 8–9, 10, 13, 18–19, 20–1, 55, 57; nineteenth century, 48, 49; twentieth century, 215, 216–7, 242
class character of Britain, 29, 211–14
class conflict, 5, 8, 26, 215, 252; in Sheffield, 36–41
class consciousness/identity, 5–6, 10–12, 26; nineteenth century, 57, 64, 73, 78; in Huddersfield, 20, 104, 105, 106; in Leeds, 44; in Sheffield, 41; twentieth century, 214; in Birmingham, 285; in Chicago, 289; service class, 225–6, 245, 252–3
class dealignment, 207, 227–32
class demarcation, *see* social segregation
class formation: concept of, 5–6, 7–8, 26–7, 57; geography of, xiii, 12–19, 25–9, 207–14
class organisation(s), xiii, 7, 8–10, 26, 29, 51, 53–4, 57–8; twentieth century, 214, 215, 226, 274, 306, 327; *see also* working class organisation(s)
class perception, 10, 106
class politics, 212–3, 227–32, 308; *see also* working class politics
class relations, xiii, 2–4, 15, 25; in Birmingham and Chicago, 276, 294–5, 297; service class, 216, 255–6, 274–5; *see also* social relations
class settlement, 306
class solidarity, *see* solidarity
class structure, 5–7, 59; eighteenth century, 164–5; nineteenth century, 27, 73, 78–9, 177, 178, 184–5, 281; in Huddersfield, 79, 97, 105, 106; in Leeds, 44; in Sheffield,, 35–6; twentieth century Britain, 208–9, 214, 227–8, 285, 304, 331–2; in USA, 257
class struggle, 8, 26; nineteenth century, 20, 51–2, 53–4, 57, 59–61, 64–7, 201; twentieth century, 207, 216, 254–6, 257–8, 273–5
cleanliness, *see* hygiene
clerks/clerical workers: nineteenth century, 75, 76; in Huddersfield, 92, 94, 104; twentieth century, 207, 208, 217; *see also* white collar workers
clubs: gentlemen's, 183, 196; mine, 138; sick, 32
coal industry, 310; USA, 256, 260
collective action, 9, 20, 52, 53–4, 56–7, 60, 61–3, 65, 67, 202–3; in Cornwall, 134–5, 147, 150
collectivities-in-struggle, 9, 274–5
commerce, 27, 163–4, 325
commodities, fetishism of, 56
commodity status of the home, 125, 156, 157, 171, 186, 192–3, 202
common land, 114; in Cornwall, 119, 135, 139, 149
communications, 67, 68n; nineteenth century, 20, 28–9, 52, 54, 60, 62–3, 71n; twentieth century, 18, 210, 232; *see also* transport
communism, 122, 280–1; in France, 208
community: and class, 51, 52, 57–8, 61, 65, 66, 105, 332; and the family, 165; housing estates, 350; and neighbourhood, 99, 105, 291–3, 296; and property, 279–82, 289–91, 296, 297, 300; and work, 53, 55, 64, 66
commuting, 235–6, 242, 248–9, 335; Bristol, 338, 353; Plymouth, 249, 250–2; Winchester, 245, 246
competition, 312, 313, 314, 315, 317, 320, 321–2, 324, 325, 326, 328; for space, 297
componentry, 310, 313, 314
concentration, 210, 260, 307, 308, 309, 310, 328; re-, 326, 327; *see also* centralisation
conception (planning) and execution, 259, 265, 274, 324
Congregational Church, 102, 103–5
connectedness, *see* class capacity
consciousness, 11–12, 15–16, 21, 331; black, 288; Chicago, 293; Cornish, 150, 151; *see also* class consciousness
conservation, 230–1, 252
Conservatism, 227, 228, 231–2; in Huddersfield, 101, 103, 104; in Birmingham, 277–8, 285, 287, 289, 298, 299–300, 301, 304
construction, *see* building
consumer goods, 28, 29, 310, 311, 321–2, 323
consumer services, 232–3, 315
consumption, 25, 52, 53; eighteenth century, 164, 167–9, 172; nineteenth

century, 173, 186, 202; twentieth century, 209, 210–11, 212, 214
consumption, politics of, 212–13
consumption cleavages/sectors, 228–31, 330, 332
consumption cultures and lifestyle, 212, 223–5, 237, 242–3; in Winchester, 247
contracting: internal, 256–7; sub-, 76, 326
contradictory class locations, 208–9, 257
control: of the home, 202; of labour, 6, 179, (USA) 256–9, 266, 272, 273; of places, 279; *see also* authority; male dominance
Conybeare, CAV, 122, 150–1
co-ordination, *see* integration
copper mining, 108–9, 122, 123, 127, 130, 131–2, 140
core employees, and housing, 332, 334, 355, 357
Cornwall, 20, 108–53, 319
corporate capital, 263, 270
corporate capitalism, 6
corporations: origins, 54, 58, 59; twentieth century, 211, 213, 214, 216, 232, 310; in USA, 260, 262–3, 270; *see also* multinational corporations
corridors, 168
cottages, 353; in Cornwall, *see under* building; home-ownership
cotton industry, 74, 79–80, 97
council housing/public rental sector, 157, 330, 331, 332, 333, 338; subsidies, 355, 356
craftsmen, *see* master craftsmen; skilled workers
credentialism, 208, 215, 216, 255, 271, 340
Crosland, T.P., 100–1
culture(s), 8, 29; in Sheffield, 32, 39; *see also* consumption cultures; production cultures
currencies, 310–11, 328
curtains, 191, 193, 195, 196
cutlery industry, 31, 32, 34, 35

Daley, Richard J., 286, 301–2
Dawson, William, 301
death and disability: Cornish miners, 138, 145, 147, 148; *see also* mortality
decentralisation, 232–3, 238–42, 325, 326, 328
decoration, 193, 194
de-industrialisation, 308; in Cornwall, 109, 110, 142, 148, 149, 150
democracy, 278; capitalist, 52, 64–7, 276–82, 292–5, 296, 300, 303–4; direct, 65, 66, 67
Democratic organisation: in Chicago, 278, 284, 286, 288, 293, 298, 301, 303
depopulation: in Cornwall, 109
design, *see* house design
deskilling, 74, 208, 214, 217, 321, 325–6; and scientific management, 254, 255, 259, 266, 267, 273, 274
detached houses, 191, 195, 245, 337
development: economic, 306, 307; urban, *see* town planning
direct and indirect relationships, 51–60, 64–7
direct democracy, 65, 66, 67
disability, *see* death and disability
disease, *see* health/sickness
disorganised capitalism, 306, 307, 308–9, 310–11, 328
dissipation/intemperance, 180, 188, 189
distanciation, 17–18
distribution, 25, 52, 163, 232
division of labour, 3, 6, 15, 26, 163–4, 165, 191, 216–17; international, 13, 71n, 308; sexual, 159; social, 214, 216, 220, 263, 274; spatial, 15, 308, 316, 321–2
divorce, 160, 176–7, 210
domestic appliances, 194, 309–10
domestic economy, *see* family economy
domestic ideal, 174
domestic management, 174–5
domestic production, 28, 173, 174, 185, 209; *see also* outworkers; work(place) and home
domestic property: in Cornwall, 110–1, 137–9, 148–9, 151–2
domestic science, 194–5
domestic servants, 27–8, 178, 181, 193, 195; management of, 173, 182, 184; social relations, 182, 183, 186, 294; as status indicators, 84, 86, 89, 185

domestic technology, 193–5
domination, 3, 6, 58; *see also* authority; male dominance
Dowlais, 199
'dual politics' thesis, 212–13, 227–32
dumb waiter, 168
Durham, 199
dwellings, *see* housing

earnings/incomes: eighteenth century, 164, 170; nineteenth century, 84, 179, 197; Cornish miners, 109–10, 112, 120, 125, 129–39, 141, 143–4, 145–6, 149–50; twentieth century, 209, 259, 277, 321; and housing, 211, 334, 335, 340, 353, 354, 355, 358; service class, 216, 217, 222, 223, 247
economic development, 306, 307
economic planning, 309, 325, 326
economic restructuring, 307, 315, 316–27, 328, 331–2
economies: nineteenth century Britain, 27, 28; twentieth century, 306–12; Britain, 207–8, UK, 315, 321–4, 325–7; *see also* regional economies
economies of scale, 321, 325, 326
economies of scope, 327
education/schooling, 12; eighteenth century, 167; nineteenth century, 27, 75, 76, 84, 181–2, 183, 185, 196–7; in Huddersfield, 94, 101; in Leeds, 47, 85; in Oldham, 77; women, 174–5; twentieth century, 212, 222; and housing, 346, 348, 349, 351–2, 353, 354; service class, 216, 223, 228–9, 237, 242, 246–7; USA, 255, 263, 270–1, 274
efficiency, 264
elections, *see* voting behaviour
electorate, *see* franchise
electrical engineering, 262, 270, 309–10, 321–2
electrical industry, 270, 274
electricity, 194, 195
electronics, 313–14, 328
élites, 51; artisan, 74, 76; housing, 21–2, 355, 358; managerial, 332, 335; urban, 171
emigration, *see* migration
employment: nineteenth century, 27, 198; Cornish miners, 117, 141–2, 148, 150–1; in Leeds, 42–4; in Sheffield, 34; twentieth century, 214, 217–20, 306, 308, 310, 321–3; Birmingham, 283, 299, 300; in Chicago, 283; in Plymouth, 249–50; in USA, 268; in Winchester, 245–6; *see also* children; family economy; labour; occupations; unemployment; women; work
employment and housing, *see* labour market and housing; work(place) and home
employment relation, 15
enclosure(s), 114–16, 124, 135, 165
engineers/engineering: in UK, 321–2, 323; in Leeds, 31, 43, 47; in Sheffield, 33–4; in USA, 256, 262–3, 266, 268, 269–71, 272, 310
Englishness, 293–5, 296–7, 304
entertainment, 194, 202
entrepreneurship, 326, 327, 335, 336–7
environment, maturity of, 322–4
environmental issues, 212, 226, 230–1
ethnic groups/ethnicity, 4, 7, 25–6, 154; in Birmingham and Chicago, 21, 276, 286–9, 291–5, 296–7, 300–1; in Britain, 209, 222, 327, 357; in USA, 256–7, 261; *see also* race
ethnographic studies, 214, 333
Europe: class, 306; emigration, 288, 301; industry, 310, 312, 313, 314, 317, 323
exchange, 3, 25, 55; *see also* market(s)
exchange rates, 310–11
executives: housing, 337, 338, 354, 356
exploitation, 3, 4, 6, 53, 59, 280; nineteenth century, 185, 186, 257; twentieth century, 208–9
exports, *see* trade

factories, 57, 60, 179–80, 211, 256, 327; in Leeds, 41–4; in Sheffield, 34, 35, 39
factors, 35
family, 159–60; eighteenth century, 165, 166, 167, 169; nineteenth century, 173–82, 186, 200, 281; twentieth century, 209–10; and housing, 334, 335–6, 339, 353, 357, 358
family businesses, 91, 92–4, 354, 358

family/domestic economy, 179; in Cornwall, 109–10, 131–3, 135–41, 142–5, 147–8, 149, 150
family wage, 159, 179, 201
farming, *see* agriculture
fashion, 192, 193, 243
feminist perspectives, 11, 332
feudalism, 58
fetishism of commodities, 56
fetishism of organisations, 56
finance: employment, 219–20, 354–5, 356–7; home-ownership, 192, 330, 351
financial capital, 307, 310–11, 325
financial services, 225
fishing industry: in Cornwall, 109, 113, 120, 136
flax industry: in Leeds, 42–3
food industry, 260, 274
food prices: in Cornwall, 125, 135
food riots, 134–5, 166
Ford/Fordism, 310, 311, 323, 324
foremen: in USA, 256, 257
France, 11, 56, 68n, 71n, 208, 271, 309–10, 325
franchise/suffrage: in Camborne, 150–1; in Huddersfield, 86, 89, 99; in Leeds, 45, 46; in Sheffield, 39, 41
'free mining', 112, 129
'free social spaces', 52, 66
freedom, 156, 157, 183; *see also* choice
freehold/leasehold tenure, 121–2, 192; in Cornwall, 109, 110, 115–16, 117, 122–8, 133–4, 137, 139, 144–5, 148–9, 150; in Huddersfield, 81, 82–3
'freestanding' towns, 235, 242
friendly societies, 47, 75, 199–200
fulfilment, 278–9, 290–1, 292, 297, 302–3
functionalism, 160, 202, 331
furnishings and furniture, 39–40, 164, 183, 193, 196

gardens, 200; in Cornwall, 124, 125, 137, 144–5
gas, 194, 195
Gateshead, 199
gazumping, 346
gender, 7, 15, 25–6, 154, 204n, 214–15; and employment, 27–8, 209, 257, 327, 357; and the home, 17, 20–1, 154, 158, 174, 183–4, 196, 200–1, 202; *see also* sex ratio; women
General Motors (GM), 310, 311
gentrification: inner city, 242, 252–3; rural, 252
geographical mobility, 167, 334, 354; service class, 216, 217, 225, 235–7, 242; *see also* residential movement
geography of class formation, xiii, 12–19; nineteenth-century Britain, 25–9; twentieth century Britain, 207–14; service class, 232, 235–45
'geological metaphor', 316, 319
Germany, 11, 56; industry, 271–2, 273, 309–10, 313, 321
ghettoes, 211, 327
gold mining, 142–4
government, *see* local government; state
gradational theories of class, 2
Green Belt, 327
ground rents: in Cornwall, 116, 124, 125, 126, 137; in Huddersfield, 81
group cultures, 279

Halifax, 163; home-ownership, 106n, 199
Hawick, 199
health/sickness, disease, 171, 172, 173, 185, 187, 188, 189, 190, 198; Cornish miners, 138, 145, 147, 148; *see also* mortality
health care: employees, 219–20, 222; *see also* medical profession
heating, 193, 194
heavy trades: in Sheffield, 33–4, 38, 41
Hegel, 59
'helping professions', 272–3
heritage, 226, 230, 247, 248
Hillhouse, *see* Huddersfield
Hispanic people, in Chicago, 288–9, 298, 303, 305n
historical geography, 13–14
home, 17, 20–1, 154–61; history, 161–203; *see also* domestic appliances, *etc.*; work(place) and home
Home Counties, 327
home-ownership/owner-occupation, 161; nineteenth century, 106n, 192–3, 198–200, 201, 202; in Cornwall, 111, 117, 123, 124, 125, 128, 137–9,

home-ownership (*cont.*): 140, 143, 144–5, 148–9, 151–2; in Huddersfield, 81–3, 96; twentieth century, 94, 157, 279, 299, 330–1, 332–58; service class, 223, 228–9; *see also* freehold/leasehold
homelessness, 203
Hong Kong, 314
house building, *see* building
house design and decoration: eighteenth century, 167–8, 169, 171–2; nineteenth century, 193, 194, 195–6; twentieth century, 245, 337
'house farming', 192
house maintenance, 197, 356
house prices, *see* housing costs
households, 25, 154, 155–6, 157, 160; eighteenth century, 165, 167; nineteenth century, 28, 89, 140–1; twentieth century, 209–10, 297, 331, 332, 335–7, 352–8
housewives, 158, 159, 174–5, 195, 200–1
housing, 167–72, 186, 191–6, 331–2; in Bristol, 337–8; in Cornwall, *see* building; in Huddersfield, 81–3; *see also* middle-class housing; working-class housing
housing, location of, 156, 157–8, 353–4; *see also* residential choice; residential segregation
housing and class, 157–8
housing and employment, *see* labour market
housing choice, *see* residential choice
housing conditions/living conditions, 84, 186–9, 191, 196–7, 203, 353; in Birmingham, 285, 290–1, 292, 296, 299
housing costs/prices/values: eighteenth century, 169, 171; nineteenth century, 185, 186, 192–3; in Cornwall, 119–20, 144–5; twentieth century, 334, 335, 341, 344–51, 353, 355, 356; in Bristol, 337–8; in Plymouth area, 252; in Winchester, 248; *see also* rents
housing élite, 21–2, 355, 358
housing estates, 211, 225, 245, 350–1; in Plymouth area, 250, 252; in Sheffield, 34
housing histories: Bristol, 338–58
housing ladder, 336–7, 353, 355, 358
housing market(s), 192–3, 331, 333–7, 352–8
housing moves/mobility, *see* residential movement
housing needs, 186, 192, 197, 336
housing practices/projects, 358
housing search, 353, 355
housing space, 186, 336, 353
housing speculation, 336
housing standards, *see* housing conditions
housing status, 335, 338, 353
housing subsidies and grants, 285, 334, 355–7
housing tenure, 157, 158; nineteenth century, 84, 186, 192, 197, 198; twentieth century, 230, 330–1, 335, 358; *see also* home-ownership; rented housing
housing values, *see* housing costs
Huddersfield, 77–8, 79, 80–3, 99–102, 105; Hillhouse district, 20, 81, 82–3, 85–94, 96–7, 99–100, 101, 102–6
hygiene/cleanliness, 168–9, 186, 188–9, 193, 194

identity, 9, 279, 330; class, *see* class consciousness
ideology, 12
immigration, *see* migration
imperialism, 307, 327–8; British, 293–4, 295
incomes, *see* earnings
independence: Cornish miners, 111–12, 119, 123, 129, 133, 149–50, 151; *see also* individuality
Independent Labour Party, 48, 64
India: car production, 313
individuality/individualism, 11–12; Cornish miners, 109–10, 112, 123, 134, 151; and the home, 155, 203; and home-ownership, 161, 331; lower middle class, 75; women and family, 165, 166, 175; *see also* independence; privacy
industrial output, 306, 308, 310; cars, 312–13; *see also* productivity
industrial proletariat, 34, 128–9
industrial relations, 262, 325

Industrial Reorganisation Corporation, 321
industrial revolution(s), 51, 52, 54, 60–1, 74, 164, 173, 174, 179, 189–90
'Industrial Society', 307
industry/industrialisation: eighteenth century, 163–4, 170–1; nineteenth century, 61, 189, 191, 199; in Leeds, 41–4; in USA, 256–7; twentieth century, 211, 213, 23–7, 257–75, 277, 283, 306–28; *see also* de-industrialisation
industry, location of, 235–7, 322–4
informal economy, 214, 332
infrastructure, 52, 54, 61–3; *see also* communications
inheritance, 156, 335–6
inner cities, 297, 308, 321–2, 326, 327; Birmingham, 287; gentrification, 242, 252–3
institutions, 6, 7, 16–19, 29, 84, 209; in Huddersfield, 80, 86; in Leeds, 47–8; in Sheffield, 32, 39; *see also* organisations
insurance, 125, 138, 357
insurgency, 59, 60, 66
integration/integrity, xiii, 18–19, 20, 54–61, 62–4, 66–7, 71n; in Leeds and Sheffield, 31, 49
intensification, 318
interest mediation, 308
interest rates, 334, 355, 357
'intermediate' classes, 255
internationalisation, 52–3, 217, 308, 314–5
invasion: class, 221; housing areas, 191, 252
investment, 6; housing, 94, 197, 353, 355; industry, 316, 319, 325, 326
Irish, 188, 209, 294; Birmingham, 286–7; Chicago, 286, 288, 301; Cornwall, 115; Huddersfield, 86; Leeds, 43, 46, 47; Oldham, 77
Ironside, Isaac, 40
Italy, 11, 309

Japanese industry, 273, 311, 317, 321, 326; micro-electronics, 313, 314; motor vehicles, 312–13, 317–18
job information and job search, 235–7
job security, 215, 216
jobs, *see* careers; employment
John Brown & Co., 34
journals, *see* newspapers

Kelly, Edward, 301
Kent: amenity societies, 231
Kentish London, 76, 78
kinship, 165
kitchens, 195
knowledge, appropriation of, 216, 257–8, 261, 265, 270–1, 273, 274

labour: and capital, *see* capital and labour; casual, 198, 310, 323, 326; direct/indirect, 259; division of, *see* division of labour; living/dead, 320, 321, 322, 323, 324; mental/manual, 263; and modernisation, 325; non-productive, 215, 216, 257; and scientific management, 254–63, 265–6, 269, 273, 274; subsumption of, 27, 256; *see also* wage labour
labour aristocracy, 27, 74–8, 94, 96–7; *see also* artisan élite
labour consciousness, 10, 41
labour costs, 308, 322, 325–6, 327
labour force, *see* employment
labour market, 6; and housing, 331–2, 333–4, 335–7, 352–8; local, 214, 323, 331; segregation 159; spatial extent, 235–7
labour migration, *see* migration
labour mobility, 334
labour organisation(s), 63–4, 308, 309, 324; in Cornwall, 150; in USA, 262; *see also* working class organisation(s)
Labour Party, 49–50, 64, 228, 231–2, 321; in Birmingham, 285–6, 287–8, 291, 292, 296, 298–9, 303–4; in Camborne, 151; in Sheffield, 40
labour power/supply, 6, 15, 213–14; service class, 235, 245
labour process, 6, 15; mining, 111–12, 129–31, 133, 149; *see also* deskilling
labour reserve, 145–6, 147, 323
labouring classes, *see* working class(es)
ladies, 174, 200
Lancashire, 79, 97, 98–9
land tenure, 114, 121–2, 128–9, 152n, 165, 176, 192; in Cornwall, 109, 113, 114–19, 122–8, 135, 144–5, 151–2

Latin America: cars, 313
Laura Ashley, 210, 226
leakages, 355
leasehold, *see* freehold/leasehold
leasehold reform movement, 109, 121–3, 127–8, 150
Leatham, Edward, 100, 101
Leeds, 28, 29–30, 31, 41–8, 49, 50, 84–5, 95–6
leisure/recreation, 32, 167, 183, 223
leisured classes, 163, 167–9, 171
Liberal Party, 121–2; in Cornwall, 109, 122–3, 151; in Huddersfield, 100–1, 103, 104–5; in Leeds, 46, 47; in Sheffield, 40; and the SDP, 226, 227, 228, 232
life chances, 3, 26–7, 189, 232, 332
life expectancy, *see* mortality
life-lease system, 115–16, 122–3, 125–6, 127–8, 145, 149
lifestyle, 26–7, 84, 332; artisans, 90, 185; genteel, 173; service class, 223–6, 232
light trades: Sheffield, 31–8
lighting, 193, 194
little masters, 75, 76, 96–7; in Huddersfield, 74, 83, 94, 96, 101, 103; in Oldham, 77, 79–80; in Sheffield, 35, 39, 40; *see also* master craftsmen
Liverpool, 73, 163
living conditions, *see* housing conditions
living standards, 10, 353; of Cornish miners, 125, 133, 140, 150, 151
loans: housing, 355, 356, 357
local government and politics, 66; nineteenth century, 19, 49–50, 77, 197; in Leeds, 46–7; in Sheffield, 40; twentieth century, 212–13, 229, 231; in Birmingham and Chicago, 277–8, 285–6, 287–9, 294–304; in Tavistock, 252; in Winchester, 248
locale, 16–17, 73–4, 154
locality, 17–18, 51–2, 53, 62–3, 66, 67, 253, 279, 327, 336
location: housing, *see* housing, location of; industry, 235–6, 322–4; labour power, 213–14; service industry, 232–5
lodgers/lodgings, 28, 84, 89, 171, 191, 197
London: eighteenth century, 162–3, 170; nineteenth century, 28, 29, 76, 78; housing, 75, 121, 126, 189, 199; twentieth century, 252–3, 283, 314–5, 338; commuters, 245, 246; housing, 334, 353; industry, 309–10, 323
London, City of, 27, 207, 232, 245, 287
'lower class', 84
lower middle class(es), 74, 75–6; in Huddersfield, 86–106; in Leeds, 46–7, 84, 85; *see also* petty bourgeoisie

machinery/mechanisation, 30–1, 37, 74, 262, 326; mining, 149; textiles, 79
'machinofacture', 31
male dominance: eighteenth century, 165–7, 171; nineteenth century, 173–7, 179, 183–4, 191, 196, 200–1; twentieth century, 158–9, 352–3
management/managers, 58, 59; nineteenth century, 75, 76; in Huddersfield, 83, 94; in USA, 256–7; twentieth century, 207, 208, 215, 216, 220, 236, 254–6, 257–75
managerial élites, 332, 334, 335
Manchester, 28, 39, 163, 187, 189, 192
manual labour, 263, 277
'manufacture', 31
manufacturing industry/manufacturers: nineteenth century Britain, 27, 28, 55, 76, 84, 179; in Huddersfield, 94, 99, 101; in Leeds, 44; twentieth century, 308, 315, 322–3; in Birmingham and Chicago, 277, 283; in Britain, 207, 218, 220, 225, 232–3, 235, 321–2, 325, 326; in USA, 260, 268, 269
market(s), 55; eighteenth century, 164, 165; nineteenth century, 27, 28, 62–3, 327–8; twentieth century, 309, 315, 326, 327; *see also* trade
market relations, 3, 4, 53, 58, 215–16
marriage, 159; eighteenth century, 165; nineteenth century, 73, 174, 176–7, 184; in Huddersfield, 96–7, 104; twentieth century, 210; and housing, 337, 338, 339, 353
Marx/Marxist theory, 3–5, 6, 7, 8, 10–12, 13–14, 25, 51–60, 68n, 69n, 110, 185, 208, 212, 256, 280–1, 331–2

mass production, 260, 309, 310, 321, 325, 326, 327–8; cars, 312
master craftsmen, 75, 76, 77; in Huddersfield, 80, 83, 85–6, 90, 92–4, 99, 101, 104; *see also* little masters
maturity/de-maturity, 322–4
mechanical engineering, 321–2
mechanisation, *see* machinery
medical profession, 176, 354, 355; *see* also health care
medicine, private, 228–9
membership: community/ethnic group, 276, 279, 296, 300; institution, 84
men, *see* male dominance
mental/manual labour, 263
merchants, 84; in Huddersfield, 94, 99, 101, 104; in Leeds, 44; in London, 27
mergers/takeovers, 260, 321, 325
metal trades, 43, 178, 260, 274
Methodism, in Sheffield, 32
Mexico, 306, 313
micro-electronics, 313–14, 328
middle class(es), 1, 6; eighteenth century, 164; nineteenth century, 19, 84; attitudes to working class, 175, 180–2, 185, 188–9, 198, 199–200, 201; home-life, 28, 173–8, 182–5, 200–1; in Huddersfield, 92, 94, 97, 99; in Leeds, 41, 44, 45–7, 84–5; twentieth century, 200, 208–9, 211, 222, 232, 285; in USA, 271; *see also* bourgeoisie; intermediate classes; lower middle class(es); middling classes; new middle class; service class; upper middle class
middle class housing/home-ownership, 169–70, 190–1, 192–6, 199, 202–3, 340
Middle East, 313
Middlesborough, 199
middling classes: eighteenth century, 164, 167, 169, 170; nineteenth century, 73, 75; in Leeds, 46, 47
migration/immigration/emigration, 48, 61; Birmingham, 286–8; Britain, 28, 71, 172–3, 209; Chicago, 288–9; Cornwall, 109, 115, 139–48, 151; Huddersfield, 86, 97; Leeds, 47; Sheffield, 34; USA, 140, 256–7, 260–1; *see also* residential movement
milieux, 96, 210–11, 231–2, 242–5
mine clubs, 138
mining/mines, 119; in Cornwall, 108–15, 117, 120, 123, 129–35, 138–9, 141–2, 145–7, 149–50; in South Africa, 142–4, 146, 148; in USA, 140, 261
mobility, *see* geographical mobility; social mobility
modernisation, 321–2, 325–6
money/capital gains, 300, 301
mortality/life expectancy, 125, 167, 173, 187–8, 210; *see also* death and disability
mortgages: Cornish miners, 125, 137; 'increased mortgage allowance', 345, 347, 350, 351; tax relief, 157, 355, 356
motor vehicles, 283, 309–10, 312–13, 323, 328; *see also* cars
multinational corporations, 207, 214, 308–9, 311, 313; employees, 354–5, 356–7, 358
municipal ideology: in Birmingham, 289–91, 292, 299

National Economic Development Office, 325
neighbours/neighbourhoods: in Birmingham, 300; in Chicago, 291–3, 296, 302, 303; in Huddersfield, 20, 94–6, 104–5; in Lancashire, 98–9
New Commonwealth immigrants, 287
'new middle class', 208, 209, 269, 272
New Model Unions, 63, 72n
New Towns, 327
New York, 283, 314–15
Newly Industrialising Countries (NIC), 306, 313–14, 326
newspapers/journals/periodicals, 29, 62, 180, 200, 253
nonconformity: in Huddersfield, 101–4
non-productive labour, 215, 216, 257
non-working class, 332
north-south polarisation, 232–8, 356–7
Northampton, 199
Northumberland, 199

occupations: changes, 148, 221; and class/status, 3, 83–6, 92–4, 96–7, 104–5, 217; differentiation, 324; dual, 113; and education, 271, 272; and household, 53; and unions, 63–4; *see also* employment
Oldham, 73, 74–5, 78–8, 79–80, 97, 105, 199
oligarchy, 65
operatives, 74, 323
oppression, 4
organisation(s), 52–61, 64–7; *see also* class organisation(s); institutions
organised capitalism, 306, 307–8, 309–10, 327–8
organised labour, *see* labour organisation(s)
organised resistance, *see* collective action
'outer city', 238
outworkers, 35, 42, 209
overcrowding, 187, 188, 191; in Cornwall, 126, 127
owner-occupation, *see* home-ownership
ownership: capital, 15; companies, 58, 59; *see also* housing tenure; land tenure; possession(s); property

Pacific Basin countries, 313, 315
Parliamentary representation, *see* voting behaviour
parochialism, 295
part-time work, 220, 234, 327
parties, and class, 57, 59
paternalism, 201, 203, 281, 289, 292
patriarchy, 158–9, 165–7, 184, 257; *see also* male dominance
pauperism, 145; *see also* poverty
pay, *see* earnings
Penrhyndeudrath, 199
Penzance, 145
'people, the', 280
periodicals, *see* newspapers
personal relations, 170
petty bourgeoisie: eighteenth century, 166; nineteenth century, 74, 75, 76–7, 78; in Cornwall, 128, 148, 150, 151; in Huddersfield, 81–2, 91–2, 94; in Leeds, 44; in Sheffield, 35, 38–9; twentieth century, 208, 214; in Birmingham, 299; *see also* lower middle class(es)
piecework, 258
place, attachment to, *see* attachment to place
place, politics of, 297, 304
places: twentieth-century Britain, 211–15, 232
planning, *see* economic planning; town planning
Plug Riots, 45, 46
plumbing, 193, 195
Plymouth commuter-shed, 249–52
police, 27, 200, 253
political organisation, 26
political theory, 3
politics: nineteenth century, 64; in Cornwall, 122, 149–52; in Huddersfield, 86; in Leeds, 45–6, 85; in Sheffield, 38–41; twentieth century, 157, 212–13, 226–32, 308;*see also* class politics; local government; radicalism; voting behaviour
politics, popular, 54, 60
politics of place/space, 297, 304
pollution, 187
poor, the, *see* poverty
popular politics, 54, 60
population: eighteenth century, 62, 162–3; nineteenth century, 28, 172; in Birmingham and Chicago, 284; in Cornwall, 109, 142, 147; in Leeds, 47; in Sheffield, 34; twentieth century, 19, 207, 308
population, movements of, *see* migration
'populist' movements, 66
possession(s)/possessiveness, 156–7, 165, 172, 176, 195, 202, 278–82; in Chicago, 291, 296
'post-modernist' tendencies, 327
postal service, 29, 61, 62
poverty/the poor: eighteenth century, 171; nineteenth century, 27, 74, 89–90, 180, 181, 185, 186, 187, 189, 191, 196–7; in Cornwall, 138, 145, 147; twentieth century, 323, 327; in Birmingham and Chicago, 277, 292
Powell, Enoch, 286
press, *see* newspapers
privacy/privatism/privatisation, 161; eighteenth century, 165, 168, 170, 172; nineteenth century, 173, 175–6, 177, 182, 186, 195; twentieth century,

156, 157, 203, 330–1; in Birmingham, 292, 296, 297, 299, 300, 304
private economic service, 215
private medicine/health care, 219–20, 228–9
private rented housing: eighteenth century, 170, 171; nineteenth century, 28, 191, 192, 197–8, 201, 202; in Cornwall, 125, 126, 127; in Huddersfield, 81–2, 83; twentieth century, 330, 333, 338, 353; *see also* rents
producer services, 219–20, 232–4, 314–15, 328
production: geography of, 235–7; means of, 6, 210, 215; mode of, 6, 51, 55, 129, 173, 179; organisation of, 55, 167, 190; politics of, 212; relations of, *see* relations of production; socialisation of, 59; sphere of, 26, 172, 173; submodes of, 6
production, domestic, *see* domestic production
production and consumption, 52, 53, 210–11, 214
production and reproduction, 160–1, 167, 186, 215–16; *see also* work(place) and home
production cultures, 29, 211–14
productivity, 313, 320, 321, 325
'professional managerial class', 208, 215
professions/professional workers: nineteenth century, 76, 84; in Huddersfield, 83, 86, 99; in Leeds, 44, 84–5; twentieth century, 208, 209, 215, 216, 220, 230–1, 235, 323; housing, 334, 335, 338, 354, 358; scientific management, 255, 271, 272–3, 275; women, 175, 222
profit/profitability, 151, 207, 317, 320
progressivism, 264
proletariat/proletarianisation, 49–50, 51, 61, 68, 69n, 128–9, 280–1; in Cornwall, 110, 148; in Leeds, 41, 44; in Oldham, 73; in Sheffield, 34; white-collar, 332; *see also* semi-proletarian status; working class(es)
promotion, 215, 216, 270, 354
property, domestic, *see* domestic property
property and community, 279–82, 289–91, 296, 297, 300
property relations, 111, 282, 296
property rights, 6
property values, *see* housing costs
prosperity: in Birmingham, 283, 284, 298, 300; in Chicago, 284; in Leeds, 41; *see also* affluence
protectionism, 317
Protestantism, 165
public houses, 17, 32, 48, 200
public rented housing, *see* council housing
public sector employment, 332, 338
public spending: Birmingham, 300

quality control, 312–13, 322, 326
quality of life, 212, 351

race/racism, 7, 257, 261; in Birmingham, 286, 287–8; in Chicago, 286, 288, 293, 302–3; *see also* ethnic groups
'radical regions', 17
radicalism, 59, 64, 66, 79, 121–2; in Cornwall, 122, 150; in Leeds, 45; in Oldham, 79–80; in Sheffield, 38–9
railways/trains, 28–9, 34, 62, 63, 191; in Cornwall, 135, 147; in USA, 260, 261
Ramsden estate, 81–2, 89
rateable value, 84
rates, 150–1, 299, 300
rationalisation, 274, 318–19
rattening, 36, 38
recreation, *see* leisure
redeployment, 321
redundancy, 323, 327
Redruth: housing, 123, 126, 127; land tenure, 109, 114, 117, 119, 122; mining, 113, 148; politics, 150; poverty, 145, 147
reform: political, 38, 45–6, 64; social, 181–2, 185, 189, 198
refuse disposal, 171, 187
regional economies, 308, 309–10, 321–2, 325, 326–7; West Cornwall, 148, 151–2; West Midlands and the mid west, 277 283–4
regions: class analysis, 12, 13, 15; institutions, 17–18; politics, 212, 308
reification, 52, 56, 67n
relational theories of class, 2–4

relations of consumption, 210–11, 214
relations of production, 1, 3–4, 5, 6, 13, 14–15, 25, 49, 43, 57, 73, 129, 160; twentieth century, 207, 210–11, 213, 214, 215–16; *see also* capital and labour
relations of reproduction, 7–8, 13, 14–15, 215–16
relaxation, *see* leisure
religion/religious groups, 4, 7, 25; in Leeds, 85
rented housing, 330, 337, 356; *see also* council housing; private rented housing
rents, 170, 171, 197, 198, 355; in Cornwall, 125, 145; *see also* ground rents
reproduction, 7–8, 13, 14–15, 25, 160–1; eighteenth century, 167; nineteenth century, 182–3, 185, 186; Cornish miners, 111; twentieth century, 209, 212; service class, 215–16, 237, 274; working class, 321
residence, *see* home; housing
residential choice/constraints: nineteenth century, 190, 197–8; twentieth century, 94, 211, 237, 242, 331, 334, 335–7; in Bristol, 353
residential movement and mobility: nineteenth century, 47, 94–6, 105, 190–1; twentieth century, 94, 331, 332, 334, 336, 339–40, 352–4, 357–8; assistance, 344–5, 355–7
residential segregation/differentiation, 73–4, 75–6, 83, 84–5, 157–8, 186, 189–91, 195–6, 330–5; in Huddersfield, 90–6; in Leeds, 47, 48; in Oldham, 77; in Sheffield, 34
resources, 6, 217
respectability, 30, 39–40, 73, 75, 76, 195
restructuring, *see* economic restructuring
retailers/retailing, 75, 76, 178–9, 232–3, 237; in Huddersfield, 85–6, 92, 99, 104; in Leeds, 84, 85; *see also* shopkeepers; shops
retirement: Cornish miners, 138, 148; service class, 245, 246, 250–2
revolution/revolutionary movements, 10, 38, 59, 64, 66
revolutionary consciousness, 10, 41, 60; black, 288
'revolutionary' technical change, 320
riots, 62; in Chicago, 286, 302
roads, 62, 63
rooms, 17, 169, 183
ruling/governing class, 58–9, 164–5, 280
rural areas, 210, 213, 238, 242, 248–9
'rural' historical imagery, 226
rural settlements: Plymouth area, 250, 252; *see also* villages

St Agnes, 117, 140
St Ives, 134
St Just, 113, 140
salariat, *see* service class
salary earners, 215, 340, 353, 354, 355
salesmen, 104; *see also* retailers
savings: Birmingham, 200; Cornish miners, 137–8, 140, 142, 145, 147, 150; service careers, 355
scale: class analysis, 5–6, 12; economies of, 321, 325, 326
schools/schooling, *see* education
scientific management: domestic, 194–5; industrial, 21, 254–6, 257–75
SDP, *see* Social Democratic Party
sectorial alignments/cleavages, 210, 228, 330
security, 278–9: in Birmingham and Chicago, 290–3, 297, 302–3; Cornish miners, 137–9, 144; home-ownership, 201, 330, 351; *see also* stability
security of employment, 215, 216
security of tenure, 81, 149, 150
segregation, *see* residential segregation; social segregation
self-employment, 85–6, 151, 358
self-help, 75, 105, 191, 200, 203
semi-detached houses, 195, 245
semi-proletarian status, 110, 149–50, 151–2
semi-skilled/unskilled workers: nineteenth century, 77, 84, 96–7, 178, 185; twentieth century, 261, 266, 299, 323; *see also* deskilling
servants, *see* domestic servants
service careers, 355
service class, 274–5; in Britain, 21–2, 208, 214, 215–17, 220–32, 235–45,

248–9, 252–3, 323; in Plymouth area, 249–52; in Winchester, 246–7, 248; in USA, 255–6, 260, 269–73
service industry/employment: nineteenth century, 27, 178–9, 185; twentieth century, 308, 315, 322–3; in Britain, 207, 211, 217–20, 232–5, 327; in Birmingham, 283; in Plymouth, 249; in Winchester, 245–6; in USA, 268
sewage and sewerage, 187, 189, 190, 193–4
sex ratio: in Huddersfield, 86, 89
sexual division of labour, 159, 160; *see also* gender and employment
sexual repression, 173, 176
Sheffield, 29–41, 48, 49, 50
Sheffield Outrages, 37–8
shopkeepers: eighteenth century, 170; nineteenth century, 74, 75, 76, 77; in Cornwall, 148; in Huddersfield, 91, 92, 94, 96, 101, 104; in Lancashire, 98–9; in Leeds, 44, 46, 85; in Oldham, 77; in Sheffield, 40; *see also* retailers
shops/shopping, 211, 225, 242–3, 253; in Tavistock, 252; in Winchester, 247
sick clubs: in Sheffield, 32
sickness, *see* health/sickness
Singapore, 306, 314
single parents, 210, 332
single persons, 210, 338
skilled workers: in Britain, 84, 96–7, 178; in Huddersfield, 85–6, 90, 92, 94, 97, 99–100, 101, 104; in Leeds, 43–4, 47, 84; in USA, 256, 257, 258, 261, 265–6; *see also* artisans; deskilling
slums, 123, 126, 189, 191, 198, 277, 299; clearance, 201
small businesses/businessmen: nineteenth century, 74, 75, 76, 80; twentieth century, 214, 326, 327, 336, 358
small masters, *see* little masters
smallholdings/subsistence production, 110, 121, 129, 152n; in Cornwall, 109–20, 124–5, 128, 133, 136–9, 144–51
social action, *see* collective action
social control, *see* control
social convergence, 321, 327
social demarcation and differentiation, *see* social segregation
Social Democratic Party (SDP), 228, 232; Alliance, 226, 227
'social diary', 184
social forces, 7, 155
social groups, 4, 186
social interaction, 96–7, 154, 155, 190; in Huddersfield, 79, 80, 91
social mobility, 75, 220–1, 332; in Cornwall, 148, 151; in Huddersfield, 92–4; in Sheffield, 35; in USA, 271
social movements, 66; internationalist, 308
social paradigms, 319–24, 328
social problems, 172, 189
social psychology, 11, 12
social reform/reformers, 181–2, 185, 189, 198
social relations, 2–3, 25, 26–7; and the home, 154, 155, 160–1, 182–3, 184, 186; *see also* class relations; relations of production
social relationships, *see* direct and indirect relationships
social reproduction, *see* reproduction
social segregation/demarcation/differentiation, 167, 172, 200, 330–4; *see also* status
social services, 215
social status, *see* status
social stratification, 73–4, 83–4, 186, 331–2; in Huddersfield, 85–6, 90–6; in Leeds, 84–5; in Wakefield, 84
social structure, *see* class structure
social surveys, 332, 335
social welfare, *see* welfare
socialisation, 26, 209, 257
socialism, 66–7, 262, 331; municipal, 289–91, 296
socialist countries, 311, 316
Socialist League, 48
socio-spatial processes, 307, 319–27
solidarity, 10, 51, 57, 66, 69–70n, 170; working class, 52–3, 63, 331; in Birmingham, 285, 289, 298
South Africa, 142–4, 145, 146, 148
South Korea, 306, 313, 314
South Wales, 219; coalfield, 199
space: and class formation, 12–19;

space: and class formation (*cont.*): nineteenth century Britain, 25, 28–9; twentieth century Britain, 210–11, 213, 214–15, 358
space, politics of, 297, 304
space-economies, 315, 316; UK, 315, 325–7
spatial paradigms, 318–19, 324–7, 328
spatial segregation, 334; *see also* residential segregation
spiralists, 334, 336, 340
stability: capitalist institutions, 280, 281–2; leasehold reform, 121, 122, 127, 144; service class, 226; Victorian ideal, 178, 199–200; *see also* security
starter homes, 245
state: and class, 7, 15, 25, 26, 27, 209, 235; development of, 56, 58–9; and the economy, 28, 308–9, 310, 316, 325–8; as employer, 214, 215, 216, 219–20, 228, 232, 234, 235, 262; and the family, 177–8, 181–2; and housing, 201, 334, 355, 356; and male dominance, 165–6
status, 84, 105; Huddersfield, 86, 89–96
status, and the home/housing, 154, 155–6, 157–8; eighteenth century, 172; nineteenth century, 84, 91–2, 94–6, 184, 191, 192, 198, 201, 202; twentieth century, 335, 338, 353; *see also* social segregation
status affiliations, 3
steel industry, 33–4, 256, 261, 310
streets, 32, 96, 196
strikes, 73; in Cornwall, 134; in Huddersfield, 79; in Leeds, 44–5; USA, 261–2, 265–6
struggle, 25; of Cornish miners, 149–51; *see also* class struggle
style, *see* fashion; house design
subjectivity, 5, 15–16; labour power, 320, 324
subsidies: housing, 285, 334, 355–7; industry, 327
subsistence, 132–3, 134–5, 209
subsistence plots/production, *see* smallholdings
suburbs/suburbanisation: eighteenth century, 169; nineteenth century, 28, 74, 75–6, 172, 186, 190–1, 192, 198; in Leeds, 41; in Sheffield, 34; twentieth century, 210, 238, 242, 297; in Chicago, 292–3, 302
Suffolk, 231
suffrage, *see* franchise
Sunday schools, 32, 101–2
Sunderland, 199
survival rates, *see* mortality
system integration, 18

Taiwan, 306, 313, 314
technical education, 270–1
technical experts, 215
technological paradigms, 310, 317–19, 320–1, 324, 326, 327, 328
technology: and class struggle, 54, 61, 67; and economic development, 310–11, 317–24; and the home, 186, 193–5, 209; and scientific management, 254, 260, 270–1
telecommunications, 19, 210
television, 18, 223
temperance, 75, 77, 200
tenancies-at-will, 81, 89
tenure, *see* housing tenure; land tenure
tenure, security of, 81, 149, 150
terraced housing, 196, 197; in Bristol, 337–8; in Huddersfield, 82–3, 89
tertiary sector employment, *see* service industry
textile industries, 77–8, 79–80, 178; in Leeds, 31, 41–3; and scientific management, 261, 274
Third World, 68n, 71n, 308
Thornhill estate, 81, 82–3, 89
thrift, 199–200; *see also* savings
tied accommodation, 338–9, 352, 355
time and motion studies, 264, 265
time distances, 28, 210, 211
tin-mining, 108–9, 113, 129–35, 141–2, 146–7, 151
totalisation, 54–5, 69n
town planning: in Plymouth area, 250, 252; in Winchester, 248
towns/town life, 162–4, 165, 171, 172, 185, 186–91; *see also* cities; municipal ideology
trade/exports, 308–9, 310–11, 315, 327–8; cars, 312–13; micro-electronics, 314; *see also* market(s)
'trade, the': Sheffield, 32, 37–8

trade unions/unionisation, 10, 18, 60, 61, 63–4, 75, 76, 201, 307, 310, 320, 321, 323, 326, 327; in Birmingham, 287, 292, 299; in Cornwall, 109, 134; in Leeds, 44, 47; in Sheffield, 36–8, 39, 40–1; in West Yorkshire, 79; in USA, 261, 262, 265–6
tradesmen: in Cornwall, 148; in Huddersfield, 81–2, 91–2, 96, 99, 101, 103, 104
tradition, 133–4, 149–50
trajectory of capitalist development, 13–15, 21, 111, 284
'transformation rules', 316–19, 328
transport/travel: eighteenth century, 163–4, 170; nineteenth century, 28–9, 52, 54, 60, 61–3, 186, 190, 198; twentieth century, 210, 213, 219–20, 232
tributers, 110, 112, 120, 129–31, 132, 137, 138–9, 140
tutworkers, 112, 120, 129–33
Tyne and Wear, 237–8
Tyneside, 199

USA, *see* United States
unemployment, 323, 327, 332; in Birmingham and Chicago, 277; of Cornish miners, 140, 145; in Plymouth, 249–50; in Sheffield, 34; in Winchester, 245
uneven development, 13–14, 15, 29, 211–14; in Leeds and Sheffield, 29–31, 50
Unionist Party: in Birmingham, 289–91, 296
unions, *see* trade unions
United States: car production, 312, 313, 317; European influence, 61; immigration, 140, 256–7, 260–1; industry, 309, 310; micro-electronics, 313, 314; place and ethnicity, 276, 296; scientific management, 255–75; *see also* American Dream
universities: USA, 263, 270–1
unproductive labour, 215, 216, 257
unskilled labour, *see* semi-skilled/unskilled labour
upper classes: eighteenth century, 164, 166, 167–9, 170; nineteenth century, 28, 41, 192
upper middle class, 166; in Leeds, 46, 84–5
urban areas/urbanisation, 163, 172, 189, 210; *see also* cities; towns
urban development, *see* town planning
urban 'places'/'spaces', 297
urban studies, 3
'urban villages', 95–6
Ure, Andrew, 55

value, 3, 55, 56, 186, 215; the law of, 316–17, 320, 328
values, 74–5, 85, 96, 199–200, 225–6, 331, 351–2
ventilation, 194
villages, 242; commuter, 252, 335, 338, 353; 'urban', 95–6
voting: eligibility, *see* franchise
voting behaviour, 84, 98–9, 226–32, 285; in Camborne, 150–1; in Huddersfield, 99–101, 104–5; in Sheffield, 40

wage-bargaining, 308
wage labour/wage-earners: origins, 128–9; eighteenth century, 164, 165; nineteenth century Cornwall, 149–50; twentieth century, 208, 332, 337; *see also* capital and labour; working class(es)
wages, *see* earnings
Wakefield, 84
Wales, South, 199, 319
wallpaper, 194
walls, 191, 195
Washington, Harold, 278, 289, 298, 303
water closet, 193–4
water supply, 187, 188, 193
Watton, Harry, 285–6, 292
wealth, *see* affluence
Weber/Weberians, 1, 3, 4, 53, 59
welfare/welfare state, 27, 209, 222, 306, 327, 330, 332; in Birmingham, 290–1, 296; employment, 215, 222
welfare subsidies, 355
West Indians, 287, 288
West Midlands, 277, 309–10
West Yorkshire, 79, 97, 199
white-collar workers: nineteenth century, 74, 75, 76, 77; in Huddersfield, 92,

white-collar workers (*cont.*): 94, 96, 97, 99, 103, 104; twentieth century, 214, 217, 220, 262, 308, 332; *see also* clerks
Winchester, 245–8
windows, 195–6
Wolverhampton, 73
women, 4; and the home and family, 158–60, 165–7, 173–7, 182, 184, 200–1; in Cornwall, 136, 137, 141, 147; *see also* child-bearing; gender; male dominance
women, employment of: eighteenth century, 171; nineteenth century, 27–8, 84, 89–90, 178–81, 185, 191; in Cornwall, 120, 132, 133, 136; in Huddersfield, 90, 91; in Leeds, 43, 47; in Sheffield, 32; twentieth century, 200–1, 209, 214, 221–2, 234, 319, 321–2, 323, 325–6, 327, 353, 357
woollen industry, 42, 43, 79, 80, 97
work: and community, 53, 55, 64, 66; and non-work, 175, 191, 202; nature of, 272; part-time, 220, 234, 327; *see also* employment
'workers' control', 257
working class(es)/labouring classes, 52–3, 54, 57, 280, 281; eighteenth century, 164, 166; nineteenth century, 27–8, 49–50, 175, 178–82, 185, 195, 296; in Huddersfield, 99–100; in Leeds, 31, 41–50, 84; twentieth century, 208, 214, 215, 217, 223, 321, 323; in Birmingham, 285, 296, 298–9, 300; USA, 261–2, 271; *see also* labour; proletariat
working-class housing/home-ownership: eighteenth century, 167, 170–2; nineteenth century, 28, 172–3, 188–9, 190, 191, 193, 195–200, 201, 202–3; in Huddersfield, 81; in Leeds, 95–6; twentieth century, 331
working-class organisation(s), 54, 56; in Birmingham, 298; in Cornwall, 319; in Leeds, 47; *see also* labour organisation(s)
working-class politics, 8, 49–50, 60, 61, 64, 231–2; in Birmingham, 299; in Leeds, 31, 45, 47–8; in Sheffield, 38; in West Yorkshire, 79
workplace, 15, 17, 154, 155; control of, 29, 36, 42, 43, 256–9, 266
work(place) and home, 161; eighteenth century, 167, 169–70, 171, 179; nineteenth century, 91–2, 182, 186, 195, 197–9, 202; twentieth century, 332; *see also* domestic production; labour market and housing
World War I, 262
World War II, 303, 318, 321, 352

York, 163, 199
Yorkshire, 231; West Riding, 79, 97, 199